THE NAT

The National Frame

ART AND STATE VIOLENCE IN TURKEY AND GERMANY

Banu Karaca

FORDHAM UNIVERSITY PRESS NEW YORK 2021

Fordham University Press also publishes its books in a variety of electronic formats. Some content that appears in print may not be available in electronic books.

Visit us online at www.fordhampress.com.

Library of Congress Cataloging-in-Publication Data available online at https://catalog.loc.gov.

Printed in the United States of America

23 22 21 5 4 3 2 1

First edition

Contents

THE NATIONAL FRAME

Introduction

Intimate Encounters

Istanbul, October 5, 1993. Enter Kenan Evren, retired chief of the military staff and leader of the infamous 1980 coup d'état. During his presidency (1980–1989) and under his direct orders, 650,000 people were taken into custody and tortured, at least three hundred died or disappeared under unknown circumstances, tens of thousands had to leave the country, more than one and a half million were blacklisted, fifty people received the death penalty, nine hundred films were banned, and unions and associational life in Turkey were completely disbanded.[1] But on this day, he did not don his military uniform, nor was he receiving accolades for this political "service." He was celebrating his first solo show at Aksanat. The gallery had opened only a few months prior, designed to be the cultural flagship of Akbank, the banking arm of the Sabancı conglomerate. The exhibition, it seemed, was well received. Politicians, business leaders, and retired army officers were in attendance, the press interest was lively, and at least one painting was sold for the sensationally high price of 500 million lira (about $35,592 at the time, and a hefty sum for the local art market in those days). One notable absence, however, marked the event: Artists and curators, incensed by the exhibition, had decided to boycott the opening. We would hear from them the next day, in a review written by the art critic Ahu Antmen (1993) for the daily *Cumhuriyet*: The painter Mehmet Güleryüz suggested that Evren had better chosen a prison to show his paintings. The artist Gülsün Karamustafa found it inconceivable to "accept Evren as a colleague," and Orhan Taylan went even further, noting that it was "shameful" for the entire discipline of painting that Evren, the "enemy of democracy" incarnate, had taken to "paint and brush."

How can one explain the discomfort and outrage that this exhibition induced? It was the obvious connection between art and power, politics and money, the unmasked presence of the military-industrial complex in the art world. The outrage was directed at the effort of an ex-dictator to legitimize, even absolve, himself through the recognition of the art world. It was, most likely, further fueled by the fact that when in office, Evren had personally intervened in art exhibitions and openly professed his distaste for abstract and conceptual art. Perhaps it was also that he reinforced the almost stereotypical image of the artist-dictator (Michaud 2004) or that he repudiated the curiously powerful idea that someone "sensitive to art" cannot possibly be "such a bad person."[2]

Fast forward to Berlin, April 2004. Another arts institution, another controversy. The Hamburger Bahnhof, part of the national gallery network of the State of Berlin, announced that it had secured a seven-year loan from the collection of Friedrich Christian Flick. Having negotiated the loan, the German government presented it as a win for the city and its inhabitants. The financially squeezed German capital had long been hampered in its pursuit for new acquisitions for its museums, and this loan would enhance the state collection. The first exhibition curated from the Flick loan was to be presented in 2005. But then, news emerged that Flick had assembled his collection of 2,500 pieces of contemporary art and modern masters with the Nazi fortune accumulated by his grandfather, Friedrich Flick. The latter had successfully avoided paying reparations to the thousands of forced laborers, mostly Eastern European Jews, he had exploited during the Third Reich, and this despite his conviction at the Nuremberg Trials. Berlin's art world was up in arms. For the local artists' association Friedrich Christian Flick's deal with the Hamburger Bahnhof was nothing short of an attempt to whitewash his family name through art. To make matters worse, he had managed to do so by having his collection exhibited in a public museum, and hence at the taxpayers' expense, as the upkeep, storage, and insurance of the artworks in question would be covered by the state.

I take these two examples, the tensions and unease they produced, as ethnographic occasions to tackle understandings of art and its emancipatory potential, of art as a reflection of Enlightenment values, and an avenue for critique and self-reflection. Today, art is described through a wide range of theories and positions, yet the majority, if not all, of public and official discourses on the national (the state) and supranational level (for example, UNESCO or the European Union) share the assumption that art is inherently good. This idea of the inherent goodness of art, its daily trials and tribulations, be they structural or contingent, forms the basis of this book.[3] While transnationalism and globalization are increasingly at the forefront of both artistic practices and the scholarly analysis of art—and for good reason—I propose to reexamine what it means that the idea of the emancipatory potential of art has been intrinsically bound up with the history of the nation-state and, hence, understandings of what it means to be modern, indeed what it means to be "civilized." Wrestling with the paradox that within a globalized art world dominant understandings of art remain refracted through the national frame, this book interrogates the assumption of the inherent goodness of art through, against, and across the national contexts of Turkey and Germany. It does so by exploring instances that cast doubts on the assumed civilizing power of art, that unsettle discourses on art as a vanguard of freedom and democracy. It proposes that exclusionary narratives of national art histories, censorship, and the role of economic dispossession in the assemblage of art collections, that is, different forms of state violence, are as important to understanding art as is its emancipatory potential.

The National Frame

Today, assertions that credit art with "heighten[ing] consciousness" (Royce 2004) or as an avenue of self-reflection that enables "agency" (MacClancy 1997) are taken for granted. While these discourses on art are frequently attributed to those who see art as a form of critique (and hence as oppositional), the state notably and just as often uses the very same formulations that center the emancipatory potential of art. Yet, apart from a few examples (Fabian 1996, Myers 2002, Svašek 2002, Winegar 2006, Price 2007, Stokes 2010), the state and, with it, official cultural policy remain underrepresented in the anthropology of art. This is even more so when it comes to the interconnections between the making of art (and the art world) and state violence. Although a considerable body of scholarship exists on the historical importance of aesthetic expression in nationalist movements and nation-building processes, anthropology, like cultural studies, has mainly been interested in artistic appropriation and the "agency" and identity formation of individual and collective actors in the field of cultural production (MacClancy 1997, Schneider 2006, Schneider and Wright 2010). Overall it seems that anthropological analyses of the art world have been more comfortable with cultural politics "from below" than cultural policies "from above." This suspicious stance, as Stuart Cunningham (1992) notes, has contributed to framing cultural policy as a tool of manipulation rather than actively engaging with its potential for cultural critique.

Nation-states have aimed to regulate the arts from their very inception. Aesthetics have played an exponent role in the "making of national culture" (Fox 1990) and in rendering the nation tangible (Hobsbawm 1992, Smith 2013). With the establishment of the Turkish Republic, the idea of the "Turkish synthesis" (Gökalp 1959) aimed to refine "Turkish" folk culture following "Western standards." This rapprochement to the West employed Orientalist motifs in its argument that Turkish art was to distinguish itself from other "Eastern" artistic repertoires, deemed irrational and overly emotional (Stokes 1992, Öztürkmen 2002). However, ambivalences arose trying to reconcile "the modern" and its universalistic claims with the "national" assertion of distinctiveness. Similarly, the quest for German particularism thrived on strong antimodernist sentiment (Mommsen 2000) regarding modern, international conceptions of art as incommensurable with "German-ness." Although, for instance, the expressionist avant-garde radically broke with these premises in the early twentieth century, it was only after World War II that the German state has favored cultural policies that situated it firmly in the artistic heritage of classical "Western" canons (Belting 1993, Naumann 2001). As the literature elaborates on these respective historical trajectories, the question arises how these past developments are shaping the conditions of contemporary artistic production, presentation, and circulation.

In her study on the contemporary art world in Egypt, Jessica Winegar (2006, 21) sees "the nation as a major category of practice in Egyptian artistic and intellectual life" in the process of postsocialist transition. I would like to push this argument further by proposing that in Turkey and Germany too, we talk about art as a decidedly transnational phenomenon within national frameworks. I show why art remains vitally bound to these national frameworks, however differently configured they might be. Indeed, one major argument of this study is that as the conditions of artistic production index national histories, artists have to exhibit certain sensibilities with regard to these histories. Despite the transnational networks of people, monies, and "things" that characterize the intensified circulation of art—and artists—under the auspices of globalization (Marcus and Myers 1995, Appadurai 1996, Wulff 1998), the national arena continues to delimit the boundaries of what is deemed acceptable or imaginable in the arts. The mediating discourse of the greater good, although at times invoking "the good of humanity" in universal terms, generally is employed with an attendant—"the needs of the people"—that refers to a national population that, however imagined, is characterized by national particularities. It is through this dynamic that the national prism continues to refract the production and perception of art, even for artists and other actors in the art world who employ "the national" as an analytical lens for critique or who mobilize universalist claims of art in their work.

I trace the refraction of art through the national frame via two key dynamics. The first takes up Norbert Elias's (1969) notion of "decivilizing moments," that is, moments in which the seeming linearity of the civilizing process is called into question, and applies it to those that challenge the idea of the inherent goodness of art and its idealized connotation as a greater good. This challenge can at times be induced by artworks themselves, by the materiality of individual works, particular styles, or schools of art. Or, as in the two opening vignettes, this challenge can emerge from the conditions under which art is produced, bought and sold, circulated, and presented, that is, the conditions that ultimately frame the perception of art(works).

This more disconcerting dimension of art might be nowhere more forcefully expressed than in Walter Benjamin's (1968, 256) famous proposition that "there has never been a document of culture, which is not simultaneously one of barbarism."[4] Written in 1940, it was historically astute in describing the "great cultural and artistic achievements" of the past as predicated on exploitation, war, and other kinds of violence. It was also prophetic of what was still to come, as along with the Nazi killing machine the greatest art theft in history was advancing through Europe, a theft that has shaped the German art world to this day. Benjamin might not have envisioned the many ways his words would resonate not just in his native Germany but also "down in Turkey, far away" (to use Anderson's evocative 2007 title on Wilhelmine Germany's perspective on the Armenian genocide). Yet here too, historical episodes of economic dispossession and state violence continue to configure the production and circulation of art in the present.

In examining what happens when the many claims and assumptions about art are unsettled through the concept of decivilizing art, I do not mean to reinforce a dichotomy between civilization and barbarism but to emphasize that the "myth" of modernity is constituted by the claim of defeating barbarism (Bauman 1989, 12). Some kinds of "barbarism" abound in the arts, where destruction (referred to as vandalism when executed by those not in power) is part and parcel of the making of "new civilizations," especially since the French Revolution (Gamboni 1997). Although frequently misunderstood, Elias did not see the civilizing process as a linear and triumphal development but as an imaginary of moral superiority that is fragile, always in danger of reversal and—every so often—of revealing the structural violence that it is predicated upon (Dunning and Mennell 1998). Decivilizing moments in the arts, then, are moments when the ideas of the moral superiority of art—its emancipatory potential—are called into question, even become untenable. They are not instances of "uncivilized" or "primitive art," since they cannot be delegated to a supposed far and distant other (although this is often attempted), but are inextricably and undeniably part of "the self," or the national histories out of which they emerge. Different modulations of decivilizing art often work hand in hand. Censorship, for instance, can be understood as an ascriptive operation of decivilizing art, in that an artwork is identified as unsettling official history (and at times the moral or public order) and hence needs to be suppressed. At the same time, censorship is a decivilizing operation in itself in that it fundamentally contradicts the foundation of the modern, liberal democratic state, while cloaking itself as a necessary measure to sustain civility and, by extension, "civilized artistic expression." Decivilizing art is not solely a negative operation but can also be a vehicle for critique in that it might consciously aim to unearth what has been forgotten, suppressed, and obscured—in ways often deemed more effective than politics or scholarship, for that matter. Neither is it a fixed category: What is regarded as decivilizing art at one moment in (art) history might very well be considered a civilizational achievement in another.

The interpellation of art into the national frame is established through a second dynamic, that of dispossession. In his work on the interplay between indigenous and colonial art, Nicholas Thomas (1999) argues that both categories are, especially in the case of settler colonialism, predicated on processes of dispossession. These processes are not limited to past acts of expropriation and of suppressing cultural expressions but have engendered a legacy in which the right to self-representation and the question of "who owns culture" continue to be highly contested (Berman 2012, Myers 2002). The subject of dispossession has thus far been omitted in anthropological considerations of contemporary artistic production outside of the realm of the postcolony and the narrower field of "indigenous art." And yet, different kinds of symbolic, material, and economic dispossession have shaped the makeup of the contemporary art world in Turkey and Germany. In fact, this book anchors its analysis in two cities in which multiple kinds of dispossession are deeply intertwined with the history of art and its institutions. The exclusion of minorities from national art histories, the discounting of socialist art in the reunited Germany, and the link between large-scale economic expropriation on the heels of war, genocide (the Holocaust in the case of Germany and the Armenian genocide in that of Turkey), and other forms of state violence in the assemblage of art capital (that is, capital sustaining the art world) and prominent art collections all constitute practices of dispossession that are rarely discussed as such within interrogations of the contemporary art world. The only exception to this omission is gentrification—a process that characterizes the role of art in urban space. I argue that these processes remain largely obscured because they circumstantiate decivilizing moments. They become tabooed in national histories as moments that do not adhere to the civilizing narrative of the state, of modernity and progress, or as operations in the art world that contradict idealized notions of art. The silences that sustain their obscuration create an investment into the official narrative of the nation-state, and hence into national belonging, and with it a complicity that keeps calling art back into the national frame.

I examine this curious dynamic through a comparative ethnography of the art world in Istanbul and Berlin, two locations especially well-suited to explore this—for lack of a better word—darker, much neglected side of art. I propose that thinking though Turkey and Germany together allows for recognizing that its decivilizing capacity is as constitutive for our understanding of art as it is for the structural makeup of the art world. This is not to say that this entire book is a horror story about art or an effort to deny its transformative potential. Rather, I situate decivilizing moments within the daily workings of the art world and the practices with which artistic expression is governed, produced, and talked about. As such, the study is indebted to the argument that the emancipatory potential of art can only be (re)claimed by vigorously analyzing the conditions of its production, presentation, and circulation and by recognizing that our perception of art is always also mediated, and often delimited, by these conditions (Benjamin 2003 [1936], Adorno and Horkheimer 1969, Rancière 2010).

This comparative look at the art worlds of Berlin and Istanbul is motivated by the notable similarities in how cultural policies have been formulated in Germany and Turkey as both contexts have struggled with art as a vehicle for expressing modern nationhood. These congruencies are all the more striking when we consider that current art from Germany and from Turkey is evaluated differentially, mirroring the place that each country occupies in dominant geopolitical and civilizational imaginaries, imaginaries that continue to construe the world in terms of "West" and "East" or, more recently, of "Christianity" and "Islam" as separate and incommensurable entities. Despite this differential perception, I encountered a shared vocabulary with regard to the social, political, and cultural function of art when talking to artists, policy makers, critics, funding agencies, and others engaged in the art world. The commonalities of this vocabulary were most pronounced whenever there was conflict over the form, content, or instrumentalization of art, as all objections and criticism were invariably fought off using one master narrative: "All we are trying to do is contribute to the greater good!"

While taken for granted, the idea that art serves the greater good and is inherently beneficial deserves closer attention. Anthropologists have increasingly drawn on Alfred Gell's (1998, 4) proposition that "the anthropology of art cannot be the study of the aesthetic principles of this or that culture, but of the mobilization of aesthetic principles (or something like them) in the course of social interaction." Talking about art is a substantial part of art making because discourses on art do not just provide a context for distinguishing art from non-art (that is, making things recognizable as art) but also for negotiating the conditions under which art is produced, sold, bought, and presented. I take Gell's intervention as a cue to trace how different aesthetic theories, and particularly those pertaining to the assumed civilizing power of art—most prominently expressed in the idea of art as a greater good—are mobilized in the daily workings of the art world. It is in this vein that the study builds on insights gained from Howard Becker's *Art Worlds* (1982), in which he translated the institutional theory of art into a comprehensive sociological study.[5] Becker's meticulous survey of the different actors within the art world, most of whom had been unaccounted for in the sociology of art, demonstrates that "the making of art" requires collaboration and is dependent on institutional networks. Yet Becker's emphasis on collaboration tends to underplay the power differentials that are, in fact, constitutive for the art world. To better capture this dynamic my approach extends Arthur Danto's (1964) definition of the art world as an interplay of institutional spaces, practices, and authoritative theories to an assemblage of diverging intents and motivations of the many actors that together constitute the art world. I thus understand the art world as a terrain of struggle in which the inherent goodness of art is constantly constructed and disrupted.

Conducted mainly between 2005 and 2011, the fieldwork that informs this study aimed to capture how the different art world actors navigate national legacies and mediate their varying intentions and interests in the production and reception of art. It follows conversations with artists, critics, curators, art historians, art managers, corporate sponsors, and foundation and government officials about their respective understandings of art and their working practices. Historical and present evaluations of the local art scene and rationales behind sponsorship, funding, and cultural policies further guided my questions. I traced different understandings of art and artistic positions through participant observations at art openings, which provide meeting points for the art world, including audiences. Apart from attending exhibitions, conferences, and collectors' meetings, I followed arts publications along with the arts and culture pages of the daily news media, on- and offline. I reviewed policy papers to understand how official memory regimes underwrite legal and political discourses on art and to explore tensions between policy precepts and actual state practices. Artists, whom I met inside and outside their studios and who shared their experiences and their works in progress as well as their trials and tribulations, at times overtly and at others inadvertently directed my attention to the civilizing impact of art as a mediating discourse. Although the focus of this study is primarily on the visual arts, I interviewed a number of performance and theater artists, dancers, and filmmakers to better understand the similarities and differences between these artistic genres and gain further insights into the constitution of the art world in Istanbul and Berlin. After an initial mapping of each arts setting, I started to follow controversies, conflicts, and cases of censorship more closely. Some of these were reflected in the press; others were relayed to me through informal channels. I examined how artists tried to circumvent market rationales or undermine official history and why they protested the politics of certain arts institutions. To get a better grasp of the political economy of art, I tracked the money—by now as much a sensationalized facet of the art world as a persistent source of discomfort—as economic calculations are often regarded as adversarial to the civic power and emancipatory potential accorded to art.

It is based on these research experiences that I came to focus on the structural paradoxes that characterize the modern conception of art. I will detail these contradictions in the remainder of this introduction but will preliminarily sketch them as follows: In the framework of the state, but not only there, art is understood as a characteristically national. Yet art is also deemed a universal expression—while simultaneously being conceptualized as a deeply personal articulation. Art ostensibly "belongs to the people" and is a common good, but it is also a commodity that can be accumulated in private hands. This process—although vital for the art market and hence for the development of art and artists' livelihoods, is sometimes understood as a loss for the public. These contradictions are in need of constant mediation in the daily workings of the art world. Jacques Rancière (2004) proposes that the contemporary definition of art both arises from the modern condition and is taken as a manifestation of Enlightenment thought, thus producing a complex and at times perplexing self-referentiality in constant need of (re)affirmation. Emphasizing the decivilizing capacity of art provides an analytical lens to break this self-referentiality in the form of immanent critique. As such, the civilizing and decivilizing of art are not mutually exclusive processes but dialectic in nature. They are predicated upon each other in a web of relationships and practices that constantly veil the actual conditions under which art is produced, circulated, presented, bought, and sold; they need to be veiled in order to keep idealized understandings of art intact. Here, as throughout the study, I use the formulation "idealized understandings of art" not to romanticize art or certain artistic practices but to indicate widely shared, discursively legitimated, and historically situated understandings of the inherent goodness of art that serve to obscure a whole range of contradictions. These understandings are as constitutive for the political role of art as they are for the art market and for artists' self-perception, in short for all outlets of the art world. The idealized connotations of art pose a challenge to those working in the art world, often on a daily basis. Troubling the assumption of the goodness of art to varying degrees, it is these challenges that I take up in this book, along with historical episodes in which artworks are deemed harmful or are perceived as incompatible with the modern image that the state aims to present. These episodes and artworks are either suppressed in official history or portrayed as temporary deviations from the modernizing project. Before delving further into the conceptual framework of the book, let's turn to the art settings of Istanbul and Berlin.

In the Art World: Sites

Although Istanbul and Berlin may seem like "natural" choices for a comparative angle on Turkey and Germany, it should be noted that both cities are characterized by an extensive infrastructure of arts venues. Both have gained considerable attention in the international art market over the past two decades, in part from the acclaimed biennials that they host. And both draw artists from throughout the country as well as from abroad.

After its postwar reconstruction and the erecting of the Berlin Wall in 1961, West Berlin, cut off from its agrarian and industrial hinterlands, became a heavily subsidized cultural showcase, charged with displaying "democracy" and "freedom" to the other half of the city and the other, socialist Germany (see Borneman 1992). These measures were also intended to ameliorate West Berlin's isolation from "the mainland" of the Federal Republic. It was, however, also this very isolation that produced a certain subcultural flair that from the late 1960s onward attracted predominantly young people to a city made even more attractive by the exemption from compulsory military service (which remained in effect in the reunited Germany till 2011) for men residing in West Berlin. As Berlin had lost a considerable part of its population and labor force in the war and from the subsequent division, it became a major destination for labor migrants beginning in the late 1950s, first from

Italy and Spain and then Greece and Turkey, which added new dimensions to the city's cultural scene, although immigrants' cultural activities were mostly supported by informal networks until the rise of multiculturalism in the 1980s. With the reunification of the two Germanys in 1990 came the decision to reinstate Berlin as the capital. An array of programs was established to rekindle the city's status as a cosmopolitan center for the arts, frequently invoking the "glory days" of the Weimar Republic, which ended with the National Socialists' rise to power. One of these programs is the Capital Cultural Fund (Hauptstadtkulturfonds) financed by the federal government, for which the city has become a flagship project, the symbol of a young and vibrant Berliner Republik. Artists in Berlin are also eligible for another federal fund, the Kulturstiftung des Bundes (the German Federal Cultural Foundation), as well as project grants by the Berlin Senate and funding sources on the district level. In addition, Berlin has an array of public and private museums and galleries as well as nonprofit arts spaces. Along with other European countries, Germany has initiated significant cutbacks to its formerly much-famed arts funding structure since 2006; previous waves of rollbacks had occurred in the 1980s and 1990s. A significant difference from Turkey is that German artists who gain regular income from their artistic work can enroll in a special social security program called *Künstlersozialkasse* (artists' social fund). But as regular income from artistic work is hard to come by, many artists I met took on jobs in the service industry or applied for unemployment benefits and, sometimes, welfare.

Although not the formal capital, Istanbul has long been a center for the arts in Turkey, as it had been in its imperial formation. With a range of exhibition and performance venues, art academies, and arts foundations, it continues to attract artists from all provinces. Many of Istanbul's new arts institutions and museums have emerged through private rather than state initiatives and have flourished in the wake of the economic liberalization policies solidified by the military coup d'état of 1980. Independent art spaces and artists' initiatives have emerged, or rather reemerged, in the 1990s and throughout the 2000s, when the strict ban on civil society associations and cultural organizations enacted by the military junta was gradually lifted. Artistic expressions of domestic migrants, coming in waves in the 1950s and then again the 1960s, and internally displaced Kurds fleeing forty years of armed conflict have been an integral, if often neglected, part of Istanbul's cultural makeup. Similarly to Germany, there are state-administered as well as municipal and local funding categories, along with the cultural initiatives of political parties. But as artists and cultural managers often note, Turkey's state funding system is difficult to navigate, particularly for visual artists outside the state structures.

Since the 1980s, funds for contemporary art have been, comparatively speaking, minuscule. This had slowly been changing as Turkish authorities discovered the "soft power" of arts and culture programs in diplomatic efforts, especially in the framework of the now largely stalled European Union accession negotiations. As a result, funds for exhibitions abroad, and to a lesser extent in Turkey, have been made available. Exact numbers are hard to come by as representatives of the Ministry of Culture and Tourism admitted to me as recently as October 2013, in part because of the ad hoc decisions with regard to budget spending, which in any case is more geared toward tourism than the arts, and inadequate itemization in the ministry's yearly reports. The low level of government support for the arts also explains the vital role played by foreign cultural institutions located in Istanbul, such as the Goethe Institute, the Swedish Consulate, and the Institut Français. Artists who cannot make ends meet generally seek jobs in teaching at universities and schools or as private instructors. Others take on web design or translation work, but generally they prefer not to talk about their subsistence strategies. For most artists, working as a bartender—as do some of their colleagues in Berlin—seemed unthinkable given the low regard (and pay) for the service sector in Turkey. While generalizations are hard to make, it is nonetheless possible to say that in most cases—and in both locations—art remains a solidly middle-class affair, not least when it comes to cultural capital and educational background.

Notably, the cities of Berlin and Istanbul play distinct but parallel roles in their national imaginaries. Both are taken to symbolize past and present East-West divisions—and the bridging thereof—one being a capital of the past, that is, the Ottoman Empire, the other the capital of a once again united Germany. It is, of course, important to remember that "Istanbul is not Turkey" and "Berlin is not Germany," as so many of my interlocutors frequently emphasized. The concentration on these two metropolises means that in the German case less attention is given to the manifestations of German federalism—especially when it comes to cultural policy. In the case of Berlin, I am ultimately looking at a city where much art is produced but, in contrast to Cologne, Düsseldorf, and Munich, little is sold. Unlike these established centers of Germany's post–World War II "economic miracle," Berlin has struggled and for the most part failed to become an economic hub; for much of the 2000s the city of Berlin was teetering on the brink of bankruptcy. Its budget, deemed unconstitutional by German courts, inspired Berlin's long-time mayor Klaus Wowereit (2001–2014) to coin the phrase "*arm aber sexy*" (poor but sexy) to advertise his city's cultural vibrancy despite—or because of—its destitution. The focus on Berlin also means omitting details on the fate of the old West German capital, Bonn, where the Bundeskunsthalle (the Art and Exhibition Hall of the Federal Republic of Germany) still stands, as well as Kassel, which has hosted the internationally acclaimed *documenta* since 1955, an event specifically designed to situate Germany within the canon of modernism after World War II. Thus there is in this study a certain lack of attention to the makeup of pre- and postunification East Germany, to the disinvestment it experienced, and to newer phenomena, like the "New Leipzig School" for painting, which rose to (inter)national fame throughout the 1990s and 2000s. The focus on Istanbul in the Turkish case eclipses another established center, Ankara, which throughout its republican history has hosted important art academies and public art projects yet today mostly lacks public spaces for contemporary art, as does Izmir—a city once renowned for its artistic production. There are many newer centers of contemporary artistic production, such as Diyarbakır, not least because of a number of artists who have chosen to stay there and keep their jobs as elementary and high school art teachers while still shaping the contemporary art scene in Turkey significantly. Diyarbakır has been joined by such seemingly unlikely cities as Çanakkale, Mardin, and Sinop, where independent art festivals and biennials, museums, and local cultural policy initiatives have thrived over the past fifteen years or so.

Having ventured into this research in 2005, I witnessed how political, personal, and artistic alliances in Istanbul and Berlin's art world were forged or broken. Long-standing patterns, both spatial and organizational, changed course, sometimes unexpectedly. By mid-2008, for instance, Berlin's post-Wall art scene began moving back into the western parts of the city, a development that would have been hard to fathom during my initial research. While throughout my time in Berlin the fact that the city did not have a *Kunsthalle* or another institution with the financial means to exhibit current art produced in the city, including those of international acclaim, caused broad discontent, Thomas Demand finally opened his first solo show in the Neue Nationalgalerie in September 2009 (notably four years after an exhibition dedicated to his work had taken place at the MoMA).[6] Istanbul, in turn, has continued to see an explosion in the number of its commercial galleries, independent arts spaces, and initiatives. Few thought these projects would be able to survive given the lack of public funding, yet some continue to prosper. Others have dissolved, changed form, or struggle to hold on. New ones continue to spring up. When I began my research on cultural policy in Istanbul, the term "multiculturalism" was often used timidly by officials. By the end of my fieldwork it was part and parcel of all cultural policy discourses and beyond.

None of these examples comes to mean that "all has changed," nor do they in themselves signify major paradigm shifts. Yet each of my research stays drove home the much belabored but nonetheless valid point that ethnographic contemplations are but snapshots that capture particular moments. The following interrogation is thus based on the realization that despite the pace of the global art world when it comes to its constellations and conceptual preoccupations, certain discourses have endured and left traces in both Germany and Turkey that are worth exploring. Some of these discourses may speak more to the general constitution of cultural policy in modern nation-states than the two urban locations, Istanbul and Berlin, while others are very much rooted in their historical particularities and contexts. Both of these dynamics are also at play in more recent developments, namely, the rising authoritarianism and war in Turkey and the resurgence of right-wing politics and violence in Germany, which will be taken up in the concluding chapter. Their implications for the art world, hard to fathom during the completion of this study, while still emerging, speak once again to how nationalism in Europe and around the world keeps calling local formations of the global art world into the national frame.

In the Art World: Stories

Clifford Geertz (1975) famously defined culture as "the stories we tell ourselves about ourselves," and the ways that actors in both cities talked about the local art world, the stories they told themselves about themselves, were notable in their own right. When I began my fieldwork in Istanbul in the summer of 2005 and announced that I would initially be staying for seven months, it was not uncommon to hear that the Istanbul art world is "so small" that it should take me no more than a couple of weeks, "a month, tops," to talk to "everybody." My own assessment was, however, that I had barely scratched the surface, not least because I could only make it to a fraction of the exhibitions, conferences, panel discussions, and other art-related events that took place every week. The same was true for Berlin. I have often wondered where this perception of small scale might have come from and why it persists in Istanbul despite the rapid increase in art spaces over the last decade. One explanation might be the concentration of the contemporary art scene on the—geographically speaking—European side of the city, many of them in Beyoğlu, some in Nişantaşı and Levent. This perspective discounts a range of activities in other parts of the city, including Kadiköy on the Asian shore. Another way of making sense of the perception of small scale, however, might be that in contrast to what many Berlin artists described as an atmosphere of *Nebeneinander*, that is, a state of being next to one another that suggests a low level of mutual engagement, artists in Istanbul are frequently said (and say of themselves) to be "in one another's business." My sense is that differences in sociability in Berlin and

Istanbul derive, in part, from distinctive experiences of state support or the lack thereof. Especially after the 1980 coup d'état, state institutions were seen as unreliable—or for political reasons undesirable to work with in Turkey. This led to a situation where a few key curators, critics, and sponsors emerged who for many artists presented the only alternative for facilitating local exposure and fostering international connections. While in Berlin too, artists emphasize the importance of personal and professional networks in order to secure grants, exhibition opportunities, and international circulation, the lack of public funding makes these connections all the more important in Istanbul. However, the multiplication and diversification of independent and institutional actors in Istanbul's art world since the beginning of the 2000s has reconfigured the playing field considerably. Still, I witnessed firsthand that these kinds of dependency structures in the art world make gossip as much a favorite pastime as a source of crucial information. The same is true for Berlin, where gossip, rumors, and off-the-record remarks play an important role, not least because they present ways to counteract or highlight interdependencies between artists, curators, and critics and to navigate the internal politics of the art world. It is because of said dependency structures that off-the-record remarks referred to in the study are correlated only with the professional designations of respective interlocutors in order to maintain their anonymity. As research progressed, I learned that it was vital to make clear that I was not aligned with any of the often antagonistic camps in each setting (see Kosnick 2007). This often included remaining as vague as possible about to whom I had spoken previously, as interlocutors scrutinized not only my choices but also the order in which I proceeded.

Having grown up in Germany with parents who had immigrated in the later 1960s and early 1970s, a trajectory that in Turkey is associated with the derogatory label "*almanci*,"[7] I expected some unpleasant encounters with regard to my background. This was indeed at times the case but remained mostly anchored around the "German accent" my Turkish revealed for a number of people—while my coming via New York as a researcher just as frequently mitigated this situation. The fact that since 2004 there has been an increased interest in immigrant cultural production from Germany on the international scene (the award-winning films of Fatih Akin were frequently credited for the changing perception of emigrants from Turkey and their descendants) also played into the dynamics of my fieldwork interactions. Yet I found myself somewhat taken aback by the circumstance that this part of my personal background had turned into some kind of cultural currency. My arrival in Berlin, in turn, coincided with one of many waves of public controversies on immigration and "integration," in which immigrants from Turkey and their descendants featured once again prominently, especially as in the aftermath of September 11 the terms "Muslim" and "immigrant" have become synonymous in Germany (see also Mandel 2008). At the time, discussions galvanized around propositions to make speaking German mandatory in schoolyards, a so-called Muslim test designed to ascertain that Muslim immigrants who applied for naturalization were committed to the German constitution (featuring such questions as "would you allow your daughter to wear a mini-skirt?," see also Ewing 2008), and the then still ongoing Danish caricature scandal[8] that led many politicians and journalists alike to conclude that Islam and democracy were utterly incompatible. These debates had been followed closely in the art world, with the result that many interlocutors wanted to discuss these and other issues of my personal background with me. Here it was especially my "accent-free" German that raised attention and was frequently remarked on. The fact that "an immigrant kid" appeared in the shape of a researcher from the United States seemed to pose somewhat of a conceptual impossibility for a number of people I interviewed. After an initial phase of frustration, I decided to conduct my interviews in English whenever I could foresee one-time meetings, to avoid these kinds of lengthy discussions that my designation as an *Ausländer* (foreign national)[9] seemed to invite. The reactions I encountered in both locations are as much a facet of the historical interrelation between Turkey and Germany, sketched in more detail in the sections that follow, as they are part of the interplay between the categories of "insider" and "outsider," "native" or "non-native" of any fieldwork experience, so eloquently analyzed by Kirin Narayan (1993).[10]

The Enduring Power of Asymmetric Perception

In their video work *Road to Tate Modern* (2003), Şener Özmen and Erkan Özgen appear to us as present-day versions of Don Quixote and Sancho Panza. Donning suits and ties, they are on horse- and donkeyback respectively, with Özmen carrying the iconic Quixotian spear—in his case, a long stick. Riding through the mountainous outskirts of Diyarbakir, where both artists hail from, they seem weary. A soft song hummed in the background accompanies them. Tired from the long journey—forty days and forty nights, according to Özgen/Panza—they decide to refresh themselves at a little stream that cuts through the arid landscape. Once back in the saddle and a little farther along the way, they cross paths with another traveler. Addressing him in Kurdish, they say that they have lost their way and ask which path to take to reach the Tate Modern. With gestures and words, the traveler directs them up the mountain. "Is it far?" they ask. "Yes," he replies, "yes, it is very far, but you can make it." *Road to the Tate Modern* humorously yet forcefully questions the possibility of arriving at the center of the global art world—exemplified by the seemingly unreachable Tate Modern—when producing in its double "periphery." Here, the notion of periphery denotes not merely Turkey, or Istanbul for that matter, but the war-torn Kurdish landscape. Özmen and Özgen's work poignantly addresses the fact that where artists come from not only affects the conditions of artistic production but continues to shape the perception of their work. The global hierarchy of value (Herzfeld 2003, see also Winegar 2006, Wu 2009) pervades the transnational circulation of contemporary art through dichotomies of "East" and "West," "ethnic art" and "art proper," "artistic centers" and "peripheries." And this despite the fact that with Edward Said's *Orientalism* (1978) and the critiques of visual representations of the Other it has inspired (Lewis 2004, Price 2007, Mitchell 2009), the end of such hierarchizations has been postulated many times over.

The stubbornness with which these dichotomies are reproduced and the asymmetries they have created has led to art from Turkey long being judged according to its merging of "traditional" and "modern" currents, thus implying that "modernity proper" is external to Turkey. This is as much the case for historical evaluations as it is for contemporary art. A more recent inflection of this assessment is the notion that art from Turkey is first and foremost "political"—with political denoting local or national concerns. In contrast, German art is now understood as unquestionably modern *and* as not (or at least not necessarily or primarily) related to national politics. "Now" is the operative term here, since this has not always been the case, not least in the official German imagination, in which modernism in the arts was long identified as decidedly "un-German." It was, after all, not until the 1950s that West Germany adopted explicitly Occidental cultural policies to transcend long-standing anti-Western and antimodernist currents as part of its post–World War II rehabilitation into the international community, a process that the historian Konrad Jarausch (2006) has described as "recivilizing Germany"—a term I will return to in more detail in the course of the book. What makes this asymmetric perception even more notable is that Turkey embarked on aligning itself with the "West" by "modernizing" its artistic canon as early as 1923. As Ottoman art, like all aspects of its cultural landscape, was deemed unfit for the modern nation-state in the eyes of its new leaders, modernism was officially, if contradictorily, embraced. Whereas Germany's position has been normalized—that is, it has been accepted as part of the modern West—the question of what makes for Turkey' s modernness in the arts and beyond has remained a matter of contention ever since.

Despite these notable divergences and the long-standing emphasis on alterity between Turkey and Germany in politics, scholarship, and public discourses, both locations share intriguing historical and structural similarities.

Arriving relatively late on the nation-state scene and long maintaining authoritarian governing structures, ideas of cultural commonality and ethnicity, rather than civic citizenship, were emphasized in both Germany and Turkey (Stolcke 1995, Akçam 2004). This notion of culture comprised artistic production as an integral expression of peoplehood and emerged in distinction to either a "foreign" civilization or a discredited civilization of the past. For Germany, the formative Other in the field of culture and art was France (Elias 1978) and then, after 1945, Nazism (Knoblich 2001); for Turkey, it has long been the Ottoman Empire. The emphasis on cultural commonality in German and Turkish nationalism also entailed comparable searches for a distinctive artistic style to create internal cohesion, assert modern nationhood, and—ultimately—Western belonging (Belting 1993, Bozdoğan 2001). I use the phrase "assert modern nationhood" here to indicate once again that against prevalent notions, both locales have at different times been confronted with considerable doubts concerning their "modernness." When I talk about the historical legacies of the doubts and insecurities regarding the modernness of Turkey and Germany, I do not mean to perpetuate tropes of Germany's *Sonderweg*—the special path—as Germany's modernization process has been described or of Turkey's continual belatedness, a trope that prevails across scholarship on Turkey. On the contrary, one substantial task of this study is to show how these two discourses of exceptionalism have served to obscure a range of political predicaments and inequities in both national contexts and how they have been reflected in the governance of art.

In both locales pronounced state support for the arts has been bound to the idea that aesthetic education is a civilizing agent formative for modern personhood (Glaser 1997, Sağlar 1994). Turkish and German cultural policies have equally claimed that such support serves to secure freedom, democracy, and pluralism, all regarded as political manifestations of idealized notions of modernity (Hamilton 1996).[11] Given these congruencies, this study interrogates how cultural policies and their legacies are affecting the production and reception of art in the present. Without obscuring the vicissitudes of Turkey's modernization project, manifest in limitations of the freedom of expression and the fragility of democratic governance structures, the comparative perspective put forth here operates from an understanding of modernity not as a contained phenomenon but as a shared trajectory encompassing politics, economy, society, and culture in divergent locations (Kahn 2001). While imperial orders and colonial politics have long connected people in faraway places, and quite intimately so (Lowe 2015), the coevalness of modernity (Fabian 1983), beyond the specific cases of Germany and Turkey, has been constantly disavowed.

Encounters

Along with historical parallels, this intimacy too informs my inquiry, an intimacy produced through a series of entanglements between the Ottoman Empire, and later the Republic of Turkey, and its German counterparts. Germany and Turkey share a long and often troubling history of economic and intellectual exchange and political allegiance, to which the cities Istanbul and Berlin bear witness. Yet these connections remain largely obscured in politics and public memory, with the result that contemporary encounters between Germany and Turkey, be they in the political arena or academia, on TV programs or in the art world, are always accompanied by professions of both difference and unfamiliarity (raising the question: How are "we" to ascertain difference if "we" do not know each other?). It is against this background that discussions of German-Turkish relations have mostly focused on the unidirectional labor migration from Turkey to Germany starting in the 1960s, modulations of "guest" and "host," and the question whether "Turks" could be "integrated into German society." This focus has obscured the two-way stream of traveling military personnel, political refugees, monies, scholars, artists, and ideas that preceded the "guest worker treaty" (Marchand 1996b, Böer et al. 2002, Emre 200). In the course of the nineteenth century, German entrepreneurs and workers, military generals, adventurers, and archaeologists sought opportunities or offered their services in an empire for which imperial Germany had its own economic and political designs (Fuhrmann 2011). Traces of these interactions can be found, for instance, when strolling through the Monumentenfriedhof in Berlin-Schöneberg, where a number of tombstones dating back to the late nineteenth and early twentieth century mark the graves of those who ventured from Berlin to Istanbul. During the same time period, Ottoman orphans were placed as apprentices with German craftsmen. When Ottoman university students produced a socialist paper in their offices just a block away from Berlin's famous Ku'damm boulevard in 1919, military men who had come to Prussia to get insights for reforming the Ottoman army (first official military exchanges date back to 1789), diplomats, merchants, and journalists had already established a presence in Germany. For the newly unified German Kaiserreich (1871), foreign cultural policy in Ottoman Empire presented the testing ground for operationalizing culture in the domestic sphere, that is, developing a cohesive national cultural policy at home. Earlier anecdotes, such as those about Protestant Bavarian farmers who joined the Ottoman army to flee religious oppression in their homelands in the sixteenth century, also shine a different light on the shared history of the Ottoman Empire and the Germanys (Andrews and Kalpaklı 2005, 27). While the alliance that the Ottoman Empire entered with Germany during World War I is still remembered—notably more so in Turkey than in Germany—the trade debts that Germany defaulted on in the process are rarely, if ever, publicly acknowledged today (Güçlü 2000). Neither are German efforts to frame this military alliance in terms of a Holy War—that is, as a call to jihad (Hagen 2004). There are other troubling aspects of Germany and Turkey's joint history: German race theory, before being applied to Jewish and other "unwanted" populations during the Third Reich, was first elaborated upon Ottoman Armenians, regarded as major competitors—and hence obstacles—to German economic and political aspirations in Anatolia, especially along the route of the Berlin–Baghdad Railway (Kaiser 1997, Anderson 2007, McMeekin 2010).[12] Ottoman-Armenian and German history converged once again, this time in Berlin, when Talat Pasha, one of the architects of the Armenian genocide, fled to the German capital to avoid prosecution and was shot there by Soghomon Tehlirian, the sole survivor of his family, in 1921.[13] Turkey often prides itself for taking in Jewish refugees during World War II (Reisman 2006), among them Ernst Reuter, who went on to become Berlin's mayor (1948–1953), and Erich Auerbach, who wrote *Mimesis* while teaching at Istanbul University (Konuk 2010). But while it has been acknowledged that Turkish diplomats acting on individual initiative issued Turkish passports to Jews, the fact that the Turkish state did little to protect its Jewish expatriates in Berlin and elsewhere in Europe from Nazi persecution has received little attention (Guttstadt 2008). I point to these encounters not to establish simple connections or haphazard convergences in history. Rather, I see them as indicative of a constitutive intimacy between Turkey's and Germany's imperial and national formations, between what is generally considered "East" and "West." These encounters unsettle not just the temporality that these dichotomies suggest. They also unsettle notions of radical alterity and mutual unfamiliarity that pervade the imaginaries of contemporary Turkey and Germany, while denying their interrelations. They are forgotten today because they no longer have political currency, in contrast to the late nineteenth century, when Germany—in light of its imperial designs—hailed its ties to the Ottoman Empire as closer than those to any "other *European* country" (Gross 1979, 167, emphasis mine). While some of these encounters play into specific episodes in the decivilizing of art taken up in the course of this book, there is another issue that I want to get at here. The method of comparison has a long tradition in the social sciences, yet this project frequently induced unease. This unease would have not necessarily come up if I had compared voting patterns, EU integration policies, or even minority regimes. It stems from the proposition that together with the politics of art, artistic production from Turkey is commensurable and comparable with that from Germany. Today, German art is unquestionably (and unmarked) "Art," whereas art from Turkey continues to be "Turkish art." Falling outside "the topos of West European . . . superiority" (Böröcz 2006, 112), how artistic production from Turkey is evaluated today frequently mirrors the projection of radical otherness that has marked much of the scholarship on the Ottoman Empire and the Turkish Republic. This is a problematic notion, since much seems to suggest that the Ottoman Empire saw itself and was perceived "very much [as] part of Early Modern Europe" (Deringil 2007, 713). Analyzing the long-time, if shifting, alliances between Ottoman and Christian-European officials, the historian Selim Deringil (like Gross) argues that thinking of Europe and the Ottoman Empire as "two separate and irreconcilable entities" is a fallacy in the "historicity" it projects. What emerges instead is a process in which the image of the "barbarous Turk" and "the fad of Turqueries that swept across Enlightenment Europe," abjection and admiration, frequently traded places. A similar dynamic was at work in Ottoman evaluations of Christian Europe. It was only in the second part of the eighteenth century that negative tropes of the Ottoman Empire were foregrounded (Bevilacqua and Pfeifer 2013). This negative image alone is hardly sufficient to evidence the Otherness of the Ottoman Empire. After all, the relationship between imperial Germany and France, or France and England for that matter, could be described in similar terms. Notably, interventions such as Deringil's have done little to unsettle the narrative that with the onset of the Renaissance, Western Europe reigned in an era of progress and reason while the Near and Middle East remained mired in tradition and despotism. This understanding has long informed art history as a discipline tending to "Western art," one based on a canon in which the Renaissance presents both an ontological and a geopolitical marker. Here too, a closer look reveals that the relationship between "the West" and the Ottoman realm was actually much closer throughout the Renaissance than formerly assumed, that it was characterized by encounters, interlocution, and parallelisms. The art historians Lisa Jardine and Jerry Brotton (2000) are among those who firmly situate the origins of Renaissance culture in a "two-way material exchange" between the Ottoman Empire and Christian European powers, thus contradicting the standardized notion of the Ottoman Empire as merely a formative Other to a nascent understanding of "Europeanness." Instead, they propose that elites in the Ottoman Empire and Christian Europe laid claims to the same heritage, including a shared iconography. As the same artists enjoyed the patronage of the Ottoman and other European courts, paintings, commemorative coins, and other "cultural currencies" were exchanged in the course of diplomatic missions. These exchanges were both based on a mutually intelligible visual repertoire and further developed common imaginaries.[14] Shared motifs not only existed in the visual arts but also in literary production, making the normalization of conceptions of radical alterity all the more notable. Focusing on the "long sixteenth century" as a period of cultural, political, and social upheavals and of "intense mutual attention" from the perspective of comparative literature, Walter G. Andrews and Mehmet Kalpaklı (2005, 26–27) identify a shared interest in self-sacrificing love for the absolute ruler, god, and "beloveds of all sorts." They argue that analogous sociopolitical conditions and the common grounding in Hellenic heritage expressed themselves through parallels in the genre of devotional poetry in the urban centers of the Ottoman Empire as well as in Rome, Venice, and London. Often describing the affection between two men, this devotional poetry was subject to similar onslaughts of moral panic in all of these locations. Despite these interventions that highlight mutuality, exchange, vivid competition, and a multidirectional transfer of knowledge (Mack 2002), the reductive understanding of Islam as a "carrier civilization" (Asad 2002, 217) that preserved but did not develop classic art and scholarship[15] continues to shape evaluations of Near and Middle Eastern art. Drawing on Ann Stoler's (2006, 6) argument that the assumption of "incomparability compels forgetting," I propose that the suppression of the histories and memories of these encounters feeds into the asymmetry through which Germany and Turkey are conceptualized geopolitically—and artistically.

In this study, comparison is thus not conceptualized in the classic anthropological sense pioneered by the structural functionalists, who identified "discrete"' cultural or social units that could be compared and contrasted cross-culturally, examined the diffusion of certain artistic styles, or asked if the very notion of art can be transposed from one society to another (Boas 1955, Anderson 1992, Morphy and Perkins 2006). I neither propose that the artistic heritage and lineages of Turkey and German exhibit the same inherent "qualities," aesthetically or otherwise, nor that preoccupations with different styles and schools of art were the same at all times. Instead, I begin with the assumption of familiarity—even intimacy—and hence comparability of Turkey and Germany, Berlin and Istanbul, as a way to think through a set of interrelated questions regarding the civilizing function accorded to art and the moments when art is seen to cede this function. For this reason, the comparative perspective is woven throughout the entirety of the study, in a side-by-side reading of nation building and modernization through the lens of art; of formulations of cultural policies; practices of producing, presenting, selling, and collecting art; and of delimitations of the freedom of the arts in both locations. In trying to escape the enduring power and allure of asymmetric perception and the conceptual limitations it has produced, I follow the historian and postcolonial theorist Dipesh Chakrabarty's (2000, 34–35) suggestion to destabilize "the themes of 'failure,' 'lack,' and 'inadequacy'" that are as ubiquitous in academic treatments on India as they are in those on Turkey, by employing "a gesture of inversion," to "read 'plentitude' and 'creativity' where this narrative has made us read 'lack' and 'inadequacy.'" Taking up this "gesture of inversion," the study moves away from the notions of lack and failure in Turkish modernization not solely by attributing "plentitude" and "creativity" to the aesthetic expressions and the multitude of debates on art from Turkey but by accounting for the fact that in Germany, too, similar preoccupations regarding the mutual expressiveness of art and modernity have existed and continue to do so. And this, even though Germany's efforts at establishing its Western belonging have been highly successful and its artistic standing is no longer questioned. This kind of retelling of the Turkish and German experience of modernity through art opens the path for a second inversion. By focusing not on the civilizing but decivilizing capacity of art, we can begin to rethink our assumptions about art and gain more contoured insights into how art is constituted institutionally and politically. I hence emphasize periodic ruptures in the modernization narratives of Turkey and Germany in which different modulations of decivilized art figure prominently. Thinking through the German and Turkish cases together, I argue that—all historical specificities notwithstanding—both present struggles with the normativity of modern power. The mutually dependent projects of nationalism and modernity have informed and structured discourses on the arts and produced a joint vocabulary that serves to reconcile the contradictions inherent in the modern conception of art and to disavow the entanglements of art in state violence.

The Modern Conception of Art

At this point, it might be helpful to dwell a bit more on the modern conception of art and how it emerged. Elaborated in Enlightenment thought, this notion, with all its contradictions, still shapes understandings of art today. It is in its formation that the idea of the inherent goodness of art is situated, an idea that forms the basis of a range of aesthetic theories that are mobilized whenever tensions arise between the proposed beneficial nature of art and its many political and economic uses.

One very productive way of tracing the modern conception of art is through the commodification of literature in the eighteenth century as proposed by the art theorist Martha Woodmansee (1994).[16] Woodmansee describes how the developing book market, while lending unprecedented exposure to literary works, fueled an antagonism between authors and book dealers. Since, at the time, artistic works were understood as renderings of the world that was ultimately accessible to everyone (a notion that corresponds with the imitation theory of art already sketched in ancient philosophy), artists often received only a nominal honorarium for their labor. It was the quality of this imitation that distinguished individual works of art from one another as well as art from non-art. Artists' subsistence strategies were further undermined by the absence of copyright regulations, resulting in numerous unauthorized reprints of their work and a price war among "pirating" publishers. It was in this context, Woodmansee argues, that a debate about the very character of art arose. Rather than seeing art as the skilled representation of what is "out there," it gradually became an imaginative creation in its own right, one that, originating from the artist's individual "genius," transcended nature. While this conceptual shift strengthened artists' positions vis-à-vis the market, it simultaneously obscured the embeddedness of artistic developments (and indeed of the modern concept of art itself) *in* the market, including the conceptualization of art as a profession (Baxandall 1972, Kempers 1987).[17] As the commodification of literature leveled the way for art to be negotiated in terms of demand and supply, writers and thinkers became acutely distrustful of the effect of the market on artistic expression. In an attempt to counter the manipulative force of the market, they developed different modes of defining works of art as self-sufficient, meaning that art was understood as both indifferent to and autonomous from the conditions of its production. In these elaborations, aesthetic value was no longer based on the reality out of which an artwork arose but on the relationships between its "component parts" (Woodmansee 1994, 16). This interpretative move was popularized in France in the first and in England the second half of the nineteenth century through formulations such as *l'art pour l'art* (art for art's sake), "the uselessness of art," or "aestheticism," all of which suggested that solely aesthetic markers such as inner harmony and symmetry should be measures for artistic accomplishment and value. Although the question of what makes for "purely" aesthetic markers has remained a matter of contention, these understandings laid the groundwork for what would become known as the formalist school of art in the twentieth century (Greenberg 1961, Eldridge 1995 [1985]).

It is notable that the emphasis on disinterest, that is, the idea that art should serve no other end than itself, idealized art as incommensurable with the market at the exact moment when art was integrated into the market as a particular kind of commodity. Incommensurability with the market in turn also meant incommensurability with the masses. It is through these interpretative shifts that the question of taste, and hence of the audience, came increasingly to the fore. To be more exact, what emerged was a stratified view on taste, a distinction, as Pierre Bourdieu (1984) would later describe it, between the masses that consumed "popular art" and the few "men of rarified taste" (and these connoisseurs, just as the artists, were always imagined as men, as Woodmansee and others remind us), who were able to exercise true appreciation thanks to their expertise on Art with a capital A (Zolberg 1990, 155–61). At other times, the autonomy of art has been understood as setting art apart from other kinds of expressions and thus shielding it from interventions, for instance, from politics. That the notion of the autonomy of art presents a vehicle to argue for a wide range of often conflicting ends also crystallizes in one of its most well-known formulations, that of Immanuel Kant. In his *Critique of Judgment*, Kant conceptualized art as expressing "purposiveness without purpose" (*Zweckmässigkeit ohne Zweck*). At the same time, he elaborated on art's potential for "subliminal instruction," in which the contemplation of beauty as "a symbol of morality" (1987 [1790], 228, §59) provides a cognitive tool through which we can realize our common humanity (also see Mortensen 1997, 160). He thus proposed a link between the beautiful and the moral, arguing that "trained receptivity to beauty can aid the growth of morals, and, conversely, that moral growth can dispose us to beauty" (Bell-Villada 1996, 23–24). It is this linkage that ideas of art as a conduit for civic cultivation frequently draw on, even though the extent to which art is open to explicit pedagogization remains debated, exactly because of its proposed autonomy.

The modern conception of art needs to be correlated with the rise of the nation-state not only because of its embeddedness in the capitalist market. Terry Eagleton (1990, 9) has argued that the centrality of aesthetics in European philosophy since the Enlightenment was a vital part of the bourgeois class project, especially as "the idea of autonomy—of a mode of being which is entirely self-regulating and self-determining—provides the middle class with just the ideological model of subjectivity it requires for its material operation." On the often violent road to the nation-state, art was no longer an expression of the divine but a symbol through which competing social and political groups sought to legitimize their claims to power through the aesthetic, perhaps even the sublime (Kempers 1987).

The contradictions inherent in the modern conception of art are thus inherent in modernity itself: As art becomes framed as a highly individual expression it is also—especially under the impetus of Romanticism—increasingly interpreted as a manifestation of the national collective. It is at this historical conjuncture that art is defined as increasingly autonomous from both society and the market. While art is accorded universal value, only the few, the "select," are deemed able to appreciate it for "what it really is." As will emerge repeatedly throughout this study, art is often seen as an expression of shared experiences, yet its appreciation requires formal knowledge. At times, art is understood as an educative tool, yet it should not yield itself to didacticism or—worse—instrumentalization. The more art is viewed as a civilizing—or disciplining—force, the more it is also identified as a means to transform society as well as to escape from society: a means of governance as well as a challenge to it. When art is talked about in the daily settings of the art world these seemingly discrete—and historically situated—theoretical takes on art are frequently merged in order to reconcile the tensions arising from the contradictory facets of the modern conception of art. This merging expresses itself in shorthands, such as that of art as a greater good and as inherently beneficial, as advancing critical thinking and democracy, and as an expression of "our common humanity." All of these formulations vernacularize an entire history of thinking about art and aesthetics, condensing heterogeneous lines of thought that are taken for granted and only questioned—if at all—in moments of crisis. It is in these moments of crisis that I locate the decivilizing aspects and capacities of art, moments that ever so often reveal that articulations of modernity and progress, civility and enlightenment in the making of the nation-state, as in discourses on art, are deeply intertwined with and predicated upon different kinds of violence.

Outline of the Book

Chapter 1, "Modernity, Nationalism, and Civilizing the Arts," further elaborates on the grounds of comparison and the conceptual framework of this study by discussing parallels and differences between the German and Turkish modernization projects in which cultural policy has played an exponent role. Drawing on postcolonial critiques of modernization theories, the chapter examines what tropes of "belatedness" and "exception" actually reveal and obscure in each case. At the heart of this inquiry are the emblematic controversies over how to create "national art" and how art has been used to represent modern nationhood against persisting doubts from within and without Turkey and Germany. The controversies surrounding "national art" discussed in this chapter show how ideas of modernity and civility remain indebted to processes of violence that art must always disavow.

"Art Worlds: Of Friends, Foes, and Working for the Greater Good," Chapter 2, takes us deeper into the art world, mapping the ways that art world actors relate to one another in the arts setting of both cities. It traces how aesthetic theories are mobilized in the daily workings of the art world to reconcile conflicting understandings of art. As relationships between artists, audiences, critics, curators, and art dealers are frequently personalized through a friend/

foe binary, I argue that motifs of amity and enmity serve to mediate structural dependencies and power differentials in the art world that are rooted in the inherent contradictions of the modern conception of art. A second mediating discourse, often employed by collectors and sponsors, reconciles divergent interests through the trope of art's civilizing capacities and hence of art as a "greater good" that is ultimately framed in national terms.

This trope is mirrored in Turkish and German cultural policies that have been based on the modernist notions of aesthetic education as a civilizing agent and as essential for modern personhood. How these notions have been translated into cultural policy is the topic of Chapter 3, "Governing Culture, Producing Modern Citizens." Here I focus on the tension between art as a supposedly functionless good and the many ways that art is operationalized by the state. I highlight major debates and turning points in Turkish and German cultural policies, including now obscured episodes that have shaped them significantly. These include the multifaceted debates on the relationship between art and politics in the early Turkish Republic and the fact that engagements abroad, including arts initiatives in the Ottoman Empire, were formative for domestic German cultural policy.

"The Art of Forgetting," Chapter 4, examines decivilizing moments that constitute silences in national art histories, such as those surrounding art collections that are historically related to the dispossession of minorities—including the Holocaust, the Armenian genocide, and the wealth tax (1942–1943) for non-Muslims. It discusses how East German art was not simply devalued but came to be seen as a deviation from the modern paradigm in a reunited Germany so much so that it was declared both aesthetically and morally bankrupt and equated to Nazi cultural production. Similarly, works created during the Anatolian painting tours (1938–1943) that "failed" to adequately represent Turkey's modernization have been lost to this day. I discuss how artists reify or break these silences on historical instances deemed unspeakable within the civilizing narrative of the state.

A different facet of art deemed outside of the boundaries of the civilizing discourse is the focus of Chapter 5, "The Politics of Art and Censorship." Here, I look at the attempts to censor the exhibitions *Regarding Terror,* thematizing media perceptions of the Red Army Faction (Berlin) and *Free Kick* (Istanbul), mainly featuring works on the Kurdish question and other instances of state violence. Under the shadow of the "global war on terror" and each country's historical challenges with "security politics," critics of each exhibition casted doubts on the assumed benefits of art and construed arts and politics as incommensurable. Outlining how freedom of expression is circumscribed by official memory regimes in both countries, the chapter analyzes different modes of censorship and the variety of actors engaged in it. I highlight that silencing efforts use the argument of the autonomy of art not to shield art from political intervention but to suppress political expression through the arts.

Chapter 6, "Enterprising Art, Aestheticizing Business," explores the political economy of art in urban spaces marked by waves of dispossession and social segmentation. Formerly inhabited by minorities, the physical "voids" of Istanbul and Berlin (Huyssen 2003) have become nexuses for the tenacious dualism of enterprising art and aestheticizing business, with gentrification being just one—but the most visible—component of this dynamic, in which artists are both complicit and resistant. Anchoring the discussion in the biennials that both cities host, I argue that the spectacularization of art in urban space has been vital in veiling the decivilizing histories of post-coup Turkey and the specter of Nazism that loomed over Germany's reunification. Finally, the chapter takes a look at the counterstrategies that artists developed to (re-)claim urban spaces for artistic interventions as well as for engagements with their difficult pasts.

1
Modernity, Nationalism, and Civilizing the Arts

> You will find that the questions that you are asking are of minor—if any—relevance for the German context.
>
> —SENIOR GERMAN ANTHROPOLOGIST, BERLIN, 2006

> The difference between the arts settings of Berlin and Istanbul? What difference? There is none.
>
> —VASIF KORTUN, ISTANBUL, 2005

"Germany and Turkey are incomparable." "That's like comparing apples and oranges . . . it just doesn't work—you can't do that! Especially when it comes to art." These were the initial reactions I received after presenting my research project to colleagues in Germany. These statements might be expected given that, especially within the current European imagination, Germany and Turkey are conceptualized in terms of radical alterity. The former is frequently cited as a model for successful modernization, while the latter is regarded as seriously flawed, if not a failure altogether. Similarly, Germany's artistic lineages are now firmly established within the Western canon, while those of the Ottoman Empire and modern Turkey are considered to be outside thereof.

In what follows I am further elaborating the grounds of comparison, that is, the ways that I propose to think through and think together the cases of Turkey and Germany. Discussing parallels and differences in nation-state building in the two contexts, this chapter traces how the national frame and its different iterations have historically been constituted. As I am comparing and contrasting two narratives on the role of art in claiming and consolidating modern nationhood, I am less focusing on individual artists or specific schools of art and more on the discussions among state actors and public intellectuals in both locations. Thus, I address art mostly in the generalized way that is frequently inherent in these debates, namely, as a civilizing vehicle, to show how different conceptions of art have been mobilized in the making of modern Germany and Turkey.

Taking Vasıf Kortun's[1] assertion on the "sameness" of the art world in Istanbul and Berlin as a point of departure, I draw on poststructuralist and postcolonial critiques that have tackled the concept of modernity with regard to the prevalent understandings of the periodization and of the "location of modernity" (Mitchell 2000, Deeb and Winegar 2012). These critiques have fundamentally unsettled the idea of a linearly developing modernity and its emancipatory potential by showing that discourses on modernity and civilization have served both to legitimize and disavow epistemological, structural, and physical violence in its many forms. Dominant historiographies have long spatialized and ascribed the philosophical tenets, economic processes, and political institutions of modernity to the West (or, alternatively, the "global North"). Consequently, the "Rest" of the world, to take Stuart Hall's expression for a reified notion of the East and the "underdeveloped" South, was merely left to follow its model, struggling to catch up (Hall 1996, Ahıska 2003). To be clear, the joint reading proposed here does not argue for "alternative" or "multiple modernities" (e.g., Hannerz 1996, Gaonkar 2001) in the two national frameworks. Instead, it analyzes respective experiences of the "normativity" of modern power (Scott 1999) through the interlocution between the processes of state formation and discourses on art as a national expression.

Despite dominant notions, there have been considerable contingencies and insecurities regarding both Germany and Turkey's modernness, insecurities that continue to shape the governance of art. This chapter thus analyzes two tropes of exceptionalism through which Germany and Turkey, their state-formations and geopolitical positions, have been described. It asks what these tropes reveal and obscure and how they continue to be, seemingly contradictorily, both present and disavowed. The notion of "belated modernity" has provided an explanatory model for a range of predicaments in Turkey. The idea of the German *Sonderweg*—a conceptual attempt to grapple with Germany's own historical sense of belatedness—has been both refuted and reified in scholarship and politics. These two discourses of exceptionalism are intimately intertwined with how nationalism and modernity have been reflected in debates on the arts in Germany and Turkey.

National Formations: Convergences and Divergences

Étienne Balibar (1991b, 86–87) argues that myths of national origin derive their ideological efficacy from claiming to be manifestations of a people's "destiny," in which the nation-state form becomes the embodiment of "a people's" will to self-determination. It is on the basis of such proclaimed peoplehood that the nation-state is portrayed as the culmination of a rational "project" that unfolds linearly and cohesively. Yet in the German as in the Turkish case, as with nationalist movements in general, the very delimitation and definition of "the people" has been a contentious issue. The myth of "the nation" and hence of national homogeneity is far from being a one-time process but has been constantly made and remade in Turkey and Germany, and these periodic consolidation efforts have also inscribed themselves in the discourses on the arts.

Turkish nationhood was formally legitimized in the international arena by the ratification of the Lausanne Treaty, which established the Republic of Turkey in 1923. In practice, however, the construction of the nation has been a conflicted and violent process that has to be analyzed with regard to the transition from a highly heterogeneous empire to a homogeneously conceptualized republic. Turkey was produced actively through genocidal violence against Armenians, Assyrians, and Pontian and Anatolian Greeks (largely perpetrated between 1915 and 1917); the expulsion of entire populations; and other far-reaching methods of demographic and social engineering.

In order to achieve nationhood, Germany had to bridge the fragmentation between a conglomerate of principalities and free cities that had emerged out of the remnants of the Holy Roman Empire. These geopolitical entities were frequently denominationally divided and maintained their own borders and taxation systems until a unified German state was founded with the end of the Franco-Prussian War in 1871. The demographic policies of the National Socialist regime that culminated in the Holocaust fundamentally homogenized Germany's population and can in part be understood as an effort in state consolidation, furthered by the integration of expelled ethnic Germans from Poland and other Eastern Bloc countries after World War II.

Although the establishment of the respective states, Germany's unification in 1871 and the establishment of the Turkish Republic in 1923, were fifty-two years apart, both national histories are frequently characterized through the trope of belated arrival on the nation-state scene. Often seen to have caused a sense of inferiority and insecurities regarding their position in "the modern world," this trope has been employed as an explanatory device for the compensatory politics exhibited in both cases, that is, the proneness for authoritarianism and, consequently, state-led modernization.

At times, unified Germany is described as having developed by way of "defensive modernization," a term that suggests a somewhat flawed process, reactive rather than active, born out of necessity rather than volition. Despite the widespread usage of this term, this "flaw" is rarely, if ever, addressed as such. Instead, scholars continue to discuss Germany's modernization under the heading of the *Sonderweg*—an idea elaborated in the nineteenth and early twentieth century from within Germany that diagnosed a "special path" for the country's modernization, thanks to its particular history, which set it apart from Western powers (Kocka 1999, Lepenies 2006, see also Blackbourn and Eley 1984).[2] Indeed, not unlike Turkey (often described as a bridge between East and West), Germany long equated its geographical location with its political orientation, describing itself as a cultural and geopolitical intermediary power (*Mittelmacht*) between the East (especially Russia) and the West. In Turkey, the discourse of the "need to catch up" to an ever-leading West has persisted not only throughout more than ninety years of the Republic but can be traced back to the eighteenth-century Ottoman Empire. The trope of Turkey's continual belatedness has obscured the pronounced incongruence between policy discourses and practices in the realm of culture. It has also produced historical erasures and blind spots in art history, especially with regard to the persecution of minorities and the impact that the series of military coups has had on artistic production and cultural policies. Alongside persistent economic and structural problems these issues help explain why Turkish cultural policy has remained "unsuccessful" in its quest for becoming recognizably modern.

There is another, related convergence between Turkey and Germany. In both cases the turn to culture and art in the national project emerged from the experience of military defeat but took different shapes. Germany's experience of failed revolution (1848–1849) and its late unification fed into motifs of inwardness in intellectual and artistic production, paired with a Romantic longing for national unity. In contrast, a series of territorial losses initiated the periodic outward orientation of the ruling elites of the Ottoman Empire beginning in the late eighteenth century. This westward gaze—at times fixed on France and at others on the Germanys, especially Prussia—was to overcome perceived military and cultural shortcomings. That the narrative of belatedness is, for the most part, a closed chapter in Germany's history results not simply from its divergent artistic production or its socioeconomic and political standing but is clearly related to the "restorative" cultural policies and interventions of the Allied forces following another military defeat of Germany, that of World War II.

German and Turkish nationalism have shared an awareness that art presented in the national frame can be employed to instill and reflect a "collective identity," to express "the culture" that demarcates a people. It is in this context that artistic production has often been conceptualized as performing a legitimizing bond to a supposedly coherent and communal past, very much like the "invented traditions" that the historians Eric Hobsbawm and Terence Ranger (1992) described as an outstanding feature of modern state formation.[3]

"German Particularism" and the Search for Distinctly German Art

In the beginning was Napoleon.

Thomas Nipperdey

The art historian Hans Belting (1998) proposes that the search for a distinctly German art by the Romantics in the later eighteenth century has to be understood as an attempt to culturally bridge Germany's multitude of semi-independent principalities. Together with the Reformation, this political fragmentation had produced regionalism in the arts. The visual arts were particularly affected by the Reformation. Painting was generally banned in Protestant Germany, and only a limited number of official positions for painters were available, leaving artists with little room for experimentation outside the prescribed modes of representation. This led to a "divided German artistic tradition"—the emergence of two kinds of German art (*Zweierlei deutsche Kunst*), Protestant on the one hand, and Catholic (notably often referred to as "Mediterranean")[4] art on the other. In order to overcome this division, some artists began to draw on classical rather than religious themes. Linking themselves to Greek styles and motifs, they turned to antiquity in the hopes of establishing aesthetic cohesion across the Germanys.

The search for a uniquely German artistic style gained heightened urgency with the rise of German nationalism, which became more contoured with the experience of the Napoleonic occupation (1804–1815). With the failure of a revolutionary unification attempt in 1848–1849 the "project of aligning Germany's cultural identity with the putative modernity of the French Revolution . . . collapsed" as well (Mah 1990, 60). The historian Harold Mah argues that for German intellectuals such as Georg Wilhelm Friedrich Hegel (1770–1831) and Heinrich Heine (1797–1856), the French Revolution had marked the realization of Enlightenment and the arrival of modernity, since it "eliminated traditional obstacles to social equality and constitutional government," even if they were shocked about the violent turn the revolution had taken. They were faced with the question if and when Germany itself would arrive on the modern stage. There were increasing doubts as to whether Germany was equipped to meet the "standard of reason and modernity" (5) exhibited by France, especially since the reforms that had been instated during Napoleonic rule were promptly dismantled by Prussian reactionism. In a parallel argumentative move, first Hegel and twenty years later Heine tried to align German philosophy and thought with French political practice, and it was through this equation that Germany's modernity was claimed by both. Yet questions remained about how to explain the discrepancy between thought and practice, theory and politics, as well as about the nonexistence of a specifically German art style. For many German thinkers the answer to these questions lay in the experience of the Reformation, which emphasized inwardness—*Innerlichkeit*—rather than outward action.

Innerlichkeit was seen as intrinsic to German political life as to its art. That this inwardness was regarded as both a possible path and an obstacle to Germany's modernization can already be traced in Friedrich Schiller's *Aesthetic Letters* (which he began to write in the mid-1790s). Two projects can be identified in Schiller's writings. At times, Schiller was in line with Enlightenment thinking emphasizing the emancipatory potential of aesthetic education as a facilitator for a rational state, for self-government, and, ultimately, freedom. This seemingly subversive stance was contrasted by the position he developed in the second part of the *Letters*. Here freedom is not located in the external political context but takes the form of an inward aesthetic experience that produces internal freedom and "consoles" the individual in the face of the repressive regimes, alienation, and social disintegration that characterize the modern condition (especially in *Letters* 5 and 6; see also Woodmansee 1994, 73). In this second elaboration, aesthetic experience accommodates the sociopolitical status quo rather than challenging it.

Germany's self-image of the country of poets and thinkers (*Dichter und Denker*) developed in distinction to "French civilization" and its political and cultural hegemony in continental Europe. Indeed it was in this context that German culture—*Kultur*—was increasingly understood as antithetical to the notion of civilization (Elias 1969, Lepenies 2006).[5] By emphasizing the cultural autonomy and uniqueness of the German spirit (*Geist*) and its physical manifestation in the *Volk*, that is, an ethnicized conception of peoplehood, Germany distinguished itself from France and England, both seen to represent the cold rationalization and calculating nature of the modern world: "Kaufmannsgeist und kalte Verfeinerung" (Naumann 2001, 53). The historian Wolfgang Mommsen (2000, 257–58) shows that this current of ethnic-nationalist (*völkisch*) orientation in the arts was at times succinctly antimodernist and relied on anti-Western polemics, despite the opposition of various artists' movements, such as the impressionist and later expressionist painters.

Whereas Germany strived to be on par with France and England in its military and economic capabilities and imperial ambitions, it did not see itself as part of the West. It was only after World War II, and only gradually, that "modernity" and "Western belonging" were attributed to and claimed by Germany.

In an atmosphere shaped by insecurities about Germany's position in the modern world *and* about what constitutes the "German artistic tradition," the emergence of modernism, a decidedly international movement, in the late nineteenth and early twentieth century, only polarized the German art world further. The notion of *Überfremdung* (literally: overforeignization, now commonly connoted with an "excess" of immigration) as well as that of "degeneracy"[6] as threatening both German art and the German "national character" became commonplace in official discourses on the arts. Yet Emperor Wilhelm II's (1888–1918) expectation of "arts in the service of the state" (*Kunst im Dienst der Staatsidee*) was not necessarily met with approval by artists either, especially since the arts became increasingly restricted by censorship. Mommsen (2000, 8) shows that modernism in the arts, slowly winning ground in Germany, often expressed the fragmentation between the liberal and nationalist wings of the emerging bourgeoisie, while voicing discomforts about the modern condition. These tensions,

> prompted Wilhelm II to denounce modern art saying that "it does nothing more than portray misery as more loathsome than it is." This was even more incomprehensible to the Kaiser, since "we the German people, have made great ideals part of the public good, while these same ideals have disappeared more or less from other nations." . . . Anti-modernists of those years advised artists to look to German art of the past for models to imitate. For them, *modern art was as un-German* as the Gothic and the renaissance, which art historians would have so liked to define as German.
>
> (Belting 1998, 62–63, emphasis mine)

Another facet of the debate about Germanness in the arts became heated toward the end of the nineteenth and the beginning of the twentieth century. For instance, German artists began to critique the acquisition practices of the National Gallery in Berlin, established in 1896 and tellingly dedicated "To German Art" ("Der Deutschen Kunst"), when it added non-German artists to its collection.[7] The protests gathered further momentum during the Bremen art controversy of 1911. After the purchase of a van Gogh painting by the Bremen Museum, the manifesto entitled "Ein Protest deutscher Künstler" (A protest of German artists) portrayed this acquisition as endangering German traditions and revealed concerns regarding state patronage of the arts in Germany. Investment into "foreign works of art" was seen not only as resources lost for German artists but as hampering the national art market and hence the development of German art.

The "Turkish Synthesis": Rationalizing the Arts

> If a nation is rich in art and its people skilled in the arts, it can achieve a full life of its own. A nation that cannot do this is like a man who is lame or lacks a limb, who is invalid and crippled. But for what I have to say, even this comparison is not adequate. If a nation is cut off from the arts, one of its vital arteries is severed.
>
> Mustafa Kemal Atatürk

There is a notable divergence between Germany and Turkey that is worth noting before delving into the interlocution of nation-state building and the arts in Turkey. While imperial Germany pursued expansionist policies, trying to gain colonial influence outside of its borders, even if to varying degrees of "success," the Ottoman Empire was shrinking. The successive territorial losses caused by the emergence of independence movements across the Balkans, Greece, and the Middle East along with the looming threat of being divided up among the Entente powers fueled nascent Turkish nationalism (Keyder 1997). With its disintegration, the empire lost many of its centers of artistic innovation and production, such as Damascus, Baghdad, and Thessalonica, during the late eighteenth and early nineteenth centuries. In addition, large-scale genocidal violence and ethnic homogenization policies led to the killing and exiling of Armenian and Greek painters and other minority artists; the history of the impact of this loss still needs to be written. Whereas the newly united Germany saw the rapid expansion of its bourgeoisie, a "Turkish bourgeoisie" was still in its violent making, its absence considerably hampering the art market.

It is against this background that the Turkish Republic started out on a slightly different path in the search for national artistic expression. In his theoretical writings, Ziya Gökalp (1876–1924), a Kurdish poet and sociologist and one of the chief ideologues of Turkish nationalism, tried to detach Turkish nationality from descent as well as from the Ottoman past—which for him, as for many Young Turks, was long discredited.[8] Instead, he enthusiastically envisioned the creation of a "new people" encompassing *all* former Ottoman citizens. This seemingly inclusive proposition and the civic notion of citizenship it suggests proved rather fragile in practice and soon moved into ethnicized conceptualizations of Turkishness on the basis of religion. The seeds for this understanding of "Turkish culture" and "national art"—the necessity of which was so forcefully declared by Atatürk in ableist terms—were sown with the establishment of the Turkish Hearths (Türk Ocakları) in 1913. Ziya Gökalp, Halide Edip Adivar, and Yahya Kemal were among the founding members, along with other artists and intellectuals affiliated with the Committee of Union and Progress (CUP). The Hearths' mission was to ignite a "Turkish national awakening" through popular education, language, art, and literature. The shifting notions of Turkishness initially advanced by the Hearths soon solidified into pan-Turanist, overtly chauvinist tendencies (Üstel 1997), making them undesirable after the establishment of the Republic.

Since the criteria for national belonging could not be entirely based on future orientation, that is, a completely reformed language, culture, and society, as initially projected, Gökalp (1959, 107) developed the idea of the "Turkish synthesis." His argument, not unlike that of Johann Gottfried Herder for the German context (1744–1803), distinguished between civilization—*medeniyet*—and culture—*hars*[9]—and thus between Ottoman civilization and "authentic Turkish culture." Subsequently, Ottoman civilization was portrayed as a complete travesty and not genuine to Turkey because it was, according to Gökalp, essentially based on mimicking Persian and Arabic cultural practices, especially in the field of art (262). Turkish modernization discourse hence employed Orientalist motifs in its critiques of the Ottoman Empire.

Ottoman "backwardness" was most commonly attributed to Islam, or at least a version of Islam that prevented "development" because it was infused with unreason and superstition. In contrast, "Western civilization" and especially "Western science" were regarded as exemplary.[10] Yet the Turkish synthesis was not imagined as a complete emulation either. Rather it was to provide a framework for refining "Turkish" folk culture according to "Western standards."[11] Although bearing structural similarities to reforms during the Tanzimat period (1839–1876; Deringil 1998a, Ertürk 2011), these earlier efforts were discounted as elitist imitations of "Western" culture that were detached from people's everyday experience. Taking folk culture as a basis from which to build a new "Turkish civilization" would not only entail the recovery of a Turkish culture "out there" but a modification thereof. The anthropologist Yael Navaro-Yashin (2002, 11–12) argues that this modernization effort was based on a process of discovery (or recovery) and "refinement," in the course of which "Turkishness" was at once portrayed as compatible with modernity as well as congruent with it. Anatolian folklore was to provide the material for Turkish culture and to prove Turkish affinities to European civilizations while also distinguishing Turkey from its Arab neighbors.[12] Identifying Anatolia as the heartland of Turkey was not without its problems, however, given that the Balkans "had been central to the Ottoman polity" until their breakaway in 1912–1913 (46). It was, after all, not least because of the centrality of the Balkans for the Ottoman imagination—and economy—that the empire had seen itself as a part of Europe. In contrast, Anatolia, along with many of the Arab provinces, had from the Tanzimat period onward become a focus for the Ottoman civilizing mission.[13] While Anatolia was now designated as the source for cultural renewal, it would also continue to be identified as the source of its ever-incomplete modernization. For decades, this discourse has faulted Anatolia's communities, rather than state policies of systematic disinvestment and failure to secure citizenship rights, for stifling Turkey's modernization and preventing its acceptance into the European Union.

The establishment of the Turkish Republic had been enabled by major waves of "demographic engineering," first through genocidal violence largely in the shadow of World War I[14] and then through the compulsory population exchanges stipulated by the Lausanne Treaty in 1923–1924 (Hirschon 2003, Iğsız 2018). As the forced migration of "Greeks" and "Turks" was organized around religious affiliation (leaving out other factors, such as language, for instance), this measure further paved the way for a homogenized nation-state. While Turkey applied the provisions on minorities in the Lausanne Treaty to Armenian, Greek, and Jewish populations (Özgül 2014),[15] the founders of the Republic "projected for all Muslim citizens of Turkey a Turkish national identity" (Kirişci 1998, 228). This means that despite the purported secular makeup of the Turkish state, citizenship and minority rights have been based on religious affiliation—or, rather, a limited definition thereof—one that does not recognize Alevis or Assyrians, for example. This too was not enough, however. The creation a "new people"—a "Turkish nation"—according to the founders of the Republic, among them first and foremost Mustafa Kemal, required far-reaching reeducation efforts. The early years of the republic hence were accompanied by a range of sociocultural engineering measures, among them the introduction of the Latin alphabet (1928), a move that cut off generations to come from primary Ottoman sources, including those dealing with art and literary theory. The modernization and implementation of a centrally directed school system in 1929 (Kaplan 2006) was accompanied by the reshaping of the built environment (Bozdoğan 2001, Akcan 2012). As in the Tanzimat period, the body of the citizen itself became the focus of the internal civilizing mission (Makdisi 2002, Deringil 2003). Fezzes, turbans, and shalvars had to be replaced by Western attire. Men were to wear suits; veiling was forbidden for women. The state also tried to regulate religious practice by assuming control of the religious education of imams. While official discourses portrayed this move as ensuring "moderation," it also presented an attempt to bring religious authorities firmly under the auspices of the state, even if with varying success (e.g., see Meeker 2002). As modernization and Turkification were equated, expressions of difference, be they ethnic, linguistic, or religious, became a conceptual threat to the very foundation—and sovereignty—of the Turkish state.[16]

Like other aspects of Ottoman civilization, Ottoman art was branded backward by the new republican elite, and the idea of the "Turkish synthesis" was applied to the arts as well. To uncover the "Turkish genius," as Gökalp formulated it, Turkish artists had the choice of drawing on Western, folk, or Eastern artistic repertoires. While the latter was regarded as morbid, the former two were to become the basis for a new national and modern art. The "harmonious blend" that was to emerge from this synthesis would at the same time be a distinctly "Turkish art" (Gökalp 1959, And 1984). Perhaps the most striking feature of early Turkish cultural policy was the embrace of modernist aesthetics in art and architecture if accompanied by concerted efforts to divorce modernism from its critique of modernity (Köksal 2004). But here too a synthesis was envisioned that would allow for reworking modernism into an authentically "Turkish" repertoire.

But what did the Turkish synthesis look like in practice? In the case of music, one measure highlighted by the anthropologist Martin Stokes in his *The Arabesk Debate* (1992) is the Turkification of lyrics. Within the national project, homogenization was regarded as essential for modernization, while ethnic heterogeneity indicated a supposed affinity to a "backward Orient" governed by what could be called the "aesthetics of irrationality." Western music expressed "logical, systematic, and rational thinking," whereas Eastern music was deemed irrational, morbid, and overly emotional (12). In this attempt to civilize music, acclaimed "Western" composers such as Paul Hindemith and Béla Bartók were invited to Turkey in 1932 in order to assemble a national orchestra and modernize the musical notation system. Folk music had to be reformed following Western musical conventions, namely, by introducing polyphony: "Folk tunes were to be collected, categorized, reworked according to Western methods, and made polyphonic" (Tekelioğlu 2001, 95). The 1927 ban on monophonic music education was short-lived, as these reforms did not go unchallenged. Musicians and audiences "showed little interest in polyphonic music being composed by the Turkish composers or the Western classical music played in free concerts or broadcast on radio" (Stokes 1992, 96). To counter the growing popularity of Egyptian musical films, the Turkish government even resorted to a temporary, if likewise unsuccessful, ban thereof in 1948.[17] "Unable to hear the music that they enjoyed, [listeners] either turned off their [radio] sets . . .

or tuned into Egyptian radio, which was easily available as a result of its high broadcasting frequency" (93).

In the field of folk dance, homogenization and rationalization aimed at "refining" movement repertoires: Here, refinement meant codifying the customary improvisational sequences by limiting the patterns from which they could draw to eliminate "randomness" and make dances more "rigid" (Öztürkmen 2002, 129). As the performance scholar Arzu Öztürkmen demonstrates, these "modernized" dance forms were renamed so as to index "geographical administrative units rather than ethnic ones" (132). By negating their often disparate cultural or ethnic roots, movement repertoires were merged and modified into new canons. Even in dance practices ethnic difference was regarded as disruptive for the nation-state process, while regional differences offered a "tamed" frame for diversity.

Rapprochement and Distinction

While the motif of distinction from "the West" was elaborated by German intellectuals and politicians very much till the end of World War II, we find that their Turkish counterparts employed the idea of rapprochement in their nationalized conception of art, an approximation to "the West" through the "rationalization," and hence modernization, of aesthetics. What both cases shared, however, was the idea that religion was at fault for stifling national artistic developments and for their artistic repertoires falling behind those of other European powers.

The prevalent republican narrative proposes that Ottoman art fell behind Western art some time over the course of the sixteenth century, that is, the Renaissance. The exact dates vary but are often correlated with the end of the reign of Suleiman I, also known as Suleiman the Magnificent (1494–1566), or the Ottoman retreat from the siege of Vienna (1529). Either way, the empire's withering military might and dogmatic readings of Islam were to blame. The reason for this backslide is often sought in the supposed prohibition of depicting persons in Sunni Islam and its notion that god's creation could not be mirrored (Topuz 1998, Öndin 2003). This assumption of generalized iconophobia neither differentiates between different periods nor accounts for the advent of figurative painting in the medieval Ottoman Empire (Flood 2013). It also obscures the existence of actors who were exempt from these religious precepts, for instance Armenian painters (Kürkman 2004) and others who diverged from these understandings. After all, Ottoman rulers themselves became increasingly interested in single-perspective painting, portraiture, and, later, photography (Topuz 1998, Shaw 2011). Even less polemic commentators long tended to see Ottoman art as limited and considered miniature and calligraphy as merely "decorative genres" incommensurable with trajectory of visual art in Western Europe.[18] Such evaluations discount the long-existing dialogue and the exchange patterns of artifacts, paintings, and commemorative coins between the Ottoman Empire and Western European powers. Taking place throughout the Renaissance, these exchanges are evidence of a shared visual vocabulary, not the exclusion of the Ottoman Empire from Europe's geopolitical formation (Jardine and Brotton 2000).[19]

As mentioned earlier, the Reformation was long seen as having stifled the development of a "truly" German art because it had brought about a "divided tradition" in painting. It was this process that hindered Germany (especially in the visual arts and, to a lesser extent, in the realms of letters and music) from stepping out of what nationalist commentators perceived as the shadow of French civilization, from which German *Kultur* was so desperate to distinguish itself.

These diverging conceptualizations of the impact of religion on art can be illustrated through Max Weber's (1958 [1915]) thoughts on the relationship between modernity, rationality, art, and religion. Weber proposed that with the rationalization of life in the modern condition "art becomes a cosmos of more and more consciously grasped independent values, which exist in their own right. Art takes over this-worldly salvation, no matter how this might be interpreted. It provides a *salvation* from the pressures of theoretical and practical rationalism" (342). While art takes on the function of relief from the rationalism of the modern world in the German context, there is a concerted effort to achieve rationality in artistic expression in order to establish modernity in Turkey.

Yet both quests for a national aesthetic were legitimized through their respective definition of culture. In Germany, this culture was construed in distinction to a "foreign" civilization, that is, France, while the Turkish Republic sought to distinguish itself from a civilization of the past, the Ottoman Empire. French and Ottoman civilization, respectively, were characterized as corrupting and oppressive influences to which all ties had to be severed, not least through strategies of systematic forgetting. To understand how these trajectories continue to shape contemporary discussions on the arts and cultural policy in Germany and Turkey *and* their asymmetric perception, I would like to dwell briefly on two interrelated processes of systematic forgetting—or partial silencing—of some historical lineages and the normalization of others (see Trouillot 1995). Here, I use the term "normalization" to indicate not solely the disavowal of past episodes of state violence but the denial of the continued workings of this violence in the present. Together forgetting and normalization have facilitated the Occidentalization of Germany and the Turkification of Turkey.

Occidentalizing Germany, or, How Did Germany Become Western?

The discourse of German particularism in the arts was largely discredited in the decades following the end of World War II. In the process of "recivilizing Germany" (Jarausch 2006), German art was reinterpreted as "European art in a western tradition" (Belting 1998, 34). Significantly aided by the cultural policy directives of the Allied forces (Nickel and Schrön 2002), German cultural policy (*Kulturpolitik*) after 1945 exhibited a systematic effort to omit the ethnic-nationalist currents in the history of German art in favor of "restorative cultural policies" that aimed at situating Germany firmly within the artistic heritage of the West (Knoblich 2001, 7). This Occidental shift disavowed and ultimately concealed the long history of antimodernist and anti-Western sentiment within German arts and politics and was facilitated by "the political restoration of western Europe after the war, which was premised on the existence of the eastern block [*sic*]" (Belting 1998, 37). By taking Germany "into the fold," Europe emerged as a geopolitical entity based on cultural affinity. But the affirmation of Germany's western belonging did more than that. It allowed for obfuscating Europe's collective violent past, including centuries of religious warfare, class divisions, and two world wars. The many complicities in Nazism—which had just a few years earlier united the continent—were just the latest instance of a history ordained to be forgotten (Judt 1996, Mazower 1998). It is in this manner that the civilizational narrative of the European idea is dependent on Germany's Occidentalism. This discursive move of tying Germany into the lineage of both the geopolitical configuration of Western Europe and the canon of modern art was "successful" in that its Western belonging is largely unquestioned today.[20] The usage of the term "restorative" is misleading in that it obscures a substantial interpretative shift; Germany did not simply revert back to pre–National Socialist fault lines but in part suppressed and in part reconfigured former debates in public memory and official discourse. Yet both suppression and reconfiguration were shaped by the Nazi past and often imbued in it. Akin to Hannah Feldman's (2014) insightful critique of "postwar" French modernism as actually being intensely informed by France's wars in the decolonizing arena, Germany's postwar Occidentalism (while no longer at war, at least for some time) continued to be significantly shaped by the experience of the Third Reich.

Yet there have been considerable doubts among European powers regarding Germany's modernity given this trajectory and its National Socialist past, and they have resurfaced periodically after World War II. These doubts crystallized during Germany's rearmament beginning in 1955, the emergence of left-wing militancy in the 1970s (see Chapter 5), Germany's reunification, and the rise of anti-immigrant violence and the Neo-Nazi movements in the early 1990s. Especially in the lead-up to the reunification widespread concerns were voiced that a once more strong and territorially integrated Germany might come with a renewed potential—and desire—for military aggression.[21] In an article entitled "Uneasy about the Germans," the playwright Arthur Miller (1990), while professing to be in favor of reunification, expressed his doubts with regard to German modernness by asking, "Does the Federal Republic of Germany arouse lofty democratic feelings in its citizens' minds, or is it a system that is simply a matter of historical convenience invented by foreigners?" After all, he argued, the Federal Republic came into being without shedding "a drop of blood" for democracy; instead democracy was merely "handed to the Germans." Miller questioned how committed Germany really could be to this form of governance, which it had attained without struggling for it.

In its reunification treaty, Germany countered these anxieties by defining itself as a *Kulturstaat*—a cultural state—in contrast to its pre-1945 predecessors' term "*Kulturnation*" (for a more detailed discussion, see Chapter 3). The latter had distinct Prussian, Wilhelmine, and National Socialist connotations, in the context of which both "*Kultur*" and "nation" signified expansionist policies and military aggression. This refashioning was not only employed to diffuse concerns about a reunified Germany abroad. According to Michael Naumann, the former secretary of state for culture (1998–2000), it also provided a degree of domestic self-assurance because the treaty guaranteed cultural pluralism, which interestingly referred to the cultural heritage of the German Democratic Republic and not, as one might assume, to the "multicultural" makeup of Germany that has emerged from the labor immigration from the 1960s onward. Although today the antithetical conceptualization of civilization and culture is often portrayed to have been reconciled in Germany (Lepenies 2006), this conceptual rift has produced an enduring legacy in understandings of German citizenship that privilege cultural bonds over civic ones. As the reunification treaty remains ambivalent about what this "German culture" is or entails, it has—recent changes to the naturalization law notwithstanding—also perpetuated organicist understandings of German citizenship in which the innateness of culture is emphasized over processes of socialization (Stolcke 1995). Given this historical background, the employment of the culture concept as a basis of the German state leaves open the possibility of conflating culture and ethnicity and thus a *völkisch* notion of *Kultur* that was supposed to have been discarded after 1945. A telling example in this context is the discussion around German *Leitkultur*—"leading" or "guiding" culture—that was initiated during the national election campaign in 2000 (Mandel 2008, Ewing 2008) and has periodically flared up since. Originally intended to make a statement about "German core values" that immigrants were supposed to adhere to, it backfired once politicians were asked to define this "essence of Germanness." Usually their definitions circled around concepts of liberal democracy, secularism, and the Judeo-Christian tradition—all elements that, while in keeping with the dominant narrative of modernity and Western belonging, have been strongly contested in Germany's path to modernity.

The extent to which this normalization had taken hold manifested itself in the rarity of reference to this history or the national framework in my conversations with visual artists in Berlin. The representations of their artworks and practices oscillated very much between local connectedness and references to the international art world. Cultural policy officials like Torsten Wöhlert, then press secretary of the Science, Research, and Culture Division of the Berlin Senate, however, very much reflected on Germany's troubled modernization trajectory. When I asked him about his opinion of the role of private sponsorship in the German arts sector, he noted that Germany—in contrast to the United States—could not rely on private monies to sustain arts and cultural programs, since it had "destroyed its finance bourgeoisie [*Finanzbürgertum*] in 1933." This process, in his opinion, had irreversibly marked Germany, and especially Berlin and its art world, in a particular fashion. While one could contend that Wöhlert's take on the issue is informed by his East German upbringing (it was, after all, a foundational narrative of the German Democratic Republic that East Germany was born out of antifascism), educational formation, and the fact that he represented a city government composed of Social Democrats (SPD) and Socialists (PDS), his view is congruent with that of Michael Naumann (2001). He too sees Germany's Occidental orientation and cultural policies as arising from the political responsibility of the country's National Socialist past.

Turkifying Turkey, or, How Did Turkey Become Turkish?

While Germany has largely succeeded in normalizing its Western belonging, Turkey has sought to normalize another series of ruptures, first and foremost those created by Turkification, a process underwritten by state violence and social engineering. Turkification has led to the systematic forgetting of the non-Muslim backgrounds of important artists and architects—such as the Balyans, a family of architects who are responsible for many of Istanbul's eighteenth- and nineteenth-century landmark Ottoman buildings, including the Dolmabahçe Palace in Istanbul—and to neglecting artifacts and artworks that contradict official historiography. (It is not so long ago that tour guides in the Dolmabahçe Palace would identify the Balyans as a family of Italian architects.)

I have already indicated that in Turkey the mutually dependent projects of nationalism and modernity have been tied to the idea of ethnic homogeneity, so much so that any reference to ethnic diversity has long had the potential to become a conceptual threat. However, this process entailed a fundamental redefinition of the notion "Turk." As Şerif Mardin notes:

> Between 1918 and 1939 Turks embarked on a major identity switch. This involved a change in status, from subjects of a multi-ethnic, cosmopolitan empire to citizens of a republic that set down and affirmed its true Turkishness. . . . This process was met by Western commentators with either spirited or tacit approval, the change being seen as a step towards Turkish modernisation. Such approval however, has eluded an important question: how was this transition possible? . . . After all, the antithetical quality of "Ottoman" and "Turk" was a theme all knowledgeable commentators on Turkey had asserted in the past.
> (Mardin 2002, 115)[22]

That this shift was not as easy as the term "switch" proposes can be discerned from an array of intermittent efforts to consolidate and reify the nation-state, such as the "Citizen speak Turkish!" campaign in the 1930s, which criminalized the usage of "foreign" languages in public. Language as a means and expression of national unity, like other cultural expressions, was portrayed both as authentically Turkish *and* as disjointed from its Ottoman heritage. To this end, the Turkish Language Association (Türk Dil Kurumu) was founded in 1932, with the inaugural mission to eliminate loanwords from Arabic, Persian, and other languages referencing the Ottoman past. Another indicator that the reforms to construct a new people did not take hold as easily as projected was the establishment of the Turkish Historical Society (Türk Tarih Kurumu) in 1931. The Turkish Historical Society has periodically intervened in public discussions by elaborating narratives on national homogeneity and revising "Turkish history" in order to accommodate official ideology. One of its more outlandish theories, the "mountain Turk thesis," was propagated during the rise of the Kurdish rights struggle in the 1980s and 1990s. According to this thesis, Kurds do not actually represent an ethnic group or groups but are "mountain Turks" who (somehow left behind during the migration from

Central Asia) had "forgotten" their original language and were left speaking a broken form of Arabic.[23] In its reification of a common "Turkish identity," the Turkish Historical Society has endorsed explanatory models relying on scientific racism that contradict the inclusive conceptualization of Turkish citizenship envisioned by Gökalp, for instance. Quite similar to the German notion of citizenship, this move always left open the possibility of returning to "ethnic," "biologized," and hence exclusionary understandings of citizenship. Although the early Republic seemed to try to forge a sense of belonging apart from ethnicity, the authoritarian process of "nationalization from above," as Keyder (1997, 42) argues, did not allow for a conceptualization of the population as an "aggregate of individuals." Consequently, this "collectivist vision"—or, as Taha Parla (1985) frames it, corporatist integration of state and society—was expressed in organicist terms and from the 1930s onward relied increasingly on a homogeneity in terms of ethnicity.

Since the later 1990s, there have been efforts to reinterpret Ottoman history on the part of official Turkish channels, a trend that has become ever more contoured since the Justice and Development Party (Adalet ve Kalkınma Partisi, AKP) came to power in 2002. These reevaluations mostly circle around the Ottoman Empire's grandeur. With the upsurge in discussions around Turkey's historical and present-day diverse ethnic and religious makeup, the purported "cosmopolitanism"[24] of the Ottoman Empire has also been emphasized in politics, scholarship, activism, and the arts. I found a growing awareness among artists in Istanbul of the ill-fitting pieces of Turkish (art) history stemming from the wholesale dismissal of the Ottoman past and its artistic heritage. The growing interest in the Ottoman past has also paved the way for questions regarding Turkey's more recent history, which too has been obscured and within which the 1980 coup d'état presents a notable rupture. Dissatisfied with the long-perpetuated idea that contemporary art only began in the 1990s in Turkey, some have become interested in the artistic production of the 1950s, 1960s, and 1970s to rediscover the rise of popular culture in the wake of massive domestic and international labor migration, or the experimental video art with pioneered by Nil Yalter in the late 1970s. Others have begun to explore the connections between artists and revolutionary social movements that characterized the 1970s. The mounting dissatisfaction with the fragmented history and Eurocentric narrative of modern art that continues to dominate the international scene has expressed itself in a growing interest in the recovery and reworking of different artistic heritages from Anatolia as well as alternative ways of writing the art history of Turkey. Those who focus on "Turkish art"—itself a notable construction out of Ottoman heritage—are slowly discovering the controversies, debates, and developments that have been obscured in official historiography.

Given this brief overview on how the contingencies of modernity and Western belonging as civilizational markers have been reflected in the discourses on the arts in nation-state making in Turkey and Germany, the following questions arise: How can one explain the persisting asymmetry in the perception of Turkish and German art, given that Turkey's attempt to align itself with Western modernity by rationalizing artistic expression in the 1920s predates West Germany's shift to Occidental cultural policies that were only established after 1945? How is this asymmetry produced and sustained, and what purpose does it serve? To approach these questions, the following passages deepen the account of how modernity is conceptualized in the social sciences and how these conceptualizations relate to theorizations of past and present political, economic, and cultural conditions of the "non-West" and, more specifically, the Ottoman Empire and Turkey. I will thus return once more to the two discourses of exceptionalism and the ways that they have configured conceptualizations of modernity with regard to contemporary Turkey and Germany. These conceptualizations are also mirrored in the idea of Europe—itself a fragile feat—and how it has been construed as both a geopolitical entity and a civilizational context that included Germany and excluded Turkey since the mid–twentieth century.

"Belated Modernity" and Its Impasses

> After all, we come from a tradition of belated modernity . . .
>
> Elif Shafak

Like the writer Elif Shafak, many scholars from within and without Turkey continue to frame Turkish modernization as a belated and flawed appropriation of modern political thought or even as a historical failure. Scholars who engage in the diagnosis of Turkey's perpetually deficient modernization generally attribute this failure to its state-directed, or top-down, modernization process—a kind of governance that is opposed to the idea of a modernity "proper" (Kasaba 1997, 31). As Germany's state-led modernization trajectory is often described in a similar manner, albeit with vastly different outcomes, this purported causality alone cannot explain why the trope of belatedness has been central for the entirety of Turkey's republican history as well as the last century of the Ottoman Empire. That Turkey's history and current political, economic, and sociocultural makeup, and consequently its artistic production, has long been exclusively evaluated under the paradigm of "belated modernity" has created many blind spots. Much of the theorizing on Turkey still is conceptually rooted in the discipline of Orientalist studies and thus in a body of knowledge production that, as Talal Asad and Roger Owen (1980, 35) put it, describes non-European "political life by looking for absent kinds of concepts—'liberty,' 'progress,' 'humanism'—which are supposed to be distinctive of Western civilization" (see also Chakrabarty 2000). The notion of "belated modernity" has become an explanatory model for almost all political, economic, and social predicaments in Turkey. This standardized narrative has led not only to obscuring continuities, for instance, of citizenship laws between the Ottoman Empire and present-day Turkey, histories of dispossession, and mechanisms of state violence but also of the historical entanglements with the wider European context.

Meltem Ahıska (2003) argues that the reification of an "always-already late" political structure has served to deflect attention from long-standing political issues, such as the "Kurdish question"[25] or uneven development within Turkey, by correlating them with the purported conservatism and traditionalism of the eastern provinces rather than with governmental policies: "Instead of concentrating on the present problems and their solutions the hegemonic imaginary looks beyond the present with the aid of an already-late and always postponed ideal" (352). This discourse of belated modernity does not only displace the root causes of an array of socioeconomic and political inequalities but creates a sense of stasis that contradicts the very understanding of modernity. To put it in Johannes Fabian's (1983) terms, coevalness between Turkey and "the West" is denied from both within and without. Reflecting on the internal perpetuation of Orientalist tropes within Turkey, Ahıska further notes that "just as the West always refers to the notion of the East to assert its hegemony, Turkey reproduces the reified images of the West to justify its regime of power in its boundary management of dividing spheres, regions and people along the axis of East and West" (2003, 368).

This statement has implications beyond the ways that past and present governance is justified in Turkey. It can also be read as a critique of the (sometimes inadvertent) complicity of scholarship that reifies the trope of belated modernity as an explanatory model that ultimately displaces the temporality of modernity onto a "polarity of East and West" (Ahıska 2003, 368). It is this displacement that has been normalized, and with it dichotomies of East and West, modernity and tradition.

Even nuanced approaches, exemplified by the sociologist Çağlar Keyder (1997), tend to reinforce rather crude dichotomies of modernity and tradition. Keyder argues that the statist equation of modernization with Westernization prevented the elaboration of what could have been a "Turkish modernity," one that, for example, could have been developed out of rethinking Islam (37). Although he attempts to break away from the idea of a mere mimicking of modernity, his frequent usage of the "local" still juxtaposes the modern to a local that appropriates modernity instead of developing correspondingly. Not only does this kind of argument presuppose a modern, distinct West, but concepts such as modernity and tradition become reified once over. In his interrogation of nationalism in the postcolonial setting of Southeast Asia, Partha Chatterjee (1986) has cautioned against naturalizing the formation of nation-states as the political manifestation of a homogenous modernity and against seeing later forms of nationalism as mere imitations of Western models. Especially works that have emerged in the field of subaltern and postcolonial studies have shown that European modernity was not only facilitated by colonial exploitation but that modern conceptions of race, gender, and nationhood as well as techniques of governance and policing actually emerged out of and were originally developed within the colonial encounter (e.g., Tolen 1991, Stoler 1992). Yet, as Timothy Mitchell (2000, 3) convincingly argues, to stop the argument at seeing "modernity as a product not of the West but of its interaction with the non-West" is to conceptually reinvest into a "European-centered dualism." To decenter this perspective, one must take into account that the West has likewise appropriated knowledge gained from occupied societies and incorporated it in their modernization projects "back home."

In the case of Turkey, the question of who actually represents the modernizing force is complicated further when one takes into account the "competing claims for modernity" (Atasoy 1996). Historically, Islam has been identified as an obstacle to Turkey's modernization, in an argument that by sweeping generalization has equated Islam with rural Anatolia and frequently has attributed to Islamists an understanding of modernity as limited to Western technology (Kasaba 1997). The rise to power of political Islam has posed a series of conceptual problems for this narrative, not least because it has been accompanied by what Esra Özyürek (2006) calls "nostalgia for the modern," in which the early republican past is taken to symbolize "true modernity." This discourse could be regarded as a recent manifestation—or variation—of the trope of belatedness. Özyürek indicates that what is at stake is more than the place of Islam in public life and politics. Rather this nostalgia for the modern presents a longing for the early republican period that corresponds with class-structural attachments. It is most "fervently promoted" by the former bureaucratic elites of Turkey, who experienced a considerable loss in social standing, political power, and economic capital when the neoliberalization measures introduced under the military rule of 1980–1983 began to favor an emergent devout business elite.

The portrayal of the rise of political Islam as a regressive development was for some commentators temporarily destabilized when, from 2002 onward, the current AKP government began to pass legislation that granted minorities the right to broadcast, publicize, and educate in their respective languages. The reforms also entailed the lifting of martial law in the Kurdish provinces and the removal of the death penalty. Initially hailed as important steps toward the demands of domestic and international human rights organizations as well those of the European Union, these reform packages proved precarious at best—long before Turkey's spiral into authoritarianism and violence in 2015.[26] Even in the late 2000s and early 2010s, when Turkey was frequently touted as a possible model for "Muslim democracy" in the region, it remained the country with the most convictions at the European Court of Human Rights (ECHR). As they are worded much like their European counterparts, it is often noted that it is not the laws themselves but their application that is problematic in Turkey. Yet I would argue that rather than failures of the state, the de facto circumscription of freedom of expression and deficiencies in democratic governance are practices of "successful" state making in that they consolidate the power of the state. They are not indices of a dichotomy of tradition and modernity between which Turkey is caught but part of the "Turkish experience of modernity" (Bozdoğan and Kasaba 1997, 3).

Heightened Modernization or Antimodernism?

While there had already been considerable ambiguities in Germany's path to modernity before 1933, National Socialism is regarded as *the* rupture in Germany's modernization trajectory—one that continues to generate periodic concerns about Germany's belonging to the "civilized West." Broadly speaking, there are two poles along which this phase of German history is conceptualized and discussed. On the one hand, the Holocaust emerges as a unique and singular event based on a specific constellation in German history, culture, and politics that ultimately can only be explained outside of the modern condition. National Socialism is thus understood as a temporary deviation from modernity, a deviation entrenched in German particularism (Repp 2000). On the other end of the spectrum, the Holocaust is understood as a "heightened version of the norm," that is, as an event ultimately rooted in the modern condition and especially its bureaucratic apparatus (Bauman 1989). The following elaborates on a number of positions that are located along this spectrum and shows how they inform contemporary understandings of German modernity and Western belonging.

In his *Modernity and the Holocaust* (1989), the sociologist and philosopher Zygmunt Bauman firmly situates the Holocaust within modernity. In his analysis, modernity emerges as a "necessary condition" of the Holocaust as an industrialized, rationalized, and bureaucratic endeavor. Starting from the premise that the Holocaust cannot be explained by solely pathologizing the perpetrators, he posits that moral indifference was produced through routine bureaucratic procedures, allowing "ordinary people" to transform into the perpetrators of horrendous acts. Bauman argues that when this capability converges with a racist ideology that promises "a better, more reasonable, and rational social order," genocide occurs (95).[27] In the conclusion of his study, Bauman's argument takes an interesting turn when he asserts that it was Germany's existence as a modernity without democracy, that is, the absence of democratic checks and balances, that enabled the Holocaust. However, he does not reflect on the implications of his argument for dominant understandings of "modernity" or of the "West."

I would like to juxtapose Bauman's argument with the anthropologist Uli Linke's *German Bodies: Race and Representation after Hitler* (1999), since she similarly aims to emphasize continuities rather than ruptures between National Socialist ideology and German history before 1933 and after 1945. Yet her premise forms a counterpoint to Bauman in that Linke sees a continuum in terms of an ambivalence toward modernity that is specifically "German" and primarily expressed through the site of the body. Linke draws on psychoanalytical notions such as pathology and the unconscious, rather than the rationality of modern bureaucracy that Bauman highlights. Her analysis thus resonates with Eric Wolf's (1999, 197–98) proposition that National Socialist Germany is "better understood as a movement akin to the cargo cults and ghost dances studied by anthropologists than as a rational deployment of means to pragmatic ends." Linke (1999, 65) posits that nudity in German *Freikörperkultur* (free body culture) was part of the symbolic "postwar [World War I] rejection of modernity," where corporeality was juxtaposed to the "unnatural, decadence and impermanence" of modernity. Here, nakedness was not only employed as a symbol against consumerism and bourgeois authority but became the site of racial violence. German nationalism could insert itself into this body cult because it converged with the antiurban rejection of modernity through the rediscovery of the pure, natural body, one that was set apart from the bodies of "others" through racist ideology. According to Linke, this imagery continues to live on in present-day political representations. Yet, like Bauman, she acknowledges the conception of race as a modern invention and concurs that the Holocaust relied on the interlocution of modern science, technology, and bureaucracy. But in contrast to Baumann, Linke locates the possibility of the

Holocaust more pronouncedly in an ambivalence toward modernity rather than in modernity itself. For Linke, aligning the Holocaust with modernity has "both the potential of distancing as well as making everyone complicit" (215). Rather than exploring this tension further, it seems that both possibilities inherent in her argument seem too troubling for her to pursue.

The historian Kevin Repp (2000, 2), in turn, attempts to reassess German history by conceptualizing it as an "alternative route to modernity." Setting out with a description that reflects the uneven development within Germany after 1871, he posits the existence of a "dual Germany," one that at once exhibits "anachronistic political structures" (and hence "the absence of liberal, democratic traditions") combined with modern welfare state policies. This search for alternatives, so his argument goes, can only be traced outside the political apparatus, in the realm of reformist approaches in German associational life. "Decrying the rationalizing, alienation, depersonalizing forces of modern industrial capitalism as the evisceration of living *Kultur* by mechanistic *Zivilization* at the same time as they sang the praises of modern science and technology, Wilhelmine reformers felt just as at home with the discourse of cultural despair as they did with the discourse of progressive optimism" (14). That the joining of modern technology and German *Kultur* was a difficult endeavor, however, becomes evident in the historian Jeffrey Herf's (1984, 157ff.) interrogation of "reactionary modernism," as he labels the balancing act that characterized both the Weimar Republic and the Third Reich's attempts to reframe modern technology not only as reconcilable with but actually arising from *Kultur.* Bearing structural resemblances to the conception of the "Turkish synthesis," this proposition, however, did not solve the long-held antinomy between *Kultur* and modernity in German thought.

On quite the other end of the spectrum, we find Steven Ozment's (2004) take on German history and modernization. He explicitly wants to move away from defining Germany based on the twelve years of Nazi reign and from diagnosing a disposition for genocide in the peculiarities of German history. Trying to "emancipate" Germany from this part of its past, he argues for placing the German experience into the larger European framework. In contrast to Mark Mazower's (1998) examination of European complicities in Nazism and contingencies in the emergence of liberal democracies in Europe, however, Ozment conceptualizes the Third Reich as a temporary breakdown in Europe's triumphant trajectory by identifying the Nazi regime—horrific as it was—as an outlier of "the new experiments of the 20th century." While, according to Ozment, the Napoleonic occupation of the Rhineland (1794–1813) furthered democratic ideals, Germany has "always feared anarchy more than tyranny," as "the Germans" did not share the American and French "optimism" in the capabilities in humankind, which explains why neither the French nor the American revolution were fit to be models for the Germanys.

Problematic as Ozment's propositions might be, his interjection, along with those of Bauman and Linke, plays into the larger context of the German historians' debate (*Historikerstreit*) of the 1980s that was originally prompted by Ernst Nolte's proposition that Nazism has to be understood as an extreme reaction to communism and especially Stalinism. Two main camps emerged in the ensuing debate. The revisionist fraction aimed at normalizing National Socialism (that is, disavowing its workings in the present) as part of the totalitarian regimes in Europe. The critical historians, however, maintained that while the Holocaust needs to be analyzed within the European context it also has to be understood as rooted in the particularities of German history (Eley 1988). These discussions were reignited after Germany's reunification, when the search for a "new national self-understanding" (*neues nationales Selbstverständnis*) set in and the question of Germany's geopolitical belonging came up anew. While Hans-Helmuth Knütter, for example, diagnosed an "overidentification" of Germany with the West after 1945 that devalued German achievements of the past (Berger 1995, 202–3), Stefan Berger (1995, 215) posited that "the central achievement of the Federal Republic after 1945, namely Western orientation, should not be given up by the reunified Germany." These statements deserve attention because they once again emphasize that, historically speaking, Germany was not part of the West per se. "Western orientation" was not or simply a given but had to be actively produced.

In the aftermath of this controversy and with German reunification, East German history was completely marginalized, and the East German experience was negated in the realm of the everyday (Berdahl 1999) as well as in its political and artistic lineages. This discrediting of the German Democratic Republic was both an outcome of the revisionist project to "renationalize" German identity and a condition "to overcom[e] the reunification crisis" (Berger 1995, 207), which expressed itself in uneven development and the discontent this caused in the general population. Within the revisionist argument, German critical historiography, instead of totalitarianism or the Holocaust, was faulted for the difficulties in the reunification process because it contributed to the tabooing of nationalist sentiments in Germany—which now so many wanted to consider as a once again legitimate expression, even a right. In the search for a "usable past" (Moeller 1996) on which to construct the new Germany and endow it with a positive image, the history of division became increasingly obscured, yet it continues to shape German politics and cultural policy.

Modularity or Normativity?

One way to avoid the many trappings of the discourses of exceptionalism, beyond notions of "alternative" or "multiple modernities," is to interrogate the trajectories of Germany and Turkey within a shared trajectory that encompasses politics, economy, society, and culture in divergent locations (Kahn 2001) and thus as struggles with the normativity of modern power.

In the introduction to his highly influential *Imagined Communities*, Benedict Anderson (1983, 4) argues that nationalism "became 'modular,' capable of being transplanted with varying degrees of self-consciousness, to a great variety of social terrains to merge and be merged with a correspondingly wide variety of political and ideological constellations." His notion that the model of the nation-state, once it was established, became available for "pirating" leaves out the implications of power differentials that led to the objectification of nationalism as the political manifestation of modernity. It is in this context that I find the anthropologist David Scott's (1999, 17) thoughts on modern power to be especially productive, since he tries to account for these power differentials by emphasizing that the narrative of "modernity was always-already inserted into a normative discourse." Drawing on the understandings of modern power developed by Michel Foucault and Talal Asad, Scott argues that modern power relies on and produces a political rationality in which "premodern possibilities are not only no longer conceptually approachable except in the language of the modern, but are now no longer available as practical historical options" (23).[28]

This perspective opens a different path for approaching Turkish and German nationalism and their respective modernization processes. It makes a comparison on equal footing, a joint reading of Turkey and Germany, possible. It allows us to keep in mind that Germany's capability for modernity was not only questioned but that modernity was long outright rejected in the fields of both politics and the arts. Viewed in this vein, periodic insecurities about Germany's modernity, as in 1945 or 1989–1990, appear not as deviations but as constitutive for the German political and cultural landscape. This perspective also avoids reducing Turkey's history to a sheer mimicking of Western European models and allows for comparing the trajectories of both the German and Turkish art worlds, their aesthetic approximation to "the West," and their attempts at claiming modern nationhood and hence civility through aesthetics. Highlighting the normativity of modern power emphasizes continuities within respective historical trajectories as well as narrative ruptures, similarities, and differences in the two discussed locales without resorting solely to tropes of accomplished or failed modernization. As divergent as their historical sociopolitical situations have been, both countries have struggled—and continue to do so—with similar issues that emerge from the normativity of modern power, even though Germany is now firmly established in the West and Turkey still regarded outside of it.

The following chapter maps the present-day constellations of the art world in Istanbul and Berlin. More specifically, it investigates how the relationships between and among different art world actors are framed in both locations. It begins to give insights into how the official modernization narratives and their normalization in the form of dominant discourses play out in the settings of Istanbul and Berlin. Despite the pronounced international character of contemporary art, it is at the intersection of these narratives with the day-to-day operations of the art world that references to the "national" reinsert themselves, at times implicitly and at others explicitly. This reinsertion appears as much when art is discussed in the abstract as when practices integral to the art world, such as reviewing, selling, collecting, and sponsoring art, are concerned.

2

Art Worlds

Of Friends, Foes, and Working for the Greater Good

This chapter maps the art world and the ways that art world actors, primarily artists, gallerists,[1] collectors, museum officials, and sponsors, describe their work and relate to one another in the arts settings of Istanbul and Berlin. It traces how aesthetic theories are mobilized in the daily workings of the art world to reconcile conflicting understandings of art. When art is talked about in the daily settings of the art world, a set of larger, historical discourses pertaining to the "nature of art" are always invoked as well. From the legacies of classical thought that have addressed art both as corruptive and enriching, distracting and cathartic to Enlightenment elaborations on the civilizing impact of art, from the critique of the Frankfurt School to formalism and institutional theory, these seemingly discrete theories are frequently merged in the day-to-day operations of the art world. Other motifs, such as the autonomy of art, are regularly employed both in the art world and the broader public without reference to the historical contexts out of which they arose. Instead they too are invoked through pragmatic shorthands.

I posit that those relationships in the art world that are frequently framed in terms of amity and enmity do not simply or necessarily reflect interpersonal issues or individual conflicts of interests but are indicative of structural dependencies and power differentials in the art world that are rooted in the inherent contradictions of the modern conception of art.[2] The friend/foe binary serves to mediate these dependencies and contradictions, or to disavow them, or, rather, their structural character, altogether. Here, the notion of foe does not necessarily signify personalized ill will (although it sometimes does). Rather it is an umbrella term to express different registers of discontent and experiences of frustration that arise from different and contradictory positionalities within the art world that emerge as adversarial to another's interests. Similarly, the notion of friendship does not necessarily point to personal attachments but to the mediation of power differentials.

A second mediating discourse, often employed by collectors and sponsors, reconciles divergent interests through the trope of art's civilizing capacities and hence of art as a "greater good." The constant need to affirm these ideas grows exponentially the further removed the actors are from the actual process of artistic production. This dynamic is basically the same in Istanbul and Berlin, but subtle differences emerge in the explanations of what constitutes the greater good not least because the "peoples'" or "society's cultural needs" are explained through national particularities.

Art and Its Audiences

Theoretical approaches to art rest on presumptions about the effect and affect of art, about what happens in the eye of the observer. While artists and audiences are often discussed as separate entities, the philosopher Robin Collingwood (1969 [1945], 484–95) has countered claims about the autonomy of art by conceptualizing art as a fundamentally collaborative process between artists and audiences. This collaboration lies not only in the response of the audience to a work of art but in the consideration of the audience during the creation of an artwork. For Collingwood, it is not by way of expertise, that is, formal knowledge, that an audience enters into this process. All they need is "intelligence" and "determination" (486), although these are rather vague qualifications of a potential audience's properties. In contrast to the philosopher George Dickie's (1995 [1984]) view, the audience is not just a "role bearer" in the institution of the art world. Instead, audiences are construed as active participants in the production and reception of art, based on an empathetic process that draws on shared emotions and concerns that the artist expresses on their behalf. It is these shared emotions that mark the audience as a community, Collingwood suggests.

The question if and what kind of prior knowledge audiences need in order to enter into this interaction remains a matter of contention. When the relationship between art and audiences is discussed in Turkey and Germany, understandings of art appreciation as intrinsically human are weighed against considerations of arts education and "acquired taste." Arthur Danto (1964, 571) proposes that much of art today is conceptualized as exhibiting aspects of reality that remain otherwise unseen, a proposition he illustrates through the analogy of the mirror image. Susanne Neumann (Berlin, Figures 1–3) and

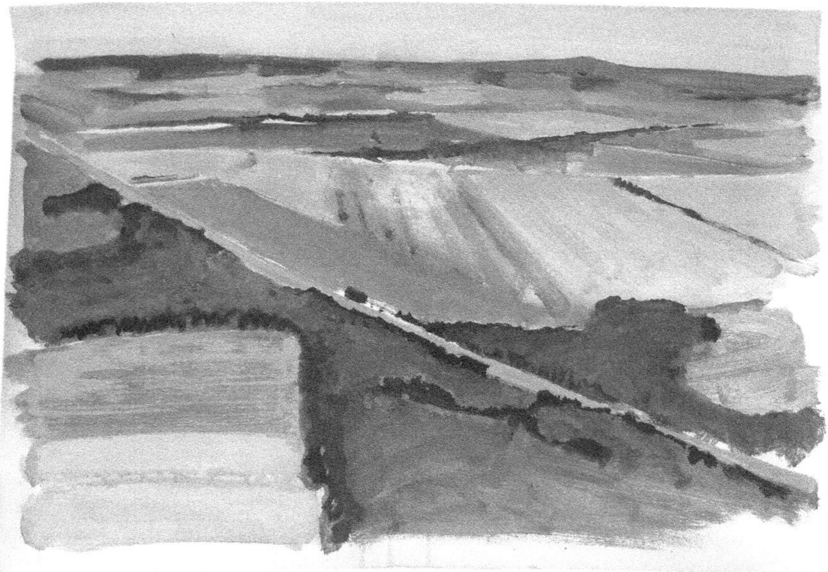

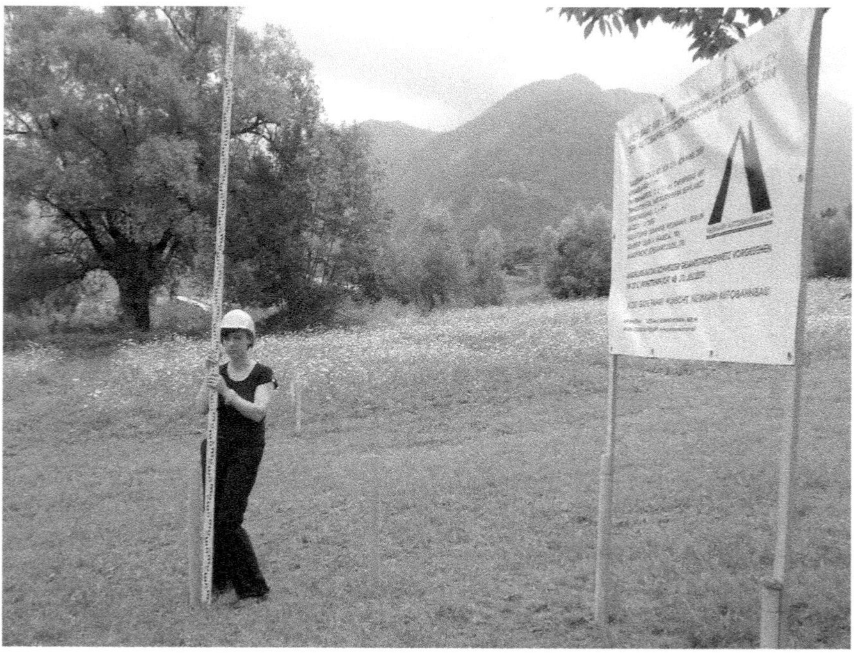

Figures 1–3. (*continued*)

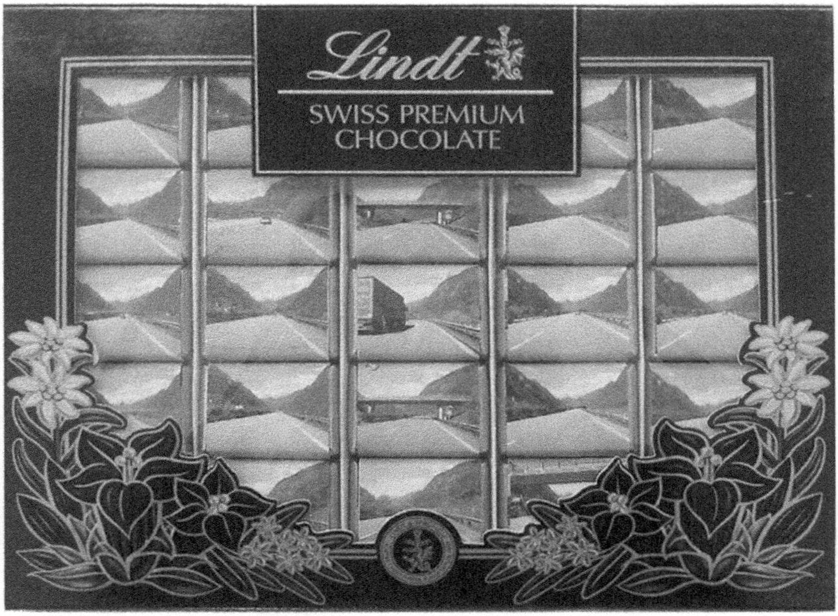

Figures 1–3. Susanne Neumann's work for the sculpture park openArt in Roveredo, Switzerland, 2004–2006. For this work, Neumann photographed the local segment of a cross-country autobahn, which she then transformed into paintings, postcards, and other memorabilia, such as the chocolates depicted here. The installation included a model replica of a fifteen-meter-long stretch of the autobahn in the sculpture park. Fig. 1: *autobahn*, 2004–2006, acrylic on paper, 50×70 cm; Fig. 2: Susanne Neumann conducting geometrical leveling with fictitious construction sign, openArt, Roveredo, Switzerland, 2005; Fig. 3: *Schoggi*, 2004–2006, imprinted chocolate souvenirs from Switzerland, 20×30 cm. Courtesy of the artist.

Ahmet Öğüt (Istanbul, Figures 4–5) are two examples of artists who explicitly draw on familiar images and everyday situations in many of their works, citing exactly this reason.

When asked about the role the audience plays in their creative processes, most artists considered the viewer's gaze a vital factor. Prior knowledge of art history or theory was often regarded as helpful but not necessary, especially when the expression of shared experiences was emphasized. As İnci Eviner (Figures 6 and 7) explains, however, capturing a moment that constitutes a "shared experience" and is intensely personal at the same time can be challenging. "I want to be very personal, yet I want to be one and the same with others, I want to be alone and together. I want to speak out of the shadow of others. In my practice there is always a moment in which these contradictory

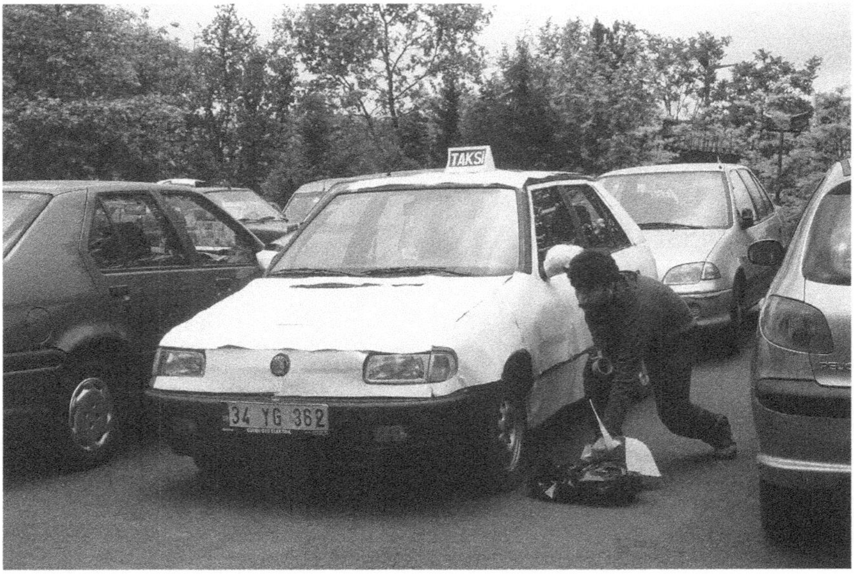

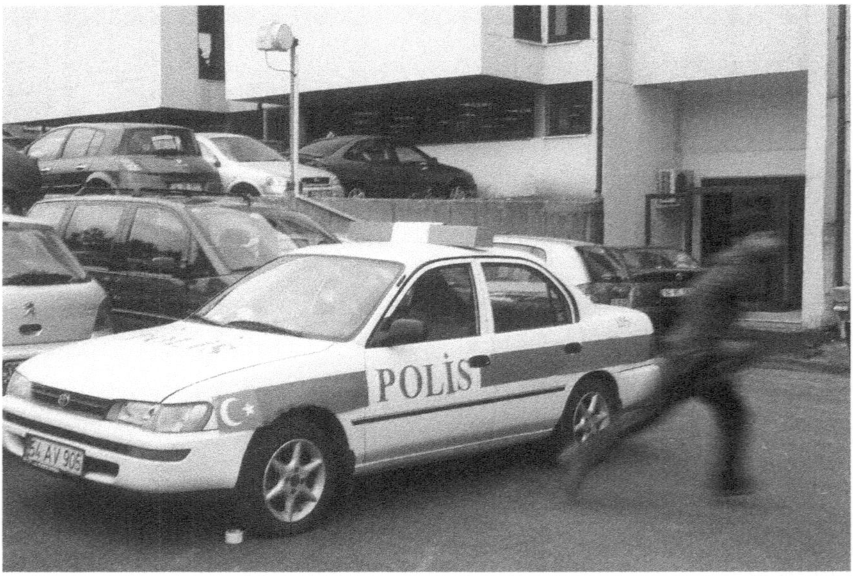

Figures 4–5. Ahmet Öğüt's *Somebody Else's Car*, 2005 (slide projection, 20 pieces, photo series), documents how Öğüt transforms the cars of unsuspecting strangers into taxicabs and police cars. Courtesy of the artist.

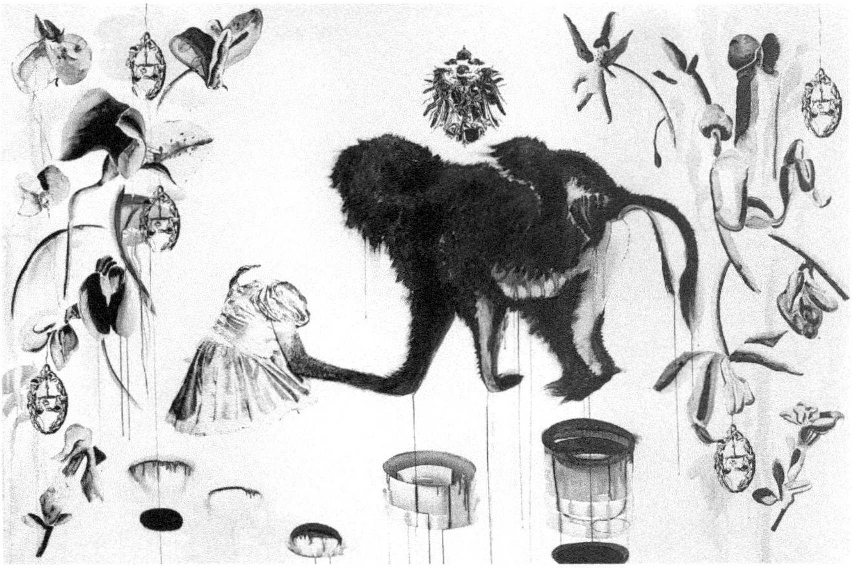

Figure 6. İnci Eviner, *Beauty and Beast*, 2007, acrylic and silkscreen on canvas, 220×320 cm. Photo: CHROMA. Courtesy of the artist and Galeri Nev İstanbul.

positions come together. It is a short moment, but that is the moment I need to capture. It is this moment that is both me and the other."

Others emphasize that thinking about the potential audience and how they perceive a piece can stifle their creativity and note that striking a balance between a personal artistic expression and broader intelligibility is often a delicate endeavor. Christian Niccoli (Figures 8–11) describes his process by saying: "The viewer plays a role, of course. I always ask myself, will the viewer get this point? If not, then I am doing something wrong. I want to communicate with the viewer, but this does not mean that I want to take the viewer by the hand. . . . The problem with contemporary art is that it is difficult to understand. Most of the time it is absolutely incomprehensible, especially if you don't know the history. So you have to keep that in mind as an artist."

A number of artists I spoke to in both cities try consciously to overcome the division between artist and audience by developing decidedly collaborative or participatory projects. ODA Projesi (Room Project), an artist collective established by Özge Açıkkol, Güneş Savaş, and Seçil Yersel in 2000, embodies these kinds of efforts. Renting a shared apartment in the neighborhood of Galata (Istanbul), they opened their home for a variety of projects that, according to Yersel, were guided by the following questions: "How do relationships determine a space? How can we share a room with others? Are we, as artists,

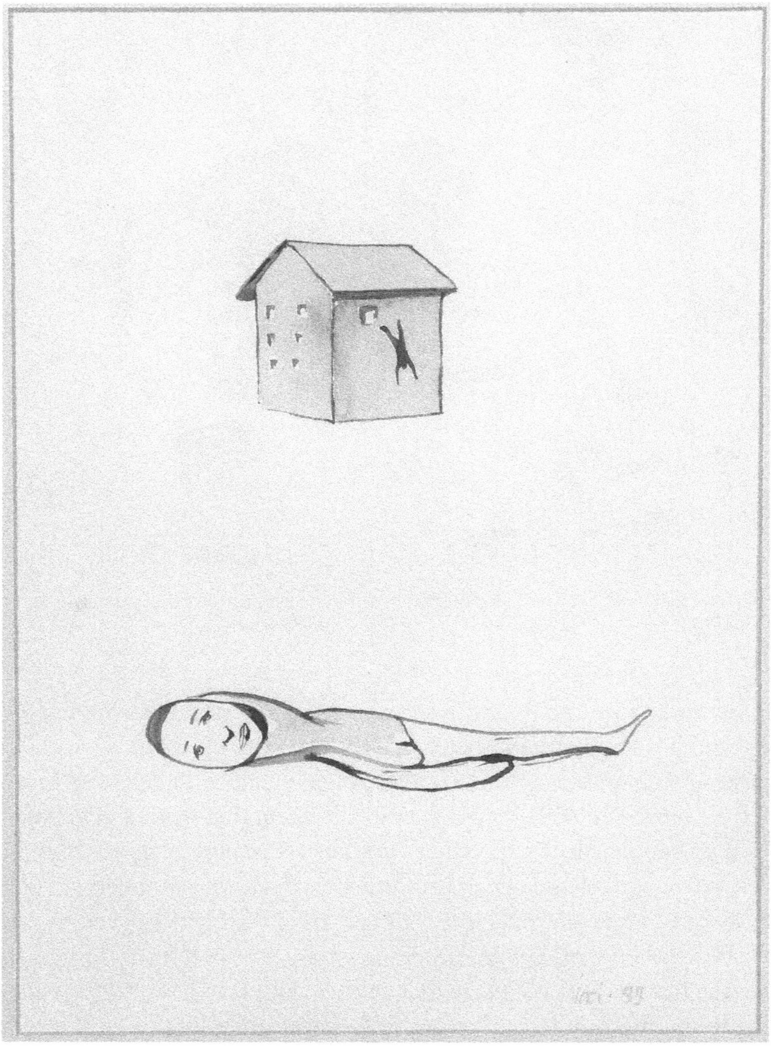

Figure 7. İnci Eviner, *The Sea*, 1994, watercolor on paper, 31×23 cm. Courtesy of the artist and Galeri Nev İstanbul.

hosts, or are we neighbors? How can we use the space outside of normalized exhibition formats?" Rather than producing artworks or performances in the narrower sense, the collective invited neighbors, colleagues, and academics to use their space. Projects such as *Birthday and Wedding* (2000), during which the artists and children from the quarter planned a birthday celebration for

Açıkkol and also invited a young woman who was preparing for her wedding, were explicitly based on generating conversations on the shared experience of celebrations. Although the day was photographically documented, the "art project" ultimately resided in the encounters facilitated that day.[3] While participatory or collaborative art—arguably buzzwords of the last two decades—project alternative ways of how art, artists, and audiences relate to one another outside of the marketplace of art, the conditions of such participation and the aesthetic parameters under which they can be discussed have been fiercely contested, including by many artists who describe their work in this vein (Bishop 2012, Kester 2011).

Questions of how to create spaces that lie outside of the established institutional outlets of the art world also guide the Berlin-based artist Susanne Bosch, whose work is mostly located in public space. She stresses that she does not treat public space as an "extension of the gallery, where something is exhibited for an audience." Instead her projects are often participatory in nature and entail negotiations with those who inhabit and use these spaces on a daily basis. Experiences of working in public space have motivated Bosch to take courses in conflict management, which she sees as an important tool for the kinds of debates she is trying to facilitate. Her installation *Mensch weg/Insan yitmis/Meri helazbune/Person disappeared* (2004), for instance, was exhibited in the display windows of SOX36, a club and cultural staple on Berlin's Oranienstrasse in Kreuzberg. The district inhabited mainly by immigrants from Turkey, a large part of them Kurdish. The collages represented persons who had either been forcibly disappeared in their home countries or had vanished in the course of attempting to immigrate, without documents, to Germany. The work also featured the narratives of their families, many living in Kreuzberg, who were searching for their missing relatives.

The way that Bosch conceives of public space and differentiates it from the gallery setting entails a distancing from the institutionalized outlets of the art world. Artists often voice disapproval of what they perceive as the insularity and self-referentiality of the art world and take pride in seeing their works resonate "outside the boundaries of the arts setting," as the Berlin-based artist Bernardo Giorgi put it. Both he and Florian Zeyfang stated on different occasions that the art world is often "more involved in taxing itself" than in "generating productive conversations." While there is a certain amount of antagonism toward the art world across the board, there is also an interesting push and pull in this relationship between individual artists and art world institutions. Many artists note that much of their time is spent on professional networking in order to get projects under way or to meet curators, evidencing

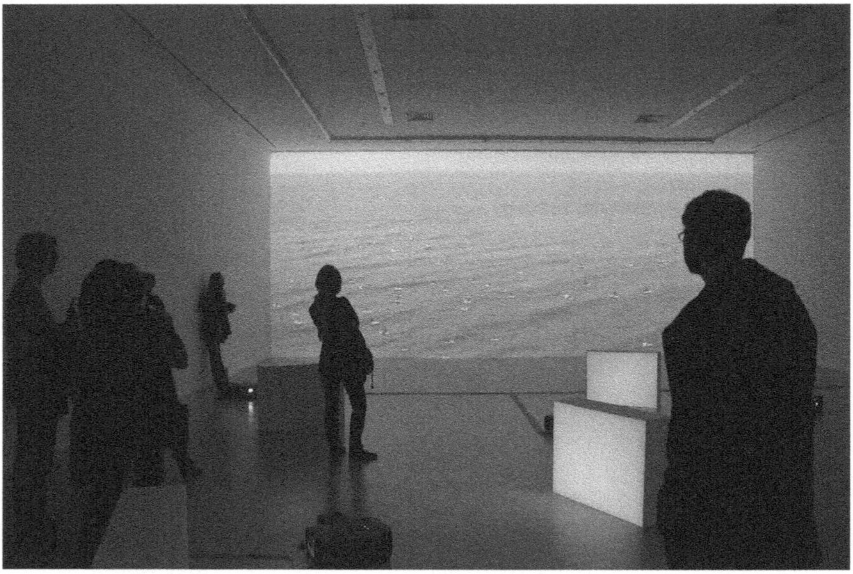

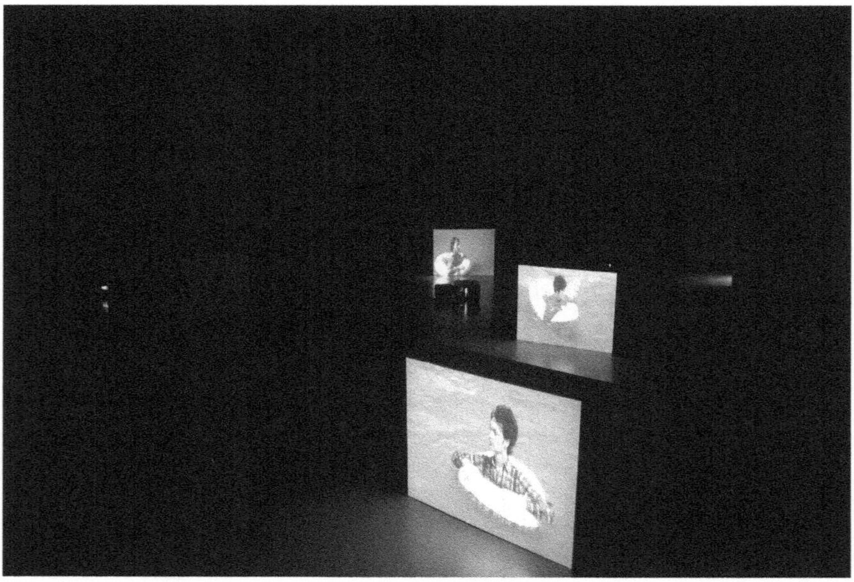

Figures 8–11. (*continued*)

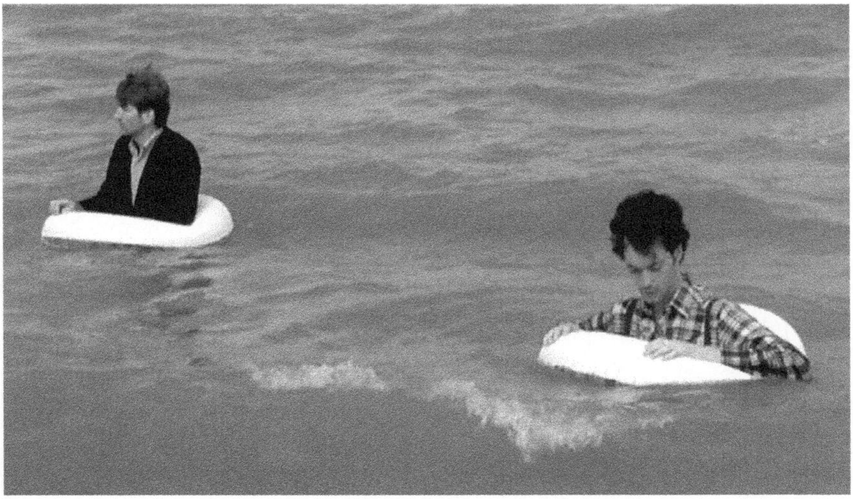

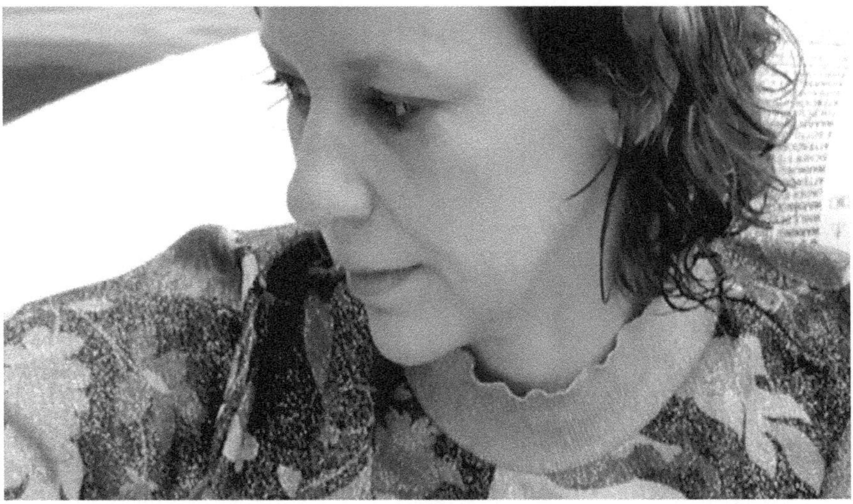

Figures 8–11. Installation images and video stills from Christian Niccoli's *Plantschen/Splash* at Künstlerhaus Bethanien (Berlin, 2008). In connection to this work, Niccoli said he wanted to capture the drifting state of many young Berlin-based artists that "might dress and live well but have very little hope for the future in terms of employment and social security." 2008, 16mm reversed on DV-PAL, two formats: 1-channel video, 5:05 minutes; 7-channel video installation, 1:25 minutes. Courtesy of the artist.

the interdependency that characterizes the art world, where socializing is experienced as a necessity but also as a burden.

A slightly different take on the limitations but also the possibilities of the institutional arts setting is presented by Banu Cennetoğlu. Talking about her project *The List*, which exhibited on public billboards throughout Amsterdam the names of seven thousand refugees who had died trying to reach "Fortress Europe," she notes: "When I came across this list, I thought, how much can I achieve as Banu Cennetoğlu, as a 'simple citizen,' so to speak, to make this list visible? Quite little, really. That's why I used my professional connections, my art network. In this project, I specifically took into account the audience. It is not really about my work but about making the list reach people." In this instance the disciplinary and institutional boundaries of art did not present an obstacle for communicating with a broader public. Rather Cennetoğlu strategically used her position as an artist to transcend the art world in its narrower sense.

Mediating between Artists and Audiences: Critics and Curators

As art has its own disciplinary history and presents a field in which knowledge and connoisseurship play an exponent role, it is also in need of mediation, both in terms of exposing audiences to works of art (that they might or might not be able to see in person) and providing the context within which works are discussed. In this mediation between artists and audiences, critics, or arts writers, as some prefer to be called, assume a vital role. In the international art world, the "death of the critic" has been proclaimed repeatedly since the 1960s, and artists have increasingly taken to writing about their own works. Some of them do so simply because "no one else does" or "does it well." One artist from Istanbul explained: "I prefer to write about my own works, instead of waiting for writeups that, even if positive, completely miss the point." Others take to writing because the worldwide grant economy requires them to submit "artist statements" in which they describe their work process and conceptual approaches. Still, artists very much rely on reviews by art magazines and the daily press to enhance their visibility and to generate interpretative frameworks for their work. Major German newspapers such as the *Frankfurter Allgemeine Zeitung* (FAZ), *Die Süddeutsche*, the Berlin-based *Tageszeitung* (TAZ), and the weekly *Die Zeit* include culture and arts pages (called feuilletons) that feature art reviews and are forums for cultural critique. Berlin artists have mixed feelings about the number and thrust of the feuilletons. One curator remarked,

"The feuilleton is a place where everyone thinks they can say something about art because they think they understand what it's about and how we should do our work. That's why we have so many feuilletons."

In Istanbul some respondents posited that true art criticism does not exist in Turkey, pointing to the fact that some newspapers tend to run event announcements rather than analyses of exhibitions and performances. However, at the time, the dailies *Cumhurriyet*, *Radikal*, *Milliyet*, *Taraf*, and even the smaller left-leaning *Birgün* and the Kurdish *Özgür Gündem* as well as weekly papers, such as *Agos*, had arts sections. *Hürriyet* and *Milliyet* also published monthly journals exclusively dedicated to art. In addition, a fluctuating number of arts journals exist both in print and online, some of which are affiliated with corporate arts centers—and thus run the danger of having somewhat promotional qualities. Another notable issue in the context of Istanbul is that a number of prominent curators regularly write reviews. How this particular concentration of power plays out in the daily workings of the art world was for the most part avoided by respondents. However, some noted that the dependency structures in Istanbul's art world made it difficult for people to criticize one another, especially given the high likelihood that one would have to work together again on other occasions. In contrast to Germany, where the grievance is that "everyone's a critic," discontent in Turkey was expressed through the notion of lack. Naturalized by the political and scholarly discourses of belated modernity, these grievances obscure the more concrete issues of interdependency and power differentials that in fact shape the manifestation of art criticism.[4]

Yet there are also shared formulations of grievances when it comes to the form and content of arts writing. A considerable number of artists note that they find most of it aloof, "overly abstract," or simply "bad." An internationally successful, midcareer artist from Berlin put it in unequivocal terms: "If I have to read another art magazine I am going to throw up." A gallery worker who had just recently quit her position conceded, "One good thing about leaving the gallery world is that I don't have to read that stuff anymore." Yet there are always exceptions to formulations of antagonism in the art world, namely, those concrete relationships and interactions that are deemed "successful." It is thus not surprising that "good" arts writers are highly respected, and some artists, for example Susanne Neumann, take on part of the responsibility for the state of art criticism by maintaining that the more information artists provide the better informed reviewers' assessments will be. When I asked Brigitte Werneburg, editor of the arts and culture section of the *TAZ*, how she ensures that her reviews do artworks and artists justice, she responded: "You can really only work with what people offer you. How good is the press material? How well is the concept explained to me? That is really the duty of the gallerist or the curator. It is their task to make the artist look good or even better than she is." But Werneburg also echoed the sentiments alluded to earlier: "Anyone who reads reviews or catalogue texts knows that the problem lies in the dense usage of theory. These texts are not written in any understandable way, let alone clear German." Werneburg sees her role as providing insights into the local and international art scene for the broader audience of a daily newspaper. "Our goal is to build a bridge," she says, "between the reader and the art world."

The interplay of collaboration and antagonism, interdependency and power asymmetries also dominates artists' accounts of curators. The rising authority of the curator has been subject to critique over the past two decades in the international art world (Rogoff 2002, Obrist 2008). This critique is mirrored in Istanbul and Berlin; artists in both cities noted that curators are ever more interested in their own fame and fortune than in the work of the artist. Yet curators remain important mediators between artists, artworks, and audiences: They provide the conceptual framework in which works are presented and discussed. Curators select and bring together different artists and their works under a specific theme or set of questions. Unless they are institutionally affiliated, they often take on the task of securing a space, raising funds, and dealing with the logistics of an exhibition. Writing press releases, preparing catalogues, and working on outreach for a given event can also fall into their purview. A common discontent expressed with regard to curators in both cities is that they are, somewhat paradoxically so, rather uninterested in the specific work that an artist contributes. They are often said to adhere to "hip themes" that are superimposed on the works instead of seriously engaging with them. But as with other arenas of antagonism in the art world, once asked more concretely, artists also volunteer stories about curators (some world renowned and others working on more local scales) whose perspective they appreciate, always stressing their exceptionality. On this topic a Berlin-based artist remarked:

> Curators are really somewhere between business and idealism. Yet you have to rely on them, get them interested in your work, and this dependency can make for rather tense, and sometimes even depressing, situations. You might have noticed that in the art world everyone is really friendly on the surface. You can't fight, you can't have a controversial discussion. Like in the business world, you never know if you need this person in the future. So you can't really be friends with them, can't really share your thoughts. There are of course exceptions,

> like Anselm Franke. He is one of the rare curators who is all about the art, who really wants to discuss issues, and for whom this is not just a business.

Curators themselves frame their work as facilitating the communication between arts spaces, audiences, artists, artworks, and, sometimes, sponsors. This mediating function also makes for their authority to frame the perception of artworks, even if this frame diverges from the artists' intentions. While the reference to business corresponds with one of the actual roles that curators sometimes assume, it is also a shorthand that reveals the power asymmetries between artists and curators.

Disgruntlement with the power differentials vis-à-vis curators, commercial galleries, and other institutions of the art world, such as museums, has also led artists to search for alternative exhibiting strategies. In Berlin this has manifested itself from the late 1990s onward in the establishment of producer galleries (*Produzentengallerien*) formed by groups of artists who create their own exhibitions spaces and often *employ* curators to work for *them*.[5] In Istanbul this development has been mirrored by the formation of artists' initiatives or collectives but also by artists taking on the task of curating exhibitions with and for their peers. Talking about her experience of *Free Kick* (2005), an exhibition curated by the artist Halil Altındere, İnci Eviner notes: "Instead of moving into existing spaces, we can create our own. Curators of course do not feel the need for that, and they should not have to; either way they would not care. Instead of waiting for a gallerist or a curator, artists today are creating their own spaces."

In the Gallery: Friendship, Trust, and Risk

Gallerists are both much sought after and under constant scrutiny by artists. Their motives are always questioned. After all, their interests and those of the artist and might not always align. Artists in Istanbul as well as Berlin talk of their attempts to find a gallery as anxiety-inducing endeavors. It was not uncommon to hear from interlocutors how they were excitedly working away on their portfolios to show to potential gallerists, but a few weeks later, after having tackled the fear of rejection and then experienced it, retreated to the hope of "simply" being discovered and picked up for representation. Others stated that they would try again, once they had worked up the courage, but "not now." Some, like Banu Cennetoğlu, at the time quite consciously steered away from galleries because the commercial apparatus they are embedded in does not really correspond with their artistic practices: "I don't work with galleries these days. I found that although I work in a format that excites gallerists—after all, photography has a real market—it does not really work for me. I do not work with photography's valued mechanisms of high-resolution prints and limited editions. Gallerists want very clean, very commercial stuff. I mainly work through copies. I often tear up the photos once the installation is over, so I am not really a profitable artist for a gallery. This does not mean that I categorically reject to work with galleries. Maybe I just have not found the right one yet."[6]

Needless to say, for those who at some point had gallery representation and then were dropped because their works did not sell as expected, the topic was especially uncomfortable. The same is true for those who left their galleries because they did not feel sufficiently represented or cared for.

Those who have gallery representation often describe their individual relationships with gallerists as comforting and the gallery as providing a safe haven where the business side of things is taken care of. Gallerists can shape careers, for example, by building up an artist's reputation slowly and regulating the amount of works by an artist that are out on the market at any given time, in order to avoid a sudden drop in prices. Having a gallery affiliation means not only relative security in terms of being granted periodic exhibitions but also having representation at the year-round cycle of art fairs, where much of the buying and selling of art is done these days. Artists often frame their relationship with gallerists as friendships and in terms of mutual respect and personal fondness. But as one gallery worker in Berlin explained, "Not all artists want to be coddled—although many do, and some even ask for a considerable amount of attention by calling the gallerist every two weeks to invite them for studio visits to show their newest work. Others are quite content with a distant, business-like relationship in which the gallery is just another trading place for them."

Apart from gallery owners, assistants play an important role in the day-to-day operations of the gallery and are responsible for a range of areas, from accounting to press releases. Off the record, gallery assistants often recount long working hours and little pay in what one assistant called a work environment consisting of "egocentric, moody people and penny pinchers." In Germany assistants are often referred to as *Galleriemäuse*—the gendered nature of the word "mouse" in German points to the fact that gallery assistants are predominantly women. Many of them see the difficult working conditions as part of paying their dues in the art world. Like other actors in the art world, they too frame their labor as a service to art and to society and often take pride in their supportive role in the artistic process.

There are also stories that feature "other gallerists" who treat "their artists unfairly and are only after quick financial gains." In these descriptions gallerists and artists appear antithetical to each other, as one is interested in business and the other in art proper; artists and gallerists are construed in antagonistic terms, and this although their existence is symbiotic in nature. Favoritism is another trope that comes up repeatedly. There are always other artists who "receive more care" and traction because the gallerist invests more time in promoting them to potential buyers.

Without the work of the artist, the gallerist cannot exist. As gallerists deal directly with economic transactions and public relations, secure shows, and help represent artists in their dealings with public and private institutions, artists both aspire to have gallery representation while also dreading the dependency it creates. The going gallery commission teeters around 50 percent, with gallerists generally determining the price of an artwork[7] and allowing for up to a 20 percent collector's discount at their discretion. Yet gallerists rarely address the business character of their activities. Instead gallerists frame their work as a service to artists (Turkish: *hizmet*, German: *Dienst am Künstler*) as well as to buyers, frequently employing the language of friendship. Nuran Terzioğlu of Galeri Apel (Istanbul) exemplifies this stance: "The relationships we have with our artists are very amicable, they are friendships, really. When you look at our website you will see that we list their direct contact information. We have endless trust toward each other, like a family. When you look at other galleries, their relationships with artists are more business-like. It is impossible to get an email address or the phone number of the artist through them. In contrast, we have a very respectful relationship." Murat Pilevneli, then owner of Galerist (Istanbul), described the relationship between gallerists and artists in a similar fashion: "We are the representatives of the artist. I see myself as an advocate [*savuncu*, also meaning 'defender'] for the artist and at the same time as a friend—that is the type of relationship we have. If that is not possible, I do not work with a person. At the same time, I also see myself as someone who breaks new ground for them."

Like Terzioğlu, Pilevneli emphasized that gallerists do not seek a monopoly and exclusivity with the artist. In Berlin too, gallerists highlight that artists are granted autonomy and "absolute freedom" in determining exhibition concepts and deciding which exhibitions to take part in. Mentioning that instead of "suffocating *his* artists" he helps "them get representation" with galleries abroad, Pilevneli clearly aims to distinguish himself from the stereotype of the gallerist as gatekeeper. With the strengthening of the art market, galleries have been intervening in lending negotiations with museums more forcefully. In Germany, loans from galleries are often used to prop up museum collections for thematic exhibitions, especially as the acquisition capabilities of museums decrease given drops in public funding. Britta Schmitz, of the Hamburger Bahnhof, describes the contentious relationship between museums and galleries as follows: "Galleries are important for us because they draw our attention to certain artists. But this also means that gallerists intervene much more than they used to and advise artists where to exhibit and under which conditions. There has been an extreme increase in that. I presume New York has always been like that because it's always been a very tough market. This is of course very new for us. Now it's a global phenomenon that has also made it very difficult for artists who are not represented by these big galleries."

While in Schmitz's description the power balance seems clearly to have shifted in favor of private galleries, it is important to remember that being exhibited in a museum or permanently included in a museum collection remains an important validating factor for artists. Museum approval adds value to existing and future works not least by projecting longevity in the art market. That museums use their sanctioning power quite strategically was further brought to my attention when two interlocutors who had taken part in exhibitions at the Istanbul Modern reported independently that they had been pressured to gift works to the museum. Both were presented with the argument that the short-term economic loss incurred by such a gift would be outweighed by the prestige—and thus future profits—that inclusion in a museum collection translates into.

Although admitting that their focus is on reaching potential buyers, gallerists, not unlike museum workers, frame their work as a service to the broader public. Audiences, however, frequently note that they find the atmosphere of private galleries intimidating (see also Bourdieu 1984, 273). The aesthetics of exclusion that characterizes the gallery setting is rarely if ever addressed by gallery owners; after all, they argued, they are open for all passersby. The gallerists I interviewed stressed the element of mediation between artists and (potential) buyers as their central "duty." As one Berlin-based gallerist put it: "A buyer and an artist may not necessarily get along, they may not like or understand each other. So, what we are providing for them, what we really do, is to translate between the two parties." This emphasis on translation points again to the fact that an artwork might not be self-explanatory and to the potentially divergent understandings of art held by the actors involved.

However, not all art buyers are conceived of as the same. Off the record, gallerists tend to distinguish between "serious" collectors, who, along with money, spend considerable amounts of time studying a particular artist or a specific school of art. Those who dedicate their lives to collecting and know when to buy and when to sell a piece "not to make profit" but to reinvest in other works that make a collection "stronger," that is, more coherent, are talked about with admiration. In contrast, other collectors "may have money but no taste and understand nothing of art. They only collect because it is considered good form [*zum guten Ton gehört*]. But money isn't everything." While some collectors' motivations are thus under scrutiny, gallerists' general descriptions of their relationships with buyers highlight the element of trust and speak of bonds that surpass those of mere business relations. Like their relationships with artists, gallerists couch their affiliations with buyers in the terminology of service and friendship rather than that of economic transaction.

There is another kind of collector that is frequently frowned upon by those who identify as serious collectors—the "decorative buyer." Gallery workers in Berlin and Istanbul sometimes jokingly but sometimes in an exasperated fashion refer to what a former employee of Galerie Max Hetzler described as customers with "decorative challenges." They come into the gallery with requests such as "I am looking for a contrast image in yellow to set off my furniture." This concern was seconded by the director of a midlevel gallery in Istanbul who described these kinds of buyers as "looking for something to put above the sofa" and "in dire need to be educated about art." One gallery assistant noted that she "found it aggravating when people talked about art in the same way as they are talking about cars, or what have you." Her stance reinforces that despite its commodification art remains an object of a different order—an issue that is as much at the heart of the modern conception of art as it is in the debates of the Frankfurt School.

Before delving further into how collectors themselves frame their practices and how they express their attachment to art, let me turn briefly to Stuart Plattner's ethnographic study of the St. Louis art market, *High Art Down Home* (1996). Plattner arrives at a similar portrayal of how collectors describe their relationships with art dealers as personally meaningful. He relates the existence of these highly personalized relationships to the fact that the risk in art transactions is perceived as rather high. This risk, according to Plattner, results from the asymmetrical knowledge between art dealers and buyers, especially as art prices are increasingly hard to comprehend by laypeople. Plattner thus compares the art market to another high-risk market constellation, that of peasant trading markets (200). He proposes that there, as in the art market, the emphasis on personal relationships and steady trading partners (instead of selling to the highest bidder when opportunity arises) presents a long-term strategy to lower risk. While the element of risk reduction may play a role, I propose that the expression of friendship and other modes of affective attachment do not only alleviate the perception, or actual existence, of risk. Neither do they have a solely instrumental function in establishing networks of professional favoritism (Svašek 2002). They also help mediate the contradictions that arise from treating art not as it is ideally understood, that is, as a public good, but as a commodity—a concern historically formative for the modern conception of art. Motifs of friendship and service present conduits for deproblematizing a whole range of relationships within the art world and for reconciling divergent interests in art.

A second question Plattner raises sheds further light on the tensions that the commodity character of art produces:

> But why should profiting from art be morally censured in a thoroughly capitalist society? I hypothesize that the discomfort comes about because different social classes interact in the art world: collectors who are upper middle class or affluent cannot avoid confronting the difference between themselves and the typically poor artist who makes the work they covet. So long as they concentrate on discussing their love for art and aesthetic theory, this potentially embarrassing difference can remain in the background.
>
> (Plattner 1996, 192–93)

Plattner's argument relies largely on the idea of the bohemian artist—itself a trope of the art world that warrants questioning. While individual artists might often be poor or have difficulties making a living from art alone, they predominantly come from middle-class backgrounds and thus are endowed with the attendant cultural capital. I argue that rather than stemming from class difference, the discomfort arises at the moment when artworks are unequivocally identified as commodities. Although most artists aspire to earn a living from their artistic work, they feel uncomfortable with the marketplace, not least because it marks art as an elitist realm. Viewed in this vein, tropes such as the "serious collector" and the "idealistic but poor artist" serve as discursive deflections from structural tensions in the art world, that is, the very conditions under which art is produced and consumed.

Accumulating Public Goods in Private Hands: On Collectors

Connected by way of the art market, artists, gallerists, and collectors are part of exchanges that are both necessary and conflicted. They are necessary for artists to make a living. They are conflicted because in these interactions notions of art as "making a personally valid statement," aiming "to advance our cultural vision," or offering a "transcendental aesthetic experience" (Plattner

1996, 6–7) collide with its commodity character. Scholars have examined practices of collecting under material, psychoanalytic, and symbolic perspectives, often drawing on Bourdieu's theory of distinction to explain the drive to collect (Baudrillard 1994 [1968], Pearce 1995).[8] While the following passages touch on some of these issues, I am most concerned with the problematic that arises from accumulating public goods, that is, art, in private hands, since this process illustrates many of the inherent contradictions of the modern conception of art, especially its assumed civilizing power. Taking the examples of three collectors, one from Germany (Thomas Olbricht) and two from Turkey (Sema Çağa and Ahmet Merey), I show how collectors' engagement with art is not only framed in terms of personal attachment, passion, and devotion but as a responsibility toward the artist and the public. It is this notion of responsibility that collectors cite when making their personal collections available to the public. I argue that the processes of "going public" are conceived of as a service to society and, consequently, as a contribution to the greater good. This rationalization serves to alleviate the tensions just discussed and places collecting art firmly within the parameters of philanthropic activity and thus within the conceptions of modernity, civility, and progress that philanthropy connotes.

The intersection of art with the market is regarded as equally constitutive for the art world as detrimental to it and as equally conducive to the autonomy of art as endangering artistic development. Collectors remain, along with the now globalized grant economy in the form of residencies and individual project grants, an important source of income for many artists I met. Historically speaking, private collectors of different scales were instrumental in the development of modern art by providing a counterforce to state-sanctioned and -supported art. While the art market boom of the past two decades, only shortly interrupted by the "new economy" bust in the early 2000s (and again in 2008), has brought big international collectors, such as Pinault, Lauder, and Saatchi, or Stoschek, Flick, Eczacıbaşı, and Koç, into the spotlight, smaller collectors remain a vital source of income for individual artists.

That the following examples focus on prominent collectors is not to obscure this important dimension added by occasional buyers or discount the role of those with too few resources to be registered in the glossy media outlets and annals of the art world. Rather, I concentrate on larger collectors because of their capacity to shape exhibiting practices of public institutions as well as official cultural policy. My fieldwork fell into a period during which there was much talk of the international "art bubble" produced by the unprecedented influx of money into the art market, often described through the euphemisms of "new money," "young collectors," and "speculators." As talks of the "bubble" were always accompanied by predictions of an immanent burst, a few words about the art markets of Berlin and Istanbul to preface the discussion on collectors might be useful.

Most interlocutors in Berlin emphasized that the local art boom has consisted of producing and to some extent exhibiting, rather than selling, art. The artist Florian Zeyfang was among those who correlated the upsurge in artistic activity in the city with the *Aufbruchsstimmmung* that characterized the atmosphere after the fall of the Berlin Wall. This enthusiastic embarking on new beginnings was sustained by the relatively low cost of living and the abundance of housing and studio space, especially in the then deserted parts of East Berlin. These were not only a draw for artists from other parts of Germany but also from abroad. In tandem with the continued subsidies aimed at showcasing and (re)vitalizing the capital of a reunited Germany, alternative subsistence strategies were possible for many artists who had flocked to Berlin starting in the early 1990s. A substantial number could make ends meet by bartending and waiting tables, or by freelancing in web design and for advertising agencies a few days per week, while pursuing their artistic work the rest of the time. A considerable number of the artists I interviewed in Berlin intermittently received unemployment benefits. Even under the restructured and draconian welfare category of Hartz IV,[9] the low cost of living in Berlin allowed many of them to pursue their art. The child allowance (*Kindergeld*) that the German state provides presents another source of income for artists with children, leading one artist to call her elementary-school-age son—jokingly—her "sponsor." The proliferation of performance and exhibition spaces was aided by a combination of low rents and lax regulations regarding building use that allowed for makeshift galleries. This laxity first existed by default but was to some extent institutionalized by the city's municipality, first on the initiative of Mayor Eberhard Diepgen and then by his successor, Klaus Wowereit. Both mayors saw these flexible structures as conducive to the city's creative capital and as part of a marketing device to position Berlin anew as a capital of the arts—frequently invoking the city's cultural vibrancy during the Weimar Republic. What did not take hold, however, were the attempts to bring different types of industries to Berlin, for example, publishing from Munich or advertising from Hamburg. By 2006, many German newspapers and publishers had closed their Berlin offices, leaving only correspondents and freelance contributors behind, mainly because local ad revenues necessary to maintain such offices could not be secured.

This circumstance is telling for the capital's economic state and a testament to the legacy of German federalism. While many artists live and show their works in Berlin, money from selling art is generally made elsewhere, most notably in Cologne, Düsseldorf, and Munich, in short, those cities where both old money and the beneficiaries of the post–World War II economic miracle (*Wirtschaftwunder*) reside. It was here that most of Germany's top-tier galleries were established. International buyers present an exception to this trend, as Berlin—and its art scene—present a touristic attraction.[10] Because little buying and selling of art takes place in Berlin, success elsewhere, and often abroad, is vital for artists. The same is true for their Istanbul counterparts, given the low level of public funding for contemporary art both on the national and local level.

As public funding for contemporary art is minuscule in Istanbul, budget cuts caused by global economic downturns have not aggravated the situation further, although they have affected arts sponsorship. Independent arts organizations have recently reported that corporate support, even if previously committed, has been increasingly difficult to secure. Along with project monies and grants, many artists and curators I interviewed support themselves by teaching at universities or public schools or by giving private lessons. Some have found subsistence strategies in arts and culture NGOs. Others—although hesitant to speak about their situation—seem to have to (and can) rely on personal or family means; in contrast to their German colleagues, they have little or no social security provided by the state. Despite economic turbulence, it seems that large collectors from Turkey remain in the game and are frequently seen at biennials and international art fairs, where, by all accounts, sales are still made (see Thornton 2008). Another question is, however, how the recent economic crisis has influenced the sale of artworks produced in Turkey and especially the buying habits of foreign collectors, whose number has been continuously rising—so much so that in 2005 a couple of Istanbul galleries stated that at least 50 percent of their clientele was from abroad. This fact goes against the long-held notion that art from Turkey is only of interest to the national market and illustrates the increase in attention for art from the larger region, ranging from the Balkans to the Middle East.

Collecting art is frequently portrayed as a rather new occurrence in Turkey, and the ostensible lack of collectors is often deemed to have stunted the development of art (see Winegar 2006 for a similar argument in the case of Egypt). Many propose that the emergence of collectors was underwritten by the market liberalization policies of the military junta (1980–1983) and the subsequent Özal government as well as by global economic restructuring processes. In this narrative, the purported absence of collectors is mainly attributed to a missing bourgeoisie caused by stifled economic development

(Keyder 1997). Following the standardized discourse of belated modernity discussed in the previous chapter, this argument obscures that Turkey decimated its non-Muslim bourgeoisie through genocidal violence, population exchange, and the wealth tax—the ramifications of which will be taken up in Chapter 4. Pilevneli regards this periodization of collecting in Turkey as a gross misrepresentation. Instead he proposes that "there have always been collectors, but the makeup of any given collection and how it develops depends on what you are offering them. So, what we were missing, really, were serious collectors of contemporary art from Turkey—these were the people that were in the minority. They only emerged along with spaces like Galerist that made contemporary art produced in Turkey available to them. So, it's not that we generated interest but that we established exhibition opportunities for contemporary art. That's the change we initiated."

Despite the divergent configurations of the art market, how collectors make sense of their activities is the same in both locations, as is the general problematic inherent in the practice of collecting. Collecting is framed as intensely personal, as a way of relating to the world (Baudrillard 1994 [1968], Pearce 1995). Collectors tend to speak of "their" works through the tropes of passion and love, yet the very nature of the modern conception of art as a public good differentiates artworks from other collectibles, let's say stamps or vintage cars.[11] The following passages give an insight into how art collectors portray their own activities, which are associated with both prestige and suspicion, and how experiences that are expressed as deeply personal are in notable ways refracted through the national frame.

Collecting between Passion and Profit(ability)

At an event in the Collectors' Forum series[12] in June 2006 at the Hyatt Hotel, centrally located within walking distance of Berlin's Potsdamer Platz, directors of museums and contemporary arts organizations as well as critics gathered along with around 150 well-dressed art enthusiasts, representatives of what an artist I interviewed once called "the pearl necklace brigade." Drinks and hors d'oeuvres prepared by an award-winning chef were served by a fleet of waiters at the entrance of the Grand Ballroom. The event's speaker was (and this was emphasized by the moderator) *Professor Dr. Dr.* Olbricht, an endocrinologist by training who made his fortune in pharmaceutical research. By passion, however, Olbricht is one of Germany's biggest art collectors.[13] When asked about the criteria for building his collection, Olbricht stated that he collects according to themes, with his preferences emerging mostly from his "sensibilities" (*aus meinem Gefühl*) and "the subconscious." "Just as all art, irrespective of style, deals with life, that is also what I do. I occupy myself with life. No more and no less." Olbricht's analogy between his collecting and the purview of art approximates the practice of the collector, who by way of assemblage highlights different aspects of the collected artworks, with the creative work of the artist. This mirroring process is further contoured as Olbricht elaborates on his processes for choosing artworks. Olbricht's principle seems simple: "I look for quality in an artwork; quality is the staging of something that no one sees but I notice all of a sudden." This statement is very much in line with Enlightenment ideas of art making visible what was previously unseen and to connect to the world in a new way (see Danto 1964). Walking the audience through his slideshow, Olbricht concedes that how he puts artworks in relation to one another is often quite "banal." He moves from a John Curry painting of a man gazing intently into the distance to an image of a thinly clad woman (according to Olbricht one of the first carbon color print photographs to be produced in the United States), stating: "I imagine him to be looking at something like this." Repeatedly, Olbricht takes the opportunity to reiterate that he is not knowledgeable in the arts—at least not formally: "I am not someone who, like an art historian, picks everything apart and interprets something into it, but the artist does not do that either." Again, Olbricht not only equates his own perspective to that of the artist but also approximates the practice of collecting to the artistic process. His proposition that one can understand art without necessarily explaining it references the notion that art is intrinsically human and thus accessible to all. Although collectors tend to portray their practices as requiring the serious study of art, Olbricht implies that formal knowledge can actually hamper the communication between an artwork and its viewer.

What animates his collecting, Olbricht professes, is the hunter's instinct, which in his case "reacts to color and figurative painting." Judging from the selection from his collection he showed at the event, his instinct also often reacts to erotically tinged images, a fact that while never explicitly raised by Olbricht produced periodic giggles from the audience. His description of collecting as a primal instinct speaks to Susan Pearce's (1995, 183) analysis of the motifs of collecting: "Notions like 'hunt' and 'quest,' and ideas of collections as prey or trophy, bring before us the play of dominance and control which collecting involves, painted in the brightest colors." Given the kinds of images he showed, the gendered dimensions of the hunter's quest seemed a bit too obvious for comfort. The metaphor of the hunt also plays on the motifs of "achievement through struggle" (184) and competition (Plattner 1996, 179), illustrated by Olbricht's account of his pursuit of a painting by Gerhard Richter. "I downright had to hunt it down for more than six years. I knew where it was, but just could not get it. It became more and more expensive, like the houses on Sylt.[14] It was in the possession of the art dealer who first exhibited it in his Mannheim gallery in 1967. Finally, I had my shot at it, and I got it." Notably, Olbricht did not divulge what it took him to convince the previous owner to part from this painting after almost forty years.

While professions of love and passion (see Plattner 1996, 167) play a major part in how Olbricht talks about "his" art, he admits that "personal taste alone cannot guide a collection." A balance has to be struck between "passion and reason," which means thinking about the collection in economic (*betriebswirtschaftlich*) terms. Given the present heights of the art market, Olbricht states that "even as a serious collector" it is hard to "withstand the temptation to sell a work in light of the prices that can be attained. . . . Just from an economic perspective there are some opportunities that I cannot pass up to cede a piece, even if only to invest in something new." That Olbricht uses *abgeben* (to cede or hand off) instead of "selling" brings us back to the discomfort that many art world actors face when treating artworks primarily as commodities. This issue comes up again when Olbricht further elaborates on his general selection criteria: "Does this artist already have a certain *renomé*? Which gallery is representing him? In which museums has he been shown? When you apply these criteria, you won't get an artist whose works are cheap." Here, Olbricht's language shifts from the very personal connection to an artwork to the standards of art world experts. Individual passions and desires are not first and foremost bound to the art object but refracted through the judgment of these experts. That these types of rationalizations have little to do with a particular artwork crystallizes even further as he continues: "I try to find out if the artist will have the potential to create added value for me. Many artists will be angry with me for saying so, but that's just the way it is. From a hundred artists only one will remain anyway. And after all, I have five children, and they also should be able to inherit some of my money."

Yet Olbricht goes to great lengths to distinguish himself from those who buy art solely for investment purposes. Like other collectors in Germany and elsewhere, Olbricht is quick to complain about these "speculative buyers"[15] who are "ruining it for everyone else." They are, so the story goes, not really interested in art, uninformed, and at fault for driving art prices to their current heights.[16] This trope is notable in two ways. First, it makes a distinction between collecting art for investment purposes and collecting "art for art's sake," where added value is a byproduct but not a goal. In light of Olbricht's earlier statements of his selection criteria, this seems a rather fickle distinction. Second, "speculative buyers" may very well not be interested in art in the same way as "serious collectors" claim to be, yet both groups are frequently advised by the same set of experts. This in turn points to another contradiction: Although collectors mostly speak in the first-person singular when outlining their practices, they generally work closely with advisors (gallerists, art dealers, appraisers, and art scouts). This practice tends to be one of the more obscured facets of the workings of the art market, and not a new one at that (see Rush 1961). Olbricht only made this explicit very late in his presentation and only when asked directly by an audience member during the Q&A.

Connecting to the World

The collector Sema Çağa begins the story of how she ventured into collecting modern art from Turkey with a biographical note. Çağa and her husband, Barbaros, both lawyers who met at Istanbul University, became interested in modern art when they moved into their first flat and wanted to make a home for their young family in the early 1970s. In interviews and public appearances Çağa repeatedly states that the impetus for her becoming a collector arose from the excitement that art brought to her life. While she emphasized that her family valued museum visits as part of their general education and stated that she became interested in classic modernists such as Picasso early on, she seemingly contradicted these statements by insisting that before embarking on collecting she had no prior knowledge of art. She stressed that she had received a German education and that her husband had been educated in the Anglo-Saxon system, which, she explained, afforded them the opportunity to travel to Europe frequently. There, local collectors' traditions served as further inspiration. References to personal background, education, and travel abroad are often employed as explanatory devices in the Turkish context. With or without intent, they serve as mechanisms of distinction, of class and cultural capital within the national frame that set the subject apart from the "uneducated masses." Uninterested in art and culture, they are portrayed to embody the country's "belated modernity" in dominant public discourse. These references also serve to reconcile highly personal interests with the needs of society, to which collectors are ultimately accountable and to which they make their collections accessible—but more about that a little later.

While Çağa does not employ the motif of the hunter's instinct, she frames her engagement with art in no less personal terms: "My collection is highly personal and guided by my experience of living in the city. There have been times when I have felt utterly alone in the crowd. In those periods art was a real refuge for me; in its lap I could find peace [*huzur*] and elude the loneliness of an environment full of altercations. Art opened a door for me and showed me the way." Çağa's trembling voice underlined the gravity of her emotional connection to art, the affect produced by art. Today, she continued, her outlook on life has changed. The intimacy that she feels with artistic expressions now offers a consoling loneliness that she actively seeks out. Her elaborations are not unlike those of Walter Benjamin (1968 [1931], 67), who, writing about his collection of rare books, noted that "for a collector—and I mean the real collector, a collector as he ought to be—ownership is the most intimate relationship that one can have with objects." While Benjamin's contemplation was one of decidedly inward pleasure, we will see that collecting art always has an outward component as well. Çağa's narrative on her collection encompasses art as both a mirror of modern urban life and a refuge from it, in the sense that Max Weber (1958 [1915]) describes (see Chapter 1). Collecting presents a communicative tool with which she relates to and finds a place in the world.

Collecting Art for the Greater Good: Responsibility, Sacrifice, Service

Olbricht and Çağa both highlight that art allows them to view the world through the artist's eyes. This, however, requires personal effort, immersion into artworks, and studying artists and their lives to fully appreciate their works and collect in an informed fashion. While Olbricht contends that every collector has a good amount of vanity, he, like Çağa, frequently switches registers to express humility in the face of artists' commitment to their craft. Not having formally studied art history is an important aspect in these kinds of proclamations, as is the dedication required for the practice of collecting. This also entails extensive traveling to educate oneself about historically important works as well as current art trends and to actively pursue the acquisition of works. Similar tropes are raised by Ahmet Merey, who specializes in modern and contemporary art from Turkey and whose family has been collecting for four generations.[17] Merey highlights his sacrifices in terms of the time, effort, and money that collecting involves. He notes that "it's sometimes difficult to even find something proper to wear for an event," adding that he has had to part from many personal possessions in order to be able to acquire certain paintings. When collectors make their collections public, their sacrifices are not only personal in nature but become sacrifices for the greater good of society. In the cases of Çağa and Merey, assembling and preserving works of art, specifically "Turkish art," is an endeavor that sets them apart from an "unresponsive state" that does little to preserve its artistic heritage. For Olbricht, it seems this sacrifice is borne especially by his children, who suffer losses in their future inheritance because of their father's passion for art. However, Olbricht too sees himself as a better-suited guardian of contemporary art than what he once called "Germany's dusty museum system" (cited in Lorch 2005).

All three collectors explicitly connect their efforts to local and national audiences. Olbricht, hailing from the city of Essen, works closely with the nearby Folkwang Museum and aids in bringing contemporary German artists to the Ruhr region through a residency program. Notably, he repeatedly emphasizes that it is German collectors who bring innovations to public museums and not the state; here he diverges from the long-held notion of German state support for the arts being successful. Çağa and Merey, too, speak to national cultural policy and social history. Merey diagnoses that the Turkish state's disinterest has resulted in the public's deprivation from its artistic heritage, whereas he wants to contribute to the proliferation of knowledge about modern Turkish painting. Merey repeatedly stresses that an important part of his family legacy is their early interest in figurative painting and portraits, which he sees as notable for a Muslim family that began collecting in the late nineteenth century. This narrative both counteracts and reinforces the notion that the development of art in Turkey was stifled by religious biases against figurative painting.[18] Be it her intention or not, Çağa's emphasis on coming from an old Istanbulite family follows a well-established trope employed by many of her social standing and cultural capital, setting her apart from rural migrants and displaced Kurds, who are often portrayed as having "taken over the city." Such articulations of ethnoreligious difference position Çağa and Merey as vanguards and guardians of modernization in their native contexts. Çağa proposes that her collection serves the city she loves. But she also points out that the collection is a way of inscribing her name in the local and national future, of leaving a mark in the world "along with others who build schools, hospitals, and libraries that bear their names." Although she finds it flattering to be viewed as a philanthropist, public acknowledgment is not what she is after. After all, she says, she is "just an art lover." "You may call me a philanthropist or a collector. If you want to label me I would choose to say that I am concerned with the dreams that carry us through our lives and that remain even after we are gone, after our deaths. We render ourselves visible through *our* artworks [emphasis mine]."

Many collectors contend that with a growing collection comes growing responsibility, since "collecting art is not like amassing any other kind of objects in the corner of your house." Collectors see it as their societal duty to make their collections accessible to the public—an understanding that speaks to the modern conception of art as a public good. Çağa's argument for making her collection public rests on the notion that this is required by a modern stance (*"çağdaş tavırlar gerektiriyor bunları"*) and thus articulates concerns that are prevalent in Turkey. Yet, it shares with the German context the conception of serving the greater good through art—refracted through the national frame. But how to make collections publicly accessible is in itself a contentious matter that will be further analyzed in the chapters to come. Suffice it to say here that given the decrease in public funding, board members and donors of public museums have become increasingly influential in determining the acquisition practices of museums. It is important to keep in mind that board members and members of museum donors' associations tend to be collectors themselves. Britta Schmitz explains how this shift has played out in Berlin's Nationalgalerie:

> The general consensus used to be that the director of the Nationalgalerie makes the suggestions for acquisitions and then the board agrees. Now we have a commission that comprises two seats to represent the donors' association, and they have vehemently inserted themselves into the discussion of what to acquire. This is a new situation for us, and I am unsure if this is indeed a good model. Whereas we, the museum curators and the director, know the museum collection very well, and argue from within the collection, people from outside, who have their own ambitions, now also want to have their say in the collection. I believe that this creates a certain imbalance.

Donors are likely to lobby for the acquisition of artists that they themselves collect. To relegate this tendency to personal preferences alone would be shortsighted. Rather these preferences present a strategy to ensure an increase in the value of personal collections through the sanctioning power of the museum.

A similar situation has emerged in Istanbul and is being amplified because a number of museums, most notably the Sabancı Museum, Istanbul Modern, the Pera Museum, and, more recently, the Elgiz Museum, rely on family collections for their permanent displays. Surely, the details of these cases vary: While in the case of the Sabancı, the collection has been donated to the museum, the Eczacıbaşı collection housed by the Istanbul Modern as well as the paintings exhibited in the Pera Museum, until recently, have remained in private possession and are only on loan to the museums by the respective families. This means that apart from the added value that these artworks gain, the owners can withdraw them from the institutions, that is, sell them at the added value harnessed through public exhibition, whenever they see fit. In both cases, museums as institutions intended to serve the public are either supported by public monies (Germany) or receive tax and other logistical benefits (Turkey) and are thus entangled with economic calculations of the private kind.

Social Responsibility and Economic Byproducts: Corporate Sponsorship

> It is vital to convince people in the economic sector of the importance of art and culture for our social system [*Gesellschaftssystem*] and animate them to become engaged in arts and culture. This is not only a matter of money; what is at stake here is the spirit that is needed to achieve this.
>
> Jürgen Zech, introductory remarks at the Corporate Cultural Responsibility Conference, Berlin, 2006

Few practices have come under as much scrutiny in the art world as those of corporate sponsorship, an area that even more so than collecting illustrates the antagonism and interdependency between art and the economy (Adorno and Horkheimer 1969, Lash and Urry 1994, Graw 2008).[19] Yet given the low level of state funding in Turkey, especially for independent art (that is, artistic activities not under the auspices of the state, such as art academies or municipal theaters), and the rollbacks in state funding in Germany, calls for public-private partnerships have intensified in both countries since the late 1980s. Identifying it as adversarial to the inner workings and integrity of art, individual artists are often uneasy about corporate sponsorship. Outright financial interests are seen to be in stark contrast to artists' descriptions of their own work as "deeply personal expressions," "commentaries," "interventions," and "positions"—this last term frequently used in the German context. A compounding factor in this discomfort is that arts sponsorship is usually subsumed under corporations' marketing or public relations departments. Despite diagnosing an incongruence of goals, arts organizations are often open to working with private funders and stress that private sponsorship can be most efficiently attained by fostering personal relationships, since this allows for a more direct "mediation" or "translation" between art and business.

Here I want to briefly spotlight how corporate sponsors position themselves in the arts and cultural sector and how they conceptualize their activities. In Turkey as in Germany corporate funders across the board portray themselves as upholding artistic "autonomy" and "freedom," often proposing that the state is much more likely to intervene in the arts than private sponsors. In doing so, corporations depict their sponsoring activities as divorced from their day-to-day economic operations and as politically neutral, but they also perform a notable antagonism vis-à-vis the state. In Germany there is an emphasis on art sponsorship as *Chefsache*, a formulation suggesting that sponsoring is too important a task to be left to marketing departments that only conceive of art sponsoring in terms of advertising and are unable appreciate the social importance of these projects.

In Turkey, this rhetorical distancing from advertising is, structurally speaking, slightly easier, since most corporate sponsors have their own cultural foundations or arts centers. However, here too the monies are often funneled through the corporate structure by way of PR and marketing departments. Görgün Taner, of the Istanbul Foundation for Culture and Arts (IKSV), established by the Eczacıbaşı Corporation, as well as Derya Bigalı, of the Akbank Culture and Arts Center (supported by Sabanci's banking arm Akbank), frame their activities in terms of serving (*hizmet*) the public and providing "encounters" between the arts and a mostly unspecified public. They stress that their mission is "educational" in nature. The same held true for the now dismantled SantralIstanbul (2007–2012). This exhibition complex was incorporated into Bilgi, a private university funded by the entrepreneur Oğuz Özerden, and similarly presented its relationship with the state to be weaker than it actually was. Today, sponsorship in Turkey and Germany is cast in terms of "corporate social responsibility" and based on the proclaimed insight that "corporations ought to give back" to society.

According to statistics provided by the Association of Arts and Culture of the German Economy (Kulturkreis der deutschen Wirtschaft), a division created under the umbrella of the Federation of German Industries that "advocates for culture as an indispensable resource for society," corporate funding for the arts only makes up 5 to 10 percent of culture- and arts-related spending budgets in Germany. Given this relatively low number, it was all the more surprising to witness the self-perception of German industrialists and finance giants during a conference entitled "Corporate Cultural Responsibility," organized by the Federation of German Industries in June 2006.[20] Bernd Ziesemer, then editor-in-chief of the economic daily *Das Handelsblatt* and the event's moderator, highlighted the importance of sponsorship in a decidedly national framework, in which corporate support for "German culture" contributed to its "blooming landscapes."[21] "What is still missing," he contended, "*and this is a very German condition*, is the introduction of the element of competition to motivate *Kultursponsoring* by monitoring it through rankings," citing *Businessweek*'s yearly ranking of US corporations involved in arts sponsoring.

What was certainly not surprising was that every participant was well aware that their involvement in the arts was perceived as a marketing ploy. Werner Michael Bahlsen, the director of a family-owned business that specializes in baked goods, opened his statement by saying, "Businesses today—not their owners—but the businesses are the successors of the aristocrats, the archbishops, the great noble families. It is businesses with their long traditions that have made art possible."

However, it quickly became apparent that Bahlsen's notion of supporting the arts was intimately connected to his company's branding activities, that is, the employment of artists to design packaging and print ads. He added that there is a natural synergy between artistic sensibilities and concerning yourself with a product that "has a lot to do with aesthetics"—which in his case are biscuits. Equating the often controversial approaches of artists with the development of a brand that needs to stay contemporary, Bahlsen vehemently objected to the interventions of his co-panelists, who proposed that this explicit link between art and the daily business of marketing presented an instrumentalization of art. One speaker for whom Bahlsen's take on arts sponsorship seemed too close to comfort was Frank-Peter Martin, of Bankhaus Metzler, who stressed that support for the arts should take a "disinterested" form. But how this disinterested support was to be achieved emerged as a matter of contention. Nikolaus Schweickart (Atlanta AG) proposed, "If you define arts and culture funding as a marketing tool, if art is instrumentalized in the service of a company and its products, then art is being raped. This constitutes aggressive sponsoring." While admitting that sponsoring activities are necessary "in order to attain tax advantages," he also stated that "sponsoring can get problematic. Take the example of an American orchestra that performs under the name of a corporation. Thank God, we are not at that point yet in Germany! The *instrumentalization* of art is not only misguided but also *dangerous*. A marketing department that is engaged in arts and culture always asks, what is good for business? But really, the question should be, what is good for society?"

Within the German context of Schweickart's strongly worded intervention was a clear invocation of the specter of National Socialism and its instrumentalization of art. While upholding the idealized notion that considerations of the greater good have to be at the forefront of sponsoring activities, Schweickart added, "This does not mean that a bank, a business, a corporation has to adhere to the Calvinistic principle: Do good, don't talk about it [*Tu' gutes, red' nicht drüber*]." This set off a series of back-and-forths for the rest of the panel, a veritable rollercoaster of arguments with ever-increasing stakes on the meaning of arts sponsoring that ultimately seemed unable to resolve the discomfort elicited by the convergence of art and business. Ulrich Weber, of the investment firm RAG Aktiengesellschaft, agreed that it is "only right and legitimate to advertise the cultural engagement of corporations." Yet Michael Roßnagel (Siemens Arts Program) stressed that successful sponsoring in the arts ought to orient itself toward the needs of art rather than those of the sponsoring business. He mentioned that art sponsoring enhances employees' working motivations, since it allows for positive and socially prestigious ways of identifying with the company. But this too should only be seen as a beneficial byproduct. "Art has to be the clear focus of sponsoring and cannot be instrumentalized for the aims of business, or to say it loosely based on Immanuel Kant: Art must never solely be a means but always also an end." It is no coincidence that Roßnagel chooses to refer to Kant, one of the most important German thinkers to have explored the relationship between aesthetics and ethics. That the quote is skewed by the tentativeness of the formulation "never *solely* . . . but always *also*" indicates that a noninstrumental take on art sponsorship is hard to achieve, if not impossible. Consider the following words by Bernd Ziesemer: "Walter Benjamin, wanting to characterize capitalism's impact on the realm of culture, said that we are in the era of reproduction. He meant it rather critically [*Er meinte das eher kritisch*]. I too would say that we are in the era of reproduction, and we want positive examples of arts sponsoring to be reproduced."

Like the deployment of Kant, the reference to Benjamin is skewed and unnecessary in terms of adding anything to Roßnagel's and Ziesemer's arguments. Despite their thin and clumsy use of these philosophers, there seems to be a perceived need to connect sponsoring activities to traditions of critical thinking about the role of art in society and frame sponsorship in ethical terms.

A striking parallel between corporate sponsors in Germany and in Turkey is that in both countries they cast themselves as civil society actors. As Aydın Uğur, of Bilgi University, maintained, "We do not operate like a private business at all; we really see ourselves as a civil society initiative." This sentiment is echoed by Schweickart, who stated that arts sponsorship has become a question of legitimacy and of "moral responsibility" for corporations: "We can no longer be one-dimensional economic entities, nor can we be solely shareholder oriented, but we have to think of society. Corporations, just like NGOs or foundations, are part of civil society. This understanding," he adds, "is a vital indicator for the degree of civilization [*Zivilizationsgrad*] of a society." Distancing art sponsorship from the nature of for-profit enterprise and equating corporations with civil society actors feeds into the motif of the greater good, in which advertising or connected gains, such as image enhancement or a rise in market share, appear as byproducts rather than a central consideration in sponsorship activities.

While many of the expressions of antagonism reviewed in this chapter reveal tensions that are, structurally speaking, at the heart of the modern conception of art, the personalization of the interdependent and often asymmetrical relationships within the art world and their framing as friendships presents a strategy to overcome, or at least deproblematize, these tensions. A second strategy, one that resonates with the understanding that art fundamentally contributes to the greater good, manifests itself in the notion that all art world activities, be they private or institutional, for profit or nonprofit, serve "the public." What or who constitutes "the public" in question is open to interpretation and can, depending on the position from which it is invoked, denote different geographical and sociopolitical assemblages. The public thus can connote "civilization," "society," "the nation," or different permutations of the local community—the city or the region.

At the same time, these mediating discourses merge different aesthetic theories that are at times simplified and, at others, complicated in order to accommodate and reconcile divergent understandings of art and its role in society. The vernacularized references to aesthetic theories are pragmatic in nature and call attention to a series of assumptions about art. They are both specific with regard to the historical background out of which they emerged yet also generalized and taken for granted. Their usage is evocative rather than substantive and rarely—if ever—accompanied by any more detailed explanation—nor do they seem to need to be. As these pragmatic shorthands are generally accepted without questioning, they are also extremely versatile and can be employed in the pursuit of an array of different and often contradictory interests (see Eagleton 1990). How these pragmatic processes are reflected in the formation of official cultural policies is the topic of the next chapter.

3

Governing Culture, Producing Modern Citizens

> Everyone believes that they know what literature is supposed to be good for. More often than not, the one writing has quite different problems.
>
> —JÖRG FAUSER

> Whoever speaks of culture speaks of administration as well, whether this is his intention or not.
>
> —THEODOR W. ADORNO

What is art good for? How does cultural policy reconcile the "quite different problems," to use Fauser's formulation, of the artist with that of the "social good?" After all, it is exactly the notion that art contributes to the greater social good that has rendered it a specialized branch of government. Turkish as well as German cultural policies share the notion that aesthetic education is imbued with civilizing qualities and formative for modern personhood.[1] It is this assumption that constitutes the foundation of the state's proclaimed *duty* to support the arts and to enable citizens' access to the arts.

Cultural policy is indicative of how society and individuals within that collectivity are conceptualized by state institutions at a given time and how the imagined effect and affect of art are translated into policy directives. Cultural policy is not solely a regulatory mechanism for the production of art but also *frames* its reception. This is not to say, however, that cultural policy is the only factor in the formation, duration, and impact of artistic currents and schools. Indeed, a substantial part of the history of art is characterized by the struggles against hegemonic presets. Yet the sanctioning power of the state is not to be underestimated, with one of the best-documented cases being the triumph of abstract expressionism, which was actively fostered by the US State Department to assert political and cultural dominance in the Cold War arena (Guilbault 1983).

This chapter dwells on some of the major debates and turning points in Turkish and German cultural policies, highlighting now disavowed episodes that have shaped them significantly, that is, debates that have been constitutive for the national frame and hence for how the "nation" inserts itself into contemporary debates on art. Rereading standardized narratives on cultural policy, I highlight the contradictions and persistent concerns that have marked the project of making (and remaking) the modern nation-state, and with it a "civilized people," in Turkey and Germany. I trace what at different times has been considered conducive or disruptive to the civilizing project—a project that in Germany as in Turkey is frequently portrayed in need of safeguarding against an always looming specter of reversal. The feared outcome of such a reversal differs, of course. In Germany, National Socialism has been an always lurking danger. In Turkey, it was long—and for some remains—Islam or, alternatively, "regressive interpretations of Islam" attributed to the Ottoman Empire that has been cultural policy's formative Other.

Cultural Policy's Unease

Before delving into the histories of cultural policy in Germany and Turkey, let's begin with a few general notes on the normative constitution of cultural policy in modern nation-states. Historically emerging out of the domain of education, cultural policy and its administrative units remain a testament to the pedagogical, often didactic, thrust inherent in the state's governance of the arts. Despite the administrative separation that can be found in Turkey and Germany, the domain of education has remained in dialogue with that of cultural policy, especially as officials stress that access to art is bound to levels of education. As outlined in the previous chapter, this assumption is confirmed by some and negated by others in the art world, in part because it refutes the universalistic claim of art as intrinsically human. It also yields the suspicion of elitism based on a particular kind of cultural capital and mechanisms of social distinction (see Bourdieu 1984), an assessment of art that not all respondents felt comfortable with.[2]

Generally speaking, cultural policy operates through and produces peculiar kinds of tensions. The first arises from the different registers of "culture" that cultural policy perpetually needs to reconcile. Cultural policy texts in Turkey, Germany, and elsewhere have long opened with clumsy exposés that try to navigate the "conceptual jungle" that the term "culture" denotes (Üstel 2009, 7). All of them highlight that this particular area of policy making is notoriously ill-defined. Along with divergent conceptions of art "proper," they summon anthropological definitions of culture reaching back to Malinowski, Kroeber, and Kluckhon (Kantarcıoğlu 1987, Hoffmann 1979). They invoke culture as denoting ways of life, as a communal and ultimately national referent that demarcates distinctive sets of values, heritage, and artistic production. Although anthropological definitions of culture have been instrumental in transcending dichotomies of "high" and "low" culture, cultural policy has, especially since the 1980s, lagged behind the increasing criticism of static and bounded notions of culture within the discipline itself (Wright 1998). Perhaps necessarily so, the political deployment of culture by the state as well as by supranational bodies like the European Union (Karaca 2010) remains wedded to national frameworks. Much of the political productiveness of culture as a vehicle for governance lies exactly in its conceptual capacity to continually produce and bridge slippages between these seemingly discrete definitions of culture.

A second fundamental tension arises from the gaps between the notions of art's inherent goodness and autonomy and the realities in which artistic expression is shaped, sanctioned, or delegitimized—that is, between art as a supposedly functionless good and the many ways art is operationalized—by the state. Cultural policy is at heart a bureaucratic endeavor based on the implementation of policies that reflect the state's understanding of art. While such understandings are historically contingent, modern nation-states—officially speaking—legitimize their governance of art by referencing its proposed civilizing impact. The formulation of this civilizing impact may differ—be it that "art communicates our common humanity," "allows us to reflect critically upon ourselves and the world," or "enhances democracy." The thrust is nonetheless the same. Cultural policy is underwritten by philosophical takes on aesthetics that are rarely referenced in full but presented in the form of pragmatic and reductive shorthands. The high-held ideals of the modern conception of art qua definition are contradictory, if not adversarial, to the rationales and techniques with which culture is administered. Cultural policy is proclaimed to operate outside of considerations of expediency, yet the institutional settings through which art is governed suggest otherwise—especially as art has been identified as a vital factor for economic development (Yúdice 2003). As a form of governance cultural policy is caught between transformative and functional understandings of art (Miller and Yúdice 2002). The interlocution of art and government, its shaping by power, and its regulation through bureaucratic processes have engendered long-standing discomforts. Adorno (1997 [1960], 142), however, reminds us that "the antinomy of art and administration," although signaling actual differences in operating logics, veils the interdependence between these two fields of activity. He argues that the frequently formulated call to withdraw art from the realm of administration (or vice versa) would not only endanger the livelihoods of artists but sever the connection and encounters between artwork and society that the administrative apparatus facilitates.

The unease that characterizes the marriage of art and administration is mirrored in the discourses of those who work in the field of cultural policy—a field that is as much lauded for its immense importance as it is identified as an inferior statecraft. Conceptualizing art as a guarantor of freedom and democracy, cultural policy is often described as "so much more" than just administrative procedures. It is a vocation, a labor of love, "a mindset," as I have so often heard. Yet the cultural policy scholars Toby Miller and George Yúdice (2002) note that in the case of the US State Department, "For many years, cultural diplomats were apparently selected from those in the foreign service who suffered from mental illness or severe physical disorders—also a feature of decolonizing powers such as France, where intellectual enfeeblement and chronic professional failure were qualifications for cultural governance" (71n2). I encountered similar assessments—if only in the form of rumors in Istanbul, where artists jokingly noted that the cultural ministry was filled with bureaucrats who had been "exiled" there for failing in other divisions of the state apparatus. Christina Weiss, when undersecretary for culture and the media (2002–2005), famously proclaimed that her office "was not a place to make a career," a sentiment echoed by the 2005 candidate, Norbert Lammert, who decided to take up a "real office" instead, becoming president of the German parliament.

Culture is also a peculiar animal in that no one quite wants to claim this field of policy making. Although the shaping of the cultural domain is the raison d'être of cultural policy, practitioners tend to describe their own work solely in terms of administering funds and facilitating the production, presentation, and circulation of art. Actual policies or decisions are always made elsewhere. In Germany, for instance, the *Länder*, the Ministry of the Interior, or the city senate point to one another when asked who actually makes policy decisions. Responsibility always seems to lie with other authorities or, really, "their predecessors."[3] In Berlin's Senate for Cultural Affairs the answer was unequivocally that "we do not shape cultural policy but are only responsible for selecting award committees" and that the guiding principles of Germany's cultural policy were laid out in the constitution or, alternatively, the reunification treaty. During a visit to the Ministry of Culture and Tourism in Ankara, I was told that "there have been no changes in cultural policy for the past fifty years" and that "politics should not shape culture, anyway." Here, references to the autonomy of art serve to displace responsibility from state institutions in the realm of cultural policy.

A final tension inherent in cultural policy is that between its universal and specifically national—and at times nationalist—thrust. Miller and Yúdice (2002) draw attention to the declaration of the 1982 Mondiacult conference hosted by UNESCO. Here the signatories, among them Germany and Turkey, state: "It is culture that gives man the ability to reflect upon himself. . . . It is through culture that man expresses himself, becomes aware of himself, recognizes his incompleteness, questions his own achievements, seeks untiringly for new meanings and creates works through which he transcends his limitations." This international document and its many national counterparts highlight culture as the source of self-criticism and self-appreciation. Both history and administrative units bind cultural policy to national frameworks, while the claims of cultural policy transcend—and must necessarily transcend—these boundaries, by bringing national and international developments into dialogue and to mirror each other. This interplay ensures that "the nation" and national representation continue to play a vital role in cultural policy, despite the intensified globalization of art worlds.

Cultural Policy as *Machtpolitik*: Imperial Germany

It may come as some surprise that the governance of the most German of all virtues—*Kultur*—got off to a rocky start in the newly united empire (1871). As to the nation-state stage, Germany was a late contender in the scramble for colonies. From 1884 onward, Germany pursued these interests in southwestern Africa and the Pacific violently, and in the case of Namibia through genocide.[4] Yet its expansionist designs were significantly limited by the entente cordiale (1904) and subsequent agreements designed to settle disputes between European empires and consolidate the colonial arena. In an attempt to outmaneuver these limitations, Germany turned to culture, or soft power, as it called today, as a lubricant for its power-political (*machtpolitisch*) and economic aspirations.[5] It was first and foremost the Ottoman Empire that served as a testing ground for the foreign—and by extension domestic—cultural policy of the Kaiserreich, while similar initiatives in China, Argentina, Brazil, and Chile remained smaller in scope (Dahlhaus 1990, Illich 2007). Once more in the vein of Nipperdey's famous précis on the German national awakening, "in the beginning there was Napoleon," it was in competition with French interests in particular that Germany tried to establish itself as a cultural actor in the Ottoman Empire from the late 1880s onward. France's *pénétration culturelle* had been rendered possible by the capitulations (that is, the treaties allowing the exercise of extraterritorial jurisdiction over its own citizens) and cemented by an extensive network of schools, missions, and exchange programs with the Ottoman state. Yet Germany was not to be deterred, officially hailing its ties to Ottoman Empire as closer than those to any "other European country" (Gross 1979, 167) while at the same time preparing secret game plans for parceling out an empire expected to disintegrate in the near future.[6] Having no national cultural ministry at the time, it was the kaiser himself who took the lead in this endeavor. Against the explicit wishes of Chancellor Bismarck (MacMurray 2001, 27), who advocated neutrality in Asia Minor, Wilhelm II (1888–1918) rallied nationalist and procolonial forces, while the Foreign Ministry helped cloak German colonial ambitions in the "fiction of equal partnership" between Germany and the Ottoman Empire (Marchand 1996b, 299). Public support for these initiatives relied in part on the popularity of *Orientschwärmerei* among the German bourgeoisie, that is, a fascination with the "Orient" that played as much on romanticism and exoticization as on fantasies of subjugation (see Said 1979).

Germany's cultural policy pursued three general goals in the Ottoman Empire: power politics, economic penetration, and the "extraction" of archeological assets. These goals were frequently intertwined discursively, politically, and administratively and just as often fell prey to conflicting and competing agendas of the multitude of official, military, and civilian actors that were engaged in Germany's foreign cultural policy, among them the Foreign Ministry, the Navy, the Prussian Ministry of Education, and to a lesser extent the Ministry of the Interior and faith-based groups and entrepreneurs.

The "scramble for the past" (Bahrani et al. 2011) presented a vital site of struggle. German archeological excavations, long supported by private initiatives, now were regarded as essential for the self-fashioning of the young German state and its search for "specifically German art." The aim was nothing less than to be on par with the collections of the British Museum and, of course, the Louvre (Marchand 1996a). But by the time Germany could muster the necessary funds, historical artifacts had become an increasingly politicized issue in the Ottoman Empire. Under the impetus of nascent nationalism, the Ottomans tried to establish themselves as a *Kulturnation* in their own right and enacted successive legislation from 1874 onward to protect artistic and cultural artifacts on Ottoman soil. While Germany tried to outmaneuver such legislation in 1899 by way of a secret agreement that allowed them "to keep half the antiquities found at any authorized excavation," a further revision of the antiquities law in 1906 stipulated that *all* excavated artifacts were the property of the Ottoman state (Shaw 2003, 126). Yet Germany was not to be discouraged.

The operationalization of culture for foreign policy objectives yielded certain problems, however. The first was that of its presentable objectives to deflect from colonial aspirations. For example, Germany's bid for the Berlin–Baghdad railway was envisioned to facilitate economic and political penetration, access to resources, and new markets for German products. Officially, however, the railway was described as embodying the "spiritual bond" between Germany and the Ottoman Empire and was framed as a *Kulturwerk*—a work of culture (MacMurray 2001, 100). The second pertained to the question of *how* culture was to be employed as a means of governance, especially since *Kultur* was understood as both a penchant of national belonging as well as an autonomous realm, which—in theory—limited its possible instrumentalization. This is not to say that culture and the arts were excluded from political debates in Germany; on the contrary, they presented a fiercely embattled subject.

The historian Volker Berghahn (1994, 133) notes that imperial Germany's officially sanctioned artistic production was conservative, characterized on one side of the spectrum by the rise of so-called *Heimatkunst*,[7] a genre that celebrated local and provincial attachments, and on the other by "exactitude and romanticization." Germany's unification gave rise to an unprecedented number of opportunities for artists and architects as the "young nation" commissioned an array of new ministerial buildings, schools, and museums, all of which were to be filled with expressions of its coming into being. War memorials presented a considerable portion of this productivity, and a similar fervor manifested itself in newly constituted Turkey five decades later (Bozdoğan 2001). French reparation payments (stipulated by the armistice that ended the 1870–1871 Franco-Prussian War) and rapid industrialization contributed to a growing bourgeoisie and hence an extended base for arts patronage, especially when it came to commissioning portraits. Even though the stock market plunge of 1873 destabilized the bourgeoning economy, it still entailed enough momentum to create venues for artistic experimentation outside of state patronage (von Saldern 2002). The importance of art for the newly united Germany was expressed by Wilhelm II, whose unbridled antimodernist attitude I have already outlined (Chapter 1) and who made the arts *Chefsache*, that is, a priority that should be tended to by no less than the head of state. His efforts to support the search for "German art" and contain the advance of modernism found an ally in the painter Anton von Werner, who was appointed as the inaugural director of the Berlin Academy of Arts in 1875, precisely to battle stylistic innovation. This battle was further aided by censorship regulations, such as anti-Socialist legislation, and legal provisions for *lèse majesté*, obscenity, and blasphemy charges.

It was against this background that cultural policy initiatives abroad were understood as enabling cultural renewal at home. Demonstrating the vitality of German culture to the world would rejuvenate Germany's inner cultural makeup, too. This line of thinking gained currency at the turn of the century, and not only in national-conservative camps. In the lead-up to World War I, a declaration entitled "An die Kulturwelt" (To the world of culture, 1914) was signed by ninety-three academics, artists, and other public figures, protesting the accusation that Germany was provoking war. But the declaration did more than that: It equated German military might with its cultural standing, proposing that "without German militarism, German culture would have long been effaced from the earth." The playwright Ludwig Fulda, historian Karl Lamprecht, scientist Max Planck, politician Friedrich Naumann, and archeologist and diplomat Theodor Wiegand were among the signatories. It is no coincidence that the latter two played important roles in Germany's relationship with the Ottoman Empire. Naumann had accompanied the kaiser during his first visit to the Ottoman Empire in 1889 and had contributed to the popularization of anti-Armenian sentiment, even outright racism, against a population that he saw as a major obstacle (and competition) to Germany's political and economic interests in the Ottoman Empire (Kaiser 1997). Wiegand served as the foreign director for the Berlin Museums and as science attaché at the German embassy in Istanbul from 1899 to 1911. Representing German archeological interests in the empire, he also oversaw the excavations at Bergama. Both shared an understanding of war not as a destructive, decivilizing force but as invigorating, even necessary for German political—and artistic—survival. "No Cultural Policy without Power Politics [*Keine Kulturpolitik ohne Machtpolitik*]" was a popular World War I slogan in Germany.

War, then, was welcomed on the basis of both national and aesthetic interests. The painter Max Beckmann echoed this turn, calling the advent of World War I "a wonderful catastrophe" (Mommsen 2004). The communal war effort was envisioned as a cathartic experience that would revitalize the German spirit and German art by weeding out weak aesthetic currents, leaving only those most vital and true to the "German essence" to thrive and achieve their full potential. It was this understanding that led artists such as Gerhard Hauptmann, Thomas Mann, and Max Liebermann to support Germany's war effort. For Beckmann and many of his contemporaries, the horrors of the actual experience of war fundamentally changed this perception; much of their subsequent artistic works spoke to these traumas. It is these latter positions, critical of war and violence, that they are remembered for, whereas their *völkisch*, that is, ethnonationalist, inflections that glorify war are astounding to German audiences today (Mommsen 2004).

As the First World War was nothing less than the struggle for the redistribution of power on a worldwide scale, foreign cultural policy efforts continued throughout 1914–1917. Billed as an opportunity to portray the Germans as a "people of culture" (*Kulturvolk*), the German Arts Exhibition in Constantinople was organized in 1917 by the Association for German Art Abroad. Notably, it was only possible to raise the necessary funds after the German embassy circulated the rumor that the Austro-Hungarians were planning an exhibition for the very same time period (Dahlhaus 1990, 204–5).

I have discussed this period in some detail not only because it examines little-known cultural connections between Germany and the Ottoman Empire but because it presents an attempt to grapple with the rather complex picture of the Kaiserreich's cultural policy. It was at once a power-political tool, a civilizing force beyond its territory, and a strategy for overcoming the fragmentation and challenges posed by modernism at home. Yet questions remain to what extent the German notion of *Kultur* was understood to be transferable when compared to, for instance, the French *mission civilisatrice*. The latter entails a degree of permeability and the possibility for incorporation into the French—civic—nation (manifest in present conceptions of French citizenship that allow "integration," although needless to say, racism and discrimination persist). The German understanding of *Kultur*, on the other hand, has been much more closely bound to descent as well as territory and consequently is less easily transposed outside of Germany.[8]

So what was culture to do, and how was it to be implemented abroad, since its goal was not to produce "Germans"? The leitmotif of foreign cultural policy was "trade follows language [*der Handel folgt der Sprache*]"—it was culture in its manifestation of language that was to pave the way for Germany's economic interests and aspirations of becoming a world power. As the historian Friedrich Dahlhaus (1990) notes: "At the turn of the century critical voices of German publishers and the daily press increasingly bemoaned that the dominance of French as the language of transport and administration for the Anatolian railway might lead to the *German character* insufficiently establishing itself in the expansion of the railway system" (83; emphasis mine). So, it was *the* "German character" that was to be transmitted through language and culture together with values and morals that would in turn forge connections of favorable inclination. The superiority of German culture, it was believed, would dispel the ruling Committee of Union and Progress's (CUP) resistance to German influence.

Culture Wars and Modernization Pains: The Weimar Republic

Modernism had gained momentum in Germany at the end of the nineteenth century.[9] While the turn to the classics remained on the agenda of state-supported art, modernist groups such as Der Blaue Reiter and Die Brücke found opportunities to exhibit outside of the capital, in Munich and in Hamburg, for instance, aided by the growing competition between new local and regional elites and governments.

But modernism was only one front of the culture wars that stretched across society, all the way to the podiums of the parliament. Another lay in the struggle against popular culture, particularly music and film, domains regarded as susceptible to falling prey to the "Americanization" that eroded public morals and German values. The 1926 Act to Protect Youth from Trashy and Smutty Publications, in addition to already existing if inconsistently enforced obscenity laws, was also deployed in the fight against modernism. Modernism was also battled by way of curtailing and criminalizing aesthetic expression through laws against the denigration of the republic, the army, and the church. There were also efforts at containment and incorporation that—less controversial than censorship—proposed a "moderate modernity" by democratizing access to the arts and promoting artistic approaches "rooted in the cultural life of the people and their everyday activities" (von Saldern 2002, 307). As rural-to-urban migration accelerated, unions and parties increasingly organized popular education. Political mobilization went hand in hand with the foundation of workers' choirs, theaters, and libraries, diversifying and at times radicalizing artistic production on the left as well as on the right (Berghahn 1994, 160–62).

In order to centralize arts policy, the position of arts warden was established in 1920, once again charged with producing the symbols of national beginnings, including a new national anthem, this time for the Weimar Republic (1919–1933). The art historian and literary scholar Edwin Redslob, who held the office till the Nazis disbanded it in 1933, personifies some of the tensions of this period. An ardent follower of expressionism, his policies, as per official directives, exhibited conservatism.

At the same time, movements such as Bauhaus, Dada, and the avant-garde were pushing against the authoritarian agenda, drawing foreign artists to Germany, many of them to Berlin, leading to the golden age for which the city is now nostalgically remembered. With its political and artistic experimentation, the Weimar Republic exhibited many contradictions, including a consensus between the far left and far right when it came to artistic conservatism. Both camps agreed that modernism was decadent, bourgeois, and trivial, too introspective for the left and un-German for the right. The persistence of authoritarianism complicates notions of Weimar as an "avant-garde, modern mass culture" (von Saldern 2004, 312), especially when considering the continuities in the dominant political culture before and after 1933. The November Revolution (1918–1919) had done away with the constitutional monarchy, yet Germany's cultural orientation continued to be characterized by the push and pull between the struggle for civil liberties and fervent critiques of modernism (Lamb and Phelan 1995).

Still, the Weimar Republic shared certain concerns with imperial Germany. *Kulturpropaganda*, according to former foreign minister Gottlieb von Jagow, was "the only means left to Germany after Versailles" (Dahlhaus 1990, 243). But was cultural policy indeed a substitute for economic and military might and an alternative path to pursue power politics, given the state of art at home? It was a popular assessment at the time that the Weimar Republic had not yet been able to produce "a great artist" whose work adequately reflected Germany's self-proclaimed standing in the world. Yet Dr. Schreiber of the Center Party once more echoed the need for foreign cultural policy from the floor of parliament in 1923: "The Germany of today in this postwar period, stripped to a large extent of its weapons and the means to defend itself and no longer radiating power, is bound to its position in the world to proclaim its *ethical and cultural* strength on international cultural markets and thereby influence the peoples of this planet and the *civilized world*" (cited in von Saldern 2002, 253; emphasis mine). This renewed attention to culture and the arts manifested itself in the restructuring of the German Foreign Office. In 1920, a division for the arts, music, theater, and scientific exchange was established. Due to both financial and political pressures, Germans living outside the borders of the Weimar Republic (*Auslandsdeutschtum*) became a new priority—a policy that later informed the National Socialist *Heim ins Reich* directive employed to legitimize German expansionist policies in Eastern Europe. Yet this radicalization was still to come, and for the time being, the internationalization of scientific and cultural life together with Germany's entry into the League of Nations in 1926 shifted foreign cultural policy language from unabashed propaganda to *Kulturwerbung*. This "cultural promotion," as Franz Thierfelder, the president of the German Academy in Munich, phrased it in 1931, did not aim at "Germanization" but rather at reflecting "the world . . . through German eyes" (Engel 2003, 41). But this changed dramatically from 1933 onward.

In this chapter I will not delve into cultural policy during National Socialism, which arguably presents one of the most studied periods with regard to the centrality of art and aesthetics in politics. Rather, I will return to this time period when thinking about partial silences in national (art) histories in the next chapter.

Nullstunde Deutschland: The Myth of the Zero Hour

In 1945, Germany did not simply reinstate pre–National Socialist cultural policies, nor did it immediately embrace the critical potential of art or establish the extensive support structure for the arts that West Germany became heralded for from the 1970s on. Rather, the process of "recivilizing Germany" (Jarausch 2006) entailed an element of reinvention that was carried out in part by the Allied forces. Returning émigrés likewise contributed to the formation of cultural policies in both Germanys. This formation of national cultural policy from without is rarely discussed, perhaps because it contradicts the proposed centrality that *Kultur* inhabits in the German imagination.

Along with the Allies and returning émigrés, there were those who had stayed, professing to have practiced "inner immigration," and those whom denazification passed by but who nonetheless embodied continuities with the Nazi era. For them, but not only for them, the discourse of the *Nullstunde*, the "zero hour" that projected a complete break from the twelve years of National Socialism, enabled "the beginning of the denial and willful forgetting of the past that shaped the history of both German states for decades to come" (Huyssen 2010, 212).

Nascent West German cultural policy was first and foremost marked by "a commitment to a largely bourgeois concept of culture" (Burns and van der Will 2003, 133), thus omitting antimodernist and anti-Western sentiments that had characterized much of German artistic production and cultural policy over the previous decades. Notably, Berlin's revolutionary avant-garde and German expressionism, with its penchant for "figuration, apocalyptic religiosity, and political satire," were likewise not seen as conducive to the "political codification of Cold War aesthetics" (Huyssen 2010, 210–11).[10]

The distinctly material basis to rework the memory of modernism in Germany was provided by the Association of Arts and Culture of the German Economy at the Federation of German Industries (Kulturkreis der deutschen Wirtschaft; see Chapter 2). Established in 1951, this nonprofit organization was originally managed by leading figures of the postwar economic boom, aided in no small part by the German Marshall Fund. Its initial goal was the "rebuilding" of German artistic heritage, an endeavor that was being stifled by the limited government funds for the arts (Grasskamp and Ulrich 2001). In an interview with then director of the Kulturkreis in early 2008, Stephan Frucht—a musicologist and concert violinist by training—explained this initial mission by saying "in the zero hour, Germany was in need of being tied into modernity [*Deutschland an die Moderne anzuknüpfen*]. With its rebuilding, the German economic sector assumed its cultural responsibility to bring back [modernist] works of art and to complete museum collections." Infamously organizing book burnings, the Nazis had taken a more pragmatic stance when it came to visual art. A considerable part of the confiscated modernist works from private and public collections had been sold abroad and now had to be "bought back." Furcht's choice of words, his formulation that Germany was to be *tied into modernity* rather than tied *back* into modernity, points to the fact that the Kulturkreis was not merely trying to repatriate specific works to Germany. Rather, its activities were part of a larger process of reinterpreting German artistic heritage as unequivocally located in the project of Western modernism. Providing funds for the acquisition of modernist artworks that would form the new canon of "German art," the German industry reworked its complicity in the war economy, forced labor, and systematic dispossession, transforming it instead into a modernizing and civilizing force.[11] Today, references to the specificities of the German experience have been replaced in the Kulturkreis's mission statement by efforts to divorce corporate arts sponsorship from its image as a public relations exercise, portraying it instead as akin to the arts patronage of old (*Mäzenatentum*). This shift is also indicative of another stage in Germany's disavowal of its violent past, one that moves away from identifying the "German Catastrophe," as the loss of sovereignty after World War II was long referred to, as the structuring element of cultural policy.

Overcoming the disconnect from modernism was neither quick nor easy. In 1965, the artist and academic Arnold Bode established *documenta*, an internationally acclaimed contemporary art exhibition held every five years in Kassel. *documenta* was explicitly intended to present classic modernism in a country where it "had never been shown" and to reconnect the German art world with international developments. Andreas Huyssen (2010, 215) interprets the establishment of *documenta* as well as Allied efforts in cultural policy as a move to "denationalize" the German art world, even though this internationalization was set "in a typically conservative 1950s mode" (see also Belting 2003, 42). Yet I would argue that "denationalization" thus conceived actually reinforced the national frame by way of establishing Germany's Western belonging and feeding into the myth of 1945 as the definitive rupture from the Third Reich.

The Shift to *Soziokultur*

With the political upheavals of the late 1960s, the static and elitist conceptions underlying Germany's cultural policy came under growing criticism. These critiques took up Herbert Marcuse's (2007 [1937]) analysis of the "affirmative character" of German culture, one that obscured the actual social conditions of the majority of the population. Only a break away from this idealized bourgeois canon and the extension of the culture concept to the everyday would allow for reclaiming aesthetics and unlock its potential for political critique. Cultural policy practitioners coined the term "*Soziokultur*" to describe a policy shift that would a bridge the echelons of high art and the broader public, between audiences and artists, professional arts and the alternative scene (Glaser and Stahl 1974, Knoblich 2001). This shift thus echoed early cultural policy initiatives in Turkey. The prefix *Sozio-* (rather than *Sozial-*) was to express a holistic approach that emphasized equal opportunity, access, and participation in cultural life, rather than the instrumentalization of culture for politics. The aim was a pluralization and politicization of "aesthetic practices" and a turn away from the projected neutrality of the apolitical connoisseur (Knoblich 2001, 3) that had come to signify the silences surrounding Germany's National Socialist past, which, under the guise of classicism, had first enabled and then obscured what was at heart a decivilizing process.

A central figure in rethinking cultural policy along these lines was Hilmar Hoffmann. As the commissioner of culture for Frankfurt/Main, Hoffmann summarized the proposed cultural policy shift with the slogan "Kultur für Alle." He called for a break away from established canons in order to develop a cultural democracy in which everyone would be able to partake in cultural life "meaningfully" (Hoffmann 1979, 12). This goal could only be achieved by implementing fundamental social and economic reforms, extending the infrastructure of public transportation, limiting the length of the workday, and offering affordable continuing education across cities and rural areas. It was in this manner that "the most German of distinctions," that between culture and civilization, could find an end, a distinction that according to Hoffmann had served to justify the worst barbarism of the twentieth century.

While the conception of *Soziokultur* did not bring about the far-reaching reforms it originally proposed, it did succeed at extending access to the arts and arts education to broader segments of society. *Soziokultur* intended to transform society in its entirety but ended up paving the way for framing art policies as social policies that over the past decades have been employed to purportedly mend all kinds of social ills—often inadvertently transposing questions of social justice to that of culture (Mirza 2005, Karaca 2009). This was, however, not the only contradiction that *Soziokultur* produced. It aimed to broaden the meaning of art beyond the confines of traditional, high art and to integrate everyday culture by reinterpreting it as a creative process in itself. Yet it could not—nor did it mean to—escape the notion that "art needs connoisseurs [*Kunst braucht Kenner*]," as Brecht had once put it. It also remains questionable to what extent these shifts indeed changed the connotations of culture within the German context, especially as *Kultur* and its historical baggage made its return in the 1990s, both in the reunification debate and the growing anti-immigrant rhetoric, accompanied by violence (Chapter 1).

German Reunification: From Cultural Nation to Cultural State?

The terms *Kulturnation* and *Kulturstaat*, while at times used interchangeably, index different understandings of the relationship between culture, art, and the German state. Since 1871, the notion of a cultural nation has been used to identify Germans living outside its territory, especially in Russia and the Caucasus. In the Third Reich, it signaled the desire for eastward expansion, as a way of "bringing them home" into the fold of the German state. After 1945, it expressed cultural unity of the two Germanys despite political division. With reunification Germany began to cast itself as a *Kulturstaat* to dissuade domestic and foreign fears by affirming *cultural statehood* within existing borders—as a renunciation of "German barbarism." Discourses of Germany as a cultural state highlight cultural pluralism in a particular key. Pluralism denotes first and foremost the principle of federalism and cultural sovereignty of the *Länder.* Second, it acknowledges the particularity of East Germany's cultural and artistic heritage—although as the next chapter will show, this has been mainly an issue of rhetoric.

It was against this background that the creation of the central office of a federal government commissioner for culture and the media by the Social Democratic–Green Party coalition in 1998 elicited protest—because it was seen to threaten Germany's federalist structure. Politically conservative camps charged the government with "left-wing Wilhelmism," as the late cultural critic Frank Schirrmacher famously coined it, a metaphor characterizing the planned office as an authoritarian and historically regressive move. But Chancellor Gerhard Schröder (1998–2005) was not to be dissuaded, arguing that the cultural integration of East and West Germany warranted such a central office—without acknowledging the contradiction between this narrative and that of the cultural unity of the two Germanys that had been central to West Germany's political rhetoric throughout forty years of division. Culture was once again identified as vital for Germany's standing in the European and global area, which further necessitated such a centralized office. This office was also to protect German cultural interests against the ever-looming threat of EU homogenization (Burns and van der Will and 2003, 128). But there was another aspect to this story that is connected to the memory boom of the 1980s: This office would be responsible for establishing national memorials and commemoration sites; it was to fashion the official memory regime of a reunited Germany.

Cultural policy officials such as Torsten Wöhlert and Ingrid Wagner of the Berlin Senate's cultural administration emphasized that the government agencies that award funding have no preset notion of art but are guided by notions of culture. Whenever I asked what these notions of culture entailed, they substituted it with political ideas of pluralism and freedom of expression and by pointing to the fact that not they themselves but appointed juries composed of artists and other experts as well as elected politicians selected projects for funding. Neither the criteria according to which juries were assembled (especially when it comes to artists and experts) nor the way that decisions were made were problematized. Other German officials, too, legitimize the distribution of arts funding through discourses of Germany as a *Kulturstaat*, in which "culture" is deproblematized as the basis of the nation-state. The fact that this presupposes a specific understanding of German culture is rarely questioned. Artists in Berlin tend to see state involvement in the arts as irrelevant or benign (episodes in which this assessment is broken are discussed in Chapters 4 and 5), quite in contrast to their colleagues in Istanbul. Their concerns are generally directed at cutbacks in state funding[12] or expressed periodically around the city's museums, which have long been unable and at times uninterested in including art produced in Berlin into their collections. In part, it is Berlin's wide range of municipal and federal funding and the availability of alternative venues that assuage the situation. But it is also the successful disavowal of the at times outright violent history of *Kultur* and its workings in the present that has left state involvement in the arts unscrutinized and made the history I have reviewed here largely unknown and unacknowledged.

Dismantling an Empire, "Creating a Republic of Fine Arts"

Until recently, much of the literature on cultural policy in Turkey has focused on the early republican period (1923–1938) and, to a lesser extent, the entirety of the single-party period that ended in 1950.[13] In part, this focus can be explained by the allure that declared new beginnings yield. With its foundation, Turkey claimed nothing short of a revolution—and a perpetual one at that—

and envisioned the creation of "a republic of fine arts," in the words of the politician and educator İsmail Hakkı Baltacıoğlu (1934, 6). The sheer scope of social and demographic engineering pursued under the headings of "modernization" and "Turkification" might warrant this focus, but it also reinforces the discursive rupture between the Ottoman Empire and the Republic of Turkey. Reifying the narrative of an empire that fell behind politically, economically, and artistically with the onset of the Renaissance, it settles on the notion that the Ottoman Empire did not pursue a cultural policy to speak of.

By virtue of emphasis the republican discourse was then one of creation, rather than of renewal, as in the German case, and the political establishment identified art as a necessity within this process (Öndin 2003, 70). Speaking to a belief in the transformative power of art, these proclamations make the actual policy practices and frequent lack of support for the arts throughout Turkey's history all the more notable. The following overview is thus an illustration of the problems that arise from foregrounding the transformative power of art in a political context that has struggled to maintain authoritarian control.

Against the long-held notion that the late Ottoman Empire's cultural policy is negligible (Topuz 1998), the art historian Wendy Shaw's account of the history of Ottoman painting offers cues for a different assessment of how art was governed in the late Ottoman Empire. While at the turn of the previous century it was predominantly private venues and storefront exhibitions that granted especially newly graduated artists opportunities to show and sell works, Shaw also notes that municipal and state funding could be mobilized especially for works celebrating "imperial glory and national cohesion," even—or especially—as "foreign powers increasingly threatened the Ottoman Empire" (Shaw 2011, 111). Municipal commissions and public exhibitions continued throughout World War I, broadening public access to art, as did, for instance, the annual Galatasaray exhibitions, established in 1916 by the Ottoman Painters' Association. Foreign cultural policy remained a concern during this era as well, evidenced by the initiative of the Department of Intelligence that, with the support of Abdülmecid II, commissioned works to be exhibited abroad "as a means of convincing the world that Turks were not merely good soldiers, but also had a strong civilization" (147).

The director of the Turkish Hearths, Hamdullah Suphi Tanrıöver (1885–1966), a poet, translator, and writer, served two, albeit short, terms as minster of education (eleven months in 1920–1921, while Istanbul was still occupied by Allied forces following the Armistice of Mudros, and nine months in 1925, after the establishment of the Republic), making him also responsible for arts policies. It is worth looking at Tanrıöver's activities in more detail, since how he is treated in the literature is emblematic for the state of cultural policy scholarship. Mentioned in much of this scholarship at least in passing, his activities in the Grand National Assembly of the Republic of Turkey (1923–1927) remain underexamined when it comes to cultural policy. Obscuring not only his overtly racist and discriminatory legacy, they forgo any discussion of how his parliamentary activities reflect on who was to count as "Turkish," which would have grave implications for the subjects and objects of republican cultural policy. Tanrıöver played a decisive role in rephrasing Article 88 of the constitution, the very article that defined Turkish citizenship, which in its original form stated that without distinguishing between religion and language all inhabitants of Turkey were "Turks." In the debate on said article the representative of Yozgat province, Ahmet Hamdi, requested the addition of a clause stating that those inhabitants of Turkey who accepted "Turkish culture" were to be designated as Turks. Following Hamdi's suit, Tanrıöver entered the discussion with an agenda that explicitly connected religion to citizenship and culture to property. The basis of his argument was the trope that religious minorities were clandestinely conspiring with foreign powers—and capital.[14] Drawing on the discourse of non-Muslims as "foreigners" who hampered not only national sovereignty but also the Turkification of capital necessary for the national project, Tanrıöver argued for the removal of Greeks and Armenians owning such "foreign" businesses. If they were to be unconditionally categorized as Turks, their removal would not be possible, as citizenship rights would protect them. In the end, Article 88 was reformulated, stating that all inhabitants of Turkey regardless of religion and language are regarded as Turkish *citizens*—not as Turks, however (Bali 1999, 104). Given that this constitutional decision took place on the heels of massive demographic engineering, genocidal violence against Armenians and other non-Muslim communities, and population exchanges, Tanrıöver's intervention and Article 88 became the basis of—and messenger for—further sociocultural and economic Turkification measures, including economic dispossession, that were to come in the following decades.

Incorporating the Nation

The Turkish Hearths were closed in March 1931. Seizing their assets, the Republican People's Party (Cumhuriyet Halk Partisi, CHP), under Mustafa Kemal's lead, established in their stead the Halk Evleri (People's Houses). Like the Turkish Hearths before them, the People's Houses relied on ideas of a national incorporation through education and cultural production. They also presented crucial sites for research into folklore (Öztürkmen 2002) from which a new Turkish culture was to be crafted. Somewhat paradoxically so, they were envisioned as tools for popularizing a culture that was both "already out there" and still to come into being. Likewise paradoxically, the People's Houses were presented as autonomous institutions by the people for the people yet were designed as instruments of control, bringing state (party) ideology to the people (Ahıska 2010, 213–14).

The People's Houses were to mend two diagnosed shortcomings of the Hearth movement. First, they were to function as a bridge between the *aydin* (intellectuals, or the enlightened) and the *halk* (the folk, or people). This preset produced a didacticism that from the outset contradicted the revolutionary capacity attributed to culture and art and reified the very dichotomy it aimed to transcend. Second, the Hearths were thought to have fallen short in the nationalization of culture. In order to streamline the activities of the People's Houses with the "six arrows" of the Republican Party program—republicanism, nationalism, populism, laizism, statism, and revolutionism—they were charged with facilitating the populations' appropriation of the state-led reforms.

Cultural policies of the 1930s and 1940s were populist in terms of both the sources of artistic production and its addressees. National art was to be born out of realistic depictions of "the people" and their daily lives (Köksal 2004, 101).[15] Art education pursued a twofold goal: to create amateur artists and audiences for the arts. This notion of arts training as audience building reveals one of the ways in which the effect of art was understood. It was the practice of artistic production—amateurish as it might be—that was believed to enable *access* to the arts as well as *socialization* into the nation.[16]

The Peoples' Houses exhibited a fluid understanding of folklore, crafts, and the fine arts and mandated collaborations between professional artists and amateurs in their charters. Atatürk himself did not seem to draw a strict distinction between art and folklore, artists and artisans. According to Metin And (1984, 218), his arguments were akin to Ottoman perceptions that opposed the Western European compartmentalization of art and did not distinguish between the fine and "applied" arts. However, the republican elite neither referred to this legacy nor to its socialist counterparts, with which it bore notable resemblances. Rather than interpreting the fluidity between art and artisanship as lagging behind the modern conception of art, it might be useful to analyze it in terms of its capacity for popular incorporation. This stance is illustrated by a speech Atatürk gave to artisans in Adana in March 1923, where he noted that "it is not enough to produce individual artists. Men cannot wholly successfully work alone. . . . If this collective activity is a physical necessity, it is clear that working for a common goal is essential" (cited in And 1984, 218).

Only as a collective enterprise would art contribute to the evolution of a "Turkish civilization."

The early Republic witnessed a growing cultural infrastructure. But as the artist Cemal Tollu noted, neither the emergent art market nor the state pensions that some artists received through their teaching positions generated sufficient income. Artists began to call for government support in the form of *develet himayesi* (Öndin 2003, 128). Notably, this once positive connotation of state patronage had long before my fieldwork become a highly contentious label, designating both "bad art" and political opportunism on the part of artists—especially as art in the service of the state became unimaginable for many after the 1980 coup.

There were divergent views in the early Republic on the causalities between art and development: Some argued that only an ameliorated economy would invigorate artistic production and stimulate the art market. Others posited that investing in the arts would in itself contribute to the development of the country and uplift the "new nation." In contrast to postunification Germany, nascent Turkey did not receive reparations and consequently did not experience the rapid industrialization that contributed significantly to Germany's growing bourgeoisie and art market. Artists' material concerns not only affected their livelihood but also artistic practices and art-historical documentation. The artist Elif Naci noted on the first decade of the republic: "We have neither a gallery nor documents to help us take account of these ten years. Most of our artists paint over the works of the previous year and exhibit the same canvases year after year. Thus, their salaries, so low as to not afford them new canvases, have erased the documents with which to write a history of Turkish art" (cited in Shaw 2011, 168). To remedy the situation, state-operated banks increased their arts patronage, and the Ministry of Education established scholarships for artists to study abroad.

Economic factors were not alone in curbing the advancement of art in the national arena. While the foundation of the Republic brought with it the possibility, and perceived necessity, of aesthetically reinventing the built environment, the painter Namık İsmail diagnosed that local artists "because of lack of experience" were much less called upon than those from abroad (Öndin 2003, 72). Often it was their German colleagues who were commissioned to design new government buildings, sculptures, and memorials; similarly justified preferences prevailed in the recruitment of fine arts instructors (Köksal 2004, 103). Seamlessly fitting into the tropes of "belatedness" in Turkish modernization, the argument of the "lack of experience" long remained unquestioned in Turkish art history and cultural policy research. But could these choices have been motivated by the loss of craftspeople and artists due to the horrors of World War I, the war of independence, and, most importantly, genocide, expulsion, and other demographic engineering measures? Esra Akcan points—if somewhat timidly—to this possibility by proposing that

> the republican elite refused to rely on Turkish talent, perhaps because many of the experienced architect-builders (*kalfa*) of the Ottoman Empire after the eighteenth century were members of the Armenian and Greek minority groups whose successors the last Ottoman Sultans and the new Turkish state avoided working with, and perhaps because the newly educated Turkish architects seemed too young for the task.
> Akcan (2012, 28)

Despite the by now well-documented political continuities (e.g., Akçam 2004), the appointments of foreign artists solidified the notion of rupture between the Ottoman Empire and the Turkish Republic and facilitated the exclusion of non-Muslims and other minorities from "Turkish" art and architectural history.

As previously mentioned, the project of turning Ottomans into modern Turkish citizens was from the very beginning predicated on a belief in the transformative, indeed revolutionary capacity of art, but it was also this capacity that made art potentially dangerous. One of the most striking features of early Turkish cultural policy was its embrace of avant-garde and modernist aesthetics (Bozdoğan 2001). This embrace sets it apart from its German counterpart, where modernism was long understood as a "threat to the very heart and soul of what it meant to be German" (Belting 1998, 61). Yet there were shared discomforts. In a context dominated by development rhetoric and with a new "national" bourgeoisie in the making, Turkey's political establishment faced considerable problems when it came to critiques of modernity, bourgeois values, and the way that industrialization shaped the modern condition—all central to modernist approaches. Modernization in early republican times, similarly to the German case and for similar reasons, was portrayed as a balancing act that was supposed to be nonimitative and aware of the potential social upheavals it entailed. Turkey, like Germany, was troubled by modernism's universalist claims. The debate if modernism could index national particularity and what a truly authentic "Turkish modernism" could look like raged for decades, as did the question whether a moderate modernism was possible.

Despite deep-seated anticommunism, Soviet cultural policies, especially how they conceptualized the process of "bringing art to the people," held somewhat of an allure for the CHP. Artists themselves seemed more critical, frequently rejecting state intervention and the instrumentalization of art as both antidemocratic and stifling to artistic development. To be clear, it was not the engagement with the political per se that was criticized on the part of the arts community but the fact that exhibitions like the CHP-sponsored "Exhibition on the Revolution" in Ankara (1933) portrayed art to be in the service of the state, rather than allowing art to address the revolutionary transformation of society in an aesthetically adequate manner (Köksal 2004, 102). A concrete parallel to Soviet cultural policies were the painting tours of Anatolia (*yurt gezileri*), from which the government acquired works for display in official buildings. Although wary of state manipulation, artists such as the D Group, which claimed an overtly modernist stance while trying to join cubism and "local aesthetics" (Tansuğ 1986, 179–90), welcomed the painting tours as an opportunity to absorb local knowledge and practices and create from it "a new synthesis of form with content" (Berk 1938, 5).

Intensifying Turkification: The İnönü Years

Along with the intensification of anti-Ottoman rhetoric, the regime of İsmet İnönü (1938–1950) enforced the Turkification of the economy. A widening bourgeoisie, and hence a widening segment of collectors, was produced on the back of the wealth tax (*varlik vergisi*) that targeted non-Muslim communities. I will take a closer look at this phase and how it has affected the art world, in the next chapter. For now, I want to turn to the idea of "Turkish humanism" as a way of "Turkifying" the past. The Turkish Language Association (founded in 1932) and the Turkish Historical Society (1931) were already recrafting language and history, but they continued to run up against inconsistencies, in terms of both Turkey's material landscape and its public memory.

Like other nation-states, Turkey has had to claim a historically and archeologically documented past in order to legitimize its present form and to express the "civility" connoted with the cultivation of and care for tangible heritage. But Turkey has been faced with a multitude of archeological artifacts and historical documents that contradict much of its mythical national foundation, especially when it comes to its demographic makeup and the ways that its constituency has been historically produced (also see Abu El-Haj 2001 on the case of Israel): traces of the built environments of non-Muslims and the historical Kurdish presence in Mesopotamia, for instance. The Turkish state has often dealt with artifacts, sites, and archives that prove incommensurable with its civilizational narrative through outright destruction or disinvestment, that is, by leaving them vulnerable to looting and to decay after the populations living there have been killed, deported, exiled, or their lives made unbearable.

Hasan Ali Yücel, the minister of education from 1939 to 1945, was instrumental in bringing the notion of Turkish humanism to the fore. He proposed a "Turkish Renaissance and a European-Turkish civilization" by situating the "birthplace of civilization" not in Mesopotamia (largely converging with the homeland of Armenians and Kurds) but Anatolia. Linking the latter to a Greek-Latin genealogy, Turkish humanism projected a different civilizational alignment between Turkey and Europe.[17] This allowed for the erasure of entire geopolitical areas, historical episodes, and communities now deemed evidence of uncomfortable pasts. Together with other measures and institutions instated to rework the past, Turkish humanism produced, in Navaro-Yashin's (2012) terms, a "make-believe space."[18] But as we will see, it also produced an untenable history, and its many ill-fitting pieces have been increasingly questioned in the arts and in wider society.

The İnönü government found that the People's Houses had not succeeded in integrating rural populations into the national project. To amend this failure, the Village Institutes (Köy Enstitüleri) were established in 1940. Closely tied to Yücel's Ministry of Education, these institutes trained "village teachers" and focused on literacy and development through education. The arts were again highlighted as essential in this process. In contrast to the People's Houses, however, art appreciation was seen as an avenue for elevating overall educational levels, rather than for training emergent artists or connoisseurs. Like the People's Houses, the Village Institutes were sites for researching "Turkish folklore" and "culture" as well as for incorporating rural populations into the party and state structure.[19]

Yet this effort too faced considerable practical problems. As with other initiatives in the realm of culture and education, the Village Institutes were not sufficiently accompanied by the government services to achieve the level of development the state had promised. The historian Erik Zürcher notes that while electricity provisions for rural Anatolian villages stayed under 1 percent well into the 1950s, state control in the form of tax collectors and gendarmes had clearly made their marks throughout the countryside early on. The "suppression of expressions of popular faith," a ban on trade unions and strikes that persisted until 1945, rising costs of living during World War II, budget crises, and inflation all contributed to the withering popularity of the regime (Zürcher 2004, 207). Against this background, Anatolian populations neither felt embraced by the republic nor compelled to embrace it in turn. In addition, both the People's Houses and the Village Institutes gave way to associational life that at times developed differently than intended, their reading groups and art programs diverging from the script envisioned for transforming their participants into model citizens.

The End of Cultural Policy? The Democrat Party

By the end of the single-party period the People's Houses and the Village Institutes had moved so far beyond the tight grip of the party that they had become a thorn in the eye of the conservative wing of the CHP. The now governing Democrat Party (Demokrat Parti, DP) in turn regarded both institutions either as strongholds of the CHP or as hotbeds for oppositional mobilization, especially "communist propaganda" and socialist thought. On the order of the DP, both institutions were closed down. This is how the annals of cultural policy history portray it. But a closer look reveals that the question of how to bring art to the people remained intertwined with the politics of dispossession that enabled Turkification. Both institutions' assets were seized (Zürcher 2004, 223), their archives confiscated and it seems in part destroyed.[20] We find here a script that had played out before and would play out again and again throughout republican history. The Turkish Hearths, for instance, benefited from the waves of dispossession that advanced hand in hand with the Armenian genocide (Üngör and Polatel 2011, 125), and the People's Houses in turn became "victims" of the cycle of dispossession along with the Village Institutes. The dispossession and destruction of archives of cultural production have not only targeted those identified as other, not only been the fate of acknowledged and unacknowledged minorities and marginalized groups alike, but have been exercised on the very subjects that were supposed to be the carriers of the "national awakening" as well, whenever they veered away from the national cause.

To give a more recent example, the Mesopotamia Cultural Centers (Navenda Çanda Mezopotamya) established throughout Turkey in the 1990s as the artistic and cultural arm of the Kurdish rights struggle have frequently been subject to police raids under the guise of Turkey's antiterrorism legislation. While financial assets were no longer seized (instead, financial pressure was exerted through legal fees and fines), their archives were frequently confiscated, never to be returned. Documentation of their activities and recordings of their events have been "lost." This has curtailed the writing of history of these institutions, of their artistic legacies and the social memory attached to them.[21] They present another station in the circle of dispossession that has shaped the art world in Turkey.

It is a much-rehearsed story that the DP did not pursue a cultural policy, indeed, that it was disinterested in art wholesale. This is often related to the lifting of restrictions on religious practice and education in the public sphere as a concession to its voter base (Topuz 1998, 70). But other interpretations are possible. Rather than conceptualizing the disinvestment of Democrat Party rule (1950–1960) as a nonpolicy,[22] disinvestment is itself a policy choice that becomes obscured in the historical blind spots of cultural policy research. Similarly, the long absence of cultural policy research on the time period between 1950 and the late 1980s is perplexing considering that these years span three military coups (1960, 1971, 1980) that were accompanied by the incarcerations of artists, activists, and public intellectuals. Until recently (Bek Arat 2014, Iğsız 2018), accounts on art and cultural policy have failed to capture important shifts in cultural politics and artistic expression.

The Unknowability of Turkish Art

Between 1970 and 1980 Turkey went through thirteen successive governments, often unstable minority coalitions, resulting in sporadic cultural policy practices. Three recurring discussions characterized this decade. The first centered once again on the tension between art as a universal expression and its supposed national character (Bek Arat 2014). Resembling early republican debates on if and how the universalism of modernism could be reconciled with national particularities, the discussion in the 1970s was complicated by two different inflections of "the national" in Turkey's political landscape—*milli* and *ulusal*, that is, two divergent imaginations of "the nation" by the political right and left, respectively. *Milli* is taken to express ethnicized nationalism, attributed to the Nationalist Movement Party (Milliyetçi Hareket Partisi, MHP) and movements further to the right, whereas *ulusal* indicates an anti-imperialist thrust on parts of the left that is no less bound to the framework of the nation-state. For many artists, however, the national and the universal, so forcefully debated in the political arena, were not mutually exclusive but dialectic in nature. Nurullah Berk (1973, 13), for instance, proposed that all artistic production was at once universal while also reflecting the national and local conditions out of which it emerged.

The second issue concerned the autonomy of art. The beginning of the decade witnessed the institutionalization of the Ministry of Culture as a separate entity (1971). Yet Prime Minister Bülent Ecevit suggested an independent arts council, with the state assuming a merely supporting and facilitating role. His call resonated with many artists and left-nationalist camps, increasingly wary of state manipulation, but was blocked by the MHP, which not only saw state patronage but state leadership in the arts as indispensable in the face of the ideological struggles society was facing; nothing less than the loss of "national values" was at stake.

At the same time, the question of "what actually constitutes Turkish culture" returned to the fore. Prime Minister Sadi Irmak (1974–1975), for instance, once again advocated the "research and dissemination of national culture" (*milli kültürün araştırılması ve yayılması*; Bek Arat 2014, 45). The Turkish Hearths, the People's Houses, the Village Institutes, and the paintings tours had already shared exactly this double mission; all had set out to research and disseminate "authentic Turkish culture" that was, somewhat contradictorily so, still coming into being.[23] How is one to understand this persistent "unknowability" of Turkish culture and, by extension, Turkish art, even five decades after the establishment of the Republic? Officially, it was the extent of the Ottoman corruption that was to blame. Much seems to suggest, however, that the state was unable to find what it was looking for. Anatolia was unwieldy for Ankara's projections; the once abject territory now turned heartland and its heritage continued to challenge the myth of a homogeneous Turkish culture and remained difficult to embrace.

The many returns of the unknowability of Turkish culture have persistently contradicted the state's civilizational narrative, in which everything can be captured and measured through positivist research and thereby known. They have also perpetuated dichotomous conceptualizations of West and East, modernity and tradition. It is this discrepancy that has sustained the patronizing vocabulary of "bringing art to the people," a vocabulary that stands in contrast to the bridging metaphors of *Soziokultur*, which gained ground in Germany during the same time period. Their Turkish counterparts often proclaimed similar intentions even as they inscribed the didacticism inherent in this hierarchical imaginary into the relationship between the state and the arts and ultimately between the state and its citizens. These extensive discussions were mirrored within the narrower confines of the art world, where the relationship of art to society and, particularly, to political mass movements took center stage. The decade bustled with activity: Independent arts and culture publications flourished as many proposed an organic bond between art and revolutionary movements, leading to active engagements with trade unions. Artists soon began to design their printed materials and worked on murals, and themes like "Mayday" and "General Strike" became exhibition titles.[24]

The Turkish Islamic Synthesis: The 1980 Coup and Its Aftermath

The 1980 coup disbanded associational life in Turkey and with it much of the artistic activity just described. The 1982 constitution ratified under the military regime strongly emphasized national unity and territorial integrity, not least in order to curtail the rising Kurdish rights struggle and socialist mobilization, and brought with it a renewed emphasis on Turkish language and culture. It was the military junta that merged the Ministry for Culture with that of Tourism. The Özal government (1983–1989), in accordance with its overall economic liberalization policies,[25] solidified marketing approaches to the field of arts and culture, and especially cultural tourism, along with the privatization of television and radio broadcasting that marked the European context overall in the 1980s.

In 1987, Selcuk Kantarcıoğlu, a member of the advisory council (Danışma Meclisi) that together with the National Security Council (Milli Güvenlik Konseyi) established by the military junta prepared the new constitution, published a book that brought together historical turning points and "milestones" of Turkish cultural policy. In his documentation, two discernible shifts emerge. One pertains to the extension of the culture concept that spans heritage and way of life, *hars* (culture) and *medeniyet* (civilization), the arts as well as the dimension of the everyday. He does so mainly by drawing on anthropological sources, yet one reference stands out: T. S. Eliot's *Three Senses of Culture* (1948), translated by the ministry in 1981, exemplifies the second shift.

In this essay, Eliot engages Mathew Arnold's *Culture and Anarchy* (1869) and criticizes his understanding of religion as a part of culture. Instead, Eliot argues, culture should be understood as developing in relation to religion. This is an important point when read against the reinforcement of the Turkish-Islamic synthesis by the military junta.[26] This synthesis included the instating of religious instruction at schools and reaffirmed the officially sanctioned version of Sunni Islam, and this version only, as part and parcel of being Turkish. Postulating religion as culture, it thus reiterated that non-Muslims are—and cannot be—part of "Turkish culture." Viewed in this vein, the Ministry of Culture and its policies were yet again engaged in delimiting Turkish citizenship and in reinforcing exclusionary understandings codified by Tanrıöver's intervention almost sixty years prior.

Kantarcıoğlu (1987, 17ff.) also documents the different formations that the administrative units dedicated to culture and the arts have gone through. To name just a few: In 1920, there was a special department for monuments. In 1923, *hars* and *kültür* formed a department in the Ministry of Education, but by 1933 the term *kültür* no longer appears in any of the administrative units. Instead, museums and libraries hold their own departments. In 1944, there is another structural overhaul that brings about a specialization of sub-bureaus, including a directorate for the fine arts. In 1971, culture is taken out of the educational ministry and established as an autonomous one. But in 1977 they are merged again, now under the title of National Ministry for Education and Culture. In 1978, culture and education are separated once more, with culture enjoying a stint of autonomy till it is merged into the Ministry of Culture and Tourism in 1982 and divorced again in 1990 until 2003, when the AKP combined them once more. But how to explain all this commotion? While a detailed analysis of these shifts transcends the scope of this study, it is worth remarking that the literature on cultural policy in Turkey barely notes these changes. My sense is that this forming and re-forming of different administrative units is more than mere window dressing. Rather, this constant reshuffling is indicative for the unwieldiness of art in the national project and of the state's continual attempt to gain a grip on it.

Policy by Default or Design? Contemporary Cultural Policy in Turkey

The most frequent assessment I encountered with regard to Turkish cultural policy in the mid-2000s was that it is nonexistent. The arts writer and curator Fatoş Üstek, for instance, underlined this statement by noting that only 1 percent of the Ministry for Culture and Tourism's budget was going toward contemporary art.[27] Implicitly, but less often voiced, this comes to mean that the Turkish state does not actually pursue a programmatic cultural policy but a solely regulatory approach to contemporary artistic production—most clearly expressed in state-driven censorship that despite the constitutionally guaranteed freedom of expression remained relatively normalized throughout my fieldwork and soared to new heights after. Most cultural producers, curators, and critics argue that decision-making processes on the state level are not institutionalized, often relating this lack to Turkey's "belated modernization." While I found that a substantial part of the decision-making processes in the realm of cultural policy appear arbitrary and person related, they institutionally work in favor of the state's governance of the cultural domain. In the visual arts this is exacerbated by the fact that the fine arts department in the ministry has no earmarked funds, quite in contrast to cinema and independent theater, which are catered to by separate programs. Contemporary art projects predominantly rely on private institutions and (inter)national foundations. For events outside of Turkey, they can apply to the *tanıtma fonu*, a fund supported by the Foreign Ministry and administrated by the Ministry of Culture and Tourism to "promote Turkish art abroad." Whereas the selection criteria and the composition of funding committees for theater and cinema are public knowledge, İbrahim Yazar, then deputy director general of the promotional fund, answered my question regarding the selection criteria with a flippant "we play it by ear [*kafamıza göre*]." His answer points once more to the gap between rhetoric on the importance of art and actual cultural policy practices.

In contrast to the prevalent view that Turkey "does not have an arts policy," I propose that the Turkish state—by what it does as well as what it *does not do*—actually creates a framework that *successfully* "harnesses" cultural and artistic initiatives that are either privately sponsored or independently organized. By selectively claiming these initiatives and at certain points supporting them, the Ministry of Culture and Tourism and the Istanbul Municipality were until 2013 very much in accord with recent developments in other European metropolises, such as Berlin. As such, Turkey provides a prime example that many of the developments that are relegated to the contemporary arts today can actually flourish apart from the kind of democratization they are taken to express.

The often professed disinterest in art, and especially contemporary art, is misleading when one considers the openings of two high-profile contemporary art spaces, the Istanbul Modern Museum and SantralIstanbul, which were rescheduled seemingly on the Prime Minister's Office's request to dovetail with the 2004 EU accession talks and the national elections of 2007, respectively. Apart from being granted permits and some logistical support, both projects have largely lain outside of the state subsidy.[28] Not just Erdoğan but other officials too have been successful in straddling the appropriation of artistic production and dismissing it whenever opportune. When still mayor of Istanbul, Erdoğan had famously labeled ballet "art below the belt," and during a 2012 rally in Kahramanmaraş he decried theater artists as "looking down" on "the people." Yet this at times open aversion has not hindered state representatives from emphasizing their roles in the flourishing of private arts and cultural centers over the past twenty years—without acknowledging the role of the military junta in the economic liberalization that made these private arts centers possible in the first place (Yardımcı 2005). Indeed, this symbiotic relationship has engendered a division of labor between the state and private sector in the realm of art that remains veiled by the utterances of antagonism, especially on part of the latter.

The 1980 coup cemented a turning away from the state on the part of art world. While many artists categorically reject any type of dealings with the Ministry of Culture and Tourism and its local counterparts for their projects, others have noted that it was their right to request government assistance—and accountability—in cultural matters.[29] This view was expressed, for instance, by the filmmaker Hüseyin Karabey, who maintained that one ought to engage the state continually: "Even if you only end up forcing them to reject your proposal, eventually they have to acknowledge your existence." Indeed, after ten years of failed attempts, Karabey was finally awarded a grant for his film *Gitmek: My Marlon and Brando* in 2007—although the Ministry of Culture and Tourism later tried to prevent a screening of the film at a Swiss festival (see Chapter 5).

From 2009 onward, the ruling AKP has tried to make its mark on cultural policy by turning away from long-standing state discourses rejecting Ottoman heritage and toward embracing a line that has been labeled, ever so vaguely, neo-Ottomanism. As Asli Iğsız (2015, 327) poignantly notes, apart from its nationalist currency, neo-Ottomanism has largely served "to legitimize contemporary neoliberal and cultural policies by drawing on anachronistic reinterpretations and the glorification of the Ottoman past in Turkey," specifically the pre-Tanzimat Ottoman Empire.[30] Playing on the discontent that early republican cultural policies produced, especially their patronizing thrust, this new orientation has so far expressed itself in strategic mosque renovations, the names chosen for urban redevelopment and infrastructure projects,[31] and the establishment of the Panorama 1453 History Museum, dedicated to the conquest of Constantinople. Some commentators propose that the AKP's cultural vision mainly wishes to undo "Kemalist" principles (Aksoy and Şeyben 2014). I see their deployment of dichotomies of East versus West, religious versus secular as yet another effort to gain hegemony over the unwieldiness of the cultural domain, especially as the art world and its institutions have voiced growing critiques of the government. The AKP has found two advocates for an Ottoman revival in art in the academics İskender Pala and Mustafa İsen, but questions remain as to what such a revival would look like in practice. Anecdotal evidence, some out of the ministry itself, seems to suggest that visual art in the "Islamic tradition" has found a growing market and government support, while "Islamic" playwrights, for example, have been harder to come by. Proposals to revive divan literature have yet to explain how to navigate this devotional poetry's focus on love and often bodily love between men (Andrews and Kalpaklı 2005), for instance.

4
The Art of Forgetting

> For without exception the cultural treasures he surveys have an origin, which he cannot contemplate without horror. . . . There is no document of culture, which is not at the same time a document of barbarism. And just as such a document is not free from barbarism, barbarism also taints the manner in which it is transmitted from one owner to the other.
>
> —WALTER BENJAMIN

The German noun *Überlieferung*, perhaps more so than reflected in its English translation, harbors meanings that go beyond the mere transfer of ownership. It also refers to lore, often triumphalist in nature, to stories about the past and the way they are told and retold, passed on from one generation to another (*schriftliche Überlieferung*, for instance, is often translated as "written tradition"). Benjamin was not only thinking about the spoliation and ruination of wartime victors collecting their booty or the exploitative conditions from slavery to capitalism that have enabled much of the cultural production now celebrated as "civilizational achievements." He fundamentally argued against understandings of culture as "a commodity, detached from the wider social conditions of its production" (Leslie 2008, 176). Benjamin's formulation opens a path for us to interrogate the twin processes of violence and dispossession, in which art has played a pivotal role. Both material and symbolic dispossession have shaped the art world and its historical formation in ways that warrant further attention than they have thus far received. In these processes artworks and, at times, entire collections or artistic styles become part of the politics of forgetting; the conditions of their transmission become silenced or are obscured altogether. They are forgotten, I propose, because they represent different modulations of decivilizing art, either through the interventions that artworks propose or by way of the conditions under which art is produced, accumulated, and circulated. They are instances of artistic production that do not fit into the carefully crafted narratives of the national frame that project a linear civilizing process (Elias 1969). They trouble the proclaimed emancipatory power of art and its institutions. In what follows, I highlight moments of complicity in historical silences that reify official discourses on the past, and I begin to sketch others, ones that break these silences and reveal decivilizing aspects instead of obscuring them.[1]

Missing Accountability

Like elsewhere, Turkey has experienced a "memory boom" over the past two decades (Özyürek 2007, Duft 2009, Neyzi 2011). Minority memory and heritage have played exponent roles in these processes of recovery, especially as "cultural pluralism" has emerged as a threshold for modernness, quite in contrast to earlier stages of nation building during which ethnic homogeneity indexed modernity—and despite the long-standing equation of heterogeneity with loss of sovereignty (Karaca 2010). This shift has been furthered by the role accorded to "multiculturalism" and "diversity" in the discourses of democratization and Europeanization that have significantly shaped the framing of cultural policy in Turkey and Germany. While many commentators have celebrated this recovery from the long-standing "organized amnesia" (Özyürek 2007, 3), how this recovery happens is also vital to consider. On the part of the AKP government, discourses of a "cosmopolitan Ottoman past" that has an exemplary function for peaceful coexistence in the present gained increasing political currency throughout the 2000s. Yet the question of how to address contemporary diversity has proven difficult. These difficulties have been compounded by a public sphere that has become increasingly vocal in discussing the atrocities and traumas produced by the extensive social and demographic engineering measures that brought present-day Turkey into being. The rise of artistic and cultural production thematizing mass violence and state terror has been accompanied by demands for recognition and varying calls for making amends. One such call has been to turn the former Madiamak Hotel in Sivas, the site of a pogrom against Alevi artists and intellectuals by state-sanctioned Islamist groups in 1993, into a museum.[2] However, while linking itself to discourses about facing the past and proclaiming to break with state tradition, the AKP has shied away from taking the concrete steps of holding the Turkish state structure accountable, even as the majority of these episodes of state violence lie outside of its time in government. The intricacies of navigating this dualism of partial acknowledgment and simultaneous rejection of political responsibility become visible in the public sphere, where proclamations of Turkey's multicultural makeup and antiminority rhetoric are traded off against each other on a daily basis. The same is true for official discussions on archeological artifacts and cultural patrimony. For the last few years, Prime Minister Erdoğan has reiterated that finding a few "pots and pans" at the large-scale construction sites throughout Istanbul will no longer hinder the ambitious redevelopment he pursues for the city, such as the recently completed Marmaray Tunnel, which unearthed countless Byzantine artifacts. At the same time, Minister of Culture and Tourism Ertuğrul Günay (2007–2013) made emotional appeals for the return of Ottoman artifacts from international museums. Until his last interview in office, he stressed that Turkey cared for "all Anatolian cultures and their heritage" in equal measure (*Radikal*, January 29, 2013).

These contradictions are not new. Speaking at a conference on "Imperialism, Art, and Restitution" at the Washington School of Law in 2004, the former minister of culture Talat Halman[3] bemoaned the illicit trade of "Ottoman" and "Turkish" antiquities and advocated swifter procedures for the restitution of artifacts poached from the territory that is today Turkey. A rare move at the time, he publicly conceded that the Turkish government, too, was at fault for not having afforded its cultural and artistic heritage the protection it deserved. One example he mentioned was the rejection of the Calouste Sarkis Gülbenkian collection in the early 1960s, which he qualified as "mind-boggling" (Halman 2006, 44). But is it mind-boggling indeed? Born in Istanbul in 1869, Gülbenkian, of Armenian descent, made his money in the oil trade, establishing the Turkish Petroleum Company in 1912. His enormous collection ranged from prehistorical artifacts to Egyptian, Far Eastern, Ottoman, and Christian liturgical art. Considering the proclaimed rupture between the Turkish Republic and its Ottoman predecessor, Gülbenkian's personal background and the presence of Armenian, Greek Orthodox, and Assyrian art in his collection might make the state's rejection less surprising, even though the Gülbenkian Foundation (located in Lisbon) apparently had offered not only to donate the collection but to defray all operating costs of the proposed museum. Indeed, Turkey has a long history of discarding or reinterpreting archeological finds, artifacts, and artworks that do not readily fit into the narratives of official Turkish history. While these shortcomings in the care for cultural heritage are generally explained by a lack of funding, political practices are overall in stark contrast to the importance given to art and cultural heritage on the level of political discourse. Off the record, many respondents connect this situation to a fundamental unwillingness, not financial impasses, long illustrated, for example, by the debilitated state of the Istanbul Museum of Painting and Sculpture and its archives and storage facilities. That this unwillingness reflects the conceptual problems posed by art and its production, circulation, and presentation when it transgresses the civilizational discourse of the national frame will become more contoured in the next example.

Missing Provenance

The ways that land, buildings, and monies have forcefully changed hands over the course of late Ottoman and Turkish republican history has gained increasing attention in scholarship and politics. There is also growing awareness that the genocidal violence, demographic engineering, and discriminatory practices that enabled the systematic dispossession of minorities have informed understandings of artistic heritage as well as art history in Turkey. In contrast to Germany, however, there has been to date little research on how the "Turkification of capital" has historically shaped Turkey's art economy and hence the makeup of its art world today. The extent to which actual artworks and artifacts were part of these processes of dispossession is likewise still in question. Visiting Istanbul in the 1980s and 1990s, I often heard rumors about Armenian, Greek, and Jewish household items, jewelry, and paintings being sold by the antiquities dealers in Çukurcuma, Beyoğlu—a district largely populated by non-Muslims during Ottoman times.

Provenance documentation can be read as the biography of an art object, but we can extend the same logic to art capital as well. It proves ownership and documents the ways art changes hands (sales, or inheritance, for example) as well as the locations where works have been kept—ideally since the time of creation. As provenance sheds light on the historical, social, and economic context in which collecting (or, in the case of capital, accumulation) takes place, it establishes authenticity and functions as a safeguard against the circulation of stolen objects. The fact that provenance research is largely nonexistent in Turkey poses a unique problem for those collecting art and artifacts. Although this lack is often attributed to "belated modernization" and an underdeveloped art market, I propose that missing provenance has to be understood in the context of the politics of dispossession and the role it has played in processes of nation-state building and consolidation in Turkey.

This kind of research has been hampered by the denialist stance of the Turkish state, most clearly pronounced in its denial of the Armenian genocide. But even in instances where concessions are made, the state has thus far avoided taking responsibility. Instead it has classified records as state secrets, "lost" or destroyed them, and downplayed episodes of state violence as aberrations rather than acknowledging their actual structural character. Deepening research into the provenance of art capital would involve scrutinizing land registries and title deeds, an extremely sensitive issue. Access to the respective Ottoman archives has been restricted as a matter of "national security" to shield the Republic of Turkey from far-reaching restitution claims (Üngör and Polatel 2011, x). Yet over the past decade a number of historical studies have emerged that allow us to gauge the scope of dispossession as a vehicle for Turkification (Onaran 2010, Bardakçı 2013). In the face of the immense loss of life and the devastating effects of expulsion, the time has not yet come for artworks. We can, however, begin to trace some of these dynamics that have influenced the art market, the history of collecting, and ultimately the writing of art history under these circumstances.

The massacres and deportations of Armenians and other Christian communities, Assyrians, and Greeks between 1915 and 1917 were accompanied by a concerted and coordinated effort to confiscate their "abandoned" properties. Genocidal violence was veiled through the euphemism of "relocation," and the Committee of Union and Progress (CUP) went to great pains to give the deportations a legal allure. These "highly bureaucratized procedures" were accompanied by the swift enactment of laws that established the Abandoned Property Commission (Emvâl-i Metruke Komisyonu) and the Liquidation Commission (Tasfiye Komisyonu), which kept "detailed registers of the items, properties, and capital that were confiscated from the "deportees," with the claim that they would be returned to them in their "relocated" destinations" (Der Matossian 2011, 3). The historian Bedross Der Matossian argues that the process of confiscating Armenian capital and property needs to be understood in terms of the institutional continuity in the transition from Ottoman Empire to Turkish Republic and be read together with later Turkification measures. Economically formative for the establishment of the Turkish Republic, Turkification was further aided by the wealth tax, instated in 1942. Officially billed as a measure to raise money to close the deficit in the state treasury during World War II, curtail black market activity, and inhibit war profiteering, the actual application of this one-time tax targeted overwhelmingly non-Muslims and those categorized as "crypto-Jews" and "foreigners" (Aktar 2009). In the process of collecting this tax, not only monetary assets but entire households, including goods such as antiquities and artworks, were confiscated by government officials or auctioned off by the owners under duress to meet the levied tax; their whereabouts are not subject to public knowledge today. Those who could not pay were sent to labor battalions. In the aftermath of this episode, many of the remaining non-Muslims, especially members of the Jewish and Rum (Greek) communities, left the country. Another exodus followed after what is generally known as the "events of September 6–7, 1955," a covertly organized pogrom that unleashed a wave of violence during which non-Muslim-owned businesses, along with places of worship and private homes, were ransacked and demolished by "spontaneous mobs" in order to "avenge" the purported bombing of Mustafa Kemal's birth house in Thessalonica. A nonlethal bombing had indeed taken place, but in the yard of the Turkish Consulate. This attack, like the ensuing riots, had been planned and executed by Turkish security forces in order to galvanize public sentiment around the Cyprus issue (Güven 2005). Both episodes, the wealth tax and the 1955 pogrom, albeit protested both within Turkey and from abroad, were legitimized by playing on the old motif that non-Muslims were ultimately "guests" and thus in cahoots with foreign powers in trying to undermine Turkey's sovereignty. Another episode in the Turkification of the economy followed in 1964, once again on the back of the intensifying Cyprus conflict, and once again under İnönü (see Chapter 3). Discarding both the Lausanne Treaty and the 1930 treaty that regulated free movement and trade between Greece and Turkey, the government forcefully expelled around 13,000 Greek Orthodox residents, mainly of Istanbul. They were only allowed to take twenty kilograms of luggage and twenty dollars with them. What happened to the rest of their belongings is mostly unknown today.

Confiscation of capital and property was only one part of the equation, however. As in the case of Nazi Germany, to which I turn later in the chapter, redistribution was the other (Üngör and Polatel 2011, 6). This redistribution created networks that spanned local elites and central authorities, along with special interest groups, economic or otherwise, including Muslim refugees that had been dispossessed and uprooted elsewhere, the Balkans, the Caucasus, and later Greece. Mass violence followed by structural violence forged ties of allegiance and created webs of mutual benefits, dependencies, and indebtedness. It is in this manner—through state-sponsored theft[4]—that successive waves of dispossession became an integral part of Turkish nation-state making. The silence on the connection between genocidal violence and material rewards has been broken—first timidly and then more forcefully—in scholarship on the late Ottoman Empire and Turkey (Buğra 1994; Keyder 1997, 44; Akçam 2004). What I want to emphasize here is that these networks and allegiances signal more than the motivation of economic self-interest and individual enrichment. The complicity in violence, by exertion of force or by benefitting from dispossession, presents, even embodies, an investment into "Turkishness" in terms of belonging and citizenship that simultaneously signals an investment into systematic forgetting. This investment into Turkishness is constantly modulated and reproduced in the form of the myth of the nation-state (Balibar 1991b) and rewarded with citizenship not as a right that is distributed equally but as a privilege predicated on the compliance to forget. The scope of this investment transcends the primary beneficiaries of the dualism of violence and dispossession, stretching to those who profited indirectly from the legacy of mass violence. One such example is the rags-to-riches story of the cotton trader Hacı Ömer Sabanci, founder of the Sabanci conglomerate, which, with its arts space Aksanat (established in 1993), the Sabanci Museum (2002), and regular sponsoring activities, has become one of the big players in Istanbul's art world. Sabanci arrived in Adana in the early 1920s, and despite his modest background found himself in a position to enter the cotton farming businesses, exactly because of the "voids" left by the Turkification of the economy, that is, the killing and expulsion of minority owners (Buğra 1994, 82–86; Üngör and Polatel 2011, 167; Marchand and Perrier 2014, 202–6). We will encounter other examples for the entrenchment of the art world in the politics of dispossession toward the end of this chapter.

Expropriated artworks, along with the confiscation of the property of religious communities, such as churches, monasteries, hospitals, and schools (Polatel et al. 2012), and the disinvestment, ruination, and spoliation of minority sites also meant depriving these communities of the resources of cultural production and reproduction, adding an important symbolic dimension to the practice of dispossession. The restoration of the Armenian Cathedral of the Holy Cross, located on Ahtamar Island in Lake Van, not as a place of worship but a museum under the stewardship of the Ministry of Culture and Tourism and the return of Mor Gabriel to the Assyrian community were both extensively promoted by the government as ostensibly signaling Turkey's "tolerance" toward its non-Muslim citizens. Yet both are problematic in form and scope; they co-opt minority memory rather than framing restitution and memory as questions of (historical) justice.[5] Art sold under duress, expropriated, and "lost," along with the destruction of life, signifies a cultural annihilation that is reflected by the absence of Armenian and other non-Muslim artists in Turkish art history. Together with minority farmlands and businesses, art and antiques, minority collectors, artists, and audiences have been written out of (art) history.[6]

Missing Paintings

Between 1938 and 1942 the Turkish government instated the *Yurt Gezileri* (homeland tours). Artists from the urban centers of Istanbul and Ankara were sent to different Anatolian provinces, predominantly rural areas, where they were supposed to learn about the everyday lives of local populations and act as "transfer bodies" in the modernizing project of the Republic. Ali Avni Çelebi, Zeki Ahmet Kocaman, Refik Ekipman, Nurullah Berk, and Hale Asaf, as well as Cemal Tollu, Abidin Dino, Elif Naci, and Zeki Faik İzer, Bedri Rahmi Eyüboğlu, and Eren Eyüboğlu, were among the participants in this program. Not all of these artists were necessarily in line with the government's predilections; many of them were indeed on the left of the political spectrum. What they shared, however, was the notion that the painting tours provided an opportunity to meet the "real people" of Anatolia. Staying two months or longer, artists were expected to bring six paintings to Ankara. From the recorded 650 paintings produced during these tours only eighty are "available for public view" today (Erol 1998, 72). The fate of the missing paintings is rarely questioned. Artists usually donated some of the paintings produced during their stay to the local branches of the People's Houses that hosted them. Nilüfer Öndin (2003, 172) suggests that many were lost or destroyed in the process of dismantling the People's Houses in 1951. This does not explain, however, how the substantial number of paintings allegedly stored in Ankara disappeared. Some of the artists and art historians that I spoke to suggested that the paintings were discarded because of their "minor artistic quality," a trope that forecloses any discussion on these works. They are regarded as state sanctioned and thus aesthetically corrupt from the outset. It might very well be that the artistic quality of these paintings is questionable or that the Democrat Party regime simply sought to negate the cultural legacy of the Republican People's Party, including its artistic expression. Other interpretations, however, might also warrant attention, especially since many of the artists in question were well respected then and today are deemed representatives of "Turkish" classic modernism, scoring considerable prices at national and, more recently, international auctions.

Take the example of the painter Hulusi Mercan. Returning from Tunceli (Dersim) in 1943, Mercan was faced with an official interrogation regarding one of his paintings with the title *Tezek* (dried cow dung), a multipurpose material extensively used in the village where he stayed. His interrogation suggests that while the proposed goal of these painting tours was to capture the "everyday life of the people," the subject chosen by Mercan was not really what the government had in mind. It seems that cow dung did not render itself to the governmental discourse of development, even contradicted it. From 1937 to 1938, Mercan's destination had seen a horrific wave of genocidal violence executed by the Turkish military against the local Kurdish (Zaza-Alevi) population, including forced adoptions, deportations, and resettlement measures that have marked the region to this day (van Bruinessen 1994). Given this background, the government was likely to have questions regarding Mercan's observations in the region, even if these atrocities were not reflected directly in his artwork. Similarly, the experience of Avni Arbaş, who was on a painting tour in 1942 in Siirt, a province in southeastern Turkey inhabited by Kurds, Arabs, and Turks, suggests that it was not always, or not only, the art produced but also the artists' observations during their sojourns that presented a potential problem. Many artists' experiences neither reflected the promised development nor the rural embrace of the republic so central to national discourses at the time. That there was tight government control over the written correspondence of the painting tour participants becomes clear in Arbaş's autobiography, where he notes that none of his letters describing impressions from his painting tour had made it to their addressees. He proposes that they must all have gotten lost or fallen prey to censorship (Ural 1998, 21–23). Another set of paintings that is lost to this day is Abidin Dino's *ibrik* series, which was dedicated to the long-spouted water pitcher used for water storage and transport. Just as Mercan's interest was piqued by cow dung, Dino became preoccupied with this tool of everyday life during his painting tour in Balıkesir in 1939 (Aköz 2004). Neither government officials nor art critics, such as İsmail Hakkı Baltacıoğlu (Erol 1998, 56), were too pleased with the paintings, which, again, failed to represent or—in their opinion—even unduly distorted the modernization efforts that the political establishment wished to project.

Curating Modernity from a Private Collection

The politics of forgetting are not confined to state institutions but play out in the newly founded private museums as well. Upon the request of Prime Minister Erdoğan, who was instrumental in securing the site for the museum, the Istanbul Modern opened in December 2004, coinciding with Turkey's EU accession negotiations. Relying mainly on the private collection of the chair of the board of directors, Oya Eczacıbaşı, and her husband, Bülent, the permanent exhibition was supplemented by loans from Bülent's father, Nejat Eczacıbaşı, as well as from the Nejat Eczacıbaşı Foundation. The entrance floor that houses this permanent exhibition was shortly thereafter joined by a downstairs area for temporary exhibitions, a library, and a screening room. The initial display of the permanent exhibition, shown under the title *Observation/Interpretation/Multiplicity*, did not explicitly claim to represent the history of modern painting in Turkey, nor was it organized chronologically. Still, many artists, curators, and critics had an impression to the contrary, given that the museum's name suggested it to be a reflection of the modern (city) rather than of the personal taste of a particular pool of collectors.[7] This perception was fortified by the timeline of the inaugural exhibition, which spanned the twentieth century until the early 1980s, and a curatorial statement that described the exhibition as "provid[ing] a chance to learn, explore, and feel one of the most important elements of modern Turkish art" (Akay et al. 2004, 16). When I raised the question of representation to Levent Çalıkoğlu, who co-curated the show with Ali Akay and Haşim Nur Gürel, he answered: "Just because the museum is called Istanbul Modern does not mean that we present a genealogy of modern art. That's why we suggested a thematic organization. We never claimed that we could do a historical overview." This did not really answer why the exhibition claimed to review the "most important elements of modern Turkish art." Pressed further, Çalıkoğlu stated that the criticism was to be expected when curating mostly out of a family collection and that he too wished that they could have included works from other private and institutional collections as originally planned. These, however, withdrew despite initial interest, most probably because they were planning to establish their own art spaces. Toward the end of our conversation, Çalıkoğlu suggested that the educational, cultivating impact of the Istanbul Modern on "Turkish audiences" might, under the given circumstances, trump the question of curatorial integrity. "Look, what we are doing here is basically educating the audience; this is what you have to take into consideration. Otherwise, these discussions are rather snobbish and unrealistic. . . . Of course, there can and should be criticism, but this museum is a beginning. Up to 2,500 persons visit the museum per day. I see this as a success. Of course, it is a very problematic institution. I myself acknowledged that, and this is why I only acted as the director for one month, when it was first opened."[8]

The narrative of "the modern" presented by the Istanbul Modern bears the danger of canonization, although the selection criteria for the displayed works partly lie outside of art historical considerations and are driven by other factors, such as availability. The selection criteria index dependencies that remain veiled in the everyday operations of museums. While the display of the Istanbul Modern's permanent collection has since changed multiple times and has been supplemented regularly with new acquisitions and gifts to the museum collection by the Eczacıbaşıs themselves, other questions have persisted. Among them is the discussion whether the Istanbul Modern is a public or a private institution and what these possibilities mean in terms of its mission—but more on that in a moment.

One issue that caught my attention repeatedly in the early of the Istanbul Modern was that the sociopolitical or historical context of the exhibitions and artworks was never addressed, or only in a highly selective fashion. This was particularly striking during a retrospective of Fikret Muallâ (1903–1967) in 2005. The accompanying texts focused solely on the painter's psychological state: a childhood injury that had left his right foot crippled, the early loss of his mother, his alcoholism, the loneliness he experienced in Paris, and his unrequited love for various women. Mentioned in passing was his "fear of the police" while still in Turkey, as he had been arrested in a "misunderstanding" and badly beaten while under custody. That Mualla had been an associate of the writer and poet Nâzım Hikmet, who was persecuted for "communist activities," and that torture was widespread in the case of political prisoners, then as for decades to come, was not noted anywhere. When I addressed this lack of political context in an interview with Ali Akay, who co-curated this exhibition once again with Çalıkoğlu and Gürel, his answer was stern: "These are things that people can read in books." Akay's assertion contradicts, or rather reduces, the educational impetus described by Çalıkoğlu to "purely" aesthetical matters. It is underwritten by discourses on Turkey's belatedness—in this case the belated cultivation of audiences—that are employed at strategically opportune points. Here, the interdependency between state and private institutions has created indebtedness to the state that creates blind spots and helps perpetuate official narratives as the mediating trope of "the greater good" propels a specific kind of forgetting.

In the course of my fieldwork, the Istanbul Modern has repeatedly shied away from political issues when composing Turkey-related shows. While the different modalities of censorship will be taken up in the next chapter, I want to point out that silencing mechanisms in private institutions are often less visible and harder to trace than those enacted by the state. The art historian Wendy Shaw, who had worked with the Istanbul Modern museum as a curatorial consultant in 2006–2007, for instance, recounted that the administration had asked that the word "Kurd" and its permutations be struck from exhibition texts (this was corroborated by an artist who preferred to remain anonymous). One could argue that much has changed since then and that with the beginning of the official "peace process" in 2013 not just the term "Kurd" but the expression "Kurdistan" has—or had—been decriminalized. The principle, however, remains the same. While there is a division of labor between state and private institutions in the day-to-day operations of the art world (Chapter 3), there is unity when it comes to official discourses.

The art historian Ali Artun (2008) has been one of the most forceful critics of the Istanbul Modern and other private arts organizations. Like the museums and galleries of banks and corporations, the Istanbul Modern presents itself as a public institution, but in contrast to most it is located on public land and has received logistical support from the state. The family collection gains value through public subsidies while also retaining administrative (and artistic) control over the museum it established. Once more referring to the motif of belatedness, Artun suggested that these types of imbalances arise from the weak or missing institutionalization of art in Turkey (see Pieprzak 2010 for similar discussions in postcolonial Morocco). Another reading is possible. I would suggest that institutions such as the Istanbul Modern are actually rather strong, strong enough to enact these types of obscurations so vital to official history. Alternatively, we can also understand the Istanbul Modern as a showcase for the institutional dependency between the state and private institutions. Private museums, cultural centers, and galleries that are part of banks, founded directly by corporations or industrial families, tend to have rather close ties to the state and exhibit less openly critical stances. In contrast, not only independent spaces but some personnel working at the Istanbul Painting and Sculpture Museum, who are notably themselves artists who have taken up civil service to support their artistic work, are frequently more outspoken. As the sociologist Sibel Yardımcı (2005, 105–13) shows, the Eczacıbaşı family, who has also founded the Istanbul Foundation for Culture and the Arts (İstanbul Kültür Sanat Vakfı, IKSV), has demonstrated its allegiance with the state by extensively citing Mustafa Kemal up until the 2000s in their catalogues for the Istanbul Festivals and has frequently invited state officials and military figures to their symposia on cultural policy. But the relationship between the state and the Eczacıbaşı family goes beyond the advent of what is called Kemalism. Before the occupation of his native Smyrna (Izmir) by Greek forces, Süleyman Ferit Eczacıbaşı (1885–1973), Nejat's father, was close to the Kuvâ-yi Milliye (nationalist militia forces) and later supported the Committee of Union and Progress and especially their cultural Turkification measures (Dündar 2003, 25). As Ayşe Buğra (1994) documents, the relationship of the family with the state structure has flourished throughout decades and changing regimes, and the Eczacıbaşı's economic standing today thus cannot be thought apart from these alignments.

"Not without My Nazi"

In an article entitled "Not without My Nazi,"[9] Norbert Seitz (2002) dwells on the sensationalism that inevitably accompanies the discovery of formerly unknown facts about Nazi Germany, be it biographical details of public figures (Günther Grass's short stint at the Waffen-SS and Jürgen Habermas's membership in the Hitler Youth, both revealed in the 2000s, come to mind) or political or economic continuities. Seitz wonders about the persistence of the pattern of shock, scandalization, and reestablishing forgetfulness, given the pronounced "culture of remembrance" in Germany. According to Aleida Assmann and Ute Frevert (1999), this culture of remembrance emerged after a period marked by silence and forgetting (*Vergessenheit*) in the Federal Republic and the antifascist obsession (*Versessenheit*) in East Germany. The German unification, in turn, produced a "relatively homogenous collective memory" and, I should add, shared blind spots.

Indeed, the wide-ranging engagement with the difficult past of the Third Reich in Germany is to some extent unparalleled in its scope. Yet the periodic revelations Seitz points to are reminders that neither denazification nor the official project of facing the past have been as thorough as generally projected. Recent interventions have, for example, highlighted the incomplete denazification of German legislation, which prevented many Nazi perpetrators from being convicted, as they were tried under National Socialist rather than federal law (Perels 2006). Other confrontations, too, have proceeded more timidly, like inquiries into the violent entanglements of Germany's colonial past and Nazi policies and personnel, the role of German anthropology in the Third Reich (Gerndt 1987), and the involvement of Rudolf von Laban, the "founder of modern dance in Germany," in the shaping of National Socialist cultural policies (Kant 2004). Denazification in the art world was uneven, perhaps more so than in other institutional settings (e.g., see Monod 2005), despite the fact that the legacy of the Third Reich has been formative for Germany's contemporary cultural policies. *Vergangenheitsaufarbeitung* or *Vergangenheitsbewältigung*,[10] that is, facing or mastering the Nazi past, have not only been central themes in scholarship on Germany and German politics. The experience of the Third Reich has substantially shaped cultural production: memoirs, novels, films, monuments, and artworks too numerous to be discussed here. Instead, I want to focus on the curious tension that arises between the selectivity of memory on the one hand and the wide-ranging memorialization of Nazi atrocities on the other. This tension has created notable blind spots regarding the continued impact of National Socialist arts policies on the configuration of public and private art collections, museum politics, and the writing of art history. The aestheticization of politics that Benjamin diagnosed for fascism at the end of his "The Work of Art in the Age of Mechanical Reproduction" (1936) translated into specific kinds of monumental architecture, public ritual, and National Socialist symbolism. It also translated into claiming ownership of significant works of art. For the Third Reich, art did not simply legitimize power or function as an instrument of propaganda. Art was the incarnation of power itself: Hegemony over the aesthetic realm was equated with sovereignty, and the possession of "great works of art" expressed moral—and racial—superiority. It is in this manner that artworks became part of the larger politics of expropriation with which the Nazi regime sustained itself and its violent expansion. The dispossession of "cultural goods" was legally solidified in 1938 and coordinated by a special taskforce named after and led by Alfred Rosenberg (Einsatzgruppe Reichsleiter Rosenberg), one of the Nazi Party's chief ideologues and from 1941 onward minister for the "Occupied Eastern Territories." The confiscation of art facilitated by the Nazi regime in Germany had three pillars: The first consisted of the purge of "degenerate art"[11] from public museums. The second rested on the expropriation of Jewish collectors in Germany either by outright confiscation or through sale under duress and hence under market value. Monies from these sales were used to cover the cost of emigration (in the form of the so-called flight tax) or of punitive taxes imposed by the German state on its Jewish citizens. Third, confiscated works were incorporated into state collections, sold for foreign currency to fill the war coffers of the National Socialist regime, or simply misappropriated into the personal collections of Nazi cadres.[12] In the occupied territories, the expropriation of museum collections and the dispossession of Jewish collectors worked along a similar logic, aiming at locating art that would bolster German inventories. Each military invasion was planned alongside such confiscation procedures, making the "protection," appropriation, and transfer of art to the German heartland integral to the reordering of Europe under Nazi rule (Engel 2003, 431; Nicholas 1994; Petropoulos 1996; Feliciano 1998). Just as in imperial Germany's maxim "no power politics without cultural policy" (see Chapter 3), military might anchored itself once more in art. But this time, delusions of "racial superiority" merged with the desire to produce and possess certain artworks. The Thousand-Year Reich, this much was clear, would depend on it.[13]

A number of high-profile restitutions of Nazi-looted art have been celebrated, such as the return of Gustav Klimt's portrait of Adele Bloch-Bauer from the Austrian State Gallery, a case that has been captured on celluloid numerous times.[14] The same is true for the Monuments Men, the military unit charged with protecting cultural heritage in the European war theater, which also created the basis for restitution by securing art depots in which the Nazis had hidden their treasure from the aerial bombings of approaching Allied forces. Their mission is described as nothing less than saving "the greatest cultural and artistic achievements of civilization."[15] Yet periodic finds of Nazi-looted art continue to rock the art world. One such discovery was made 2012 at the Munich home of Cornelius Gurlitt. The 1,400 works in his possession had been amassed by his father, the art dealer Hildebrand Gurlitt, whose career in the Third Reich was not without contradictions. Finding himself an outcast because of a Jewish grandmother on his father's side, and as a former museum director who had supported modernist painters, he was branded an "art bolshevist" (*Kunstbolschewist*) from 1933 onward. In an unexpected turn, Gurlitt's services were then required by the führer. Hitler was seeking an experienced art dealer to locate artworks for his vanity project, a German art museum in his hometown, Linz. This position afforded Gurlitt privileges in buying artworks sold under duress. In addition, friends—collectors and artists—hoping to save their now "degenerate" artworks from the Nazis, entrusted him with their care. Failing to return these works after the war, the Gurlitts supported themselves by selling them off, piece by piece, over decades.

A closer look beyond the headlines of these sensationalized finds reveals that since the end of World War II a large web of actors has worked to make the trade in Nazi-looted art an extremely lucrative business. This web spans former Nazi functionaries, national and international auction houses, art dealers, galleries, and museums and stretches to former members of the Protestant Art Service,[16] art appraisers, and art historians, who have continued to profit from what has been labeled "the biggest art theft in history" (Koldehoff 2014, Tatzkow and Schnabel 2008). The German state and many national and international arts institutions long turned a blind eye to these issues and could do so not least because the 1938 law that regulated the confiscation of artworks has never been revoked. Germany has signed both the Washington (1998) and the Berlin Declarations (1999), both of which suggest guidelines for restitution but are not legally binding. It was only in the trail of the Gurlitt scandal that substantial funds were earmarked for provenance research at German state museums in order to investigate if they had Nazi-looted art in their holdings.

Within this legal void, indemnification[17] has been presented as a moral imperative, and art restitution, like restitution overall, is understood as "justice, [that] is in part, a form of remembrance" (Booth 2001, 777; Levy and Sznaider 2006; see also Slyomovics 2012). These artworks were not just stolen, not subject to a simple heist, but were part of a willful and highly organized system of dispossession facilitated by mass murder. They were part of the material basis of the dehumanization that made genocide possible. This, however, is not just an issue of the past. National Socialist cultural and economic policies continue to shape present-day practices of collecting and exhibiting art, and I will illustrate this through a discussion of the controversies over two collections, one a temporary, the other a permanent loan to the Hamburger Bahnhof Museum in Berlin.

"Dirty Money": The Flick Collection and the Hamburger Bahnhof

> The enormous amount of money required to build an art collection, be it the old masters or contemporary art, needs to be earned first. And the way in which it is earned is never clean.
>
> Brigitte Werneburg, Berlin, 2006

Long before Friedrich Christian Flick made headlines by seeking a home for his collection, the German tabloids were fascinated by his jet-set lifestyle, supported by his multimillion deutschmark inheritance from the Flick conglomerate. Founded by his grandfather Friedrich Karl (1883–1972), the Flick empire began with steel and expanded to coal. Once Flick senior ventured into the business of transportation in the early 1930s, he was well positioned for the rearmament contracts of the Nazi regime that would soon come to power. Donating to the National Socialist party, he quickly became Germany's largest weapons producer (Kessen 2004, 56) and was inducted into the Freundeskreis Reichsführer SS. This circle of "friends," consisting of businessmen around Heinrich Himmler, received preferential treatment for government contracts and was the main benefactor of "aryanization" procedures, that is, the expropriation of Jewish-owned businesses and the redistribution of their assets (Stallbaumer 1995; Hayes 1998, 13). In 1947, Flick was put on trial in Nuremberg. The charges revealed that in addition to profiting from the war of aggression waged by the Nazis, he had enriched himself by exploiting 48,000 forced laborers, mostly Eastern European Jews. He was sentenced to seven years of imprisonment, of which he only completed three—thanks to the amnesty enacted by the American occupation forces, soon more concerned with Cold War power constellations than with the National Socialist legacy of the German industries. While still in prison, Flick largely managed to circumvent the Allied decartelization directives. Voided by Chancellor Adenauer in 1951, they presented another concession of the Allied forces in favor of the German economic miracle (*Wirtschaftswunder*), regarded as a bulwark against communism. During his lifetime, Flick refused to pay the 5 million DM compensation, amounting to 2,000 DM per surviving—and eligible—forced laborer, that his representatives had negotiated with the Jewish Claims Conference (Kessen 2004, 81). The charges at Nuremberg and his refusal to pay compensation notwithstanding, Flick was awarded the Great Federal Cross of Merit (the only federal German state honor) for his accomplishments in advancing the German industries. Still, scandal followed the Flicks, as it became known that both the company and the family had been engaged in a tax-fraud scheme aided by a network of bribed politicians in the early 1980s. The theme of tax evasion has remained with the family ever since: Some Flick heirs took on Austrian nationality to enjoy tax advantages while continuing to profit from their German investments. His grandson, Friedrich Christian Flick, has long taken up residence in the tax haven of Switzerland for the same reason.

Friedrich Christian Flick maintains that he began to collect old masters in the late 1970s and ventured into contemporary art in the mid-1980s (Frehner and Steiner 2001). Independent researchers, however, posit that he only turned to contemporary art in 1995 and within five years amassed 2,500 works of art, among them entire series by Bruce Nauman and Martin Kippenberger (Kessen 2004, Werneburg 2004). When news of his "bulk purchases" emerged, many commentators suspected that Flick was seeking to "whitewash" his fortune and distance himself from his unflattering image as a "spoiled party boy" by turning himself into a patron of the arts. Indeed, Flick himself went on record proclaiming that he wanted to change the public perception of his family name and counteract persisting Nazi connotations. In a 1997 letter to his uncle, Flick stated that "the art collection will give my children and descendants a constructive and meaningful possibility to build a new identification with our name" (cited in Ramge 2004, 265–66). To achieve this, however, the collection needed to be shown in public. Flick offered it to his hometown of Zurich. But the city's authorities declined, shying away from anticipated controversy. During the three years that he co-managed the company, Flick—like his grandfather and father—had refused to pay into the compensation fund and turned down requests to donate into the forced labor fund from his personal fortune. The topic had gained renewed urgency when with the fall of the Iron Curtain former forced laborers residing in Eastern Europe had become eligible for compensation payments. Predominantly living in impoverished conditions and suffering from the long-term health issues incurred during the hard labor and exposure to chemicals used in the production of hand grenades, for instance, they were in dire need of financial assistance.[18]

Flick saw himself confronted with the situation of having 2,500 artworks and nowhere to show them. According to the research of the Berlin-based artists Renata Stih and Frieder Schnock, help came in the form of Flick's financial advisor, Eberhard von Koerber, a board member of the Association of Arts and Culture of the German Economy (Kulturkreis der deutschen Wirtschaft), which we have already encountered in previous chapters. Koerber was also a close friend of then chancellor Gerhard Schröder, and together they came up with the plan to bring the collection to Berlin, to the Hamburger Bahnhof Museum.

When news of the impending arrangement between Flick and the Hamburger Bahnhof, facilitated by people in high places, surfaced, Stih and Schnock felt that the issue needed to be addressed from within the art world, and they created artistic interventions "to draw attention to the fact that the Nazi heirs basically still run the country" and "that the Flick conglomerate never investigated its history during the Third Reich."[19] Frieder Schnock explained their assessment of the Flick loan further by saying, "A tax evader lets his collection be shown in Germany, subsidized by public institutions, leaving them with even less money for other projects. The lender is a limited company registered in the tax haven of Guernsey." Indeed, Flick does not officially own the works but buys, lends, and sells them through his company Contemporary Art Ltd. This fact alone, as Stih interjected, should have foreclosed any legal arrangements between Flick, the city of Berlin, and the state museum because it violates EU guidelines. Both Stih and Schnock emphasized that they had no doubts that Flick's primary goal was to enhance the value of his collection by exhibiting it in a public institution.

In trying to secure funding for their intervention, Stih and Schnock presented a proposal to the New Society for Visual Arts (neue Gesellschaft für bildende Kunst, nGbK), a grassroots arts organization composed of artists, critics, curators, and other art world actors.[20] They had to move carefully, however, since the grants administered by the nGbK are financed by the national lottery. The committee of this funding body, in turn, comprised some of the very same politicians who had signed off on the "secret contract" detailing Flick's loan to the city. Schnock recounts: "We gave our proposal the codename 'The White Knight,' a term used for the candidate of choice [*Wunschkandidat*] designated to take over an ailing business in order to rescue it, as a stand-in for the big collector who was now poised to save Berlin's debilitated art scene."

Stih and Schnock's project consisted of two parts: a publication entitled *The Art of Collecting*, chronicling the controversies surrounding the Flick fortune and collection, and the posters depicted in Figures 12 and 13. Using billboards, they turned the notion of advertising on its head and displayed them in the vicinity of the Hamburger Bahnhof and throughout the city, including in front of the Chancellery.[21]

Not everyone was enthused by the project. Even then nGbK directorate is said to have feared risks for future collaborations with the city and other state institutions. Such trepidations highlight once again the very real interdependency between art and power, an interdependency that is unsettling to idealized understandings of art yet affects the art world on a daily basis (see Chapter 2). The Hamburger Bahnhof was not pleased either—although Stih and Schnock found allies within the institution, too. "Flick himself," Stih said, "did not try to intervene against our project because this would have outed him as an enemy of art [*Kunstfeind*]. Thus, it was vital for us in this case that our work was perceived as art."

The public discussion became more heated when the weekly *Der Spiegel* ran images of the posters by Stih and Schnock in an article on the Flick loan. Chancellor Schröder, compelled to take a stance, noted in his opening speech for the first Flick exhibition in September 2004: "Art, to be sure, is not a

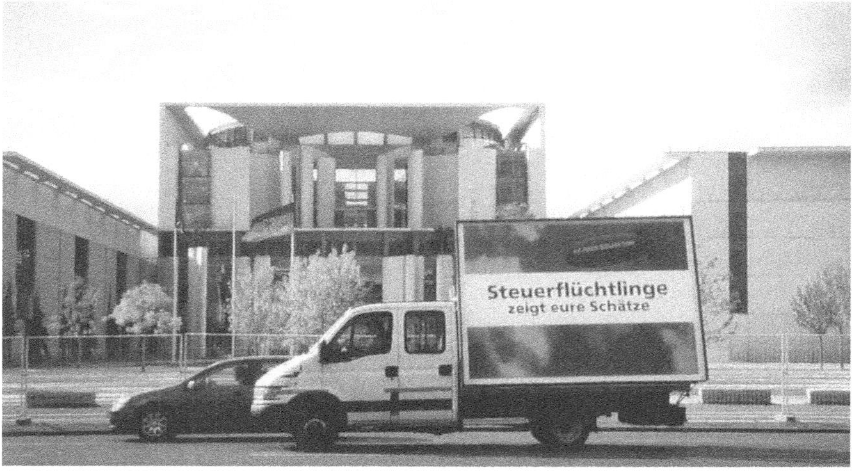

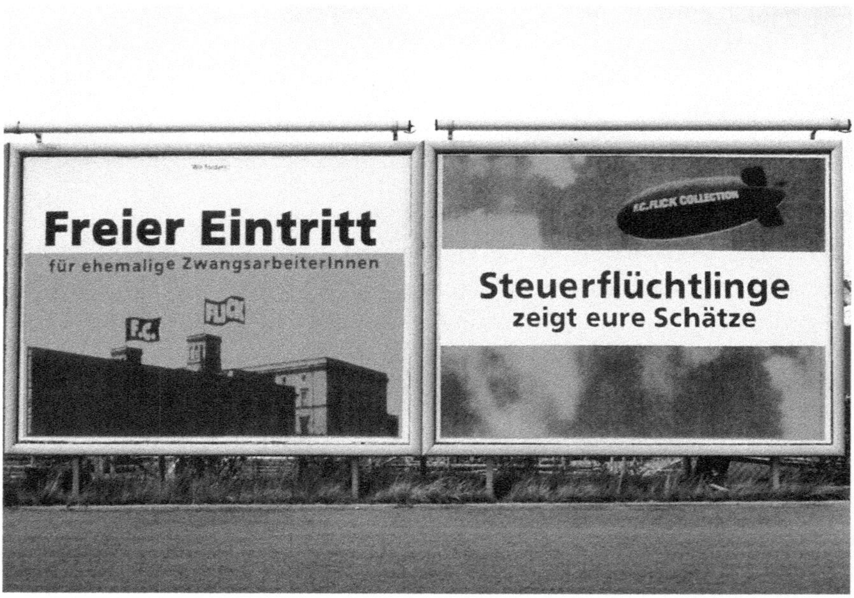

Figures 12 and 13. *Tax Evaders Show Your Treasures*, in front of the Chancellery in Berlin, 2004; and *We Demand: Free Admittance for Former Forced Laborers*, located on Invalidenstrasse, close to the Hamburger Bahnhof. Renata Stih & Frieder Schnock, *The Art of Collecting—Flick in Berlin*, 2004, © VG Bild-Kunst Bonn/Berlin, ARS NYC.

monument [*Mahnmal*]. . . . We would punish people if we were not to show this collection."[22] Schröder's statement is notable because it negates the importance given to art as a vehicle for remembrance in German cultural policy. Art's capacity for memory work has been so often praised in other contexts within and without Germany, including the long debates surrounding the central Memorial to the Murdered Jews of Europe (Kramer 1996, 282–92; Till 2005; see also Macdonald 2009). Instead, he retreated to a position in which art is independent of the conditions of its accumulation and presentation. He glossed over the fact that indemnification has been tied to an imperative to remember and cemented in policy measures as much as in artistic production. Schröder misconstrued the critical interrogation of the conditions of how art circulates, of how it is entrenched in difficult pasts of state violence, by equating such interrogations with depriving the public of historically important works. Just as in the case of the Istanbul Modern, the mediating trope of "the greater good" is used once more to propel forgetting.

Peter-Klaus Schuster, the director of the Berlin State Museums at the time, came forward to argue that the Flick collection presented an invaluable opportunity that—evidence to the contrary—"won't cost the city a cent" and proposed that Flick should be commended for dedicating himself to art that would have been "burned in Nazi times" (Kessen 2004, 119). As the art critic Brigitte Wernerburg maintained during our interview, the installation of the first exhibition from the Flick collection alone cost the city around 144,000 euros, including travel, accommodation, and honoraria for the exhibited artists and their assistants. In an effort to divert public attention from the costs of the Flick deal and deproblematize its assemblage, Undersecretary for Culture and Media Christina Weiss, too, resorted to highlighting the aesthetic positions of the exhibited works, noting that Martin Kippenberger and Bruce Nauman criticized the dehumanizing conditions of the modern world and thus were helping heal the wounds of Nazism (Goehler 2006, 216).

The original contract of the Flick loan, it seems, allowed Flick to sell off works from the collection at the Hamburger Bahnhof and to add new acquisitions as he saw fit. This also seems to be the case for the ten-year extension of the loan, signed in 2011. While the debates were raging, Flick stood firm on this position on forced labor compensation. He did, however, establish a foundation in his name in Potsdam with the mission to fight "racism, xenophobia, and intolerance," in order to build "something for the future, rather than the past." Eight months after the opening, Flick changed his stance unexpectedly and paid into the forced labor fund. "Of course, we can't help but think that we have contributed to Flick's change of heart," Schnock remarked humorously. Stih added: "The pressure really came from New York, where people said, 'If you do not pay into this fund you will not sell a single picture here again.'" In 2007, Flick donated a series of works to the museum as a show of good form and as a move to foreclose further criticism.

Why has there been so little attention given to the relationship between private art collections and National Socialist economic policies, especially given that other aspects of the Nazi reign have been so well exposed? One of the reasons might be found in the historian Götz Aly's study *Hitler's Beneficiaries* (2005). Aly argues against the dichotomous conceptualization of Nazi perpetrators and those to whom the regime was "merely" a matter of convenience rather than ideological alignment. Instead, he suggests that the systematic dispossession of Jews (and others deemed unwanted) in Germany and the occupied territories supported not only the war machinery and the Nazi welfare state but also ensured that broader segments of society could partake in middle-class consumption on the basis of confiscated goods and living quarters.[23] In his opinion, this mass entanglement in redistributed property accounts for the selective memory regarding the longitudinal impact of Nazi economic policies. Like in the case of Turkey, dispossession facilitated an investment into systematic forgetting. Art capital, that is, monies used to establish art collections (or arts institutions), and actual artworks were part of these processes of dispossession and redistribution, and it is in this manner that dispossessed artworks index something beyond their aesthetic positions. They reference genocide and large-scale structural violence that has made their accumulation possible and shaped their circulation in a way that fundamentally opposes idealized understandings of how art should be sold, bought, presented, and safeguarded. Making visible the complex interrelations between art and the Nazi regime's politics of dispossessions, slave labor, and war profiteering, Stih and Schnock's intervention troubled the discourses of the Flick Collection as benefiting the city of Berlin. It showed that the mediating discourse of "the greater good" is predicated on a decivilizing moment. Their billboards brought these entanglements both discursively and literally (in terms of physical proximity) to the German state, the Chancellery, and the Hamburger Bahnhof.

Given these wide-ranging entanglements and layers of complicity, it may come to little surprise that David R. Litchfield's chronicle of the Thyssen family's rise to fortune and nobility, which was substantially aided by their role in the Third Reich, mostly gained public attention because of a short episode presented in his *The Thyssen Art Macabre* (2006). Litchfield suggests that the sister of the prolific art collector Hans Heinrich "Heini" Thyssen-Bornemisza, Margit Batthyány, was present at the execution of two hundred Jewish forced laborers at her castle in Reichnitz, Austria. According to Litchfield, the massacre was the "grand finale" to a last dinner party hosted by Batthyány before fleeing the immanent arrival of Allied troops. The details of this episode are gruesome, to say the least, and the loss of life deserves attention beyond the sensationalist take outlined by Seitz at the beginning of this chapter. Little discussed, however, was that the art collection that continues to bear the Thyssen family name was expanded significantly by Thyssen senior from the late 1920s till the end of World War II. It features works of missing provenance and others that were bought cheaply from Jewish collectors under duress in the Nazi era. The obituary of the German press agency (DPA) on Hans-Heinrich Thyssen-Bornemisza on April 28, 2002, read, "A great collector is dead." No mention of the controversies surrounding the collection, controversies that were well known even before Litchfield's book appeared. Silence on what he owed his fortune to and on the circumstances that brought the collection to Madrid,[24] where it remains a major tourist destination after Thyssen-Bornemisza sold it to the Spanish state in 1993. Not even an allusion to the connection between the activities of the "great collector" and the politics of Nazi dispossession and how they continue to put their mark on the political economy of art, of museums, and private collections in contemporary Germany. Yet as I learned during my fieldwork, it is exactly this legacy that made the Flick Collection desirable for Berlin in the first place. As Germany has up until recently struggled to reacquire the purged modernist artworks for its public museums, the presentation of contemporary art has mainly been shouldered by private collectors, some of whom are heirs to Nazi fortunes. This dynamic was masked by Schröder and others. Their repeated references to the critical potential of art perpetuated the silences about these decivilizing processes. Other aspects of this dynamic will become clearer when turning to another collection housed by the Hamburger Bahnhof, that of Erich Marx.

A Marriage of Convenience? The Marx Collection at the Hamburger Bahnhof

The Hamburger Bahnhof, by self-description, is a museum for current art (*aktuelle Kunst*) and focuses on works from the 1960s onward. It is part of Berlin's national gallery network, which comprises four main institutions: the Alte Nationalgalerie, housing a nineteenth-century collection; the Neue Nationalgalerie, featuring classic works of modern art; the Collection Berggruen; and the Hamburger Bahnhof—all of which are under the umbrella of the Prussian Cultural Heritage Foundation.[25] While the Alte Nationalgalerie reopened as early as 1949—its collection mainly intact, since the Nazis had not found it objectionable—other public museums in Berlin and throughout the country found themselves confronted with a situation in which modern art had been largely expunged from Germany. When the Neue Nationalgalerie was founded, the objective became the so-called resupply (*Nachkauf*) of artworks from this lost period. Intimately related to Germany's struggle to establish itself as part of the "West," its quest for "normalization" in the post–World War II era (see Chapter 1), this process has been marked by obscurity. Here, normalization once more does not simply signal a disavowal of the past but a disavowal of how decivilizing episodes in German history continue to shape the present. Although the term "resupply" suggests a simple reacquisition of modernist art, of merely bringing back what once was there, very little is known about how modernism was (re)constituted in Germany, that is, how decisions were made about which works to buy and integrate into state collections.[26]

As Britta Schmitz, senior curator at the Hamburger Bahnhof, explained, the strategy of "resupply" dominated the 1970s and 1980s, leaving contemporary art on the sidelines. In the late 1980s, the Neue Nationalgalerie was finally at a point to venture into current art. Although the museum could do so only on a financially modest scale, it became evident that its space was too small to accommodate new acquisitions. At the time, the Berlin-based entrepreneur Erich Marx, a real estate developer, owner of a chain of rehabilitation clinics, and avid collector of Andy Warhol, Cy Twombly, Anselm Kiefer, and Joseph Beuys, offered his collection as a permanent loan to the state of Berlin. His art dealer, Heiner Bastian, facilitated advantageous connections for Marx in Berlin's art world, putting him on the board of a number of museums. In addition, Marx's business ventures provided him with an extensive political network. The Berlin Senate, seeing this offer as a match of great convenience and a fortuitous opportunity to fill significant gaps in its emergent collection of contemporary art, not only accepted the offer but made the integration of the Marx collection a precondition for establishing the Hamburger Bahnhof. Schmitz mentioned that some commentators feared early on that the power couple might highjack the museum's agenda. According to Stih and Schnock, the Flick controversy raised awareness that the conditions of the Marx loan had never been made public in their entirety. What is known is that Marx stipulated his collection to be part of the permanent display, with rotating shows curated out of its holdings by Bastian. This has left "the museum's own, if modest, collection a bit marginalized, not least because the Marx Collection occupies the largest rooms in the museum," Schmitz remarked.[27] Just as in the case of the Istanbul Modern, the Marx collection at the Hamburger Bahnhof bears the danger of canonizing private tastes.

The tensions surrounding the Marx Collection are exemplary for the interdependencies and antagonisms between public museums and private collectors. In Germany, these tensions are compounded by the fact that the resupply of modern art, along with successive austerity measures over the last three decades, has significantly limited museums' abilities to extend and update their collections. Individual collectors are interested in having "their" works shown in museums for several reasons: Loan agreements defray storage and insurance costs, entail tax breaks for collectors, and increase the value of exhibited works. Storage and insurance tend to be costly endeavors, and tax breaks are granted because loans to museums are classified as *gemeinnützig*—that is, serving the public good—and hence as charitable giving. It is notable that this dynamic has only very recently come into discussions in Germany (Graw 2008). Neither have ethnographic and sociological approaches to the art world (Becker 1982, Plattner 1996) addressed this interplay, although all of these works—just as institutional theories of art (Danto 1964, Fraser 1985)—note how important it is for visual artists to be exhibited in museums, both for gaining professional *renommé* and for achieving higher prices in the art market. In addition, a museum presence enhances artists' chances in the global grants economy, which has become a vital subsistence strategy for many. Despite the often-cited rise of the art market, museums retain much of their sanctioning power. However, as Schmitz diagnosed, the balance has tipped in favor of big collectors, who have the necessary financial means to buy large-scale installations and outbid museums in the secondary markets. While much of this dynamic is also at work outside Germany, it is important to keep in mind that the legacy of the Third Reich further circumscribes the power differentials between public museums and private collections. Less gory and sensational then the fallouts of Nazi-looted assets, this dynamic nonetheless presents another facet of the decivilizing aspect of art. It is unsettling in its own right, as museum politics continually veil the actual conditions under which artworks are accumulated and exhibited. These interdependencies and their manifestations, if often quietly, counteract the mediating discourse of art as a "greater good." They frame the perception of artworks, determine what kind of art is available to the public and even how it is displayed—and thus shape the writing of art history.

Deviation from the Modern Paradigm: The "Other" German Art

In 1999, when Weimar acted as the European Capital of Culture, the Weimar State Museum organized an exhibition entitled *The Rise and Fall of the Modern*. The show was divided into three sections. The first, according to its curator Achim Preiß (1999, 10), featured "academic conservative art" of the early twentieth century. The second focused on Nazi-sanctioned image production, mainly paintings that emerged between 1933 and 1945, including works from Adolf Hitler's private collection, displayed for the first time in postwar Germany. The final section was dedicated to East German artworks as representations of socialist realism, covering the post–World War II period up until Germany's reunification.[28]

In her review of the exhibition and the protests it elicited, the anthropologist Barbara Wolbert (2001, 57–58) remarks that the very location of Weimar made the show a loaded event from the get-go: "Weimar, home to Schiller and Goethe, founding place of the first German Republic, and the town in walking distance from the concentration camp Buchenwald, is itself a politically vexing place." While the artworks from the early twentieth century were properly framed and mounted on the walls, the paintings from Hitler's private collection were arranged as if they were in an art depot, with paintings resting against boards arranged on the floor. The artworks from the German Democratic Republic were similarly presented.[29] In addition, the latter were either unframed and shown with their original trimmings or framed with heavy unfinished wood. Resting on the concrete floor, they appeared as if they had just been taken down. This last part of the exhibition, Wolbert argues, left East German visitors (that is, former GDR citizens) with the impression that they were witnessing the dismantling of their past. The president of the German Parliament, Wolfgang Thierse, born and raised in the GDR, along with some members of the Academy of Arts protested the wholesale devaluation of "East German culture" and artistic heritage. Some interpreted the exhibition's aesthetic as yet another manifestation of West Germans' persisting arrogance and "triumphalism" over the East and its population (Rauterberg 1999). Two artists initiated court proceedings against the exhibitor, arguing that the manner of display was violating their personal dignity. One of the lenders, the bank Leipziger Sparkasse, likewise dissatisfied with the display, withdrew a painting by Hans-Hendrik Grimmling. Twenty-nine additional paintings followed suit in this exodus, recalled either by collectors or by the artists themselves. The curator went on record proclaiming that those protesting the show were simply unable—or unwilling—to face "their" recent history, the GDR past. The fact that the "installation strategies suggested connections between Nazi-sanctioned and official GDR art" (Barron 2009, 14), even equated them, was not addressed by the curator. This equation of National Socialist artistic production with that of the GDR parallels the transference of vocabulary established for facing the Nazi past to engagements with East German history. As Daphne Berdahl (1999, 215ff.) shows, the debates on the comparability between fascism and Stalinism that were at the heart of the German historians' debate (see Chapter 1) were soon extended to East German socialism. Consequently, addressing the GDR past was framed as *Vergangheitsbewältigung*, a process in which the past is understood as something that needs to be mastered and overcome. The categorization of socialist art as antimodern has very much become commonplace since 1990, neglecting long-standing critiques by thinkers such as Georg Lukács, who as early as 1938 questioned the proposed lineage from naturalism and impressionism to expression and surrealism as the only way to conceptualize the lineage of modern art. To suggest that only an increasing tendency of deviating from realism rendered art modern, he argued, would obscure the impact on modern literature of such authors as Maxim Gorki, Thomas Mann, and Heinrich Mann (Lukács 1955, 212).

Knowledge on the GDR cultural scene has remained rather limited, mostly focusing on dissidents, such as Heiner Müller, or those who at some point fled to the Federal Republic, like Gerhard Richter. In many of my interviews, West and East Germans were generally quick to dismiss any kind of visual or performance art of the GDR as artistically bankrupt or, as one curator put it, simply "lagging decades behind their Western counterparts." This ascription of belatedness and the denial of artistic merit resemble the tropes on art from the country tours discussed in the Turkish case. Hans Gerhard Hannesen, of the Academy of the Arts in Berlin, which was "merged" with its East German sister institution in 1993, noted that art produced in the GDR was at best a historical documentation and mostly "outdated [*überholt*]." I put "merged" in quotation marks here, since this process was in fact an absorption that mirrored the dismantling of GDR cultural institutions and heritage—and the fate of the "other Germany" overall.

The art historian and curator Eckhart Gillen has long been a notable exception to this trend and has pioneered comprehensive overviews of visual art production from the German Democratic Republic. Before German reunification was even imaginable, Gillen began research on an exhibition entitled *Deutschlandbilder* (Images of Germany), which after twelve years of preparation opened at Berlin's Martin Gropius Bau in 1997. In this exhibition, Gillen took a longitudinal approach, positing that another division had preceded the separation of the Allied-occupied Western and Soviet-occupied Eastern sectors, ultimately cemented by the Berlin Wall in 1961: A dual Germany began to exist in 1933, marked by those who stayed and arranged themselves with the Nazi regime and those who had to leave, the émigrés, some of whom were never to return. Gillen maintained that this prior division, obscured by the Cold War vocabulary of East and West, was no less important in understanding the development of German art. Noting that while the Russian and Eastern

European avant-gardes have now been integrated in Western art history, socialist art—or art produced in the Eastern bloc—continues to be discounted on principle. "There is," he suggested,

> a seeming unwillingness to really study East German artists. People just can't be bothered. It is easy to discount Bernard Heissig, for instance, as an official GDR state artist [*Staatskünstler*]. But a closer look reveals that while Heissig produced state-commissioned pieces, he also painted several pictures that never saw, could not see the light of day in the GDR. In one of the panel discussions that accompanied *Deutschlandbilder*, Heissig recounted how he practiced self-censorship, camouflaged some of his works by painting over them, or, at times, destroyed works after their completion.

Gillen highlighted another understudied aspect of the GDR art world. Prominent artists like Heissig often ensured that their students in the arts academy had "more freedom" and tried to "protect" them from the authorities. These stories, Gillen maintained, have yet to be documented, along with a more nuanced look at the diverse artistic developments in different eastern European countries (Crowley and Reid 2000, Svašek 2002), which often included coded political critiques (Barron 2009, 22). Gillen proposed that the "unwillingness" to reevaluate East German artistic production is not only perpetuated by the echelons of West German high art but by former GDR artists as well. For some artists, like Georg Baselitz, who fled to the Federal Republic when the East German government ordered him to leave the academy and work in a coal mine for a year, the feeling of injury still ran deep. He explicitly stated that he would not take part in *Deutschlandbilder* if any state-sanctioned GDR artists would be included in the show. When I asked Gillen how he had managed to include Baselitz after all, he replied: "I simply shrugged it off, and went through private collectors of his works, and they were happy to lend them to me."

The silences on the East German past might not be surprising when one considers the vast literature on forgetting in the realm of nation building. However, it is worth pointing out that artistic reunification was envisioned as much easier, since the two German states were thought to share an "inalienable cultural heritage" (Burns and van der Will 2003, 144). This idea was inscribed in the Federal Republic's discourses of Germany as a *Kulturnation* that signaled cultural unity with the GDR despite the political division (Borneman 1992). The erasure of East German art as art—and its unequivocal framing as propaganda—is notable in at least three additional ways: As Gillen pointed out, artists, curators, and museum directors had always been strong communicators in the dual German context. Eternalized in his Café Deutschland series (1977–1984), Jörg Immendorff's travels to East Berlin and his actual and imagined meetings and visual dialogues with the artist A. R. Penk come to mind, for instance. Penk in turn was a representative of another kind of modernism in the GDR and continuously produced art, although he was famously rejected from the art academy four times. Second, this erasure engenders a retrospective homogenization of the different official and unofficial artistic practices that existed throughout GDR history. And finally, it obscures different phases in East German cultural policy, which initially was marked by efforts to keep artistic alliances with the Western sector alive and to "preserve a cultural policy for a united Germany." It was only in the 1960s that a framework for a distinctly East German "national culture" was established (Stephan et al. 1974, 74).[30]

Following Gillen's lead, reevaluations of East German art have been offered by the 2009 exhibition *Art of Two Germanys/Cold War Cultures*, at the Los Angeles County Museum of Art, and the database *Picture Atlas: Art in the GDR*, established in 2012. But both projects have once again brought forth commentators that claim that GDR art has not stood the test of time. Questions remain, however, to what extent this is indeed an aesthetic judgment. The wholesale dismissal of the GDR reduces its artistic production to a deviation from the modern paradigm, one devoid of the civilizing power of art, rather than contextualizing it as an alternative claim to modernity. This latter option is not even considered.

Instances of Recovery

While art at times reflects and at others is subject to decivilizing moments, it can also animate recovery, remembrance, and commemoration. Frieder Schnock and Renata Stih's intervention against the Flick Collection presents such an instance. Other works they have produced also inscribe memory and "unofficial" knowledge of the past back into the everyday life of the city. Their permanent project *Bavarian Quarter* in Berlin-Schöneberg, for example, displays anti-Jewish legislation enacted during the Third Reich in the form of inconspicuous street signs. Instead of envisioning a permanent site, their entry for the competition for the Holocaust Memorial in Berlin proposed a *Bus Stop* offering regular transport to nearby sites of concentration camps free of charge.

On the occasion of the Eleventh Istanbul Biennial (2011), the Kamusal Sanat Laboratuvarı (Public Art Laboratory, KSL) distributed cards to the attendants of the opening festivities (Figures 14–16). At first glance they looked like the

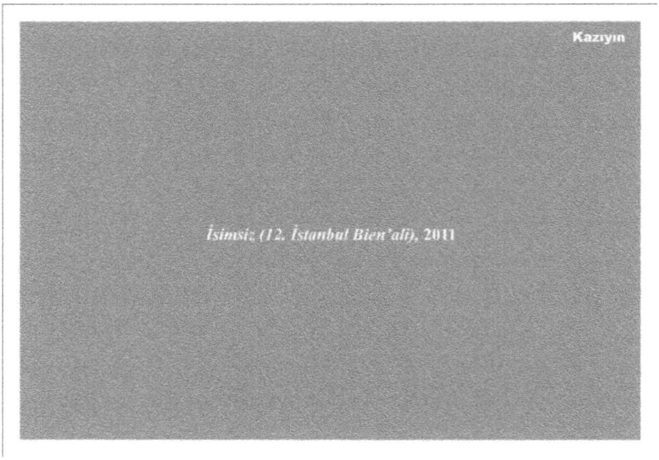

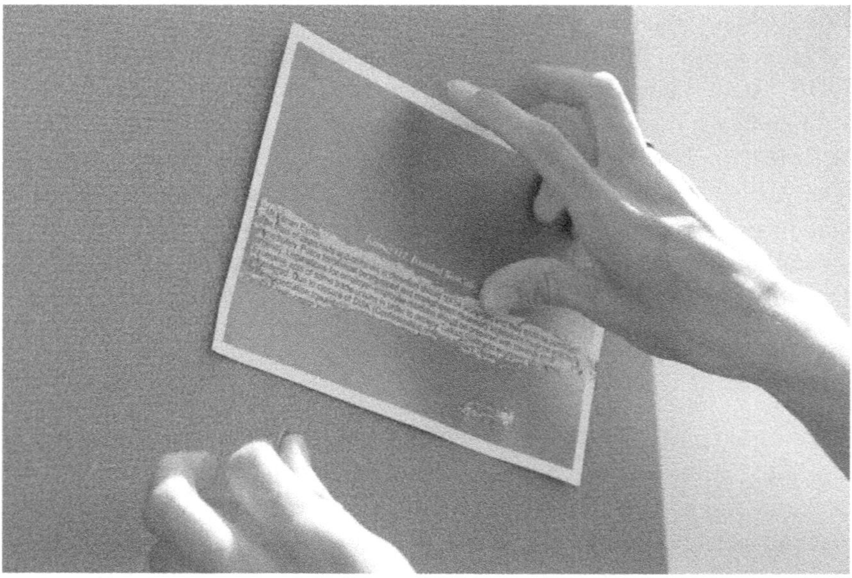

Figures 14–16. (*continued*)

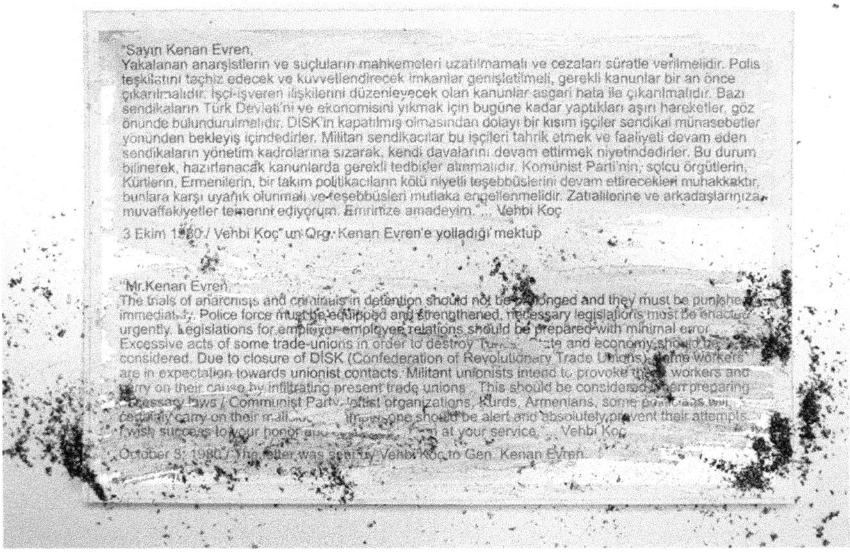

Figures 14–16. *İsimsiz Mektup (Bienal)/Untitled Letter (Biennial)*, scratch ticket distributed by Kamusal Sanat Laboratuvarı (Public Art Laboratory, KSL) during the opening ceremony of the Eleventh Istanbul Biennial (2011). Courtesy of Ezgi Bakçay.

official invitations for the event, but on closer inspection they turned out to be scratch tickets. Once the surface was taken off, a letter written by Vehbi Koç (1901–1996), founder of the Koç Corporation, was revealed. The Koç Corporation had just recently agreed to serve as the institutional sponsor of the biennial for the next decade. The letter was addressed to the junta leader Kenan Evren a mere three weeks after the 1980 coup d'état. In the letter, Koç demands swift trials for "anarchists and criminals." Although unions had already been shut down, Koç warns that their members, even if underground, were eagerly awaiting an opportunity to "destroy the Turkish economy." Finally, he asks Evren to remain vigilant: "Some left-wing organizations, the communist party, Kurds, and Armenians" continued to plot against the state. The letter ends with the salutation, "I am at your service."

The intervention of KSL initiated a discussion of the Koç Corporation beyond its stance regarding the military coup, even though many established arts journals, fearing the loss of advertising revenue, shied away from reporting on the performance. Koç's role in the defense industry[31] had already been thematized during the previous biennial in 2009 (Harutyunyan, Ozgün, and Goodfield 2011), when activists tried to raise awareness of the ethics of sponsorship in the art world. The roots of the Koç fortune, however, remain to be addressed publicly. Starting his working life in his father's grocery shop in Ankara, the Turkification of the economy allowed Vehbi Koç to become a transnational entrepreneur, for instance by taking over businesses and properties sold under duress during the wealth-tax period (Bali 2012, 72). Beyond the question of personal responsibility borne by Koç or that of the institutional accountability of his business empire, now headed by his heirs, this entanglement in the politics of dispossession brings us once more to the structural role of "dirty money" and the "enormous amounts"—to use Werneburg's phrase—necessary to build art collections and found arts spaces. It is against the background of these all-encapsulating conditions of dispossession that Vehbi Koç's heirs were able to open the contemporary arts space Arter in 2010, with support of the Vehbi Koç Foundation.

The last part of the manifesto accompanying the scratch card by KSL read: "The ability to make us forget is the biggest weapon of power. But we have never forgotten. . . . To bring the truth to the light of day, don't be shy away from SCRATCHING the shiny veneer. You will see that this country's past is its present and its future." The intervention questioned if art presented under these long-obscured and unacknowledged conditions, even if critical, is not also compromised and implicated in past injustices.

While some artworks and interventions are about revealing what has been forgotten, others, in Benjamin's terms, "transmit" stories that unsettle well-rehearsed narratives of national (art) history. Dilek Winchester's installation *Three First Turkish Novels* (2009) displays the hand-copied versions of the first three chapters of three different novels. Written in the mid–nineteenth century, each of these works is assumed to be "the first Turkish novel" by different experts. One is written in Armenian (Armeno-Turkish), one in Greek (Karamanli), and the third in Ottoman (a composite of Arabic and Persian letters) script, representing three practices of literacy that were delegitimized by the foundation of the Turkish Republic. Most Turkish speakers can understand them only when they are transliterated into Latin script or read aloud. They leave the viewer to wonder which is indeed "the first Turkish novel." Winchester's practice ultimately questions the implicatedness of art and art history in histories of violence and forgetting, probing the loss of literary practices through the language reform enacted in 1928.[32]

Another example of recovery is *Scared of Murals*, conceived by SALT (2013), which documented a forgotten period in the history of the Turkish art world. The research exhibition brought together documentations on artistic practices and publications, artists' rights struggles, and mobilization within the labor movement in Turkey between 1976 and 1980. The contemporary artist Neriman Polat noted that she was amazed to see some of her teachers from the academy in the pictures, taking part in May Day demonstrations or writing pamphlets on artists' rights. They had "never talked about this period. Neither in our theory classes nor the many hours that we spent together in the studio." As Polat has long been active in the artists' collective Hafriyat (Excavation) and the art group Kirmizi Kart (taking the punitive red card in soccer as a metaphor for feminist interventions) and in mobilizing artists around rights struggles, she was all the more surprised that this rather recent past had been completely unknown to her and her peers.

The capacity of art to address difficult pasts is not limited to individual artworks or artistic interventions. As we will see in the next chapter, art and its institutions are often regarded as "protected spaces" that should not be subject to the restrictions that other settings or expressions might incur. It is for this reason that especially independent arts spaces take on historical exhibitions focusing on long-standing taboos that established museums shy away from. One such example is *Crimes of the Wehrmacht—Dimensions of the War of Annihilation, 1941–1944*, which, to much protest, broke with the myth that only the SS (Schutzstaffel, Protection Squadrons of the Nazi Party) had been involved in crimes against humanity during World War II. It showed that the German Army directly and indirectly supported genocidal violence and, in violation of international conventions, conducted massacres against civilians and prisoners of war. An earlier version of the exhibition had toured some thirty-eight cities (1995–1999), but it was only after an updated format was shown by the contemporary arts space Kunst-Werke, Berlin (2001), that it was moved to the German Historical Museum in 2004.[33] *The Events of 6–7 September, 1955* (2005), at Karşı Sanat gallery in Istanbul, worked in a similar fashion. A documentation of the pogrom, the exhibition for the first time presented photographs of the personal archive of Fahri Çoker, the judge who had presided over one of the three martial law courts established in Istanbul immediately after the events. As the gallery was then located on İstiklal Street, one of the main sites of the pogrom, the vantage points of the violence displayed in the pictures matched the views from the building in which Karşı Sanat was located. This doubling became even more eerie when the exhibition was attacked by a right-wing mob, destroying part of the display.[34] Similarly, the historian Osman Köker has curated a series of historical exhibitions at Depo and other independent arts spaces that document the everyday lives of Armenians and non-Muslim communities in Anatolia. The photographs and postcards allowed visitors to reintegrate the stories of those murdered and expelled into their own memories of the depicted places and sites.

These are only a few examples of artworks and exhibitions that trouble official narratives, unearth decivilizing moments, and reinscribe and "connect" (Hirsch 2012) forgotten pasts to the present. This is not always an easy process, and not only because it counteracts official narratives. Historical exhibitions in art spaces struggle with the conceptual problem that, by definition, art has a different relationship to "truth" and "reality" than history—or historical museums for that matter (Conrads and Gutmair 2002). Artworks, in turn, are faced with the challenge of displacing the historical to the aesthetic realm (Crapanzano 2004, 169). This process holds unique possibilities for art, indeed is often seen to make art art. Yet, it can also run danger of decontextualizing difficult pasts and of becoming trapped in hegemonic framings of perception.

5 The Politics of Art and Censorship

The previous chapter began to look at artistic interventions that break through the systematic forgetting of decivilizing moments inscribed in official discourses on the past. I want to push this inquiry further by dwelling on explicitly political art that in the process of recovery also makes visible contentious presents. Leading to cracks in the civilizing narrative in which the national frame seeks to arrest art, these artistic interventions present instances in which the discourse of "the greater good" can no longer seamlessly mediate between different understandings of art. In these instances the assumption that art is inherently good is broken. By virtue of doing so, these artworks and exhibitions themselves become perceived as decivilizing expressions. It is in this process of displacement that censorship mechanisms are set in motion in order to deflect the decivilizing aspect from the subject of aesthetic critique to its representation.

The very existence of an array of regulatory mechanisms and practices that form censorship apparatuses upholding the limits of the assumed goodness of art speaks to the transformative power accorded to the aesthetic and to the need to control and delimit this transformative potential. Here, I employ censorship as an umbrella term for the many effective ways that different actors employ "different, dispersed kinds of regulations" in the "administration of aesthetics" (Burt 1994, xi), be it the direct involvement of state institutions or individuals who invoke "national" interests refracted through the state apparatus in order to mobilize delegitimizing mechanisms. This allows for looking at censorship beyond explicit bans and suppressions of artworks by the state. In fact, such bans have become both technically speaking difficult to enforce and—as the cases discussed here show—somewhat unnecessary. Instead, I highlight processes of (partial) silencing, including incentives for self-censorship and delegitimization as well as modes of foreclosure that authoritatively frame the production and reception of artworks (Burt 1994, Butler 1998, Brown 1998).

Two 2005 exhibitions and the debates surrounding them form the core of this chapter: *Regarding Terror* (Berlin), which focused on media perceptions of the left-wing militants of the Red Army Faction, and *Free Kick* (Istanbul), which featured works referencing the "Kurdish issue," militarism, torture, and social injustice in Turkey. Both exhibitions are instructive in terms of the problems that explicitly political art poses despite official discourses that praise the critical potential of art as indispensable for modern society and politics. The strong reactions that these exhibitions evoked present interesting points of inquiry with regard to the state's mandate to support the arts and for probing the boundaries between art and politics. In both cases, critics cast doubts on the assumed benefits of art and construed arts and politics as incommensurable. I contextualize these cases within the conceptions of freedom of expression and how they are circumscribed by official memory regimes and state discourses in both countries. What emerges in both cases is that silencing efforts use the argument of the autonomy of art not to shield art from political intervention but to suppress political expression through the arts.[1]

All Is Well in the Federal Republic?

When running an exploratory literature search on censorship in Germany, one might come to the conclusion that censorship ceased with the end of World War II or, more precisely, with denazification and the establishment of the Federal Republic of Germany. What John Borneman (1992) described as the mirror-imaging process with regard to the "two Berlins" was likewise true for the two German states. It was integral to West Germany's self-understanding that "here" freedom of expression reigned, while the "other" Germany, the GDR, censored and repressed those not in line with party ideology. Yet it has been especially its National Socialist past that has shaped Germany's constitutionally guaranteed understanding of freedom of expression *and* its limits. More than just constituting the boundaries of the beneficiality of art, aesthetic expressions that connote or are categorized as "Nazi art" are characterized as outright dangerous. To this day, films produced in the Nazi era, such as Leni Riefenstahl's *Triumph of the Will* (1935) or *Jud Suess* (1940),[2] remain de facto banned in Germany because, according to German legislation, the glorification of National Socialism and anti-Semitism constitute incitements of the masses (*Volksverhetzung*).[3] Only excerpts of these films are permitted to be shown in Germany and only for educational purposes. These stipulations reveal an understanding in which the aesthetics of these films are deemed so powerful that watching them in their entirety and without contextualization is feared to be so persuasive that they might topple all education on Nazi atrocities in the German school curriculum and all indictments of the Nazi past in political discourse. That these movies can readily be accessed online seems to indicate that rather than a complete suppression, the German state aims to delegitimize National Socialist expressions.[4] The vigilance with which these bans are enforced is an important part of Germany's self-representation to the international community, an upholding of its promise of "never again." It is in this vein that Lawrence Douglas (1998, 73) identifies the criminalization of Holocaust denial in Germany as legitimizing the existence of the Federal Republic.[5] Legally cementing the imperative to remember, it severs the Republic's ties with National Socialism through a "posture of obsessive mindfulness" of its past and is vital for establishing Germany's Occidental belonging. The question of what can be identified as National Socialist aesthetics, however, has haunted postwar Germany, especially when it comes to interpreting and judging artistic expressions. To illustrate this predicament, let us turn to Rainer Werner Fassbinder's play *Garbage, the City, and Death*, a case that has been debated for decades.

Ambiguity and the Specter of Nazism

Garbage is loosely based on Gerhard Zwerenz's *Bericht aus dem Landesinneren* (Report from the heartland, 1972) and *Die Erde ist unbewohnbar wie der Mond* (The Earth is as inhabitable as the Moon, 1973)—two novels criticizing the urban redevelopment frenzy that swept through Frankfurt/Main in the 1970s, particularly the Westend. A neighborhood populated mainly by the city's Jewish bourgeoisie before 1933, the district had turned into desolate housing for low-income families and (squatting) students from the adjacent Johann Wolfgang Goethe University. When developers in concert with the municipality tried to clear the buildings of these unwanted dwellers, the so-called housing battle broke out. For the play, Fassbinder synthesized one character (called Herr Mauerstamm in the novels) into a developer named only the "Rich Jew."[6] Published in 1976, cultural critics quickly attacked the play as an allegedly anti-Semitic showcase, and it was discontinued shortly after its release. Seyla Benhabib (Markovits et al. 1986, 17) has suggested that the play's real problematic lay not in the text but in its reception. She argues that the discomfort was induced by characters voicing anti-Semitic views, sentiments Fassbinder regarded as deep-seated in German society. Going further, David Barnett (2004, 30) has interpreted the outcry that the play produced especially among members of the conservative Christian Democratic Union (CDU) as an attempt of the German right to reduce its fascist affinities and persistent anti-Semitism to its National Socialist manifestations. The city's Jewish community and its CDU majority protested the world premier, which was planned in Frankfurt in 1985, even demanding a ban of the play from Walter Wallmann, the city's mayor. Many of the city's left-leaning intellectuals, while also wary of the possible impact and direction of play, opposed a ban, and hence censorship, on principle. Instead, they proposed that the characters uttering anti-Semitic statements should wear armbands displaying Nazi symbols to distinguish them from "normal Germans" (33). Disquieted by the possible ambiguity of the play, theirs was a call to assign guilt and responsibility to a clearly demarcated perpetrator group. Notably, any doubts regarding Fassbinder's oeuvre and personal stance—if at all justified—could have been resolved by reading *Garbage* alongside his *Just a Slice of Bread*, with which it was originally published. Here, a director who tries to make a film about Auschwitz "stumbles upon a lack of empathy with the victims in his actors and his team" (40). As such, *Just a Slice of Bread* is a testament to the lackluster engagement with the Nazi past, especially with how it has shaped racism and anti-Semitism in the Federal Republic.

Part of the discomfort surrounding the play seemed to stem from its timing. The 1980s were marked by a resurgence of anti-Semitism and questions regarding Germany's (continued) commitment to democratic principles. To name but three examples that fueled this discomfort: Ernst Jünger—once regarded as a trailblazer for National Socialist ideology—was awarded the prestigious Goethe Prize for Literature in 1982. In 1985, the Bitburg controversy transpired.[7] All the while, then chancellor Helmuth Kohl (1982–1998) made headlines by repeatedly calling for the "normalization" of Germany's position within the international community. This feat, Kohl argued, could only be achieved by overcoming the ever-looming "guilt complex" of the Third Reich. Interpreted as Germany's desire to return to full sovereignty, these events were accompanied by growing anxieties regarding the course a once again strong Germany would take (Olick 1998, 556)—anxieties that flared up once more at the end of decade with the country's reunification.

There were several attempts to perform the play in Germany, but every time a theater company took it on, it was eventually cancelled under public and political pressure, even after its world premiere in New York in 1987 and a successful performance in Tel Aviv in 1999. It was only in 2009 that *Garbage* officially premiered in Germany as part of a tripartite repertoire at Mülheim's Theater an der Ruhr along with *Just a Slice of Bread* and *Blood on a Cat's Neck*.[8]

The reactions to *Garbage* raised important questions: What is the relationship between an aesthetic approach to a subject and its counterpart, its manifestation in reality? What makes for the ambiguity between (re)presenting undesired or unsanctioned political positions that index decivilizing moments and condoning them? These very questions came up again, three decades later, when the KW Institute for Contemporary Art (KW) in Berlin was preparing a concept for what was to become the exhibition *Regarding Terror: The Red Army Faction.*

Regarding Terror—How (Not) to Do an Exhibition on German Terrorism

The Red Army Faction (RAF) assembled itself in the late 1960s from disillusioned splinters of the Socialist German Student Union (Sozialistischer Deutsche Studentenbund, SDS),[9] the experience of the Frankfurt housing battles, and the reaction to the murder of the pacifist Benno Ohnesorg by a policeman during a protest against the visit of Mohammad Reza Shah Pahlavi in Berlin in 1967. It galvanized further with the growing conservative backlash against the student and protest movements. What began with bombings of shopping malls turned into violence against institutions and people who for the RAF personified Germany's collaboration with US-led imperialism—manifest in the war in Vietnam—and those who embodied the continuity between the Third Reich and the Federal Republic, a particularly German brand of well-connected industrialists, officials, and politicians. Reaching its height in what came to be known as the German Autumn (*Deutscher Herbst*) in 1977, little animated the German public imagination as much as "the war of the six against 60 million"—among them most prominently Andreas Baader, Gudrun Ensslin, Jan-Carl Raspe, and Ulrike Meinhof—as Heinrich Böll (1972) called it in an essay urging for dialogue to address the problem of left-wing German violence. Böll's interjection, like all calls for moderation that followed him, was met with outcries and accusations of being an enemy of the state (*Staatsfeind*). The RAF officially dissolved in 1998, with some its members dead and others imprisoned or still on the run. Gone were the wanted posters that had for twenty-eight years filled the walls of post offices and other public buildings. Silence shrouded the episode, which had marked homegrown terrorism for some and urban guerilla warfare for others.

In the early 2000s, the curator Ellen Blumenstein, together with Felix Ensslin, conceived an exhibition that for the first time attempted to look at the RAF through the lens of visual art. They found support from KW's director, Klaus

Biesenbach.[10] Blumenstein explained her own interest in the topic by noting that, like many of her generation, she had "worked a lot on World War II and its aftermath," but as someone who was born in 1976 she "had a very strong feeling that '68 and German terrorism had completely shaped the world" she "grew up in." Blumenstein noted that other than the bestseller *Der Baader-Meinhof Komplex* (1985),[11] "people today don't know anything about that part of German history." The team applied to the Capital Cultural Fund with a preliminary concept and was awarded funding. But while they were exploring how exactly to frame the exhibition and which media to use to bring historical accounts together with the artworks, the scandal erupted.

The controversy involved, not unlike the case of the Flick Collection, a circle of persons whose political and professional connections were deeply intertwined with German history. In ways still unknown, the preliminary exhibition proposal, with the working title *The Myth of the RAF*, was leaked to Hergard Rohwedder. Her husband, Detlev Rohwedder, had been assassinated by the RAF in 1991 while serving as the head of the Treuhand, the government agency in charge of privatizing East German public enterprises and property. Rohwedder contacted Hanns-Eberhard Schleyer, the son of the former president of the German Employers' Association and ex-Nazi functionary Hanns-Martin Schleyer, who was abducted and then killed by the RAF in 1977.[12] Together they wrote a letter in the name of the families of the RAF's victims. Addressed to Chancellor Gerhard Schröder and Minster of the Interior Otto Schily,[13] it expressed the fear that the exhibition was designed to "glorify" the RAF. This fear centered especially on one question raised in the initial proposal: "Which ideas, ideals have retained their value and cannot be discounted as naïve?" (quoted after Pfitzenmaier 2005). Equating the call for a more nuanced discussion of the RAF's motivations with condoning their actions, the letter reenacted a pattern of *Staatstreue* and *Sympathisanten*. The same dichotomization of those "loyal to the state" and "terrorist sympathizers" had characterized much of the debate on the RAF in the 1970s (Balz 2006).

The German tabloid *Die Bildzeitung* was the first to scandalize against the planned show, describing it as devoted to "crimes" and as "the pinnacle of tastelessness" (as cited in Hohmann 2005a).[14] Amid the ensuing public and political pressure, Adrienne Goehler, the director of the Capital Cultural Fund, lost her position.[15] Undersecretary for Culture and Media Christina Weiss, who had likewise been on the selection committee, retracted her approval. Along with the reconceptualization of the exhibition, she also demanded a mandatory pedagogical program to accompany it. This program was to be designed by the Federal Agency for Civic Education (Bundeszentrale für politische Bildung), an institution that answers directly to the minister of the interior.[16]

Gaby Horn, the biennale director at KW at the time, noted that they were faced with the decision either to abandon the exhibition or to relinquish control to the ministry. As both choices would have constituted dangerous precedents, KW decided to return the yet unspent funds and complete the exhibition's budget through an online auction, for which artists including Marina Abramović, Monica Bonvicini, Andreas Gursky, and Thomas Demand donated works. Although many of them were not part of the show, there was a consensus in the international art world that the government's retrospective stipulations presented an unjustifiable attack on the autonomy of art. Others interpreted the KW's refusal to work with the Federal Agency for Civic Education as a "retreat to art as such" and thus an understanding of art as divorced from political responsibility (Reichelt 2005, Spreen 2005).

The scandal was all the more surprising given that it had been preceded by the release of the art-house films *The State I Am In* (2000) and *Blackbox BRD* (2001), both dealing with the history of "German terror." My interlocutors too were unable to account for the divergence in perception between these movies and the exhibition. Maybe it was the march of this topic into one of the most distinguished contemporary art institutions of the "new" postunification capital Berlin and the fact that it was funded by a federal arts agency. In our meeting, Adrienne Goehler described the "easy hystericization of the media" as aided by the personal connections of high-profile RAF victims' families to the political establishment.[17] Blumenstein concurred, adding that these connections enabled the mobilization of the minister of the interior, the foreign minister,[18] and the chancellor—institutions that usually do not intervene in the day-to-day operations of the art world. She emphasized that this intervention had also been made possible by the deep societal rift that the RAF experience had produced. For her, the RAF had long functioned as Germany's formative other, an internal "scapegoat," as she called it, that needed to be ostracized.

The battle against the RAF produced a legacy that, while protested at first, became normalized in the course of the 1980s. This legacy includes extended powers of the state—the establishment of interrogation, wiretapping, solitary confinement, and sensory deprivation protocols—that undermined both the German constitution and international human rights conventions. It also entailed lifting the protection against self-incrimination in RAF trials, regular raids of lawyers' offices, temporary bans on meetings between defendants and lawyers, and force-feeding prisoners who went on hunger strike to protest their conditions (a practice long condemned by the World Medical Association). All of these practices bear eerie parallels to what we know about Guantanamo Bay and the practices of the "global war on terror" today (Varon 2004, 2008). Then, as now, they engender a legitimation crisis of the state. This crisis is doubly troubling in the case of Germany as these measures are at odds with the proposed ideals of liberal democracy in general and with Germany's distancing from its authoritarian past in particular. The RAF experience presents a decivilizing moment in German history both because it produced a kind of violence that was thought exorcised from the new, ostensibly recivilized Germany and because it produced state reactions that contradict the ideals of liberal democracy. It is against this background that a critical engagement with the RAF exhibition was foreclosed, making the question whether one can criticize the actions of the RAF yet reconsider the experience of German armed struggle nearly impossible. It is because of this foreclosure that debates on the exhibition manifested themselves as a replay of vocabularies thought long overcome, as no other framework to approach this particular past was available.

Between Missing Abstraction and Inadequate Renderings of Reality

Regarding Terror opened in February 2005. The new concept, according to the curators, "examined the role of the media in the making of the phantasm RAF." Artworks were juxtaposed with newspaper covers providing the "connection between facts and public memory." In addition, the exhibition featured an archive consisting of newspaper clippings, scholarly articles, and documents pertaining to the RAF. The 250 showcased artworks spanned pieces created contemporaneously with the German Autumn, the RAF trials, and the much-debated deaths of Andreas Baader, Gudrun Ensslin, and Jan-Carl Raspe, as well as commissioned works, often by younger artists—representatives, so to speak—of the "third generation" since the establishment of the RAF.

The reconceptualization of the show did little to alleviate the critiques. Many journalists, politicians, and victims' families objected to the show's alleged focus on the perpetrators instead of the victims and its likewise alleged "failure to educate the visitors on the crimes of the RAF." The curators, in turn, emphasized that the arts could not be expected to render a complete analytical picture of a political phenomenon and that their focus was on the production of *media images of the RAF* rather than a historically accurate account as such. Yet many critics suggested more or less explicitly that art exhibitions on a political issue should encompass a clearly delineated pedagogical thrust. This claim is by no means an uncontested one. It invokes an entire corpus of debates in art theory on the tension between understandings of art as a supposedly functionless good (often referred to by the term *l'art pour l'art*) and art as an educational vehicle (Belfiore and Bennett 2008), a tension to which I will return in a moment. Others faulted the curators for not having contextualized the works historically, obscuring the violence perpetrated by RAF members and hence feeding into the "myths" that the RAF had engineered about itself. Another critique, mainly expressed from within the art world, attested an artistic inconsequentiality to the exhibition, which was seen to capitalize on a spectacular topic while avoiding clear aesthetic and political positions (Fanizadeh 2005, Graw 2005, Werneburg 2005).

Each of these appraisals raised questions about the relationship between art and politics as much as about the relationship between the RAF and German society, and each camp found ample evidence in the artworks for priorities gone wrong on the part of the curators. For instance, Hans-Peter Feldmann's series *The Dead* (1967–1993), although generally lauded by art critics for its affective impact, was criticized for assembling photographs of RAF members alongside those of their victims without any commentary.

Even iconic works such as Joseph Beuys's *Dürer, I Will Guide Baader + Meinhof Personally through the Documenta V* (1972) elicited scathing reviews (Figure 17): "The exhibition also documents the credulity, the will to proselytize, and the at times boundless naïveté of artists in dealing with the protagonists of terror. Joseph Beuys really believed that the top terrorists could be reintegrated into society through the aid of art. Unfortunately, the story ended slightly differently" (Büsing and Klaas 2005). It is notable that what is billed as Beuys's naïveté actually reflects an understanding of art supported by the cultural policies of the time during which he created this piece: Taking into account that the social-democratic agenda of *Soziokultur* saw art as an avenue to cure many ills of modern society, including violence, might have allowed for a less indicting interpretation of Beuys's work.

The journalist Butz Peters's (2005) review is emblematic for many of these critiques. He reprimands Gerhard Richter's *October 18, 1977* (1988), a series based on photographs of RAF members in custody as well as pictures taken after their death, for focusing on the perpetrators. However, Peters fails to mention that these photographs had been widely circulated in the German press, often with highly sensationalist headlines. Nor does he take into account that Richter has been understood as "uniquely engag[ing] a postwar German crisis in historical memory—the doubly amnesiac postwar German present, that is, a German nation burdened by the legacy of fascism and the later, and not unrelated, phenomenon of terrorism" (Saltzmann 2005, 35).[19] Instead he brushes away an entire corpus of art-historical considerations of Richter's oeuvre as well as discourses that identify art as a privileged site for approaching otherwise difficult issues. For him this is an example of the limits of the

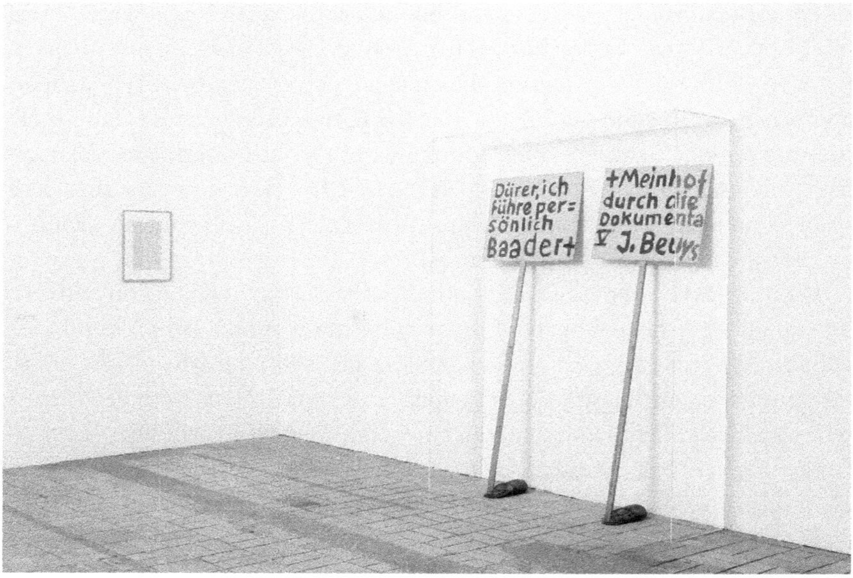

Figure 17. Joseph Beuys, *Dürer, ich führe persönlich Baader+Meinhof durch die Dokumenta V/Dürer, I Will Guide Baader+Meinhof Personally through the Documenta V*, 1972 (right-hand side of the image), KW Institute for Contemporary Art, Berlin. Regarding Terror: The RAF-Exhibition, January 30–May 16, 2005, installation view. Photo: Rainer Jordan.

emancipatory potential accorded to art, one in which art is seen to distort reality harmfully.

It is factuality or, rather, the lack thereof that seems most troubling to Peters. Turning to a painting of Meinhof by Johannes Kahrs (Figure 18), he notes: "The depiction of the prisoner in remand resembles the horrible images of KZ inmates; the tattered clothes, the hands held up. This is how Meinhof defined herself in her incarceration; she spoke of 'Auschwitzphantasies.'[[20]] The photo that served as Kahrs's template was taken in 1973 at the detention facility in Köln-Ossendorf. No one had ordered Ulrike Meinhof to raise her hands; she did it out of her own volition. However, the spectator does not sense this."

This insistence on historical accuracy and adequacy in representing reality was all the more striking given that no such calls for context or accuracy had been made for the many exhibitions that focused on (im)migration, which were as popular in Germany as in the international art world at the time (Karaca 2009). Factuality, then, it seems, becomes an issue only when the ambiguity between art and reality cannot be "tolerated." An expert on the RAF, Peters makes a string of assumptions about art that are not only contentious within art theory but mismatch the curators' intentions. Using quotation marks, he

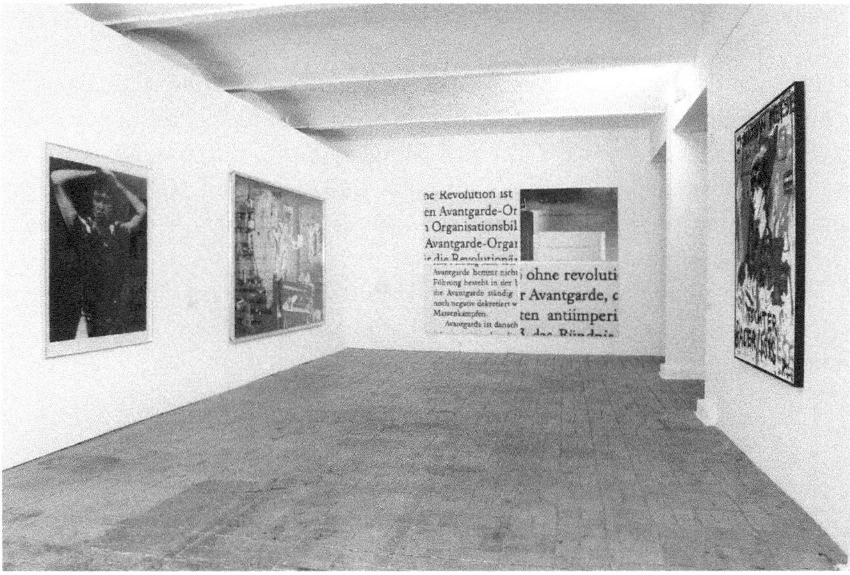

Figure 18. Johannes Kahrs, *Meinhof*, 2001 (left-hand side of the image), KW Institute for Contemporary Art, Berlin. Regarding Terror: The RAF-Exhibition, January 30–May 16, 2005, installation view. Photo: Rainer Jordan.

questions if the shown works could indeed be categorized as "art"—an often-employed strategy in censoring motions, as we will see also in the case of Turkey.

Others doubted that the RAF could be a topic for artistic engagements at all. According to Blumenstein, "politicians said what they could not have said back in the 1970s, they made a *l'art pour l'art* argument." Rather than taking up the possibility "to use the RAF to reflect on German society," these commentators negated the social relationality of art and instead construed it as located in an imagined realm of pure aesthetics. The controversy surrounding *Regarding Terror* hence played out along the tensions inherent in the modern conception of art since Kant's *Critique of Judgment*, which conceptualized art as "purposiveness without purpose" (Belfiore and Bennett 2008, 178). It is out of this formulation that understandings of art for art's sake, of the autonomy of art, developed. At times, this maxim has been interpreted in formalistic terms, that is, that art is only to be judged in terms of aesthetic parameters in the narrower sense. At others, the autonomy of art has been conceptualized as setting art apart from other kinds of expressions, thus shielding it from interventions, for instance, from politics. Yet Kant's philosophy also affirmed "an indissoluble link between the beautiful and the moral" (181) and proposed that "trained receptivity to beauty can aid the growth of morals, and, conversely, that moral growth can dispose us to beauty" (Bell-Villada 1996, 23–24). This in turn is the linkage that ideas of art as a vehicle for civic cultivation and education frequently draw on, even though the extent to which art is open to direct pedagogization remains debated. What in Kant's thinking was once an interrelated whole has since been separated into two strands and employed to argue for different kinds of relationships between art and life—and art and politics (Haskins 1989).

The attacks on the exhibition straddled these disparate understandings of art, but so did its defenses. Answering the charges that the exhibition was a transgression of "good taste," Biesenbach stated:

> It may sound conservative, but when I select works . . . I employ beauty and truth as criteria. It means that artistic quality must always be judged by the content that a work conveys. To test this has surely not been easy in the engagement with the RAF. . . . Yet it is traditionally art, in the sense of the monument [*Denkmal*], the memorial [*Mahnmal*] that does the work of mourning [*Trauerarbeit*]. You only have to look around Berlin to see which crimes and traumas of German history are visualized and made public through the arts. At stake are the victims, the grief about the victims, the processing of history, and, hopefully, learning from history. That is why the same people who usually commission monuments should not tell me in the case of the RAF: Stop, art has no business here.
>
> (Fricke and Lautenschläger 2003)[21]

Two issues stand out in this statement. First, given that Germany has a vast experience of aesthetic engagements with the past, it is all the more notable that there is no commemoration of RAF violence. Second, by invoking "beauty" (aesthetics) and "truth" (ethics) Biesenbach reaches back to a tradition that provides easily recognizable and accepted understandings of art to legitimize the RAF exhibition.[22] Although Walter Benjamin (2003 [1936], 22) argued that in the age of mechanical reproduction the formalistic maxim of "art for art's sake" had finally been revealed for what it really was, that is, mere semblance (*Schein*), the idea of the autonomy of art has remained a staple in how we talk about art, not least because of its political versatility (Eagleton 1990, 9).

A different kind of insistence on the autonomy of art was formulated by Ensslin, the co-curator of the exhibition, who maintained that art should push the boundaries of what might be regarded as acceptable: "Art does not work by taking a topic, by pedagogizing it" and "then releasing it for consumption. Such an approach," he contended, "would be apolitical" (Werneburg and

Fricke 2005). Yet despite Ensslin's intentions, art critics frequently diagnosed a lack of critical aesthetic positions in the exhibition. As such, the RAF exhibition was perceived as a transgression of art into the political sphere that was met with political delegitimization attempts as well as aesthetic critiques.

Regarding the Inconceivability of German Terror

Probing a history that has remained largely silenced, the exhibition, or rather the perception of the exhibition, could not draw on either a stable official memory regime or a critical collectivized memory. Being foreclosed in the sense that the issues it raised were designated unspeakable and illegitimate, scandalization emerged as the main avenue for addressing *Regarding Terror*. The comprehensive historical, political, and sociological processing or facing the past—*Vergangenheitsaufarbeitung*—that critics demanded from the exhibition has not been undertaken; a policy of public accountability by the state has yet to be pursued but appears ever more difficult, as there is increasing evidence that state agencies had infiltrated the RAF with undercover operatives.[23] Conservative camps have nonetheless increasingly framed discussions about the RAF with the term *Vergagenheitsbewältigung*—mastering the past. Most commonly associated with Germany's wish to return to full sovereignty, this notion was long reserved for "overcoming" the National Socialist past and later the Socialist past of the GDR.[24] As Adorno (1997 [1959]) stated, facing the past is only possible if one is fully committed to understanding and changing the conditions that have enabled it. This is difficult in the case of the RAF, as "the global war on terror" has not only reinforced the legacy of extended state powers but also renewed the legitimation crises of the state.

Facing the RAF has also been complicated by its disquieting intertwinements with Germany's National Socialist past, to which it continues to speak in multiple and often contradictory registers: by couching the history of the RAF in the terminology of dealing with the Nazi past, by acknowledging the emergence of the RAF as related to obscured facets of the National Socialist legacy, and by violently revealing the limits of denazification. This also means acknowledging the RAF's role in unmasking the personal and structural legacies of National Socialism—however misguided the RAF's manifestations in armed struggle might have been. While this was surely not the RAF's only goal, their actions contributed to the formation of the memory regime on the Nazi past as we know it today, and thus they have to be situated within the challenges to official history by the German student movement of the 1960s and the wider processes through which the past has been confronted in law, politics, scholarship, and cultural production.

The silence that surrounds the RAF stems in part from the fact that they unleashed a violence that had become unimaginable after 1945, when a peaceful and democratic Germany was to be projected at home and abroad. After all, the large-scale "recivilizing" of Germany was understood as a project that would overcome barbarism in all its forms. Many of the RAF victims had indeed profited from National Socialism, economically and politically. Some had occupied preeminent positions within the Nazi hierarchy; others were beneficiaries of the National Socialist system of exploitation and dispossession. To point to their positionalities is often read as arguing in line with the RAF. Yet this very factor might help explain why the call for mourning the victims of RAF violence has only come up very recently.

It was because of this positionality that the victims' families could mobilize government officials to exert pressure on the KW without enacting an explicit ban but through "mere" delegitimization. This delegitimization ensured, contrary to the German title of the exhibition *Zur Vorstellungen des Terrors*—with *Vorstellung* having a number of meanings ranging from "imagination" to "introduction" and "conceivability"—that the RAF as a German phenomenon remained inconceivable for most of the debate. Together with Germany's self-image as a liberal democracy, it also rendered the interventions against the exhibition unrecognizable as censorship. In the extensive press survey I conducted, only one author identified the events surrounding the exhibition as censorship, and only in the form of "censorship lite" ("*Zensur light*," Reinecke 2003).

All Is in Shambles in Turkey?

With three military coups and an overall governing structure that for the most part is qualified as authoritarian, Turkey's overall human rights record and its handling of its constitutionally guaranteed but practically embattled freedom of expression have been subject to frequent criticism, not least in the context of the now hampered EU accession negotiations. Throughout Turkey's history different types of censorship have been accompanied by state violence, imprisonments, enforced disappearances, and systematic intimidation, and these periods have alternated with more liberal ones. This back and forth has created a setting rife for self-censorship, a phenomenon notoriously hard to research. The legal reforms instated throughout the 2000s included the legalization of Kurdish broadcasting (even if preferably under state control) and publishing and involved, for example, the lifting of the ban on the letters Q, W, and X, which exist in the Kurdish but not the Turkish alphabet. These developments were hard to imagine given that only a few years earlier, in 1999, the singer-songwriter Ahmet Kaya had been bombarded with silverware upon announcing at an awards ceremony his desire to shoot a Kurdish music video. But then again, as the saying goes, much has stayed the same.

Many visual artists have been charged for political expressions, but more often than not this has been because of their activities outside rather than inside the art world. Gülsün Karamustafa, for instance, was convicted in 1971 for sheltering a political refugee (she only regained her passport and her right to travel abroad in 1987). Karamustafa long remained silent on the issue, although her works have insightfully probed the political and questions of public memory. More recently she has turned to the political trials and tribulations of the country during the 1970s and 1980s as well as her own court case.

As in the German case, Turkey's official memory regime is codified by law, albeit in a veiled manner. The 1982 constitution prepared under the military junta stresses territorial integrity (often referred to by the shorthand *Türkiye'nin bölünmez bütünlüğü*, "the indivisible unity of Turkey") and national unity while also guaranteeing freedom of expression. This has translated into judiciary practices that favor restrictive interpretations of provisions honoring freedom of expression, aided by Turkey's controversial antiterrorism legislations and Article 301 of the Turkish penal code, which in its original wording punished "insults against Turkishness."[25] While visual artists have not been convicted under this article as of yet, musicians, writers, scholars, and journalists have been battling charges on the basis of 301.[26] Turkish officials have countered criticisms of Article 301 by pointing to a range of similar laws against insulting the state and its institutions (including the national flag) in the European arena and by positing that it is not the law but its application that is problematic. Although the law was changed after the assassination of the Armenian journalist Hrant Dink, who had been made the target of a state-sanctioned hate crime through his indictment on the basis of 301, it has been a successful tool for thwarting expressions that question the official version of Turkish history. References to the Armenian genocide and Turkey's multiethnic and multilingual makeup outside the defined boundaries of "tamed diversity" (see also Tambar 2014) not only point to decivilizing moments in Turkish history but can be interpreted as threatening to Turkey's territorial integrity (postulated in Article 3 of the Turkish constitution) and thus have been equated with "separatist propaganda and terrorism." As such, all of these charges represent delimitations to the constitutionally guaranteed freedom of expression (Article 26 of the Turkish constitution) and of the freedom of the sciences and the arts (Article 27).

Satanism, vandalism, terrorism

"Satanism, Vandalism, Terrorism: I got into trouble with all three of them," Halil Altındere stated, with his mixture of good spirit and seriousness, when we met for an interview. It seemed like an irresistible pun, although nominally his last trial was not about terrorism per se but a charge of publicly denigrating the armed forces of the Republic of Turkey. It was a fitting phrase, nonetheless, as offenses bundled under Article 301 are discursively equated to terrorism and construed as threats to Turkey's territorial integrity and thus sovereignty.

In 1998, Altındere conducted an unsolicited performance at Urart Galeri, Istanbul. Spray painting a dollar sign on a painting by Esat Tekand,[27] he was handed a vandalism charge. In court Altındere argued that his intervention presented an act of artistic appropriation. The judge seemed unimpressed, rebutting his defense with a dismissive, "Who do you think you are? Picasso?" The trial hinged, however, on the account of an expert witness, the art historian John J. Cook. Testifying that Altındere's intervention was well within the framework of art history and not a destructive but constructive artistic act, Cook's affidavit showed that Tekand's piece had originally been priced at $6,500, but, since Altındere's performance, a collector had offered to acquire it for $10,000,[28] as the painting was now signed by two artists. Although this did little to console Tekand, Cook's testimony, which cast Altındere's action in terms of both artistic value and economic gain, resulted in the dismissal of the charges. The question of what constitutes art and what makes it recognizable as such were at stake once again a year later, when Altındere brought his *Deconstruction of a Death* (1997) home after an exhibition. Neighbors alerted the police after witnessing the coffin that formed the centerpiece of the installation being moved into the house but did not see it leave again, as would have been customary for a funeral service. It was under the suspicion of Satanism—at the time a source of moral panic in the Turkish media—that Altındere's home was raided. He was taken to the police station, along with his artwork, now turned evidence. Once at the police station, Altındere recalls, a deliberation between him and the police officers ensued on the nature and characteristics of an artwork. The investigation was eventually dropped, as no connection to Satanism could be ascertained. But it is the third charge that Altındere was confronted with, for curating an exhibition in the framework of the ninth Istanbul Biennial (2005), that I will turn to in more detail because, similar to the RAF case, it was perceived as a transgression of art into the political sphere that was met with both aesthetic critiques and political delegitimization attempts.

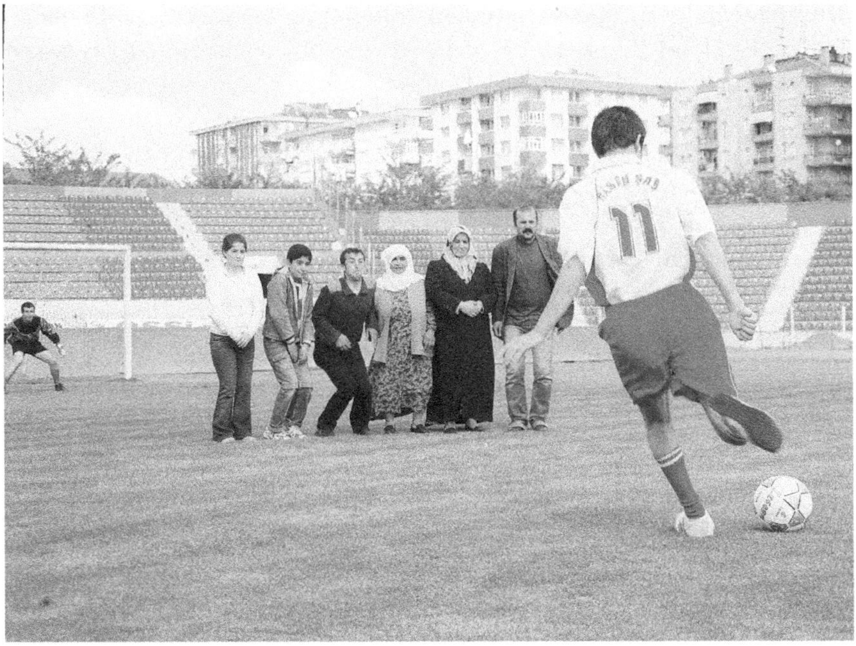

Figure 19. Cengiz Tekin, *Serbest Vuruş/Free Kick*, 2005. Courtesy of the artist.

The biennial's curators Vasıf Kortun and Charles Esche invited Halil Altındere to put together a show in the "hospitality zone" located in an old storage building adjacent to the Istanbul Modern museum, which was to host autonomous programs and exhibits alongside the biennial proper. *Free Kick* (*Serbest Vuruş*) took its name from a photograph by Cengiz Tekin, which features a football player in the Turkish national uniform taking a free kick against a "team" of assembled civilians. Even without making explicit that those featured are members of Tekin's own family, the image plays with visual codes in the Turkish context in a manner that made them identifiable as Kurdish (Figure 19).

The exhibition brought together three generations of artists, thirty-four in total, from sixteen different cities, with works that commented on Turkey's recent political history. Altındere noted that he was especially interested in artistic positions, some from established artists, that otherwise could not find a platform. Similar to *Regarding Terror*, *Free Kick* combined contemporary visual art with documentary works. It covered the experience of marginalized communities and the everyday impact of state violence, militarism, and perspectives on sexuality along with documentaries on the Cumartesi Anneleri

(Saturday Mothers)[29] and on torture in Turkish prisons. Together with the biennial, the Hospitality Zone opened its doors on September 16, 2005. Given its subject matter and that it played out against the aforementioned memory boom in Turkey, during which official history became publicly questioned, it was no surprise that the show triggered heated debates. In addition, the attack on the exhibition about the September 6–7, 1955, pogrom had recently transpired; a large international conference on Armenians at the end of Ottoman Empire had taken place amid nationalist protest; and throughout the country there was renewed attention to the "Kurdish Question."

Let me first turn to the reactions from within the art world. Having reviewed previous shows curated by Altındere favorably, the art critic Ahu Antmen (2005) noted that the "*Free Kick* is not turned into a goal" despite "putting its finger on wounds in Turkey, foremost the 'Kurdish issue,' politics, the military, military coups, torture, issues of identity, gender. Although it wants to offer a much-needed platform for debate, this exhibition falls into the trap of all 'engaged' art." What Antmen felt was missing was a sense of abstraction or, to put it in art theory terms, sublimation. This lack, she contended, reduced the exhibition to a mere pop-art aesthetic, favoring content over form and devoid of "deeper" aesthetic engagement. Antmen's assessment that there was too little abstraction from the reality the artworks drew on presents an interesting counterpoint to the critiques of the RAF exhibition, where *too much* abstraction from reality, and a one-sided abstraction at that, was identified as problematic. Her colleague Ayşegül Sönmez (2005, 10) found the show's transformative energy "hard to escape" but proposed that the works deserved a different arrangement to fully unfold their effect and come off the wall, that is, have a transcendent impact.

Altındere was aware of the criticism that his own artworks as well as his curatorial endeavors lacked aesthetic abstraction. "I have been told that my works are very narrative, and very vulgar. 'The idea of the metaphor is lost on you [*metafordan yoksunsun*]' is something that I have heard frequently." For Altındere this was a conscious choice. He noted that accessibility was crucial for him in order to allow "audiences to enter a dialogue with the work." Although he is often labeled a "political artist," Altındere describes his work in terms of his everyday experiences: "My works are influenced by the political, societal, economic, religious, and gender relations out of which they emerge, they are nurtured by the *everyday*, they emerge from it." As Altındere's works are shaped by histories of violence, art also emerges as a privileged site to reveal such histories.

As high-tempered exchanges accompanied the exhibition, not just critics but artists too felt compelled to take a stance. The artist Şener Özmen

(2005) interpreted Antmen's evaluation of the exhibition as a putdown of *Free Kick*'s curatorial program, which emphasized collectivity rather than foregrounding individual artists and works. He suggested her critique may not merely reflect aesthetic but political preferences, a take that also suggests that within the art world political inclinations may be easier to discount than aesthetic ones.

The extent to which the show induced discomfort was, perhaps, most visible in Bedri Baykam's review. A painter and pronounced left nationalist (*ulusalcı*), Baykam was outraged by the exhibition, which he proposed aimed to show Turkey in "a bad light," especially to foreign visitors. In an entry on his personal website, he went so far as to insinuate that Altındere represented the extension of the Kurdistan Workers' Party (Partiya Karkên Kurdistan, PKK) into the art world. Eliciting protest, his review has since been taken down.

In retrospect, Erden Kosova (2007) relegated negative reactions to the exhibition to a "Frankfurt School–based criticism" and the outdated distinction between high and pop(ular) art. This conservatism discounted the political thrust that had characterized Turkey's art world over the past decades. Employing the Frankfurt School as a shorthand for an elitist focus on high art, he thus reproduced a rather problematic view of Adorno and Horkheimer's (1969) critique of the culture industries, which Adorno notably revised later on (1991).

Free Kick and Goal?

About a month after the opening, an "unidentified visitor" filed a complaint against the exhibition with the public prosecutor's office, and on October 13, 2005, the 2. Beyoğlu District Criminal Court ordered the confiscation of the exhibition catalogue (Ergün 2005). The court's decision rested on three images (Figures 20–22) that depicted military persons and references such as rank insignia and uniforms on the grounds that they constituted a public denigration of the Turkish armed forces. The following day, police officers raided Altındere's office but were unable to find any catalogues, since all of them had been distributed during the opening of the exhibition.

Almost two weeks later, the 3. Beyoğlu Criminal Court of First Instance (Asliye Ceza Mahkemesi) overturned the confiscation decree after Halil Altındere's brother, the lawyer Murat Altındere, appealed it. This time the court stated that "according to the currently valid domestic legal regulations Articles 9 and 10 of the European Convention on Human Rights (ECHR) have precedent here and in accordance with these articles the confiscation decision is hereby overturned." The decision further read:

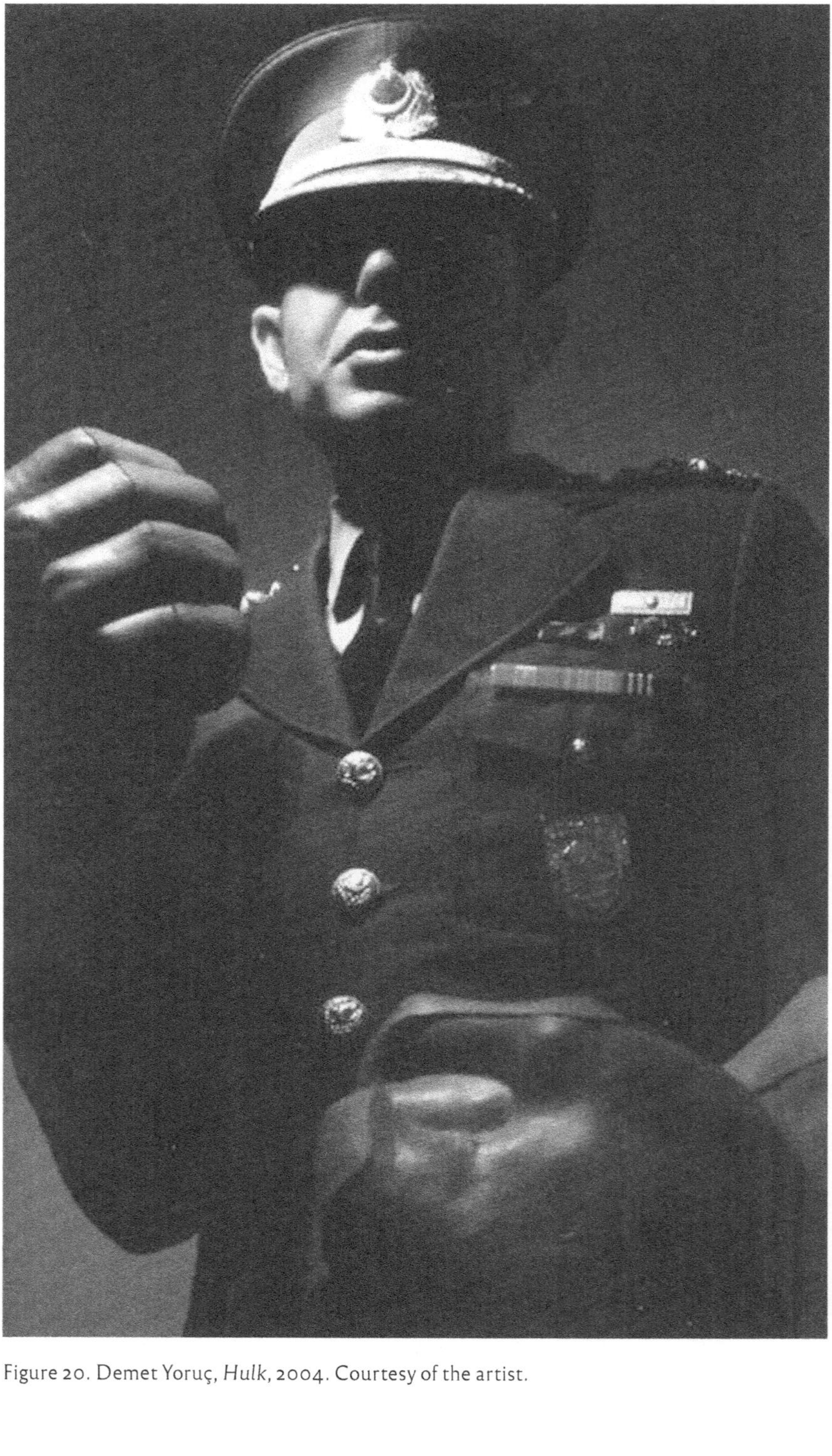

Figure 20. Demet Yoruç, *Hulk*, 2004. Courtesy of the artist.

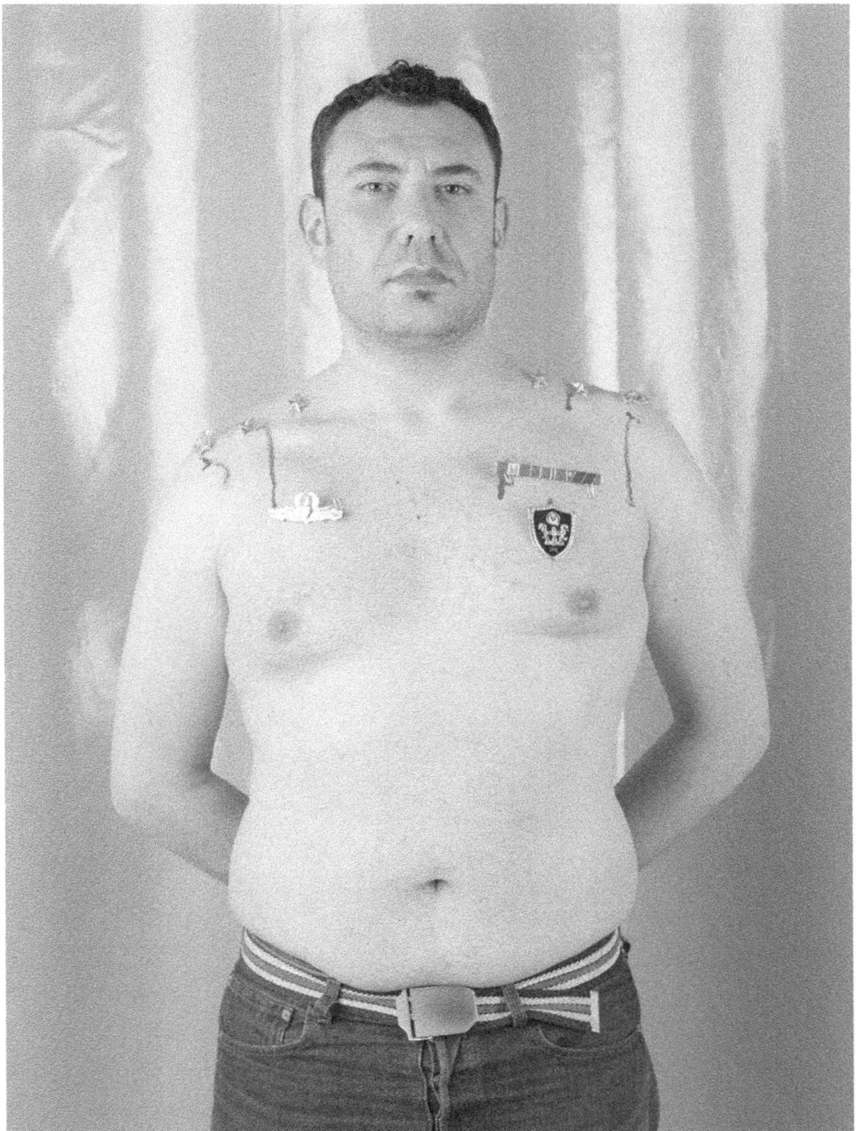

Figure 21. Murat Tosyalı, *Obedience*, 2004. Courtesy of the artist.

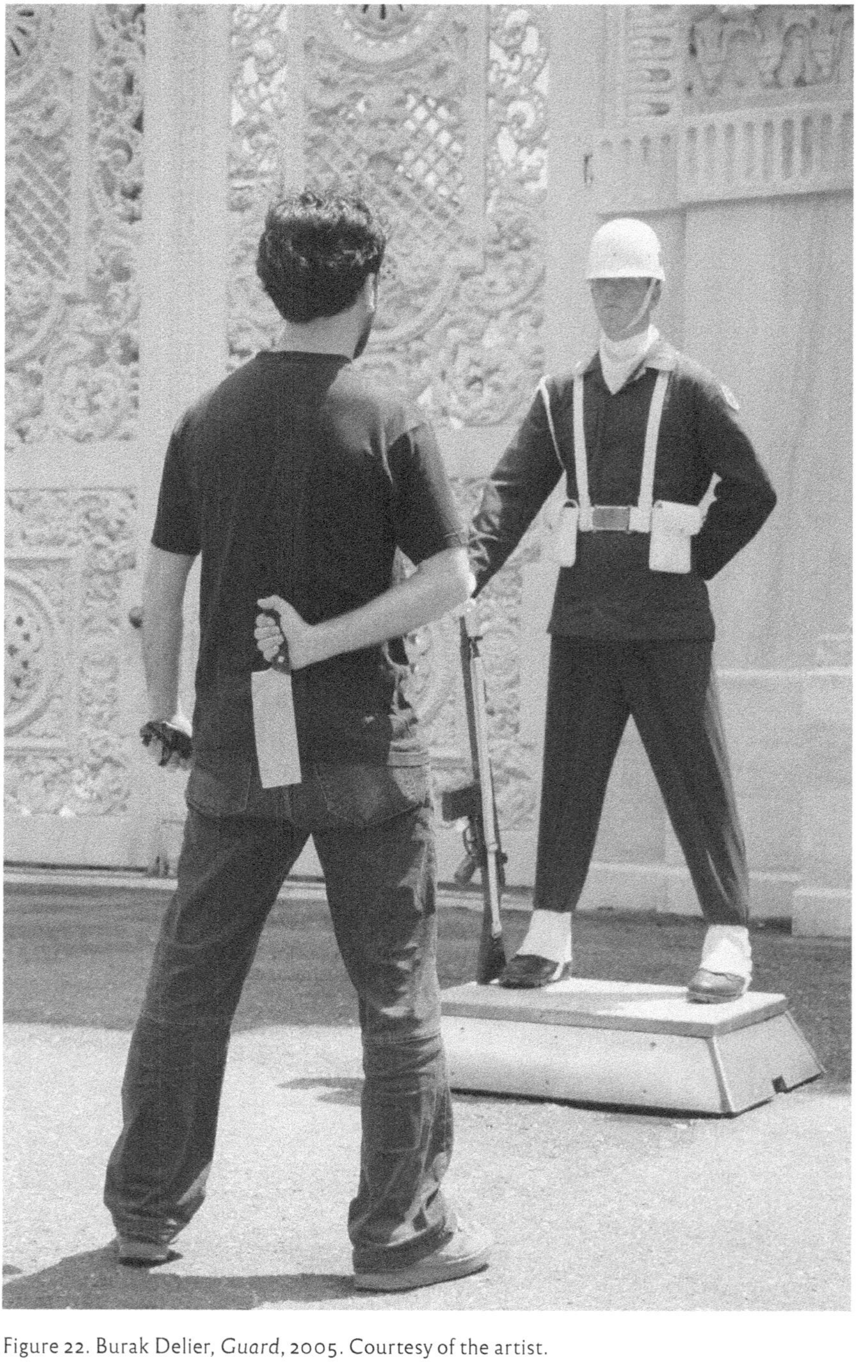

Figure 22. Burak Delier, *Guard*, 2005. Courtesy of the artist.

> None of the photographs that were cited as the grounds of the confiscation decision breached the limitations stated in these articles. Even though the artistic value of the photographs is debatable, even if they evoke the use of force, and even though they will not be met with approval by a large majority of society, as long as their content conforms to the ECHR norms, we must remember that a democracy needs to be able to endure all of these affects [*demokrasinin bütün bu duygulanımlara katlanmak olduğu unutulmamalıdır*].[30]

In our conversation, Altındere noted that this had been the first time that an art catalogue had been confiscated in Turkey. The defense, he recounted, was yet again grounded in the insistence that "the images were works of art and that it is in the nature of art to critique freely. We referred also to paragraph 4 of Article 301, in which expressions that serve to critique do not constitute an offense, and clarified that art presents what we call 'open works' [*açık yapıt*]—in the sense that they are open to interpretation. We prepared a portfolio with examples from art history, and that's how we saved ourselves from this affair."

There are several notable issues in this episode. The identity of the initial plaintiff was never revealed by the prosecution, but rumors circulated that it was lodged by a military widow or a mother who had lost her son in the army. This presents an interesting parallel to *Regarding Terror* in that affected family members, whose interests were in part congruent with that of the state, initiated silencing procedures. However, the question remains why the case initially only centered on the confiscation of a catalogue instead of on the closing of the exhibition. Was it the reprinted and easily circulatable image that was the problem here? Or was it solely out of a calculation that the motion to close an exhibition that was under the auspices of the influential and state-aligned Istanbul Foundation for Culture and Arts (IKSV) and part of a much-acclaimed biennial would have caused a major international scandal? The episode was even more curious as the confiscation attempt was not very rigorous. In fact, I was able to purchase a catalogue in a bookstore close to Altındere's office while the confiscation order was still in effect. Upheld only for a short while, enforced rather inconsistently, and quickly overturned, what did this order actually accomplish?

First, the confiscation order did succeed in delegitimizing the exhibition to a certain extent. It gave the court not only the opportunity to investigate if a denigration had indeed taken place—by probing the rather hazy boundaries between a critical artistic expression and an insulting representation—but to comment on the artistic merit of the works, the formal lack of expertise in this regard notwithstanding. Second, the temporary ban was successful insofar as it did discourage newspapers and other media outlets from reprinting the pictures in question, hence suppressing a possibly much broader circulation. Third, by categorizing the representations of militarism rather than the state practices that gave rise to these depictions as problematic, it successfully deflected the critique from the thing itself to its depiction. And finally, this delegitimizing move allowed for identifying Altındere himself as a target.

This last point became abundantly clear when the Beyoğlu Public Prosecutor's Office (Cumhuriyet Savcılığı) opened criminal proceedings, this time against Altındere personally. Redefining his role from curator to that of "instigator," the charge was again public denigration of the Turkish armed forces under Article 301. The prosecutor demanded a two-year prison sentence. Once more, Altındere's defense did not solely rely on freedom of expression but insisted that the works in question constituted art and that the critical impetus of art cannot be equated with insults. The notion that even if political in address art has to be treated differently than other kinds of expressions reiterates both the unity and the disparateness of arts and politics. As I will show in a moment, this separation, while grounded in a specific understanding of art, produces its own set of contradictions.

Altındere was acquitted of all charges on April 13, 2006. Reflecting on the trial more than a year later, a defiant Altındere expressed his surprise that it had been this particular exhibition that he had been indicted for. After all, the shows he had previously curated resembled *Free Kick* both in form and theme. One could speculate what rendered one artistic critique of the state more threatening than another or ask to what extent the international exposure of the biennial played a role in this process. But instead I want to suggest that it is the very inconsistency and arbitrariness of the silencing apparatus in Turkey that makes it so effective.

Discretionary Power

This inconsistency and arbitrariness also manifests itself in the discretionary power of officials, state-appointed provincial governors, and sometimes police forces, who are able to curtail free expression on the grounds of "threats" to the public order. This has led to a general mistrust of authorities in the art world, exacerbated by the fact that neither the Ministry of Culture and Tourism nor the cultural offices on the municipal or district levels speak out in support of artists faced with censorship.[31]

The one case in which the ministry actually did intervene, that of Hüseyin Karabey's film *Gitmek: My Marlon and Brando*, it did so in a contradictory fashion. The ministry co-funded Karabey's film, a first for the filmmaker, whose previous proposals had been rejected for ten years. Upon completion, the film was accepted to a number of prestigious international festivals, including the Tribeca Film Festival, where Karabey was awarded Best New Narrative Filmmaker. In December 2008, the film was released in Turkey to much critical acclaim. Around the same time, *Gitmek* was scheduled to be shown at Culturescapes Turkey, a Swiss festival cosponsored by the Turkish Ministry for Culture and Tourism for the substantial amount of 400,000 euros. All of a sudden, the film was removed from the program: A ministry aid, İbrahim Yazar, had threatened to withdraw the funding if the screening went ahead. In the ensuing debate it emerged that Yazar had acted on his own initiative, without an order from his superiors and, allegedly, without their knowledge. But instead of the rectification that Karabey expected, the transcript of an interview with Yazar in the *Süddeutsche Zeitung* by the journalist Kai Strittmatter emerged. In it Yazar proclaimed that in "sensitive times like these" (the bombardments of northern Iraq by the Turkish army and bombings of army vehicles and buses attributed to the PKK), the depiction of a "Turkish girl falling in love with a Kurd" was unacceptable (*Radikal* 2008).[32] During a press conference, Minister of Culture and Tourism Günay tried to diffuse the situation by stating that censorship on the part of his department was out of the question, citing the film's national release as proof. Pressed by the questions, however, he answered that it would be only natural that the Turkish state as a main sponsor of the festival would make requests pertaining to the program if they affected Turkey's image abroad. He implied that local organizers had referred to southeastern Anatolia as "Kurdistan," to which his department had not been able to remain silent (*"Türkiye'nin bir bölümünün bir başka isimle isimlendirilmesi karşısında sessiz mi kalmalıyız?"*; cited in Önderoğlu 2008). The film was eventually screened on the initiative of the cinema directors, who had already received copies of the film and could not be compelled otherwise. Again, this case exhibits many inconsistencies, and pressure was exerted even beyond the boundaries of the Turkish state, this time without recourse to legal action but by way of threatening financial repercussions.

Over the past decade or so artists have developed strategies in order to overcome state-induced discouragement and circumvent incentives for self-censorship. The formation of the 19 Ocak Kollektifi (Collective January 19) allowed for artistic interventions that protected the anonymity of participants. Established after the murder of Hrant Dink and named after the day he was assassinated, the group aimed to show solidarity with the Armenian community of Turkey in particular and with persecuted and oppressed segments of society in general. One of their projects was entitled *Münferit* (meaning "individual," "lonely," "singular"). The 2009 installation displayed the names of victims of state-sanctioned assassinations, enforced disappearances, and torture during incarceration.

The director Aydın Orak used a different but no less notable strategy to fight against censorship when his documentary *Bêrîvan—Bir Başkaldırı Destanı* (*Bêrîvan—The Legend of Rebellion*) was invited to the Batman film festival in 2009. Telling the story of the 1992 Newroz uprising in the Kurdish town of Cizre, it follows Bêrîvan, who led the struggle against the Turkish security forces.[33] The screening of the film was hindered at the last minute on orders of the governor, who—without having seen the film—declared that it "disturbed the unity of the Turkish nation" and featured "PKK propaganda." Orak took to the stage and recounted the film scene by scene to the assembled audience. The attempt to silence *Bêrîvan* seemed all the more arbitrary as it had actually been presented at the ministry's display during the Cannes film festival earlier that year.[34]

This kind of discretionary power is often used when it comes to the works of Kurdish artists. Visual artists such as Şener Özmen, Cengiz Tekin, and Berat Işık, who have consciously made the decision to stay and work in Diyarbakir, have noted that the security forces should by now be the most prolific art connoisseurs in the country, as they continue to visit and record all art events in the city. Even though preclearance procedures for arts and cultural events ceased in Diyarbakir in the early 2000s, artists who are organizationally affiliated with the Kurdish rights struggle continue to face specific kinds of challenges. This is maybe nowhere more visible than in the network of the Mesopotamia Cultural Centers, which continue to be subject to police harassment, phone taps, and regular raids; their archives have been confiscated numerous times (see Chapter 3). While members of the Mesopotamia Cultural Centers have noted an easing of control mechanisms for the events they organize in Istanbul, their activities in the Kurdish regions remain under tight oversight. ID information, *temiz kağıdı* (a police clearance certificate), and program details are habitually required of them before taking part in any event.[35]

Whereas in the German case the question of what constitutes Nazi aesthetics often involves heated, even tortuous, debates, characterizations of artistic expressions as terroristic have been employed rather promiscuously in Turkey. Minister of the Interior İdris Naim Şahin (2011–2013) infamously indicted the arts in general in a speech that identified pen and canvas as weapons and the arts as the "backyard of terrorism." Yet it has most often been Kurdish musicians who have been indicted for "offenses" ranging from singing guerilla songs to "rhythmically accompanying separatist slogans" and "keeping up morale" at rallies and demonstrations. The ongoing court cases against the artists affiliated with the Kurdish rights struggle illustrate that all utterances by Kurdish artists can potentially be construed not only as political expressions but as terrorism. In contrast to Altındere's cases, their expressions are not recognized as art but as illegitimate and decivilizing in terms of their historical and present-day references. These cases show that despite legal reforms and the supposed democratization measures that Turkey has enacted between 2004 and 2015, the collecting of potentially "incriminating" information never ceased.[36] This information, it seems, can be arbitrarily transformed into indictments in politically opportune moments (or laid to rest in a virtual or actual drawer until such opportune moments present themselves).

The (In)Visibility of the Unspeakable

The limits to the freedom of artistic expression in Germany are delineated in part by incitement laws that reference the country's Nazi past. The RAF as a phenomenon and the reactions of the German state to its emergence are problematic both because they are structurally linked or strategically likened to this past and because they unsettle the image of a (re)civilized Germany. In the Turkish case, these limits are reached when aesthetic approaches that counter official national narratives are construed as threats to the country's "territorial integrity" and sovereignty, and for decades these have been equated with terrorism. Yet the cases also show that within these fields of delimitation there are considerable contingencies: The unspeakable remains, necessarily so, unclearly mapped. After all, other types of artistic production on the RAF or works critical of official Turkish history have not been met with the same outrage or legal repercussions. An unambiguous demarcation of the unspeakable would present blatant and recognizable censorship, incompatible with "modern and civilized politics"—which is a special concern for both Germany and Turkey. The decivilized is thus marked yet also somewhat invisible.

The insistence on politics of civility is not only a question of self-perception. It is also connected to anxieties about perceptions abroad: The Fassbinder case pointed to issues of anti-Semitism and the legacy of Nazism; the RAF brought up questions of homegrown terrorism and how Germany responded to that challenge. Attacks against Altındere were often couched in statements that "the likes of him" should not be sent abroad because "they were tarnishing Turkey's image" (Evren 2008, 42).[37]

Notably, Germany's delimitation of free speech with regard to National Socialism is taken both to indicate and to hamper its modernness, to prove its

Occidental belonging (by way of taking historical responsibility) while putting its democratic maturity into question. In Turkey, those upholding the sanctity of territorial boundaries see themselves as defenders of Turkey's modernity and civility, while in the eyes of domestic opposition and the international community, censorship mechanisms indicate Turkey's deficient democratic structures.

The defense of freedom of the arts in the cases discussed in this chapter relied on conceptions of the autonomy of art. Yet this defense brings with it its own set of contradictions. The double-edged conception of the autonomy of art both protects and weakens the impact of art. Mary Devereaux (1995, 42) posits that with political art in particular we face a dilemma, in so far as we "either . . . embrace the political character of art and risk subjecting art and artists to political interference, or we protect art and its makers from political interference by insisting upon their 'autonomy,' but at the cost of denying the political character of art and its broader connection with life."

The issue is complicated by the circumstance that artists themselves at times frame the autonomy of art in formalistic terms, especially in their defense against political intervention. In his trial, Altındere insisted not on freedom of expression per se but rather on art as an expression of a different order, one free of the constraints that govern other forms of expression. Although his work might be seen as a far cry from formalistic frameworks, it is the latter that have informed the very existence of the constitutionally guaranteed freedom of art. Klaus Biesenbach moves even closer to evoking formalist principles by citing "beauty" and "truth" to justify the RAF exhibition. His critics, on the other hand, bemoaned both the show's "retreat to art" as divorced from politics as well as "a lack of critical positions," thus illustrating that the argument of the autonomy of art can be employed in the same case for diametrically opposed purposes. As such, *Regarding Terror* and *Free Kick* constituted transgressions of art into the political sphere that were met with both aesthetic critiques and political delegitimization attempts.

Judith Butler (1998, 255) proposes that just as censoring a text remains incomplete, so does uncensoring a text. Censorship reconfigures whatever it operates on, even if it is "unsuccessful" in suppressing certain expressions (Mazzarella 2013). We can see this in the case of *Regarding Terror*, where the exhibition's concept was changed yet where the controversy remained the prism that refracted (and delimited) the presentation, reception, and reviews of the exhibition that eventually emerged. We can trace the same dynamic in the news coverage on *Free Kick* that marked different incarnations of self-censorship.

Somewhat paradoxically so, the manner in which censorship and silencing mechanisms work in Turkey leads to a high visibility of censorship and thus, at times, to very visible responses. In contrast, in Germany, where the impression abounds that expression is free, censorship has largely disappeared from the public discourse and takes on forms that are often obscured, for example, on the funding level, which is more susceptible to interventions by politics (Barnett 2004, 34n23). Cultural departments in Germany generally award funding through artistic advisory committees. While the compositions of these committees are publicly announced, neither the way that committees are chosen nor their deliberations are subject to public knowledge. Much of the related silencing mechanisms thus remain invisible.[38] The de facto suppression of Fassbinder's play is rarely labeled as censorship (even at the time, only the Frankfurt's Green Party's opposition used this term). Instead it is framed as an exception arising from Germany's difficult past. It is due to the assumption that freedom of expression exists that censorship becomes unrecognizable, or misrecognized, as in the case of *Regarding Terror.* As government funding for contemporary art is limited in Turkey, possibilities for intervention in production processes are likewise limited, making postrelease silencing and delegitimization efforts the most opportune points of intervention but also much more visible (with the exception of privately funded cultural institutions, where censoring mechanisms often remain hidden).

Explicitly political art that references decivilizing moments written out of the official memory regime is seen as a transgression that breaches the boundaries within which art is supposed to operate. Lying outside the national frame, such art poses a challenge that is at certain strategic points met with silencing efforts, be they financial, political, or legal. These efforts are not necessarily complete, but they consolidate and separate the operational realms of the arts and of politics. While censorship—in and on principle—is regarded as incommensurable with modern politics in both Germany and Turkey, the enactment of silencing mechanisms in the cases assembled here are presented as guarding modernity and civility in the shadow of specific historical sensitivities that foreclose purported anti-Semitism and of the legitimation crises that characterize the "global war on terror" and each country's past challenges with "security politics." They thus silence perceived threats to territorial integrity and national sovereignty.

6
Enterprising Art, Aestheticizing Business

"A biennial," Sarah Thornton (2008, 225) notes, "is not just a show that takes place every two years; it is a goliath exhibition that is meant to capture the global artistic moment. Although institutions like the Whitney and the Tate hold national surveys that they call biennials, a true biennial is international in outlook and hosted by a city rather than a museum." This chapter takes the Istanbul and Berlin biennials of 2005 and 2006 as occasions to think through the political economy of art in the urban setting. I ask what the presentation of particular "global artistic moments" might say about the conditions of producing art in the city as well as what the different modes of artistic presentation in the urban realm might reveal about local and national histories and present-day conditions.

Biennials, their histories, claims, and projections, are a peculiar kind of formation. Today's biennials are, as is so often remarked, the descendants of the "festival exhibitions" and the "spectacular imperial displays" of world fairs first held more than 165 years ago (Ferguson et al. 2005, 48). Apart from their focus on contemporary art, they share claims to a pronounced international character, declare themselves as forums for artistic experimentation away from market pressures, and assert both globalism—and hence a kind of universalism—and site-specific uniqueness (see Harvey 2001). Throughout the 1990s and 1980s an increasing number of biennials have been launched in geopolitical locations that have long been regarded as "peripheral" (Kortun and Hanru 2003), such as São Paulo, Havana, Dakar, Gwangju, Taipei, Buenos Aires, Busan, Shanghai, Cairo, Centinje, Tirana, and Athens. Among them, the Istanbul Biennial, established in 1987, has ventured to challenge the narratives of its triumphalist historical predecessors, the Great Exhibition of London (1851), the Paris Universal Exposition (1867), or the 1893 World's Columbian Exposition in Chicago—to name just a few benchmarks in the spectacular display of industrial and colonial might (Çelik 1992). While today's biennials have asserted the desire to distinguish themselves from their imperial predecessors, they have also carried with them notable continuities in that they work through a kind of spectacularization. Never "just" an exhibition, these events are designed to deliver an encompassing experience that is accompanied by an array of programs that aim at contextualizing either the included artworks or the overall concept of the show. These additional elements range from scholarly lectures (providing the theoretical background) and films (offering a "different, more popular, and accessible medium of visualization") to the notorious DJ dance party (highlighting the fun, entertaining aspects of the whole endeavor)—and lest it be forgotten, the endless arsenal of related merchandise. Their format resonates with Guy Debord's (1994 [1967], 24) proposition that "the spectacle is capital accumulated to the point where it becomes image," in that these spectacles can be conceptualized as both the site of the commercial cooptation of art and as the expression of this cooptation.

In the case of Venice, the longest-running biennial (it was established in 1895), we can find another continuity: The Venice Biennial is still organized in the form of national pavilions. Although it has in the past incorporated a Roma (2007) and a Kurdish pavilion (2009) as well as Underconstruction (a platform initiated by the Armenian-Argentinian artist Silvina Der-Meguerditchian, 2007), as gestures to integrate stateless "nations," these interventions have remained temporary and have done little to unsettle the dynamics of national reification, that is, the national frame, in the art world. That there is growing unease with this format was expressed in the Franco-German pavilion switch during the 2013 installment of the Venice Biennial and Germany's inclusion of four artists who do not hold German citizenship.[1] Still, the national frame continues to hold its overall sway.

Like their historical predecessors, contemporary art festivals and biennials are often presented as engaging a broader public and thus as "democratizing" access to the arts when compared to "conventional" art formats. What sets them apart, however, is that in cityscapes increasingly characterized by income polarization, gentrification, and social segmentation, urban art spectacles have become a pronounced economic development strategy—a process that actually feeds into exclusionary practices in the urban realm. In the cases of Berlin and Istanbul, such exclusionary practices are compounded by histories of dispossession that are deeply intertwined with the history of art and its institutions.

But this spectacularization is not exclusive to biennials. Commercial and nonprofit art events, art fairs, and biennials increasingly have come to resemble one another. Urban art spectacles are seen to enhance the city's prestige and to provide incentives for (foreign) investment and tourism. They have produced a dualism of enterprising art and aestheticizing business that is based on a convergence and reconciliation of economic interests, cultural policy, and artistic practices, three realms generally conceptualized as pursuing opposing interests and operating logics.

Just like the joining of art and administration, the instrumentalization of art as a stimulant for the urban economy has posed a series of conceptual problems with regard to what I have called idealized understandings of art and, especially, its assumed civilizing power. The ensuing tensions are in need of constant negotiation, over the course of which the conditions under which art is produced, circulated, and exhibited are often veiled and displaced. In this process, art has not only been identified as a vital location factor and as symbolic capital in the urban environment but also as a blueprint for the neoliberalization of the economy, in which the precariousness of artists' lives is increasingly portrayed to have a model character.

The following is thus an interrogation of the artistic, political, and economic variables that contribute to the spectacularization of art—at a time when art spectacles emerge as the preferred form of presenting art in the urban setting. I use the notion of "preferred" here not to indicate artistic or curatorial predilections—although participation in biennials and international art fairs has become an indispensable stepping stone for artistic careers—but those of sponsors and municipalities who consider these events lucrative with regard to both the cultural and economic capital they produce.

Although spearheaded by different sets of actors or interest groups who seemingly occupy different positions within the local and international art world and are heirs to divergent cultural policy trajectories, this development is strikingly similar in Berlin and Istanbul. Proposing that parallels arise only in part from congruent economic, social, and political processes, I see Istanbul and Berlin as locked into an internationalized circulation of ideas pertaining to the uses, expediency, and versatility of art—and especially of art spectacles for urban renewal, image making, and city branding.

Staging the Biennials

The Istanbul and Berlin biennials took place in 2005 and 2006, respectively. The curators of the Ninth Istanbul Biennial (IB9), Vasıf Kortun and Charles Esche,[2] opened the catalogue of IB9 by proposing that

> this biennial is for and about Istanbul. We have sought *to address* the environment in which the work will be shown and to place art in a dialogue with different aspects and observations of the city itself. This has meant asking artists to stay in the city and produce *new work*, as well as selecting work that might shed light on the particularities of Istanbul in comparison with cities elsewhere. It has also meant *rejecting dramatic or historical locations in which* to show the art in *favour of more* modest living and working environments in the city. . . . It will hopefully provoke a new awareness of some common perceptions or a reassessment of the personal clichés that we all carry in our heads. This is what we believe art can do to and for us, and how it can, in its own way, change the world.
>
> (Esche and Kortun 2005, 9; emphasis mine)

While the IB9, then, had as its very theme the city of Istanbul, the Fourth Berlin Biennial (BB4), curated by Maurizio Cattelan, Massimiliano Gioni, and Ali Subotnick,[3] borrowed its title from Steinbeck's novel *Of Mice and Men*.[4] Introducing the concept, or, as they insisted tongue in cheek, the "non-concept," the BB4 curators stated:

> We believe that art is about the experiencing of possible worlds, getting diverted from or immersed in a reality we had previously overlooked. So, don't think this is a show about Berlin. Even if it takes place in one of the city's streets, it is not a show about Auguststrasse, or even about Mitte in the year 2006. If we were to be tremendously ambitious, we would say our Berlin is just a landscape of the mind, it only exists in our heads: So it could be *anywhere*—and yet it could only possibly exist here, this street is an archetype or maybe just an example: it is real and yet completely imaginary.
>
> (2006, 23; emphasis mine)

The two exhibition concepts showed parallels in the description of the possibilities that art heralds, the capacity of art to make us see what has been previously unseen, to see the present in a different light and—perhaps—imagine a different future. The relationship that the two events proposed with the city in which they were located, however, seemed to provide diametrically opposed starting points. On one side of the spectrum, the BB4 curators present "a landscape of the mind" to a seemingly undefined audience. On the other end, we find a "biennial for and about Istanbul" and, by extension, for and about the region, as Kortun and Esche emphasized during numerous panel discussions. Yet the BB4 took place in the very real environment of Berlin, and, even if it intended to, it did not escape its particular history. While employing a wider set of locations than previous installments that centered on prominent historical sites, like the cisterns of Sultanahmet, the IB9 locations, many of which it—just as its Berlin counterpart—"pioneered,"[5] were no less "dramatic" or "historical."[6]

Both biennials utilized a dispersed set of locations as exhibition venues, favoring sites usually inaccessible to the public. As many art critics and visitors noted, these sites were often more impressive than the artworks themselves (Hohmann 2005b, Stange 2006). In Istanbul, for instance, stunning—one might say spectacular—views of the city and the Bosporus competed with the works on display. In Berlin, they were shown in different locations along the 920-meter-long Auguststrasse in the Mitte district. Infamous as one of the city's most impoverished quarters in the eighteenth century, Auguststrasse later emerged as an important center for Jewish life in Berlin and as an iconic site for the Weimar Republic's art scene when Josef von Sternberg set his movie *The Blue Angel* (1930) on that street.[7]

The most evocative location in this context was the Jewish Girls School, built in 1927. Closed down by the National Socialists in 1942, it was renamed the Bertolt Brecht High School during GDR times. It was closed down yet again in the process of German reunification. Having been restituted to the Jewish Central Committee of Germany, the building was the only biennial location subject to the tight security measures for synagogues, Jewish schools, and community centers throughout Germany, measures that were augmented after waves of right-wing violence in the 1990s.

Within this site of overlapping processes of dispossession,[8] the work of the Polish artist Robert Kuśmirowski, entitled *Wagon* (2006), a life-size train wagon eerily reminiscent of the cattle cars that transported millions of people to concentration camps during the Third Reich, received a lot of attention. The work was identified as especially haunting by visitors during the guided tours that I accompanied because of its historical and spatial connotations and the juxtaposition of the light materials used in its construction with the heaviness of the memories it invoked (Figure 23).

The curators made it a point to stress that the location had remained unaltered. The desolate wallpaper, crumbling walls, and accumulated dust seemed to confirm this assertion. An interviewee involved in the production of the exhibition, however, noted that the location had been carefully staged. Walls had been moved to make room for larger artworks and redecorated to fit into the overall dilapidated, "vintage" look. As such, the staging of the exhibition space played intentionally into what could be called "the spectacle of authenticity"—an overdramatized version thereof that at times enhanced and at

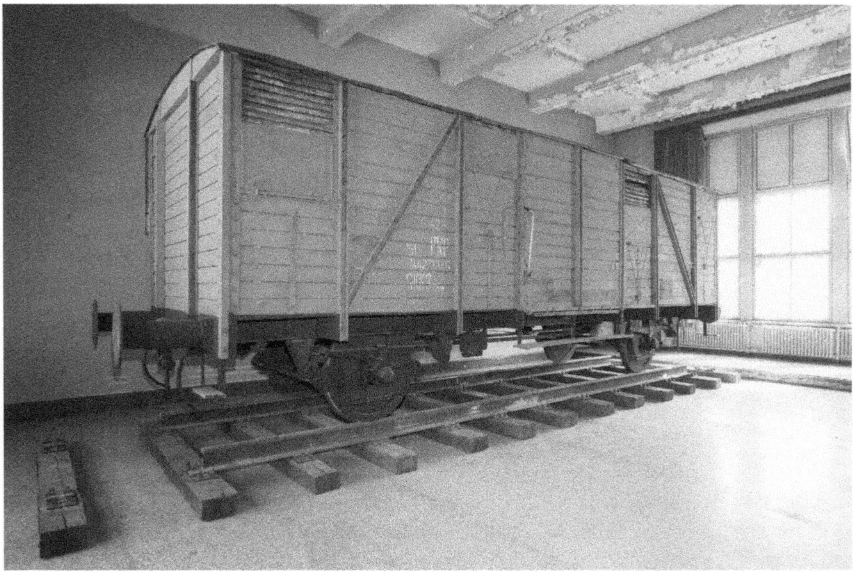

Figure 23. Robert Kuśmirowski, *Wagon*, 2006, acrylic paint, paper, cardboard, wood, 300×280×1000 cm, private collection, Kortrijk, Belgium. Courtesy of Robert Kuśmirowski; Foksal Gallery Foundation, Warsaw; Johnen Galerie, Berlin. Installation view. Photograph. Courtesy of Uwe Walter, Fourth Berlin Biennial for Contemporary Art, 2006.

others overpowered the present artworks. That the curators were highly aware of the weight that the space carried became quickly apparent in my conversation with the assistant curator Zdravka Bajović. Bajović noted that the curatorial team devoted much discussion to ascertaining which artworks could "stand up" or "hold their own" in this historically loaded environment. She also recounted that the BB4 curators—with their event opening about six months after the Istanbul Biennial—were surprised when they saw the Istanbul event and noted the structural resemblance, especially with regard to regimes of display and the selected locations. I raise this point not to imply that there was an imitative factor—quite to the contrary. The lead time for both biennials was between eighteen and twenty-three months, so both concepts had long been in the works. Rather, my sense from these two specific arts events as well as others in both cities was that the recovery of usually inaccessible places had become a desirable, at times even normative, way of presenting and experiencing art in the urban setting in the 2000s, just as the 1990s had been primarily marked by the conversion of industrial spaces that had become available with the neoliberal deindustrialization of urban environment (Zukin 1995).

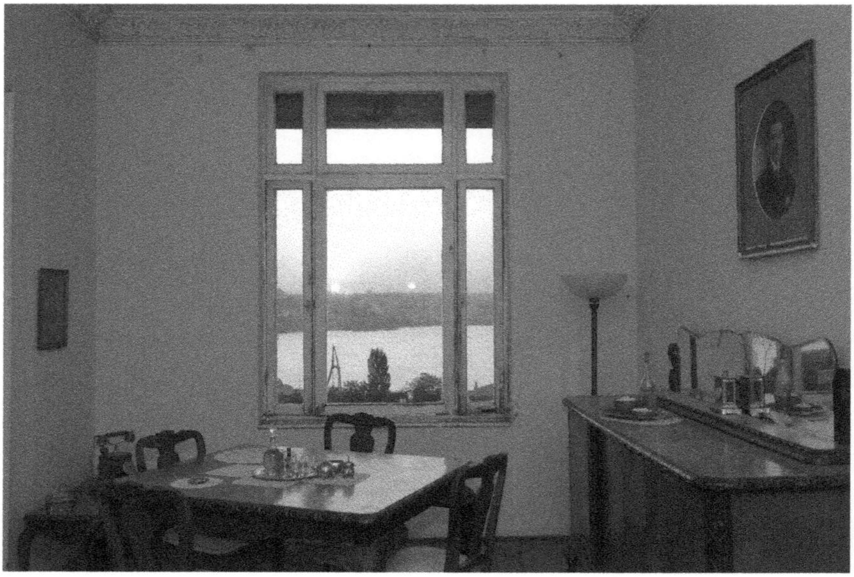

Figure 24. Michael Blum, *A Tribute to Safiye Behar*, 2005. Courtesy of IKSV Archive.

In Istanbul, the exhibition sites were dispersed—yet within walking distance—throughout the Beyoğlu district, reaching from its main pedestrian street İstiklal Caddesi over the neighborhoods of Şişhane and Tophane to the Antrepo, a former warehouse located at a now defunct loading dock at Karaköy's waterfront, adjacent to the Istanbul Modern museum. This particular *parcours* also made accessible buildings no longer in use, such as the Garibaldi building, founded by the Italian Opera Society in 1863, and a former tobacco depot.[9]

Among the locations, Deniz Palace featured a play with reality and fiction through specific (national) historical references similar yet different to those of Kuśmirowski. Michael Blum's *A Tribute to Safiye Behar* (2005) introduced the audience to a fictional character by that name and presented a "reconstruction" of her office, diaries, and photographs (Figures 24 and 25).

Behar, we learn, was not only an important feminist Marxist of Jewish descent but also a close confidant and, as the displayed correspondence between the two revealed, lover of Mustafa Kemal Atatürk, asserting considerable influence on his political thinking, especially with regard to women's rights. The detailed setup, the letters and photographs, together with a video featuring Behar's great-grandson, now a successful businessman in New York, generated many animated discussions among visitors.

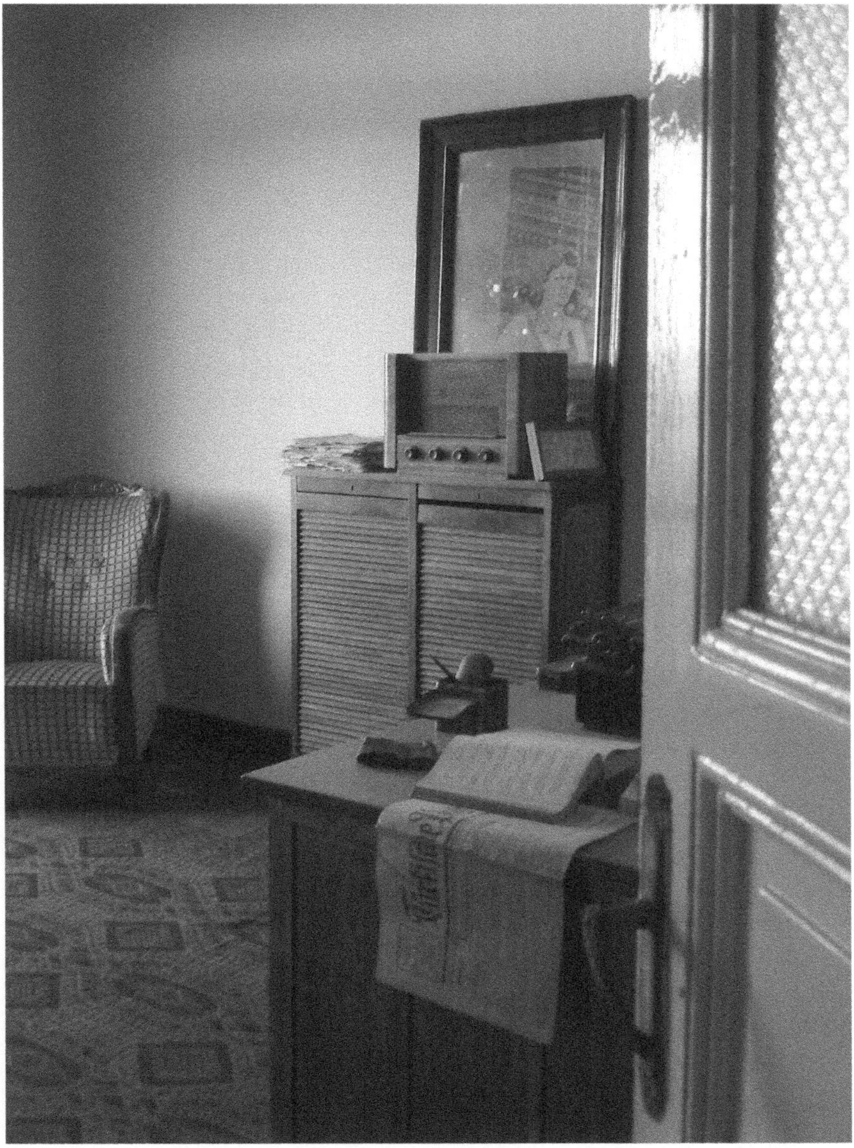

Figure 25. Michael Blum, *A Tribute to Safiye Behar*, 2005. Photograph by the author.

While Kuśmirowski reproduced or reenacted history—a history still very present in Berlin not least in the form of memorials, a number of which are within walking distance of Auguststrasse—that history was also partially silenced because it remained unaddressed by the organizers. Blum's fictionalized history, in turn, pointed to silences in the Turkish context, with Behar's emigration invoking a number of unsettling episodes of the national past in the form of the repression and persecution of its non-Muslim communities. It pointed to the discursive erasure in official Turkish history of the very existence of non-Muslims, including those once playing prominent roles in the public life of the Ottoman Empire and Turkey. Did Behar leave because of the wealth tax imposed on non-Muslims in the 1940s, because of the September 6–7, 1955, pogrom, or for entirely different reasons? Why had no one heard about this Jewish lover, confidant, and intellectual interlocutor of Atatürk before? These were some of the questions raised by visitors.

Mobilizing the memory of Jews in Europe, both works presented critical interventions that reinscribed the former Jewish presence in both Istanbul and Berlin—and by extension—Turkey and Germany. They also pointed to a notable connection between the history of Jewish absence in Berlin and Istanbul (as with non-Muslims in general, in the case of the latter) and the reconfiguration of the urban space, namely, that the "voids" left by the murder, expulsion, or dispossession of minorities frequently end up being vital spaces for urban regeneration projects, which are often pioneered by artists, who, given little available financial means, search to occupy "vacant" and "rundown" spaces in the city. In both of these examples the violent, decivilizing history of the nation-state shapes the conditions of artistic production and of the presentation of art in the urban setting.

There is another notable convergence that these two works reflect. Taken together, the pieces by Kuśmirowski and Blum point to parallel processes in which claims to authenticity and site-specific uniqueness emerge both as an aesthetic currency—in the works of art and their staging—and as an economic currency for the city that hosts the biennial. As Andreas Huyssen (2003, 18) argues, these kinds of recoveries are in fact compatible with the post-1989 marketing of memory by the cultural industries, particularly in the official, state-initiated "celebrations of diversity" that have become vital markers in the self-representation of global cities such as Istanbul and Berlin.

Exquisite Commodification or Last Resort for Artistic Experimentation?

While the Istanbul Biennial featured mostly commissioned works, the majority of the artworks shown in Berlin belonged to galleries and private collections. The sources of these works were prominently displayed on the tags accompanying each piece. Similar to the inclusion into museum collections, taking part in a biennial not only increases the value of presented artworks but the market value of participating artists overall. The curators of both biennials—well aware of this dynamic—choose different ways of dealing with this issue. In Istanbul, there was an attempt against accommodating the market, manifest, for instance, in the conceptualization of the accompanying printed material, which offered a compilation of short introductions to the exhibited artists and their displayed artworks. Emphasis was given, however, to an edited volume with artistic, curatorial, and sociological reflections on the city and to individual artists' books published under the aegis of the IB9. The publications resulted from a conscious decision to generate discussions on the conceptual framework of the biennial instead of providing potential collectors with color prints of the exhibited works. Kortun argued that although this procedure would certainly not deter potential buyers (neither, I presume, did it necessarily intend to), it also did not make it easy for them to identify in advance the works they might want to acquire and locate the galleries representing the respective artists. In Berlin, by contrast, the catalogue included large prints of the artworks along with the artists' gallery affiliations and thus resembled the sales catalogues of commercial galleries and art fairs.[10] Lenders to the Istanbul Biennial were listed in the back of the catalogue without being cross-referenced to the actual artists and works that they represented. Not without pride, Esche and Kortun repeatedly highlighted their refusal to cater to (international) collectors, museum acquisitionists, and critics, "the frequent-flyer crowd," as they called them. This strategy also entailed forgoing the usual social functions this clientele tends to expect. The effectiveness of this "tactic" (in de Certeau's [1984] sense) can surely be questioned: Indeed, their refusal might have added to the event's allure, and their decision certainly did not discourage the international arts crowd from attending. After all, who would turn down a trip to much-hyped Istanbul, especially if a home institution pays for it? In contrast, the BB4 organizers employed the exact opposite strategy, ensuring that the press covered the most exclusive parties and taking advantage of every chance for photo ops. Portraying all avenues for publicity as opportunities to invigorate Berlin's art scene, the organizers of the Berlin Biennial welcomed coverage ranging from the most upscale art magazines to airtime on Italian MTV.

A different but related issue pertaining to market pliability and internationalism was the extent to which diversity was addressed in the biennials. The persistent Orientalist tropes in the conception of international contemporary art exhibitions has been increasingly criticized both within and without the art world. The same is true for persistent Eurocentrism and unequal gender distribution; gender inequity abounds in the art world (Wu 2009). Yet the Berlin Biennial presented a lineup consisting of the usual who's-who of the Western European and US art scene, apart from a few prolific Eastern Europeans. Neither the "non-Western" plurality of Berlin nor that of the international art world was reflected, inspiring the late Nigerian curator Okwui Enwezor to declare during a panel discussion on the state of biennials worldwide: "For the first time, in a long time, I feel that I am not object of an exhibition. This show is all about white angst."

The curators of the Istanbul Biennial stated that they explicitly wanted to "stay away" from what they identified as "generic internationalism" and instead incorporated mainly artists from the Balkans as well as the Near and Middle East. *Free Kick*, a part of the biennial put together by the guest curator Halil Altındere, featuring works on Turkey's difficult past and present, including its diverse demography, elicited a lot of attention from visitors and local authorities alike (see Chapter 5). Similarly, Jakup Ferri's *An Artist Who Does Not Speak English, Is No Artist* (2005), a video in which the artist explicates this very predicament in his own broken English, thematized the artist's marginality as he lives and works in Pristina. Yet the very fact that his work was part of the biennial indicates that he had already arrived at the center of the art world—and its markets, albeit being subject to Orientalizing evaluations of his work by virtue of being a "post-socialist subject" (Muka 2004).

Throughout the Ninth Istanbul Biennial, its organizer, the Istanbul Foundation for Culture and Arts (IKSV), as well as different arts and culture groups organized public discussions, some closely related to the exhibition and its conceptual framework, others pertaining to current trends in the local and international art world. Issues such as the ethics of curating, collecting, and producing art and especially the topic of commercial cooptation and sponsorship were discussed in a controversial and often fervent manner. It was no exception that specific artists and curators were confronted with accusations by both art world actors and "lay" audiences of being handmaidens to the political and economic establishment. During a panel discussion organized within the framework of the biennial's annex at the Antrepo, harsh critiques were leveled against the institutional organizer of the biennial, IKSV, as it is funded by the Eczacıbaşı industrial group, a family that has historically strong political ties to the state establishment (Yardımcı 2005). The accusation that biennial participants were "selling out" to corporate sponsors was repeatedly raised. One audience member argued that "artists should stop cooperating with these sponsors at any cost, even if this means that they have to stop producing art or starve," and asked rather confrontationally, "what is it that you think you do for the common good, for humanity?" While this particular intervention carried much pathos and relied on idealized, even romanticized notions of art that render themselves to easy scandalization in face of the corporate sponsorship that the biennial has to rely on, the arts writer and curator Erden Kosova, himself wary of the influence of big corporations within the biennial context, tried to steer the discussion in a different direction. At the time, he proposed to accept the funding but to "bring down the system from inside" by exhibiting aesthetically and politically oppositional works and concepts. Even seemingly positive remarks such as the curator Ali Akay's interjection that the biennial had elevated Turkey's image in Europe were forcefully rebutted by the art critic Ali Artun, who stated, *"sanatın davasıyla Erdoğan'ın davası aynı olamaz"*—"the aims of art cannot be the same as those of Erdoğan." Implying that the intentions of the biennial organizers were aligned—even if only by default—with those of the government, Artun asked whom and what the Istanbul Biennial was actually for: Was the city's image at stake, serving the public or Turkey's international self-presentation, especially with regard to the European Union accession negotiations—then still high on Turkey's political agenda—by way of an artistic flagship project?

The issue of commercial cooptation was rarely, if at all, addressed in the course of the Berlin Biennial. One journalist made an implicit criticism during the opening press conference by interrupting Gaby Horn, then director of both the Berlin Biennial and the hosting institution the KW Institute for Contemporary Art (KW), while she was acknowledging the string of sponsors, saying: "This is a press conference; we are interested in the conceptual framework of the exhibition, not the sponsors!" The intervention elicited applause, and Horn, seemingly uncomfortable, promised to wrap up her speech promptly. Thomas Girst, the director of the automobile producer BMW's Cultural Communication Group, which along with the insurance giant Allianz[11] was the main private sponsor of the BB4, had preceded Gaby Horn and seemed to have anticipated this kind of reaction. Trying to make light of the contentious relationship between corporate sponsorship and the arts, he prefaced his statement to the press by stating: "I know that at these kinds of occasions, the words of the benefactors, the economic partners are always longingly awaited, which is why I will keep my remarks very short." While his words failed to elicit the good will of the audience they seemed to aim for, it is notable that Girst did not use the term "sponsor"[12] but framed BMW's support as that of a "benefactor" and "economic partner." Rather than talking about the affinity of the corporation to the respective arts event, which presents the standard way of publicly framing these types of sponsorship engagements (see Chapter 2), he quickly moved to an announcement of the Young Curators' Workshop his company was co-hosting during the biennial.

Overall, it seemed that the organizers and curators had, for lack of a better expression, either succumbed to—or embraced (or both)—commercial interests, maybe because for the first time financing had been guaranteed through a commitment of the corporate sponsors for two consecutive biennials. This embrace could also be interpreted as breaking a taboo (and thus as somewhat subversive) in that it explicitly, and not without irony, crossed the boundaries between the "pristine" or idealized realm of art and the domain of the market.[13] The lack of a need to—or the refusal to—problematize these concerns and the nonexistence of controversial debate on the spatial proximity between commercial galleries and the biennial locations was striking. After all, the Mitte district—at the time—hosted some of the major galleries of the city. One of my interlocutors who worked as a guide at the biennial frequently expressed her discomfort with high-profile visitors inquiring about where to purchase certain artists' works. This emphasis on consumption by visitors and organizers alike seemed at odds with the panel discussions at the Young Curators' Workshop. Under the heading "Does the World Need More Biennials?" the invited senior curators emphatically stressed that biennials were the sole remaining space away from market rationales that allowed for experimentation in the international art world setting. Given the particular setup of the Berlin Biennial, one wonders to what extent artistic risk taking is ensured in an environment dominated by commercial galleries.

Amid these discussions, however, it should also be noted that biennials with an almost year-round circuit covering the times between art fairs, or vice versa, have become increasingly indistinguishable from commercial art festivals, that is, art fairs.[14] In Istanbul, this approximation has been further enforced by a temporal overlap of the Contemporary Istanbul art fair and the Istanbul Biennial. Berlin's Art Forum (1996–2011),[15] which kicked off the international art fair season in late September, was, according to its director Anne Maier, proud to be able to provide each stand with an upscale "gallery look." Although the art fair, while in existence, was held in the commercial trade fair complex of Berlin's Westkreuz, the organizers had managed to secure the sole remaining vintage trade hall, a venue that according to Maier embodied an aesthetic affinity to "refined" art institutions, be they commercial or nonprofit. This art fair was notably cosponsored by public institutions for its accompanying educational programs and thus resembled nonprofit exhibitions such as the Berlin Biennial. What Lash and Urry (1994, 142) have proposed for the cultural industries, namely, that "they are becoming, not more of a business, but instead a business *service* . . . whose branding activities and content are more and more coming to resemble that of another business service, advertising," also holds true for the arts sector. Here, the realm of the art market and that of noncommercial exhibitions, that is, museums, nonprofit arts spaces, and even alternative artist-run spaces, are increasingly approximating each other. Varied as they might be from the outset, commercial on the one hand and supposed forums for artistic experimentation on the other, both art fairs and biennials today are subject to similar economic pressures, cater to collectors more than to the general public, take place in comparable settings, and employ discourses of engaging a broader audience through educational programs. As Berlin's city magazine *Zitty* runs cover stories such as "Art Is Pop. Galleries Are the New Clubs" (June 2006)[16] and as exhibition openings become the talk of the town, the dichotomy of "art for sale" and "art for the public good" has found its manifestation in the spectacularization of both. While it might be argued that this categorization is artificial to begin with, especially since the emergence of the modern conception of art was entrenched in the market, this process inherently contradicts the assumption of the civilizing impact of art and of the autonomy of art as deserving protection from both the market and the state.

Differential Perceptions

While there were considerable differences in the debates within the local arts scene on the respective biennials, the promotion and reviews of both events were bound to streamlined representations of each city. It is interesting to note, however, that the perception of international critics of the Istanbul Biennial often circled around well-rehearsed themes. In contrast to reviews of the Berlin event, which focused more strictly on the exhibition itself, they apparently could not do without drawing on the motif of Istanbul as a "bridge between East and West" (Hohmann 2005a) or alluding to the effects of the local cuisine on those unaccustomed (Herzog 2007). Not only obscuring the fact that the Istanbul Biennial, established in 1987, predates Berlin's, inaugurated in 1997, reviewers also tended to deny the "coevalness" (Fabian 1983) between the two events by emphasizing or proposing the novelty of Istanbul's arts scene.[17]

Notably, in both instances the host city did not give any (Berlin) or only nominal (Istanbul) support. This, however, did not discourage city officials from claiming the biennials for their own purposes and from translating these arts events into their own perceptions of the role of art in the urban economy—a process that points once again to the division of labor between the state and corporate sponsors, despite the often proclaimed antagonism. After highlighting the "cosmopolitanism," read as a marker of modernness, that these events established for their cities, they emphasized the media attention along with the attractiveness for tourism[18] and foreign investment that the biennials might entail. As an encompassing spectacle, the biennial was thus presented as another item in the city's public relations portfolio along with other large-scale events such as Fashion Week (Berlin) or—at the time—Formula One (Istanbul). While it might not be surprising that ascertaining the city as a brand to be marketed in order to attract tourism and other types of business is furthered by city officials, I found that curators and other actors from the art world often used the same line of reasoning when trying to establish the significance of their respective art scenes in the global circuit. In Istanbul, this was frequently done in order to counter historical particularities of the national arts scene as well as Orientalist (self-)perceptions (see Uluç et al. 2006). In Berlin, this discourse was employed to shift the city's image away from "poor but sexy" (a term coined by long-time Berlin mayor Klaus Wowereit) at best and inefficient, expensive, and "fiscally irresponsible"[19] at worst to a place where trading, the "buying and selling," of art, can be conducted, as KW's director Gaby Horn emphasized during our conversation.[20] Yet this type of integration of art into the urban economy is in part problematic for the city administrations themselves: Both the head of the Istanbul municipality's Department for Culture, Hüseyin Öztürk, as well as Hakan Bayer, the director of Kültür A.Ş., a corporation founded by the municipality that administers its cultural programs, showed themselves to be rather aware that Ankara's 2003 directive to once more subsume culture and tourism under the same institutional umbrella elicited the suspicion of instrumentalizing artistic expression for marketing purposes and of deflecting from the pronounced goal of "serving the public" to furthering international tourism and hence commercial interests. This development is especially problematic because cultural policy's raison d'être explicitly includes *shielding* the arts from market rationales. In our interviews both Öztürk and Bayer were keen to emphasize that in their view the protection of the autonomy of culture and the arts against the market were paramount. Similarly, Berlin's city officials stress that their policies have created an environment that is conducive for the art scene and propose a trickle-down effect to the nonprofit realm. Who the actual audiences are, that is, who biennials actually serve or address, however, has remained a shaky matter, in part because comprehensive audience surveys in the arts are hard to administer. In both cities, evaluations eventually tended to settle on categories like "those who are interested in art" and "cultural tourists," rather than the city's "inhabitants" or its "people."[21]

Art and the Restructuring of Urban Space

In order to understand why these market rationales can be voiced and ultimately executed today with very little protest in the case of Berlin and such little consequence—if any—in the case of Istanbul, one has to take into account how intensified global economic restructuring has articulated itself in the urban realm. It was in this process that cultural policy was redefined as a vital tool for economic development. The sociologist Sharon Zukin has argued early on that the service economy,[22] having been deprived of the concrete artifacts of industrial manufacturing by the economic restructuring waves from the 1980s onward that led to the downsizing of manufacturing and deindustrialization (Sassen 1991), has found in cultural production an abstract means of embodying its own economic growth and vitality.[23] In the course of the ensuing rise of unemployment, policy makers turned to the initially unintended effects of the arts on urban regeneration projects and began to actively include them into policy making. As Zukin (1995, viii) states: "With a continued displacement of manufacturing and development of the financial and non-profit sectors of the economy, cultural production seemed to be more and more what cities were about" (see also Jameson 1991).[24]

The format of urban arts spectacle and the discourses surrounding it thus emerged during a period marked by the liberalization of the economy on a global scale that in the urban environment has translated into growing income and hence social segmentation (Mollenkopf and Castells 1991). These processes have also accelerated the gentrification of urban space—a development in which artists are vanguard actors. But they are also among the first to be negatively affected, that is the first to be displaced. Equipped with little economic but much cultural capital, artists and arts organizations repeatedly migrate into neighborhoods that are marked by disinvestment. Once a "scene" manages to establish itself in a respective area, the mechanism of gentrification starts to set in: restaurants, coffee shops, bars, and boutiques tend to follow in art's wake. A formerly "problematic" part of town gains attractiveness and becomes an object for "redevelopment." Speculators, developers, and investors appear on the scene, converting the artistic allure into higher rents, raising the cost of living in a given neighborhood. Most artists and arts organizations as well as most of the long-term residents are not able to meet these rising costs and have to leave the neighborhood to start the cycle somewhere else, anew (Smith 1996).[25] In Istanbul as in Berlin, artists are quite aware of the theoretical critiques and practical implications of the complicities of art in gentrification processes (Deutsche and Ryan 1984). For some, this awareness informs their artistic practices in that they conceptualize collaborative projects that integrate neighborhood actors (the practices by ODA Projesi and Susanne Bosch are two such examples; see Chapter 2) instead of just using the neighborhood as a site for artistic production and in the process (inadvertently) marginalizing its inhabitants. Yet they also know that such practices alone are no safeguards against these processes. Others question the effectiveness of these kinds of initiatives altogether and note that not all artistic practices render themselves amenable to such collaborations. Many artists assume a certain automatism of the dynamics of gentrification that is difficult to break out of and contend that it is their own economic hardship—and precariousness—that makes it difficult to counteract their gentrifying presence.

During the 1990s and 2000s gentrification in Berlin was most visible in Mitte and Prenzlauer Berg, formerly parts of East Berlin. The same is—partially—true for Kreuzberg, a neighborhood in West Berlin that, enclosed by the Berlin Wall on three sides, became unattractive for its German inhabitants, who ventured further west into the city. From the 1960s onward Kreuzberg, once designated as a working-class neighborhood catering to adjacent factories, became the prime location for the city's bourgeoning punk scene, attracted artists, and transformed into an immigrant quarter. In contrast to the eastern districts of Berlin, Kreuzberg, however, long proved more difficult to gentrify given its long history of disinvestment and strong community advocacy organizations. On adjacent sides of the former Wall, all three districts—Mitte, Prenzlauer Berg, and Kreuzberg—found themselves catapulted into the geographical center of the capital of a newly unified Germany. Especially the many "deserted" spaces in Mitte and Prenzlauer Berg—with its East German inhabitants having moved west in the city or leaving Berlin altogether—offered squatting possibilities for "adventurous pioneers" as well as affordable options for makeshift galleries, clubs, and performance spaces. The very availability of these spaces, them being "free," brings us once more to the politics of dispossession. As Peter Kessen (2004, 143) notes, spaces occupied by the "young Berlin scene are indirectly based on the aryanization policies of the Hitler regime: Jewish Berliners were dispossessed, the GDR transferred the apartments into public property [*Volkseigentum*], the implosion of 'socialism as it existed in practice' [*Realsozsialismus*] then provided cheap occupiable living spaces." Attracting not only national but international attention, these neighborhoods were the first to be redeveloped given their central location and newly attained cultural attractiveness. There seemed to be little awareness that these deeper historical processes were connected to the destruction of Jewish life and culture among the city's art world actors, who generally related gentrification to the fallout surrounding Germany's reunification. The "voids of Berlin," to use Andreas Huyssen's (2003) term, that became the projection spaces of the redevelopment frenzy[26] were never just voids but actively produced through processes of dispossession. They point yet again to the decivilizing processes that in this case underwrite the production of available "empty space." They directly shape the conditions of artistic production in the form of living and working spaces affordable for artists and the presentation of art. Some of these spaces have also been witness to a different but parallel dynamic, namely, former industrial spaces that were converted into luxury lofts (Zukin 1982) after they had been made "unnecessary" and redundant by economic restructuring processes. They are manifestations in the built environment of what David Harvey (2004) has described "accumulation by dispossession" in the neoliberal key, in which people are not solely dispossessed of work and living space but also of their rights, which too become privatized and commodified—be they natural resources or social security provisions previously shouldered by the state. Urban revitalization projects and gentrification are hence playing out in what could be called "landscapes of layered dispossession."

These processes are even more contoured in Istanbul, where Galata, Tarlabaşı, and Karaköy in the district of Beyoğlu are home to many arts spaces and among the neighborhoods most affected by gentrification (Tan 2006). Here too spaces have often been described as "voids" and portrayed as "abandoned," "empty," "run down," in need of "cleaning up" and "redevelopment." Rather than being simply abandoned, they have been historically emptied by genocide, expulsion, and expropriation of minorities only to be occupied by other precarious groups arriving in the city in the process of rural-to-urban migration or seeking refuge from armed conflict—until those districts become subject to real estate speculation and they too are forced to leave. The exodus following waves of repression against the remaining Greek, Jewish, and Armenian communities that had mainly inhabited these neighborhoods along with European expatriates in Ottoman times left many buildings unoccupied.[27] With their owners either unable to claim their former property or locked in court cases over compensation, the disinvestment in the area rendered it a refuge for immigrants stranded at the walls of Fortress Europe as well as for Kurds fleeing violence in the southeast. Beyoğlu has been subject to repeated "urban regeneration" campaigns (Erdoğan, when mayor of Istanbul, was instrumental in these developments) after being claimed by the Istanbulite intelligentsia, art studios and galleries, and film and advertising executives, in whose path came cafés and restaurants (Bartu 2001, Öncü 2010). Urban redevelopment has intensified since the late 1990s, especially as the strict regulations for foreign investment in Turkey have been lifted, and with them a legal framework for expropriation in order to speed up urban redevelopment has been established (Kuyucu and Ünsal 2010). Here too, historical dispossession and neoliberal integration work hand in hand.

Art and Artists in the Service Economy

Gentrification, however, is only one—but perhaps the most visible—part of the equation of how global economic restructuring has been mirrored in the urban arena under the impetus of market liberalization and privatization. These processes have also affected the role accorded to art in the urban economy and ideas about how art should be (institutionally) governed. Last but not least, they have identified "the artist" as a model of existence under these precarious conditions.

Let me briefly explain what I suggest by this statement: In the course of governmental cutbacks of social services and welfare expenditures and given the serious dents in the endowments of funding agencies following the successive global economic crises of the 1980s, 1990s, and 2000s, nonprofit and public, that is, state-supported, arts institutions were among the first to be affected (Yúdice 1999). In Turkey, the discourse of professionalization has been employed to legitimize already low levels of public funding for contemporary art. By the same token, the reliance on private funding and sponsorship was billed not only as a measure of the extent of "professionalization" in the arts, but professionalization was also portrayed as a shortcut to overcoming the predicaments of Turkey's belated modernization in the arts. With its particular history of cultural policy, which framed art as a duty to citizens and as imperative for the education of "enlightened," critically minded subjects, German politicians and policy makers have been quick to state that they are not opposed to supporting the arts per se. Rather, these budget cuts have been portrayed as a chance to reform arts institutions that have become too cumbersome, that is, that have "too many administrative overheads" or are "fiscally irresponsible," as I was frequently told during my fieldwork. With reference to the American model of arts funding, the call for "arts management" as a "more businesslike" and "professional" working mode in the art world was voiced increasingly in Berlin and Istanbul alike. Confronted with the pressure of implementing for-profit concepts such as "professionalism" and "entrepreneurship," arts organizations as well as individual artists have found themselves in a dilemma of how to conduct "goal-oriented" work while reverting to for-profit, market-oriented frameworks (Salamon and Anheier 1997).[28]

But even more importantly, these shifts have implications for how the social and economic dimension of artistic work and the societal role of artists are conceptualized. On the one hand, economic restructuring processes and ensuing funding pressures have helped introduce business terminology and for-profit reasoning into the art world context, thus legitimizing the "harnessing" (Stevenson 1999) of what Zukin (1995, viii) calls the "the seductive influence of the arts on urban redevelopment." This increased interest in art on the side of city officials and policy makers has created a perspective in which the arts are conceptualized as a part of the urban economy and artists are ultimately viewed as service providers, rather than part of—ideally speaking—an autonomous realm (Lash and Urry 1994). This shift is perhaps most clearly expressed in a 1997 study prepared by the consulting giant McKinsey & Co. for the New York State Council on the Arts. Mainly addressed to private sponsors and investors, the authors of this study suggest that state funding of the arts should not be increased. In fact, the underfunding of the arts is portrayed as advantageous, since "underemployed" artists provide a pool of flexible labor ideal for temporary positions in the city's service economy. As artists are associated with "cultural capital" and, frequently coming from middle-class backgrounds, have received a fairly good education, they are ideal for the labor force of restaurants, galleries, offices, and temping jobs, where employers and customers alike tend to "flirt" with—and capitalize on—their creative potential. Even when these propositions do not translate into the concrete composition and availability of an actual workforce, this understanding of art and of the artist—not unlike the emergence of the modern conception of art in the eighteenth century—has a larger signifying power beyond the art world and bears similar contradictions.

Positions as blatant as the one taken by NYSCA are rejected by the majority of art world actors I interviewed in Istanbul and Berlin, although in the case of Berlin, similarly to New York, a significant part of the service sector (especially restaurant workers and advertising-related industries) indeed seems to be made up of artists trying to support their artistic work. Yet it is interesting to note that calls for professionalization are made by quite diverse actors in each location. In Istanbul, where private arts and cultural centers flourished since the 1980s, the call for the implementation of arts management techniques, institutionalization (Artun 2002), and professionalization has been voiced by those who administer the newly established arts management programs at universities as well as by some critics and curators. In part, these calls are connected to desires for more transparency in the Turkish cultural sector, where funding and sponsoring procedures remain often opaque, not least because many art and cultural centers are not incorporated under nonprofit laws. Instead they operate from the budgets of PR and communications divisions of the respective companies they are affiliated with and that are not publicly accountable either. In Berlin, they were put forward by cultural policy makers, mostly politicians from the opposition, not the governing coalition, which was composed of Social Democrats and Socialists.

There is a second plane on which cultural policy, economic interest, and artistic practice have recently converged: the concept of the "creative industries." Not to be confused with the "culture industry" (Adorno and Horkheimer 1969) long held to be cultural policy's formative other (Hesmondalgh and Pratt 2005), this shift signals the extension of the modern concept of art to commercial enterprise. The cultural policy scholar Nicholas Garnham (2005, 17) situates the emergences of this concept once again in the global economic restructuring that entailed the deregulation of the media, broadcasting, and telecommunication sector and made these private sectors eligible for public monies to support privatization processes (see also Wu 2002). Crucial to the inception of the "creative industries" and the choice of the very term "creative" was that it opened an avenue to include enterprises such as the computer software sector in the realm of cultural policy. According to Garnham (2005, 26), this allowed "software producers and the major publishing and media conglomerates to construct an alliance with cultural workers and with small-scale cultural entrepreneurs, around a strengthening of copyright protection." That copyright protection emerges as an instrumental factor in trying to establish what actually counts as creativity relies on a significant historical precedent that I have laid out in the Introduction, namely, the emergence of the modern conception of art out of conflicts over copyright and authorship over the course of the eighteenth century (Woodmansee 1994). While the reference to creativity has secured copyright protection, the overall approximation of an array of economic sectors including fashion, (web) design, advertising, and even the automobile industry (see Florida 2002) to the arts has made it possible to apply cultural protectionist policies to these sectors in the European Union and its region.[29]

While these developments have not gone unchallenged in either Berlin or Istanbul, the terminology of the "creative industries" has been peddled by cultural policy officials, who have called on artists to identify themselves as small-scale creative entrepreneurs, to varying success. Through its notable double allure (creative and entrepreneurial), this discourse is in part interpreted as an empowering shift, not least because the precariousness of artists' livelihoods is increasingly presented to have a model character in an economic environment that no longer can guarantee full-time employment. This point was prominently raised by Adrienne Goehler, the former director of the Capital Cultural Fund, who repeatedly referred to Richard Florida's work during our interview. For her, the model character of artistic practices is evident in a labor market that demands "heightened flexibility, creatively assembled patchwork careers," and "collaborating on a project basis"—all qualities that are highly developed in the artistic realm. In an era in which the principles of the *Sozialstaat* (welfare state) are no longer tenable, she argued, the economic realm has to learn from the arts, and artists have to legitimize their existence in these changing economic conditions.

Goehler's statement might help elucidate the different positions taken by artists in Turkey and Germany. Since artists in Turkey have not benefited from a history of sustained government funding (as state support has been fickle and based on personal relationships and lobbying, particularly when it comes to contemporary art), they are not subject to the same legitimization pressures faced by artists in Germany. The absence of secured government funding in the former case has granted them more leeway in positioning themselves vis-à-vis these neoliberal modulations of the art world and might explain why artists in Istanbul protest private sponsorship so fervently.

It comes as little surprise that corporate sponsors in both Turkey and Germany, however, have been quick in adopting the conceptual framework of the creative industries and their repertoires of self-representation. The vocabulary of the creative industries has further accommodated the conceptual approximation between art and the sponsorship of art but has not been able to solve the contradictions that this approximation produces. I have already outlined some of these dynamics when analyzing the portrayal of arts sponsorship as social or cultural responsibility. Here, however, I would like to extend the discussion through a couple of examples that illustrate how the kinship between the arts and the economic sector is construed by corporate sponsors and the difficulties inherent in trying to frame arts sponsorship in a noninstrumentalizing manner. Some, like Jürgen Zech (*Kulturkreis*), reflected on the *Kreativpotenzial*, the creative potential, that he deemed not only formative for the arts but portrayed as essential for business development, especially at the current economic conjuncture. Another conceptual bridge is often suggested by highlighting that "management today requires creativity and the kinds of leadership that arts exemplify through their *Grenzgängertum*," the looking and pushing across accepted boundaries and standardized procedures. This emphasis on pioneering new approaches fails to acknowledge that artistic risk taking, as an integral part of creative work, is more and more a luxury that only a few can afford in an environment marked by a continuous shortage of funding and heightened competition for sponsors and audiences. As such, the instrumentalization of art as an economic development strategy is increasingly undermining the very basis of creative and artistic production (see also Zukin 1995). Frank-Peter Martin, of Bankhaus Metzler, posited that managers can learn from the arts, for example, by asking "what kind of tasks [*Aufgaben*] does a conductor have, what can I learn from that, for my personal development." Similarly, Martin Fuchs (also from the *Kulturkreis*) proposed that engagement with the arts is an engagement with "things that speak to the soul" that also helps develop now much valued "soft skills" and "cultural competencies" that are not taught in business school but are vital in the business world today. It is through these kinds of equations that the purported civilizing impact of the arts is presented as resulting in more efficient and supposedly ethical corporate management. Such equations also serve to deproblematize corporate sponsorship activities in general. The proposition of a "synergy" between the workings of art and those of economic enterprise circumvents the issue of the instrumentalization of art. Instead, it establishes a "natural" kinship and affinity between art and business.

The Possibilities of Art

> Art in the period of its dissolution, as a movement in pursuit of its own transcendence in a historical society that is not directly lived, is at once an art of change and a pure expression of the impossibility of change.
>
> Guy Debord

Throughout this chapter, I have proposed that the arts spectacle has become the preferred articulation of the convergence between cultural policy, economic interests, and artistic practices. This is not to suggest, however, that the "spectacular" or the festival character as such impedes on any critical intent that contemporary art might have. Indeed, the art happenings of the 1960s show other uses of both criticality and spectacularization. Abbie Hoffman, for instance, interrupted the New York Stock Exchange by dropping hundreds of one-dollar bills from the visitors' balcony, leaving traders on the floor scrambling for "actual money." The Berlin-based artist Hans Winkler recounted an intervention staged with his colleague Stefan Micheel under the name of p.t.t.red, which shows how a small gesture can elicit a grand effect: After publicly slapping Mickey Mouse during a Disneyland parade in 1991, the artists were arrested on the spot. The distribution of the letter by Vehbi Koç at the opening of the Eleventh Istanbul Biennial by Kamusal Sanat Laboratuvarı (see Chapter 4) similarly played on spectacularization and happening formats.

Yet the claims that the spectacularization and festivalization of art engenders wider access or the democratization and extension of the public sphere are at least dubious, if not untenable. While city officials tend to emphasize that art festivals succeed in engaging a broader public than "conventional" art formats and thus employ an originally countercultural argument of public "space-claiming" (Stevenson 1999), this is a rather big stretch when taking the current social segmentation in the urban realm into account.

The claims of democratization are further complicated when we scrutinize the timing of the inauguration of the Istanbul and Berlin biennials. In the case of Turkey, the rise of contemporary arts festivals occurred simultaneously with repressive political practices following the 1980 coup d'état that stretched into the 1990s. The coup itself, although still often portrayed as restoring order after armed struggles between the political left and right reached critical proportions, can be better understood as the violent repression of the rising revolutionary potential and social movements that opposed exactly the neoliberal policies, IMF directives, and forays into privatization that created the present-day division of labor between the state and corporate arts foundations as well as the global economic restructuring that has found its preferred outlet in the arts spectacle. The literary critic and writer Nurdan Gürbilek contemplates this decivilizing entrenchment of the Istanbul Biennial by recounting the following anecdote:

> A few years ago, a friend of mine pitched the question: "Could it be said that the 1980s festivals served to drown out the screams rising from the prisons?" The question seemed too harsh, too point blank, too cruel for those present. It hadn't been intended to provoke soul searching, but it did, and no one wanted to answer it. Whatever would have been said would be wrong. At this point, the person who asked the question answered it themselves: "To say this would be wrong, but also wrong not to."
>
> (Gürbilek 1992, 14)[30]

Erden Kosova, too, on numerous occasions proposed that the Istanbul Biennial was instated in the process of "cleaning up Istanbul's image" after the military coup and drew parallels between the case of the Istanbul and the Berlin biennials by pointing to the latter's establishment in 1998. Although often forgotten today, Germany faced waves of anti-immigrant violence in the early 1990s, soon after reunification, that threatened to seriously hamper its newly found prominence and the international goodwill garnered from Europe and the world. In both instances, Kosova argued, these arts festivals were initially intended to dispel negative historical connotations and antidemocratic fears from within and without Turkey and Germany. This too is a dynamic through which the local, the city, is pulled back into the national frame.

Indicative of the convergence of economic interests, cultural policy, and artistic practices, the arts spectacle has come to reconcile three domains normally thought of as adhering to different interests and operating logics. Incorporating art—or at least its connotations—in the market, the increasingly normative framework of the arts spectacle and of the enterprising of art leaves the allure of its emancipatory potential intact. This development, not least expressed in the establishment of a joint vocabulary among different art world actors, raises questions around the long-held dichotomy between cultural policy as being directed from "above" and cultural politics presenting contestations from "below" (Stevenson 1999). This distinction deserves further scrutiny, especially as we are confronted with the now longstanding paradox that significant funding for contemporary art comes from corporations that are supposedly criticized by the very artists whose work they support. That the enterprising and the spectacularization of art are portrayed as both economically desirable *and* artistically viable has produced a situation in which the political and economic institutions that art critiques have not only incorporated but also commissioned works and employed artists who are critical of their governance structures and funding programs (Wu 2002).[31] The art theorist Trude Iversen reflects on the implications of this development on the tradition of institutional critique in the arts since the late 1960s by noting:

> Institutional critique is normally associated with art practices from the end of the 1960s which are defined on the basis of a criticism of its object—the art institution—which in turn refers to established, organised places where art is presented, collected and distributed. After 40 years of this art practice, which has been characterized as institutional critique for the past 20 of them, it emerges for many people as well integrated—indeed, institutionalised—in the field of art. This raises the current question with which art theory only partially has concerned itself: To what extent does institutionally critical art function *critically* when it is initiated by that which was the object of criticism? Today it is common practice for art institutions to seek and request this type of art themselves, and that raises the question concerning what differentiates the current institutional critique from institutionalised criticism/critique.
>
> (Iversen 2007, 8)

The question if what we are witnessing actually constitutes a shift from "a critique of institutions to an institution of critique" speaks to Debord's (1994 [1967], 135) assessment that under the given conditions, art is "at once an art of change and a pure expression of the impossibility of change." And yet, artists continue to challenge the instrumentalization of art in the urban economy. The Istanbul-based project *Apricot City* A4, initiated by Dilek Winchester, for instance, uses informal economic networks by distributing each of its zine-like editions through the mobile photocopiers you find on the city's street corners. Each zine is an artwork in itself created by an individual guest artist or collective. The format eludes the institutional settings of the art world, its galleries and magazines. Calling it "a parasite under the shadow of the informal economy," *Apricot City* A4, according to Winchester, has "no address" but offers "merely a possibility" as the mobile photocopiers are not sedentary but move through the streets of different neighborhoods. In 2012, a group of Berlin-based artists organized under the name Haben und Brauchen (To Have and to Need). In their manifesto, they decidedly took a stance against the "dispossession of the commons" and initiated debates about the conditions of living and working in Berlin. They asked how artists take part in the urban economy within the framework of rights to the city and how they can become part of larger movements for social justice. In doing so, they aimed to decidedly set themselves apart from the discourses of creative entrepreneurs and the creative industries. Similar discussions flared up in Istanbul a couple of years earlier and gained further momentum in the course of what came to be known as the Gezi uprising that marked the summer of 2013, in which many contemporary artists took part. It is no coincidence that the very location of Gezi Park is itself a site of layered dispossession. Once part of an Armenian cemetery (1551–1939), it hosted the first monument to the Armenian genocide, established in 1922. Confiscated from the Armenian community, it became part of a previous redevelopment frenzy—that of the early Turkish Republic—under the direct orders of Mustafa Kemal Atatürk to build a public square and a park symbolizing the new nation. The protests, which developed into a nationwide uprising, erupted when the location was to be dispossessed yet again to be turned into a multiuse residential development and shopping mall.

Instead of a Conclusion

Meeting, Again

I learned about politics at the Museum of Modern Art.

—NELSON A. ROCKEFELLER

In 2004, Christopher Tannert, director of the Künstlerhaus Bethanien, Berlin, and his co-curator, Peter Lang, began preparations for an exhibition entitled *Urban Realities—Focus Istanbul*. They traveled to Istanbul to conduct research on local artists. They met with the curators Fulya Erdemci, Erden Kosova, and Vasıf Kortun for insight into the Istanbul art world and to arrange contributions to the catalogue that was to accompany the exhibition. The organizers had already secured funding through the Cultural Capital Foundation and the Berlin Senate, and while in Istanbul they also negotiated with the Istanbul Foundation for Culture and Arts (IKSV) for additional support. All was well, it seemed. But in May 2005, when the official invitation letters, which specified the concept and announced the artists and works selected, were sent out, a vehement protest erupted in Istanbul's art world. Eleven artists, among them Halil Altındere, Gülsün Karamustafa, Hale Tenger, and Mehmet Erdener, withdrew from the exhibition. Erdemci, Kosova, and Kortun likewise declined any further involvement in the project. The refusal to participate, as it was relayed in an open letter as well as during interviews I conducted with some of the artists who pulled out of the show, was based on both conceptual disagreements and financial disparities. It seems that most artists from Istanbul were being asked to show already existing works and pay their own way to Berlin, whereas artists based outside of Turkey were receiving funding to come to Istanbul, create new works, and have all expenses covered. But it was not only economic and creative issues that were at stake. The artists argued that the official concept of the exhibition was "full of clichés about East and West, Christianity and Islam" (Altay et al. 2005, 22). They expressed discontent at being—yet again—grouped into a regionally (or locally) themed show—which many diagnosed was the only way their works were being exhibited in Western Europe.[1] "Orientalism" and being categorized as "native informants" rather than artists were also frequently voiced complaints. Tannert likewise responded with an open letter. Going on the offensive, he noted that he did not treat "artists from Turkey" as a wholesale group and that decisions about funding had been made on a case-by-case basis (Altay et al. 2005, 23–25). During our interview, Tannert refuted that Orientalism, or something akin to it, was at play in the conceptualization of the exhibition. Peter Lang, like Tannert, emphasized that they felt unduly characterized, especially "after all their efforts to study the Turkish art scene and to learn about Turkey." Yet both volunteered culturalist explanations, when they characterized the artists' collective letter as symptomatic for "Turkey's corporatist political formation under Kemalism" and as indicative for the "fragmentation" and "temper" of Istanbul's art world. They did not fail to make use of the stereotype of "Turkish artists' infighting."[2] At the same time, Tannert was quite aware, as he said, that the controversy was "ultimately a struggle around the question about the right to represent the Other." Trying to confront the issue head on, he included both letters in the exhibition catalogue and convened a panel discussion as part of the exhibition—which ended up replaying the positions just outlined and thus, at least in part, went awry. The *Focus Istanbul* affair, as it came to be known, was never resolved. It did become, however, a precedent—a benchmark, even—for many artists when considering offers from Western Europe and a cautionary tale for German curators wanting to work with artists from Turkey for years to come.

This was neither the first nor the last incident in which artists from Turkey experienced the dynamics of asymmetric perception during my research. Seçil Yersel, of ODA Projesi, noted that they had begun scrutinizing offers more carefully, to avoid being further pigeonholed as "Turkish" artists, and that the collective had even decided to abstain from invitations to Western Europe for a while. She recounted that when invited to exhibitions and arts exchange programs in Germany, Sweden, or the Netherlands, for example, their hosts frequently expected them to execute their projects in local immigrant neighborhoods, thus putting them in the position of, in her words, "social workers" rather than visiting international artists.

Yasemin Özcan, who was invited to an artists' exchange program in North Rhine Westphalia, recounted her surprise and frustration to find that most of her artist talks and panel discussions during her residency quickly turned into informational gatherings. Rather than being questioned about their current projects and artistic practices, participants from Turkey were expected to give accounts of the country's history—and current political situation—and often had to counter the rather simplistic presumptions that their hosts and German audiences voiced.[3] She summarized her experience by saying: "I never asked for nor do I ever want to be in the position of having to represent Turkey, not as an artist, not as a woman, not as an Alevi—least when abroad. During my stay, I often wondered what kind of conversations and panels would be organized if France were the guest country. I am sure that they would not have to engage in introductory French history and politics lessons."[4]

Others similarly noted that when invited to cultural or arts exchange programs they often found themselves treated less as international artists and more as within the categories of local migrant populations from Turkey in Western Europe (most of which are now notably in their fourth generation), regardless of whether they were comfortable with this ascription. And this although, like Tannert and Lang, curators tended to proclaim to be aware of Orientalist trappings and often professed the best of intentions.

That these kinds of dynamics transcend the particular case of Germany or the likewise particular relationship between Germany and Turkey emerges in Sally Price's interrogation of Jacques Chirac's vanity project, the Quai Branly Museum (2007). The museum prides itself in recategorizing objects once housed by Paris's ethnographic collections into the framework of *les arts premiers*. Analyzing the history of the museum—celebrated as a long-overdue acknowledgment of "world art"—on the background of France's *mission civilatrice* and its contemporary immigration regime, Price forcefully argues that this has done little to amend the asymmetric perception of non-Western art and its producers. The decivilizing legacies of colonialism continue to shape minority rights and immigration politics in contemporary France as much as they frame the perception of art.

This continued misrecognition of artists from and art produced in what is generally identified as the non-West can be understood by using Kira Kosnick's (2007) notion of "the whiteness of cultural policy" of "Western," and in her case specifically German, cultural institutions. Drawing on critical race theory, she shows how immigrant populations—and ultimately, I would add, artists from their countries of "origin" who are equated with them—are expected to produce "culture" not in the sense of art but of "ethnic cultural production." More often than not they are understood as "representatives" of "their communities" and by extension "their cultures" instead of as individual artists. This type of slippage between culture as aesthetics production and culture as demarcating communal difference brings us full circle to the issue of asymmetric perception with which I opened this study. In the example of the *Focus Istanbul* affair, Turkey and Germany meet once again. By always insisting that this is a new acquaintance, by over and over conjuring up dominant geopolitical and civilizational imaginaries that have construed the world in terms of "East" and "West" and see "Islam" and "Christianity" as incommensurable entities, these encounters reify the notion of incomparability that—to draw once more on Ann Stoler (2006, 6)—"compels forgetting." Reconfiguring this forgetting anew, professions of unfamiliarity obscure the long and often troubling history of encounters between Germany and Turkey and their constitutive intimacies. As such, perceptions framed along these binaries reveal little—if anything—about the actual artistic practices in question and more about conceptions of modernity. Such framings derive their power from long-suppressed histories, from a disavowal that manages, tames, or silences decivilizing moments in (art) history.

Thinking through the cases of Turkey and Germany together, trying to account for their historical encounters and entanglements, and analyzing art through decivilizing moments means to work against the kind of forgetting that assertions of incomparability engender and perpetuate. This kind of forgetting, however, is not solely reified in transnational encounters in the arts. Indeed, the preceding chapters have outlined how the dynamics of forgetting and remembering play out in the arena of cultural policy and national histories of art in Germany and Turkey, what they reveal and what they obscure, and how contradictory understandings of art and entanglements of the governance of art and state violence keep calling artistic production and reception in Germany and Turkey into the national frame.

The lens of decivilizing art enables an inquiry into the sociopolitical dimension of art by conceptualizing the art world as a terrain of struggle in which the inherent goodness of art is constantly constructed and disrupted. It allows not just for examining how artistic production is affected by state policies but for exploring how the production, circulation, and presentation—indeed our very understanding—of art are predicated on histories of violence. It is in this manner that art emerges as a privileged site for interrogating the histories of dispossession that substantially shape the terms of political and cultural life in Turkey and Germany today.

In the discussions on the capacities and expediencies of art, ranging from civic education to self-realization to economic development, understandings of society at large and what it means to be modern are revealed. While the conditions under which art is produced are entrenched in the national frame through moments of state violence as much as through references to modernity and civility, these conditions are at the same time of "diminished particularity" (Lepenies 2006); they speak beyond the cases of Turkey and Germany. It is thus no coincidence that Nelson A. Rockefeller professed to have learned about politics at the Museum of Modern Art. Remembered foremost as a collector and benefactor of the arts, as a trustee and president of MoMA, and as a moderate Republican in favor of social reform, he was also part of the Cold War military-industrial complex and the mind behind the repressive Rockefeller drug laws, stop-and-frisk policing, and the violent suppression of the Attica prison uprising.

Yet art remains a somewhat unwieldy vehicle for national projects and is as much a conduit of governance as a challenge to it. As Turkey and Germany share an acute awareness of how their political, social, and cultural makeup is perceived both by their own "publics" and abroad, artistic practices that reference state violence are frequently delegitimized by questioning the relationship between reality and the artistic rendering thereof. Such decivilizing moments become visible not only in the thematization of the RAF and the symbolic and physical violence it connoted; they also shape how certain art collections are financed and assembled. They appear as historical manifestations in the urban space, a space that bears the marks of dispossession and misappropriation on the heels of genocidal violence and discriminatory policies. While art at times (unwittingly) aids governance structures that obscure this violence, it can also pose a challenge to these very same structures. The interventions by Renata Stih and Frieder Schnock and the accounts presented by *Free Kick* are but two instances that disrupt the claims of a linearly conceptualized path to modernity by addressing ambiguities and ruptures in the constitution of modernness and imaginations of "civility." The concerns and tensions that accompany claims to modernity and "Western belonging" are expressed in a similar yet historically distinctive fashion, for example, when it comes to artworks that can be construed as challenges to national sovereignty, as in the case of Turkey, or by referring to the reverberations of National Socialism in Germany. In these processes, the state as well as other art world actors are constantly engaged in practices that transgress but also restore the boundaries between politics and art by employing the argument of the autonomy of art in a contradictory manner.

There is a continual mismatch between, on the one hand, how art is conceptualized and envisioned and, on the other, the conditions under which it is produced and the ways it is governed, presented, bought, and sold. In her essay *On Beauty and Being Just*, the literary scholar Elaine Scarry (1999, 5) makes a passionate argument for connecting beauty, or, in this case, art,[5] with justice by framing both as "an invitation to ethical fairness." Constructing an analogy between aesthetic fairness and ethical fairness by drawing on John Rawls's understanding of justice "as a symmetry of everyone's relation to another" (93), Scarry posits that both justice and beauty become invitations, calls, that one can choose to follow. There have been important critiques of Scarry's argument, critiques that have questioned its deep but undiscussed reliance on notions of symmetry, of aesthetic judgment, taste, and the sovereign subject (e.g., see Nehamas 2000). Both Scarry and her critics focus on the artwork as such rather than on the practices that enable the production of art and the broader contexts that shape its reception. Yet it seems to me that there is a potential in the call, the invitation that Scarry asks to heed. The philosopher Jacques Rancière (2001, 149) posits that art's critical potential lies in the recognition of its possibilities and limitations. Perhaps the recognition of the conditions that entrench art in different forms of state violence, be it its production, circulation, presentation, or accumulation, can—potentially—present one way to guide attention to questions of justice, an attention that can be mobilized against art being called (back) into the national frame.

Contemporary art is often described as having as its central theme the critique of representation (Groys 2005). Yet the evaluations that pervade the international art world, national cultural policy, and sometimes cultural politics arise less from the consideration of such aesthetic expressions than from the narratives that obscure power differentials and decivilizing moments through notions of "the greater good." To be able to realize searches for justice, art—as well as scholarship on art—has to face the trappings of its own representation and of the contradictions inherent in the modern conception of art. Within the anthropology of art, this is ever more pertinent: Artists have increasingly drawn on ethnographic methods, and anthropologists have highlighted parallels between art and anthropology, often calling for collaborations between the disciplines (Grimshaw and Ravetz 2004, Schneider and Wright 2010). As art continues to be called upon to engage the past and imagine different political futures, art's emancipatory potential might lie in accounting for rather than in trying to reconcile the many contradictions and tensions in the daily workings of the art world.

Postscript: Forgetting, Again

With the bulk of this fieldwork covering the period between 2005 and 2011, the present study is bound to fall short in addressing more recent developments in Istanbul and Berlin, Turkey and Germany. Some of these developments are grave; some will only unfold and show their full impact on the art world in the years to come. While an attempt at a comprehensive overview is destined to fail, I want to close by marking some turning points, selective as they might be.

Beyond the historical intimacy and different strands of historical connections, some of which I have taken up in this book, Turkey and Germany are currently entangled anew in the form of the so-called refugee deal. Making Turkey into the guardian of Fortress Europe, the deal is designed to keep those who are forced to flee hardship and war and who seek safe passage to Europe at bay and at ever greater risk. Brokered during a visit to Turkey by Chancellor Angela Merkel in late 2015, in the lead-up to a repeat election after the AKP had refused to enter into a coalition government, the deal would not only provide funds to Turkey to keep migrants from crossing into EU territory but also buy the tacit approval of Germany and the European Union for Turkey's growing authoritarianism. The Turkish army had already begun to unleash violence on Kurdish cities—that is, on civilians—a few months earlier, ending a fragile, fraught, yet hopeful peace process announced a mere two years earlier. It has since also waged war beyond its borders. I find it difficult to give a concise account of these events and their human toll or of what has ensued in Turkey since, an account that does not sound disaffected and does not simply list acts of war by the Turkish armed forces, a string of bombings claiming hundreds of lives (mainly between 2015 and 2016, and many claimed by ISIS or its Turkish affiliates), waves of prosecutions that quickly extended from those identified as responsible for the failed coup attempt of July 15, 2016 (for a nuanced discussion, see Bargu 2018) to arbitrary detentions and court cases brought against all sorts of political opposition, from journalists to artists and academics. Many of these measures have been aided by Turkey's vague antiterrorism legislation, which draws its legitimacy not only from the national but the transnational context, as the "war against terror" has become de facto international law. It comes thus to little surprise that these developments have remained largely unchallenged by the international community.

This is not the first time that Turkey has experienced a military coup; indeed, as I noted throughout this book, violent overthrows of elected governments had occurred in 1960, 1971, and 1980. (In 1997, the military intervened once more, this time by issuing a memorandum that aimed to rein in the Islamist agenda of Prime Minister Necmettin Erbakan and his Welfare Party Government, effectively forcing him out of office.) Each of these coups has engendered a rupture in Turkish political life and has profoundly affected the realms of arts and culture. What sets this time apart, however, is that the coup actually failed yet—once again—managed to foster the material and discursive conditions of forgetting that marked previous ones.

A state of emergency was declared on July 21, 2016, and remained in place for two years, creating the conditions to deepen the pressure on journalists and the media that had already set in after the Gezi uprising (2013). This pressure turned into a more and more frequent use of state-mandated media blackouts, closures of media outlets, and internet bans and has been accompanied by an ever-rising number of defamation and insult suits by the president against tens of thousands for critiquing the government on- and offline. The codification of the state of emergency into law in 2018 has further curtailed democratic structures (and possibilities) and has given way to extended state surveillance and denunciations along with censorship, self-censorship, and large-scale human rights violations.

The extension of the power of the state apparatus brought with it renewed attacks on the field of culture and the arts in general and Kurdish artistic production in particular. From September 2016 onward the AKP government ordered state-appointed trustees to take over the municipalities of several Kurdish cities that had been governed by the pro-Kurdish HDP; their mayors are now facing various charges of "aiding and abetting terrorists" and disseminating separatist propaganda. These municipalities had been supportive of Kurdish artistic production, both establishing new avenues for artists and assisting initiatives that had been built arduously through grassroots efforts during decades of violence and oppression. The trustees proceeded quickly to close galleries and theaters (like the city theater and the Amed Art Gallery in Diyarbakir), remove monuments that commemorated victims of state violence (for example, the Roboski monument in honor of the thirty-four civilians, including nineteen children, bombed by the Turkish armed forces in the southeastern province of Şırnak in 2011, also in Diyarbakir), and take down a sculpture in honor of the Kurdish politician, lawyer, and tireless human rights advocate Orhan Doğan in Cizre (see İlengiz 2019). As the investigative journalist Elif İnce reported in January 2017: "Over 1,400 associations and foundations have been shut down with state of emergency decrees. . . . Kurdish arts and culture associations with prominent theater companies, such as Seyr-î Mesel in Istanbul and various branches of the Mesopotamia Cultural Centre (MKM), are among those permanently shut." These practices have extended from municipal theaters in the Kurdish regions to theater groups and arts and cultural associations and collectives across the country. Numerous arts spaces have been closed down, their archives, props, and other equipment confiscated.[6] While some have since been reopened, their archives are yet to be returned. Along with human rights and democratic institutions, cultural and artistic memory is once again at stake and under risk of being erased in Turkey.

In October 2017, Osman Kavala, the philanthropist and founder of the arts nonprofit Anadolu Kültur, was arrested. He and thirteen others from the field of culture and civil society faced a myriad of charges, including attempting to "overthrow the government" by way of the Gezi protests in 2013. Kavala's arrest and long pretrial detention (the court case started on June 24, 2019) has sent shockwaves through the arts and culture scene in Turkey and affected anyone who, like Kavala, has been working on "emphasizing cultural diversity and cultural rights, supporting local initiatives, and strengthening regional and international collaborations and . . . projects that establish dialogue with Armenia and create spaces for the Kurdish language and culture."[7] In February 2020, Kavala and eight of his codefendants were acquitted. But shortly after his release, on his way from Silivri Prison to Istanbul to rejoin family and friends, Kavala was once again arrested, this time ostensibly for "espionage." He remains in detention, in violation of a European Court of Human Rights ruling.

Notably, throughout the violence of the past few years, the governing AKP has repeatedly voiced that they have been unable to establish "artistic hegemony"—despite their ever-increasing powers and the surge of nationalist rhetoric. President Erdoğan has likewise repeatedly vowed to overcome this "failure." Beyond the fact that restrictions alone are unable to produce art in the national key, art remains once again unwieldy to the national project. And while many artists have left Turkey, either temporarily or permanently, arts events, exhibitions, and panel discussions continue. Resilience is everywhere, against all odds.

In Germany as well, memory continues to be embattled by way of art, architecture, and cultural heritage, and I want to restrict myself to but four examples. Over the past few years, the world of arts and culture has witnessed heated debates over the Humboldt Forum, planned to be opened in the (partially) resurrected Berliner Stadtschloss (City Castle) that, largely destroyed during World War II, had been demolished by the GDR as a symbol of Prussian imperialism. Slated to open in 2020, the project is designed to bring non-European collections (that is, those of the Ethological Museum and the Museum for Asian Art) formerly located in Dahlem, in Berlin's outskirts, into the city's geographical center, the Museum Island. Billed as Germany's biggest cultural project to date (its price tag currently running at $679 million), its official descriptions are peppered with superlatives: With half a million artifacts, it wants to establish itself as "a leading cultural and museum city around the world" and promises innovative knowledge production that allows both "wonder" and "intercultural dialogue" between non-European works of art and the European masterpieces located on the Museum Island. The project has been met with important critiques regarding its reification of "Western" and "non-Western" art and cultural heritage, the lack of provenance research, and relatedly the missing debates on the restitution of objects, tens of thousands of which were looted during Germany's colonial reign and genocidal campaign in Namibia, for instance. The initiative No Humboldt21![8] has most forcefully noted that the project is nothing short of an attempt to whitewash Prussia's history and rehabilitate Germany's colonial past. As the historian and critical race scholar Fatima El-Tayeb (2016, 80ff.) so poignantly notes, this rehabilitation is attempted once more on the back of an erasure, this time spatial, of East Germany's socialist past: The reconstruction of the castle was enabled by the demolition of the GDR's Palast der Republik, home to its parliament.

But the erasures by way of German cultural policy, its reworking of the past, do not solely operate at home but in faraway places as well. Since 2016, the German Foreign Ministry and the German Archeological Institute are spearheading a project that aims to "facilitate identification of looted objects that are being traded illegally on the art market" and the "reconstruction of cultural heritage in Syria."[9] The initiative is called Stunde Null (Zero Hour); its name is the very term that has been so central to the fashioning of a postwar Germany, to the purported rupture with the Third Reich and the disavowal of the workings of the National Socialist past in the present. The project presents itself in humanitarian and scientific terms at a time during which Syrians and others fleeing war and structural violence continue to drown in the Mediterranean. Another step in "normalizing" Germany's past, it likens the Third Reich to other episodes of violence elsewhere, diminishing the particularities of the Nazi past. Here, the erasure of memory at home is connected to notions of heritage protection abroad, while the many entanglements between the fields of art, war, and state violence, indeed the very constitutiveness of violence for the art world, are obscured once more. Also obscured is the questionable provenance of large parts of the collection of artifacts from the Middle East, now turned theaters of war, that are located on Berlin's Museumsinsel. This—ultimately revisionist—iteration of the Zero Hour, no matter how well intended, adequate, or effective such a project might be, is especially unsettling given that it is playing out simultaneously with the rise of racist, right-wing politics in Germany, as in Europe overall.

The rise of the far right has been cemented with the Alternative für Deutschland's (Alternative for Germany, AfD) entry into the German parliament as the third-largest party in the 2017 elections (the first time that a party with such a platform has managed to do so since 1945). The AfD has made the arts a pronounced field of interest and advocates for a return to a decidedly "German art." Since its establishment in 2013 and successive electoral gains on the local, municipal, and state levels, the AfD has used its newfound power to target art events and artists who speak out against its policies through harassment, hate speech, and legal defamation suits (Apperly 2019). Apart from forming their own political foundation, which is poised to fund arts and cultural projects in the near future, the AfD has adopted strategies of using the *kleine Anfrage* ("minor interpellation" or "inquiry") to inundate the Ministry of Foreign Affairs's cultural department as well as other German cultural bodies (such as the Berlin Senate and the Goethe Institutes) to ask for "justifications" for current arts funding, especially support that goes abroad or to "non-German" artists (that is, artists with an immigrant background) at home. In Baden-Wuerttemberg, for instance, the AfD made such an inquiry, asking for a numerical breakdown of the "nationalities" of the dancers, actors, and singers employed in the state's theaters, orchestras, and opera houses (Apperly 2019), sending a clear message about their political preferences in the realm of art and culture. The full impact of the AfD in the federal and national decision-making committees on cultural policy as well as governmental grant-giving bodies will emerge in the coming years.

Yet growing anti-immigrant violence and racist discourses have already shaped the day-to-day politics of Germany. The Christian Union, eager to compete with the AfD for right-wing votes, has through its interior minister Horst Seehofer lobbied to turn the Interior Ministry into a Heimatministerium (its official and cumbersome name is now Bundesministeriums des Innern, für Bau und Heimat). While officially translated as Federal Ministry of the Interior, Building, and Community, it is important to keep in mind that the German notion of *Heimat* is a far cry from contemporary Anglo-Saxon usages of "community" (see Chapter 3). More than an administrative restructuring, this move has allowed the chauvinistic, exclusionary inflections of *Heimat* to make a triumphalist return on the German scene, one that enforces modes of belonging that official German cultural policy has long portrayed as overcome. This mode excludes immigrants and their descendants from being stakeholders in German *Kultur* and once more holds them responsible for all of Germany's political predicaments.

These developments present new iterations of the idea of "national art" that continues to hold its sway in politics. And once again, along with notions of modernity and civility this idea remains indebted to disavowed histories of violence. The cases of Istanbul, Berlin, Turkey, and Germany continue to provide insights into how—under the impetus of rising nationalism in Europe and around the world—local formations of the global art world are being called back into the national frame.

Acknowledgments

This book emerged between New York, Istanbul, and Berlin. In its trajectory, its sojourns and different iterations, it has incurred many debts. This book was made possible by the many artists and other practitioners in the art world who invited me into their offices, studios, and homes and shared their works, experiences, and time with me. Some of them are represented in the book through their words and works; my indebtedness to them is visible in the preceding pages. Some of them have preferred to remain unnamed or could not be named, which does not lessen their contributions or my gratitude to them.

The seeds of its ethnographic research were sown at the Graduate Center of the City University of New York. I am especially grateful to Vincent Crapanzano for his unwavering intellectual generosity and to Donald Robotham for his support. I would also like to thank Talal Asad, Michael Blim, Kate Crehan, Shirley Lindenbaum, Louise Lennihan, Jane Schneider, and Ellen DeRiso. I am grateful to Gisela Welz, whom I had the good fortune to meet while still in Frankfurt am Main. The book has benefited from colleagues who took the time to comment on very early versions of some chapters. My warmest appreciations to Ceren Özgül, Ujju Aggarwal, Nandini Sikand, Mary N. Taylor, Kee Howe Yong, Abou Farman Farmaian, Tina Lee, Christina (Tina) Harris, Nada Moumtaz, and Ted Powers. I am grateful to the late Vera L. Zolberg and to Zeynep Gürsel, who offered insightful comments at various occasions, and to Levent Soysal, who created opportunities for exchange and gritty discussion.

Other interlocutors and friends facilitated connections and helped locate valuable sources or access or created mindful refuge when refuge was needed: Bilgin Ayata, Pelin Başaran, Asena Günal, İnci Eviner, Arman Artuç, Nil Birol,

Nurten Demirbaş, Timuçin Gürer, Philippine Hoegen, Yasemin Özcan, Taha Parla, Dilek Winchester, Ayşe Köksal, Seçkin Uysal, Ayşecan Terzioğlu, Banu Cennetoğlu, Armanc Yılıdz, Christian Sälzer, and Çiçek İlengiz. I would also like to thank Seçil Yılmaz, who shared her research on the country paintings tours with me, and I am very glad to have met my colleagues from the cultural policy study group Eylem Ertürk, Esra Aysun, Aras Özgün, and Ayça İnce.

With their work and care, Christian Niccoli, Michi Knecht, and the late Stefan Beck made Berlin a more hospitable place. Along with all the "Berlin Lyrical Guerillas," I thank Deniz Utlu and Mutlu Ergün-Hamaz, who co-created "tausend Worte tief," a meeting point for BPoC writers and audiences that was and remains so needed. My warmest appreciation goes to my students at Sabanci University who participated in my seminars on political anthropology, museums, and the art world. These experiences enriched my thinking and rethinking of some of the main ideas of this book.

My time at the Forum Transregionale Studien in Berlin allowed me to present different aspects of the manuscript in progress. I would like to thank Hannah Bader and Gerhard Wolf for the environment they created in the Art Histories and Aesthetic Practices Program, the editorial team of ArtMargins, and the fellows of the Europe in the Middle and Middle East in Europe Program for their feedback and comments. At Northwestern University, I first and foremost owe my heartfelt gratitude to Penelope Deutscher and the Program in Critical Theory as well as to Ayça Alemdaroğlu and the Keyman Modern Turkish Studies Program, where I was able to present and discuss (almost) finalized parts of this book. The initial ethnographic research was made possible with a grant by the Wenner-Gren Foundation for Anthropological Research, and the Foundations for Arts Initiatives (FfAI), New York, provided a lifeline toward its completion. Back at the Forum Transregionale Studien, I am grateful to Georges Khalil, an alchemist in putting together productive and encouraging intellectual environments that helped me push the manuscript over the finishing line. And I would like to thank Jessica Metz, along with the Forum team, for their kind assistance in all things administrative, even in the midst of a global pandemic.

Encouragement and support come in a myriad of forms. For their keen eyes, incisive minds, council, and friendship I am grateful to Ceren Özgül, Meltem Ahıska, Kabir Tambar, Ayşe Öncü, Esra Özyürek, Başak Ertür, Alisa Lebow, Arlene Avakian, Martha Ayres, Leyla Neyzi, Sinan Göknur, Civan Özkanoğlu, Özden Demir, Bilgin Ayata, and Zeyno Pekünlü. For their guidance in times of seemingly insurmountable odds, I am indebted to Penelope Deutscher and Marianne Hirsch: Thank you.

Sections of Chapter 5 were first published in "Images Delegitimized and Discouraged: Explicitly Political Art and the Arbitrariness of the Unspeakable," *New Perspectives on Turkey* 45 (2013): 155–84 (special issue: "Turkishness and Its Discontents"). An earlier, partial version of Chapter 6 appeared in "The Politics of Urban Arts Events: A Comparison of Istanbul and Berlin," in *Orienting Istanbul: Cultural Capital of Europe?*, ed. D. Göktürk, L. Soysal, and I. Türeli, (Abingdon: Routledge, 2010), 234–50; also published in a Turkish translation of the volume *İstanbul Nereye? Küresel Kent, Kültür, Avrupa* (Istanbul: Metis, 2011), under the title "Kentsel Sanat Etkinlikleri Politikalar: İstanbul'la Berlin'i Karşılaştırmak, 304–24. At Fordham University Press my very warm thanks to Tom Lay and his steady hand, Eric Newman, and Rob Fellman.

I have learned to look at art first from my sister Ebru and then from my niece Hayat. It is to them and to my parents, Melek and Ergin, to whom this book is dedicated.

Notes

Introduction. Intimate Encounters

1. These numbers, provided by the Istanbul-based Hafiza Merkezi (The Truth Justice Memory Center), hardly begin to reflect the human, social, and political toll of the 1980 coup d'état. For more detailed information, see http://www.memorializeturkey.com/memorial/12th-of-september-museum-of-shame/. In 2012, Evren was tried and later convicted, but only on the count of overthrowing a democratically elected of government and not for the gross human rights violations he sanctioned. He died in May 2015, while awaiting appeal.

2. The political signaling function of artistic sensibility of persons responsible for atrocities and large-scale violence is taken up by Wolf Lepenies (2006, 3) in his *The Seduction of Culture in German History*: "It was well known in Nazi Germany that the loss of great works of art hit Hitler much harder than the destruction of large residential districts. German propagandists allowed this to be known, convinced that Hitler's reaction would be seen as a sign not of his brutal disregard for human suffering but of his artistic sensibility that the war had not been able to destroy." He notes, however, that this foregrounding of artistic sensibility is not merely "confined to authoritarian regimes (211n5).

3. There is, of course, another strand of public discourse: that of art (and the art world) as aloof or elitist. Its appearance is generally contingent on competing claims over what constitutes the "true art" of a people or a "nation" by opposing political camps. Modulations of this argument will be addressed throughout the book.

4. Some English translations of this passage replace the term "*Kultur*" in the German original with "civilization." This slip is quite notable given the conceptual distinction between culture and civilization in German thought, which will be taken up in Chapters 1 and 3.

5. Arthur Danto and George Dickie are among the pioneers of the institutional theories of art. In contrast to Danto, however, Dickie has a rather static view, in which he conceptualizes artists, audiences, and others as "role bearers" (1995 [1984], 220), paying little attention to power relations in the art world. Sarah Thornton's *Seven Days in the Art World* (2008), taking the reader on a whirlwind tour through the different sites and institutions of contemporary art and focusing mainly on its "high rollers," can be regarded as a recent incarnation of these institutional approaches.

6. The question of adequate spaces to present Berlin's public collections has occupied the city's art scene as well as local and national cultural policy makers for some time. In November 2014, Federal Government Commissioner for Culture and the Media Monika Grütters announced plans for a museum of modern art. As of the completion of this manuscript, the opening date has been repeatedly pushed back (now set for 2026), the design has been widely criticized, and the project has been marred by ever increasing costs. The same is true for the controversial Humboldt Forum, to which I will turn at the end of this study.

7. Seemingly neutral in pointing to the destination of migration, *Germaner* is a pejorative term used for those who went to Germany and their descendants, stereotypically presented as "unskilled" laborers who "tarnished Turkey's image" with their unwillingness (or inability) to fit into their "host society." The more recent, less loaded term *Almanyali* (someone from Germany) follows the terminological structure of *Türkiyeli*, i.e., a person from Turkey, used instead of the ethnicized designation "Turk" or "Turkish." Both terms have been popularized in the last decade, especially among the political left in Turkey and among minorities.

8. For an in-depth discussion of the controversy surrounding the 2005 publication of a series of cartoons depicting the Prophet Muhammad in the Danish newspaper *Jyllands-Posten*, see Asad et al. (2013).

9. The nomenclature for immigrants to Germany has shifted since the late 1980s, from *Ausländer*in* (foreigner) to *Mitbürger*in mit Migrationshintergrund* (fellow citizen with migration background) as a more general designation. For persons who, in some shape or form, have "roots" in Turkey or have Turkish citizenship, the term *Deutsch-Türken* (German Turks) is often used and just as often criticized for reinforcing the conception of Turkish ethnicity instead of acknowledging the diversity of backgrounds of those who emigrated from Turkey. In the arts and culture scene and in scholarship, the term *Post-Migranten*innen* has gained currency throughout the 2010s; it aims to draw attention to the processes that shape experiences after immigration, especially of those generations born in Germany.

10. The specificities of language use in my fieldwork interactions have formal implications: The translations of the interview excerpts cited throughout the book that were conducted in Turkish and German, along with the literature, are my own unless indicated otherwise.

11. This was notably also the case for the cultural policies of the former German Democratic Republic (Glaser 1997).

12. Anti-Armenian sentiment was further fueled by the disregard for Eastern Christianity and suspicions of possible Armenian-Russian collaboration. The liberal politician Friedrich Naumann went so far as to label the Hamidian massacres targeting Ottoman Armenians (1894–1896) "self-defense" (Anderson 2007, 101). Along with economic calculations, such sentiments also explain why the German government remained largely silent during the Armenian genocide (1915–1917).

13. Enver Pasha, the Ottoman war minister during World War I, who was instrumental to both Ottoman-German relations and the Armenian genocide, was so famed in Germany that he even had a namesake brand of cigarettes. A bridge in Potsdam bearing his name was destroyed during an aerial bombing in World War II; plans to rebuild it have—thus far—not materialized.

14. Whereas Brotton and Jardine focus on material dialogues in the early Renaissance period, Nathalie Rothman's *Brokering Empire* (2011) draws attention to the practices of "trans-imperial subjects," who as translators and mediators facilitated interlocution between Venice and Istanbul, as another example for the kinds of exchanges mapped here.

15. Among the many counterexamples to this understanding is the art historian Hans Belting's (2010) research on Ibn al-Haitham (Alhazen), who revolutionized ancient optic theory. His eleventh-century treatise on the mathematical theory of optics was widely circulated and, when translated into Latin, became the basis for the single-point perspective that laid the groundwork for the pictorial language of the Renaissance.

16. Other genealogies than the one I present here are—of course—possible, for instance, by turning to seventeenth- and eighteenth-century English and Scottish Enlightenment thinkers (Eagleton 1990, Mortensen 1997).

17. Baxandall (1972) situates the professionalization of art earlier, within fifteenth-century painting practices in Renaissance Italy. He posits that paintings emerged in collaborations between an artist and his "client" through the negotiation of work time, materials, colors, subject matters, and compensation. Kempers (1987), while also focusing on Renaissance Italy and the relationships between patrons and artists, sees the professionalization of art intimately connected to the process of state formation. Woodmansee's (1994) periodization, in turn, focuses on the convergence of the development of the book market, Enlightenment thought, and the notion of the author as an individual genius mostly through the lens of German thought on aesthetics.

1. Modernity, Nationalism, and Civilizing the Arts

1. Vasıf Kortun was the director of research and programs at SALT, established by Garanti Bank until 2017. Previously he directed the Platform Garanti Contemporary Art Center, founded in 2001, and served as founding director of the Museum of the Center for Curatorial Studies at Bard College (1994–1997).

2. For a periodization of the different permutations of the *Sonderweg* thesis, see Kocka (1999). A political program until 1945, the *Sonderweg* thesis became an object of critical scholarship after World War II in efforts to explain Germany's turn to fascism (Blackbourn and Eley 1984).

3. Hobsbawm (1992, 1) defines "invented tradition" as a "set of practices, normally governed by overtly or tacitly accepted rules and of a ritual or symbolic nature, which seek to inculcate certain values and norms of behavior by repetition, which automatically implies continuity with the past." It is then from this continuity that practices conceptualized as "tradition" derive their authority, even if the relation to the past that they project is only upheld by virtue of repetition. The term "invention" here does not necessarily imply that these practices have a fictitious basis but that their sense of continuity or antiquity is "invented."

4. That the categories "Catholic" and "Mediterranean" were so readily equated throughout the eighteenth century points to a rather different conception of Europe—and Germany's place within it—than suggested by the binaries between North and South, West and East that have habitually framed political and scholarly discussions on Europe after World War II.

5. The historian George Mosse (1985) argues that in the nationalist project the notion of German *Kultur* was also linked to rising notions of respectability. Accordingly, the opposition toward "French civilization" was frequently expressed by discrediting French morals. At the same time, he interprets the emphasis on "respectability" as a means of distinction by the rising bourgeoisie against both the lower classes and the aristocracy—the former portrayed as lazy, the latter as desolate and corrupted. This notion of respectability provided stability in an epoch of rapid change, not least by attempting to control sexuality.

6. The terms *Überfremdung* and degeneracy (*Entartung*) are frequently attributed to National Socialist ideology. However, this vocabulary (along with that of "smut and trash") already marked discussions of the state of art and popular culture in the Wilhelmine period and was widely employed during the Weimar Republic (von Saldern 2002, 311), before its usage peaked in the Third Reich. Similarly framed anxieties with regard to the popularity of Italian opera in the Germanys had already been expressed in the early eighteenth century (Applegate and Potter 2002, 4).

7. That the acquisition and exhibition practices of the National Gallery in Berlin remain contentious to this day, albeit for different reasons, will be further discussed in Chapter 4.

8. While Gökalp elaborated on cultural Turkism, he did not necessarily imagine a republican state formation (Parla 1985). Only living long enough to see the first year of the Republic, the general perception of his ideas remains refracted through Atatürk's policies.

9. The Ottoman expression "*hars*" has been replaced by the term "*kültür*," not least because of the successive language reforms that since the 1930s aimed to eliminate Arabic and Persian vocabulary. Although still in use in cultural policy

documents from the late 1980s (see Kantarcıoğlu 1987), most interlocutors were not aware that *hars* had been so broadly employed only two decades ago. More than a mere terminological shift, the notion of *kültür* bears structural resemblances to the German concept of *Kultur.*

10. The notion of "Westernization" tends to be applied retrospectively and does not necessarily have a fixed meaning. In the context of the republican era, "Western" could signify orientation toward French (e.g., language reforms), Swiss (e.g., legal code), Swedish (as in the folk-dance reform), or Hungarian models (as in the new music notation systems). In the case of the Ottoman Empire "Western" could also denote German, or rather Prussian, ties (e.g., with regard to military reorganization and engineering). For an analysis of how the terms "modern," "western," and "secular" in scholarship on Turkey actually obscure more than they explain, see Parla and Davison (2004).

11. This entailed sending urban middle-class teachers and doctors to Anatolia to collect information about "Turkish folklore" and learn about "Turkish culture" while at the same time contributing to the "modernization" of rural populations (Navaro-Yashin 2002, 48). A similar practice was put into place for painters and sculptors in the late 1930s (see Chapter 4).

12. The notion of "Arabization" (which sometimes parallels the German *Überfremdung*) has been frequently employed to devalue artistic expression from the Middle East (see Stokes 1992). I have encountered this label several times as a measurement for the quality in the genre of "oriental dancing": Arab dancers are stereotypically believed to work from a more simplified movement repertoire, while "Turkish" dancing is deemed to be more intricate and difficult to master (see also Potuoğlu-Cook 2006).

13. The formulation of an internal civilizing mission in the Ottoman Empire raises the question of how the central authority viewed its "peripheries" and whether the relationship between heartland and periphery could be conceptualized as colonial. Selim Deringil (2003, 313) attributes what he calls "borrowed colonialism" to the late Ottoman Empire, which he describes as a "survival tactic" so as not to become a colony itself. While Ussama Makdisi (2002), in contrast, speaks of "Ottoman imperialism," he and Deringil seem to concur that in their respective cases of inquiry, Mount Lebanon and Libya, modernization efforts and civilizing missions were proof that "Ottoman reformers understood [that] the modernity of their Empire depended on the reformation of the periphery as a foil to modern Ottoman identity" (47). Notably, the Ottoman modernization policies described by both Makdisi and Deringil resemble the social engineering measures implemented in the Republic of Turkey. İsmail Beşikçi (1990) has long argued that the Turkish state's relationship with its Kurdish population and territory is of a colonial nature. More recently, Uğur Ümit Üngör and Mehmet Polatel (2001) have proposed that the twin processes of the confiscation and redistribution of property in the course of the Armenian genocide present tools for what they call internal colonization.

14. For a longitudinal interrogation of demographic engineering in the late Ottoman Empire, see Üngör (2011).

15. As the anthropologist Ceren Özgül (2014) details, the Lausanne Treaty, while stipulating minority rights, "did not specify which communities would benefit from this legal recognition. . . . While Jewish, Armenian, and Greek communities within the empire were recognized as religious minorities, official minority status was denied to Christian populations native to Anatolia (such as Assyrians) and to the relatively new Christian communities such as recent converts to Protestantism. . . . Also left out were Kurds and non-Sunni Muslim sects such as the Alevis" (634).

16. It is thus not surprising that the mere assemblage of population statistics (both historical and contemporary) is a highly sensitive issue in Turkey that frequently has been met with censorship, unless it is in line with state-sanctioned narratives. Andrews and Benninghaus's (1989) long-term study surveys different Anatolian regions and lists forty-seven self-identifying ethnic and ethnoreligious groups.

17. People in western Thrace tune into Greek radio stations to this day. Tekelioğlu and Stokes are among the few authors who reveal the contestations and fervent discussions accompanying republican "reforms" in the arts. This absence is indicative of how the forgetting that characterizes official discourse is mirrored not only in public memory but also reproduced in scholarship.

18. The art historian Wendy Shaw (2011) suggests that multiple perspective and single perspective present different modalities of painting and correspond with divergent regimes of perception that still remain unexplored.

19. In contrast to the contemporary Egyptian artists discussed by Jessica Winegar (2006), early republican painters did not really have to "reckon" with the artistic legacy of a treasured civilization of the past, at least not officially. They were faced with a complete rupture rather than a comparison to cultural accomplishments of old. Similarly to the case of Egypt, however, they had to reckon with how and to what extent "western modalities" in the arts made sense in their setting (Koçak 2010, Shaw 2011).

20. In foreign policy, the term "normalization" is frequently employed to describe the amelioration of bilateral relations after World War II (not least in the context of the European Union) as well as Germany's rearmament and integration into international military missions through NATO. Chancellor Helmut Kohl's (1982–1998) notion of normalization also entailed an explicit appropriation of nationalist discourse. For a nuanced overview of what normalization has come to mean at different points in Germany's postwar history and how these modulations have affected the country's official memory regime, see Olick (1998).

21. This concern was voiced within Germany through protests under the motto "Nie wieder Deutschland" ("Never Again Germany") in the months leading up to the official reunification agreement and through the frequent reference to the French novelist François Mauriac's famous quip: "I love Germany so much that I am glad that there are two of them" (cited in Isaacson, Jackson, and Ogden 1989).

22. While Western European commentators are recorded to have referred to the Ottoman Empire as ruled by "Turks" as far back as the fifteenth century, this term was not part of the self-description employed within the empire itself. In fact, for the Ottoman elite "Turk" was for the most part a derogatory term associated with the "backwardness" and "warmongering" of their Central Asian ancestors, who had come into Anatolia with the likes of Genghis Khan (Kirişci 1998, 231).

23. Balibar (1991a, 17–18) proposes that racist theories are not just spontaneous expressions of "the masses" but have to be "rationalized by intellectuals" in a process that seeks to mirror "scientific proof." It is through this rationalization process that racist doctrines become "democratized," i.e., accessible to a national majority irrespective of class affiliations. It is along these lines that I see the Turkish Historical Society as instrumental in producing and popularizing racist narratives on Turkey's minorities.

24. As "tolerance" and "multiculturalism" have become conduits in claiming modernity, it has become somewhat commonplace to describe the diversity of the Ottoman Empire, and especially the makeup of Ottoman Istanbul, as "cosmopolitan" in recent years (Mills 2010, Brink-Danan 2011).

25. Taha Parla (2007) poignantly notes that what has long been referred to as the "Kurdish issue," just like the "Armenian issue" and a cohort of other predicaments that are on Turkey's daily agenda, are actually best understood as "Turkish issues."

26. Then as now, human rights violations, especially with regard to freedom of expression and minority rights, have been continuously reported by Turkey's Human Rights Foundation (İnsan Hakları Derneği, IHD) (http://www.ihd.org.tr/index.php/raporlar-mainmenu-86/el-raporlar-mainmenu-90.html), Human Rights Watch (http://www.hrw.org/world-report/2014/country-chapters/turkey), and EU progress reports (http://ec.europa.eu/enlargement/pdf/key_documents/2013/package/brochures/turkey_2013.pdf).

27. Götz Aly (2005) carries Baumann's argument a bit further. Rather than referring to an abstract notion of a "more reasonable and rational social order," as Bauman (1989, 95) suggests, Aly posits that the dispossession and annihilation of Jews as well as military occupation practices during World War II contributed to the broadening of the German middle class and created an investment of a large social stratum in National Socialist policies. These processes have shaped the art world significantly and will be taken up in more detail in Chapter 4.

28. Accordingly, Bruno Latour (2001) proposes that those who "resisted" this modern form of power "*became* pre-modern" (38, emphasis mine), rather than *staying* premodern.

2. Art Worlds: Of Friends, Foes, and Working for the Greater Good

1. I use the term "gallerist" (German: *Galerist*in*; Turkish: *galerici*) because it was the standard term employed by interlocutors and in the majority of art publications. In the United States, where the expression "art dealer" is more

common, "gallerist" is often understood as a European invention that deflects from the obvious connection between art and the marketplace. The German equivalent for art dealer, *Kunsthändler*in*, is generally used for those who work in the secondary art market, i.e., who resell artworks between collectors, rather than brokering sales between artists and collectors directly.

2. Since Chapters 1 and 3 deal with the state as an actor in the art world in more detail, I have for the most part omitted references to cultural policy in this chapter. However, I want to point out that artists often frame their relationship with the state as antagonistic, while state actors in turn often—and stereotypically so—portray artists as unruly children.

3. Since Oda Projesi was evicted from their apartment in the course of the gentrification of the Galata, they have continued experimenting with different media, including producing newspapers and radio shows. The fact that many of their projects do not or only secondarily produce tangible objects and are not intended as performances has led repeatedly to questions about whether their works actually constitute art. For a more detailed discussion of the concept of collaboration in the works of Oda Projesi, see Bishop (2012, 20–22).

4. This perception is in stark contrast to the landscape of criticism in early republican times, when art was very controversially discussed in the daily press (Tekelioğlu 2001, Köksal 2004, Bek Arat 2014).

5. Some of these alternative assemblages broke apart after a few years; others are trying to hold on in different formats.

6. In 2010, Banu Cennetoğlu began working with Rodeo Gallery, formerly of Istanbul (now London and Piraeus).

7. High-profile artists are an exception to this convention. As one gallerist put it: "If an artist like Jeff Koons determines an amount that he wants to receive for a work, you—as a gallerist—just count your blessings that you are representing him and don't challenge the artist's decision."

8. Pearce (1995, 159) defines a collection as "a group of objects, brought together with intention and sharing a common identity of some kind, which is regarded by its owner, as in some sense, special or set apart." Similarly to Baudrillard (1994 [1968]), she emphasizes psychoanalytic approaches to collecting, in which the affection for objects is identified as a transference of sexual desires.

9. Established in 2005 and named after Peter Hartz, the head of the government-appointed Committee for Modern Services in the Labor Market, Hartz IV has joined unemployment aid and social security. It has been critiqued for further impoverishing the unemployed instead of helping them reintegrate into the workforce.

10. In 2007, the arts writer Henricke Thomsen labeled Berlin a "transit space" for art. She explained this dynamic in part through the example of the opening of a Berlin branch of the gallery Haunch of Venison (2007–2010), a subsidiary of the auction house Christie's. As François Pinault was the majority stakeholder in both Haunch of Venison and Christie's, anxieties arose that Christie's would push into the primary art market and inflate prices in the process. While the presence of

world-class galleries might augment Berlin's image, these types of connections are likely to drive up prices, making it harder for local arts institutions, with their limited budgets, to acquire works for their permanent collections. Berlin's position as a stage for exhibiting contemporary art hence does not translate into these works being accessible to the local public—at least not in the long run.

11. While over time these types of objects can be accorded historical value because they document a common history (as indicated in the German term *Zeitzeugnis*), I would argue that art is very much understood as a public good as soon as it is completed.

12. The series was by organized by Artforum, Berlin's biggest commercial art fair at the time (see Chapter 6).

13. Spanning important contemporary artists, Olbricht's collection also stretches into works of the early sixteenth century. In 2010, he established me Collectors Room Berlin through his foundation to exhibit his works.

14. Sylt is part of the North Frisian Islands and a popular resort for German celebrities.

15. With the steady rise in art prices for most of the past two decades, art has been propagated as a relatively safe and lucrative investment, in contrast to real estate or the boom-and-bust-prone investment objects of the "new economy." Notably, collectors' handbooks such as Richard H. Rush's *Art as an Investment* make similar predictions as early as 1961. Given the special status of cultural goods in the EU arena, profit margins for reselling artworks are tax free, making their acquisition for investment purposes even more attractive. However, there have been contradictory projections regarding the future of the art market. While in 2006 a 5 to 10 percent investment in art was a standard for hedge funds (Herstatt 2006), the investment funds solely dedicated to art that popped up in the 2000s have been mostly dissolved without bringing the expected returns, not least because of the economic crisis of 2008 (Gerlis 2013). The art historian and critic Isabelle Graw (2008, 45) proposes that the emphasis on artworks as investment objects has created a conflation between the market value and the symbolic value of artworks, resulting in the maxim that "good art is art that sells." She argues that the symbolic value of an artist's body of work is increasingly based on its economic value, instead of emerging from the conversations between "art historians, critics, museums, exhibitions, and curators," which focus primarily on artistic innovation.

16. The assessment of overpricing seems to be a cyclical occurrence. In her 1960 autobiography, Peggy Guggenheim already bemoans speculative buying and ensuing price levels. Contemplating her regrets with regard to works that she sold and others that she could not afford, Guggenheim notes: "However, I comfort myself by thinking how terribly lucky I was to have been able to buy all my wonderful collection at a time when prices were still normal, before the whole picture market turned into an investment market" (110).

17. Together with his wife Merey has also established a contemporary art competition at Mimar Sinan University that grants material support and stipends for at least two students per year.

18. Similar to Çağa, Merey highlights the Western orientation of his family through education and travels during which artworks and artifacts were acquired. He emphasizes repeatedly that his great-grandparents' generation consisted of high-level military men and bureaucrats, doctors, and lawyers and that "at that time few Muslims" were in these positions. In these kinds of narratives westward orientation by default becomes a prerequisite for appreciating art. After 1909 the family collection moved into buying art of their contemporaries. Merey also mentions that his grandfather commissioned two paintings that are now part of the Istanbul Modern collection and that represent the emancipation of the "Turkish woman," gesturing once more at the collector's role as a guardian of modernization.

19. Jürgen Zech is the director of the Arbeitskreis Kultursponsoring, a working group of the Federation of German Industries. Founded in 1996, the working group encompasses representatives of more than sixty corporations. It works on sponsorship guidelines and lobbies for legal measures that regulate sponsorship procedures, including tax deductions for sponsoring corporations (see Chapter 4).

20. While the conference was entitled "Corporate Cultural Responsibility," many speakers employed the term "cultural" and "social" interchangeably. This slippage between the cultural and the social points to a conflation also inherent in the modern conception of art, with its ethical impetus and assumed civilizing power.

21. Chancellor Helmut Kohl (1982–1998) coined the term "blooming landscapes" to project economic development in the former GDR after Germany's reunification in 1990. To this day, however, uneven economic development continues to mark the inner German landscape.

3. Governing Culture, Producing Modern Citizens

1. This was just as true for former East German cultural policies, although what one was to be civilized into differed in conception.

2. Despite these organizational differences, cultural departments in Turkey and Germany share similar responsibilities. Along with visual and performing arts policy, they are concerned with museums and cultural heritage. Their fields of activity converge with other administrative units in charge of media and broadcasting regulations, publishing, and film funding. Laws on charitable giving, taxation, and questions of copyright concern the art world vitally and connect it with other domains of (supra)national governance as well as with the marketplace, since they affect the pricing and circulation of cultural and artistic goods and services and regulate private sponsorship of the arts.

3. Germany's post–World War II federal makeup has led to the principle of cultural sovereignty of the *Länder* (the German states) and hence to "an inverted hierarchy of responsibilities" in cultural policy (Burns and van der Will 2003, 134). This makeup is generally understood as an antidote to National Socialist centralization (Pommerin 1996). Most German states draw on the geopolitical precedents of former principalities, and these precedents not only reflect Germany's

pre-1871 political composition but also struggles against earlier forms of centralization under Prussian dominance. The Allied restructuring of Germany rested on these historical precedents in a concerted effort to dissolve Prussia, although it continues to have a cultural life in the form of the Stiftung Preussischer Kulturbesitz (Prussian Cultural Heritage Foundation).

4. For a detailed discussion of the Herero and Nama genocides (1904–1908), their political legacies, and how they informed the extermination policies in the Third Reich, e.g., see Madley (2005) and Ayata (2016).

5. Schooling, German-language education and press, and to a lesser extent the arts "proper," along with hospitals and missions, were categorized as foreign cultural policy areas.

6. These plans persisted during the German-Ottoman alliance of World War I. The leadership of the Committee of Union and Progress was acutely aware of Germany's ulterior motives, leading to periodic strains on this partnership.

7. Applegate (1990) proposes that provincial attachments inherent in the concept of *Heimat* (often, if inadequately so, translated as "home" or "homeland") allowed for a pluralistic imagination of the "German nation." In contrast, Waldinger (1940) argues that *Heimat*, and especially *Heimat* art, was easily integrated into the "blood and soil" ideology of the Nazis, as it joined an ethnicized understanding of homeland and nation with antimodernist calls to a "return to nature" and rising chauvinism after World War I. Von Saldern (2004), in turn, proposes that the concept of *Heimat* has been historically polyvalent but that its democratic inflections have remained underdeveloped and thus open to exclusionary understandings. In the last chapter, I will touch on how these latter understandings are, unfortunately, returning.

8. Stolcke (1995) and Balibar (1991a) argue that biology as the basis of belonging has been discredited and that culture has moved to the forefront. Yet it is important to note that how culture is employed in political discourses is versatile, in that it can move in and out of biology. As such, "biology" and "culture" are at times used interchangeably, and the German notion of *Kultur* continues to exhibit this versatility.

9. This momentum was met with opposition from within the art world, too—on the basis of both the internationalism of modernism and questions of style. For instance, in 1892 the Association of Berlin Artists voted to close an Edvard Munch exhibition because conservative members were scandalized by the artist's use of "disturbing colors and motives" (Berghahn 1994, 136). In the aftermath of this episode, the Berlin Secession formed in 1898, arguing that the academy continued to hinder artistic innovation.

10. The renewed quest for a "German art," this time firmly situated in the West, did not simply portray modernism as interrupted through the Nazi reign but once again made art historians go as far back as the Middle Ages, thinking that the art of Catholic Europe would provide a solid basis to redefine Germany's artistic position (Belting 1998, 80–89).

11. The fictitiousness of the notion of "rebuying" and how it has shaped German museum collections will be further examined in Chapter 4.

12. International bodies, such as the Council of Europe, have identified budget cuts in cultural policy as one of the prime threats to cultural pluralism in Germany.

13. The journalist Topuz (1998) has produced one of the few works dedicated solely to the history of cultural policy in Turkey, along with the art historian Nilüfer Öndin (2003). It was only with the establishment of the Cultural Policy and Management Research Center (KPY) at Bilgi University in 2010 that contemporary cultural policy research has been conducted in a systematic manner (e.g., see Ada and İnce 2010).

14. Often related back to the Ottoman capitulations, which allowed some Ottoman Christians to attain foreign nationality (Quataert 2005), the notion of non-Muslims as foreigners prevails in the guise of various conspiracy theories in nationalist camps to this day (Gürpinar 2013).

15. The activities of the People's Houses included literacy programs and classes on history, literature, the fine arts, performance, and drama, along with sports and social services.

16. The fervor with which these activities were pursued found its numerical expression in the recorded 970 art exhibitions organized in the People's Houses across Turkey between 1932 and 1940 (Özsezgin 1998, 35).

17. The Greek-Latin lineage within which Yücel tried to locate Turkey would be the exact same lineage that the European Union would claim for itself as an exclusionary mechanism vis-à-vis Turkey (see also Herzfeld 1982).

18. While Navaro-Yashin (2012) develops the concept of "make-believe space" within the context of the unrecognized state of Northern Cyprus, she notes that all nation-states share a certain make-believe quality. Given that official Turkish cultural history, like official Turkish history overall, has exhibited untenable cracks, her concept seems particularly fitting here.

19. The Village Institutes were also important tools in implementing the Land Distribution Law. In combination with low pricing and the high taxation of agricultural products, this process alienated large landowners from the regime (Zürcher 2004, 210).

20. The People's Houses were reestablished three years after the 1960 coup, this time independent of the government. They were closed down again after the 1980 coup for "revolutionary activities" and reopened in 1987 as the ban on associations was gradually lifted.

21. It might be safe to say that the biggest archive on Kurdish art is in the hands of the Turkish security forces. For a more detailed discussion, see Chapter 5.

22. A frequently noted example is the DP's discontinuation of the yearly State Painting and Sculpture Exhibitions, which used to be a vital forum for young artists to launch their careers.

23. Nurcan Toksoy (2007) begins her monograph on the People's Houses with an epigraph by Mustafa Kemal Atatürk. Lauding their research, he dwells on the

example of Diyarbakir, of which "we used to know nothing of note." It is, says Atatürk, thanks to the People's Houses that we know of Diyarbakir's economy, its history, its folklore, and no less its "Turks as if we had stayed there for months and had examined everything." Yet the discourse of not knowing Diyarbakir, like much of the Kurdish regions and, indeed, Anatolia, is often repeated in western Turkey, just as the task of "researching" and "disseminating" national culture remains in the mission statement of the Ministry of Culture and Tourism.

24. Two 2013 exhibitions, *Scared of Murals* (SALT) and *Let's Go Postering, 1963–1980: The Left's Visual Adventure* (Depo), unearthed parts of this history that had largely been forgotten. This was also a time during which independent art collectives, such as the Sanat Tanitim Toplulugu (1972), were established and state and private infrastructure for art grew.

25. Although the economic liberalization of Turkey is often attributed to Turgut Özal's regime, it is important to stress that this process had already begun and was met with left-wing opposition during the 1970s. The coup was geared toward ending this opposition to economic liberalization, which was further solidified under Özal.

26. While the military has been portrayed as staunchly secular for most of republican history, this assessment obscures that the 1980 military junta advanced the very concept of the Turkish-Islamic synthesis not in order to separate state and religion but to bring religion once more firmly under the authority of the state. For a nuanced reading of the Turkish-Islamic synthesis through the conceptual lens of "segregative biopolitics, assimilation, absorption, and dispossession," see Iğsız (2018).

27. I have not been able to verify this information, as most cultural agencies, including the Ministry of Culture and Tourism, are coy about giving out actual budgets, and those that are available to the public are not itemized in detail. During a 2013 visit, a senior official in the ministry's Directorate for Strategy Development noted that the way budgets are kept is unwieldy to such an extent that even he has problems deciphering them.

28. Although never officially confirmed, several people working at Santral relayed to me that Erdoğan asked for a preopening to coincide with his national reelection campaign in 2007. While parts of the art world welcomed the fact that Erdoğan had deemed contemporary art important enough to request these early openings, others boycotted both events, seeing them as an instrumentalization of art for political purposes. Santral was closed in early 2013, and its collection was deaccessioned under questionable circumstances.

29. Istanbul's 2010 tenure as a European Capital of Culture led to an unprecedented number of public-private partnerships. Although most did not produce sustainable programs, they raised awareness for the right to demand state support for the arts (Karaca 2013).

30. The term "pre-Tanzimat" is not used by the AKP but can be inferred from Erdoğan's frequently employed narrative of "Turkey as having been oppressed and alienated from its traditions and civilizational achievements for the past two hundred years."

31. The naming of the third Bosporus bridge, for instance, has been deeply hurtful to Turkey's Alevi populations, as its namesake, Yavuz Sultan Selim (1465–1520), ordered the massacres of forty thousand Alevis in 1514. Sparking the Gezi uprising of 2013, the most controversial urban renewal project to date (culturally speaking) has been the proposed reconstruction of the eighteenth-century Ottoman barracks in Taksim. That the project was initially conceived as a mixed-use mall indicates that Ottoman references are pragmatically employed to rally nationalist sentiment under economic considerations, rather than being concerned with specific art historical or aesthetic legacies.

4. The Art of Forgetting

1. Whereas English translations often use the term "civilization," the German original employs the term *Kultur* (which I have included here). Given the long antinomy in German thought between conceptions of culture and civilization, this slippage is notable but in this instance works within the dialectic of culture and barbarism that Benjamin proposes.

2. Thirty-three persons (and two perpetrators) died when the hotel was set on fire. Police and security forces looked on, and firemen only arrived eight hours after the attack had started. For details on the struggle to turn the site into a place for commemoration, see Çaylı (2019).

3. Taking office in 1971, Halman is often said to be Turkey's first minister of culture. However, as outlined earlier, it would be more correct to say that he was the first to head the ministry in something akin to its present form. Among his many activities in the field of culture, Halman served as a member on the UNESCO Executive Board (1991–1995).

4. Taner Akçam's (1996) work on the Istanbul trials (1919–1920) shows that along with the killing of Ottoman Armenians and dragging the empire into a war of aggression, the prosecution also indicted the unsanctioned appropriation of Armenian property.

5. Ahtamar and Mor Gabriel are only two out of thousands of expropriated community sites (Polatel et al. 2012). Given that potential restitution will be decided on a case-by-case basis, this process might take decades at the current speed and fickleness of the political establishment.

6. As the art historian Vazken Davidian noted in our conversation, Ottoman Armenian painters have been doubly obscured, since they have been written out of both Ottoman and Armenian art history. Their works remain in a limbo of invisibility and largely unacknowledged. See also Davidian (2015).

7. Many commentators questioned the overall rationale of exhibiting the family collection under these conditions. One artist forcefully noted: "What I really can't stand is this notion that 'at least we are doing something for the public,' as if that was a good thing in itself. We must stop this nonsense, either something is good, or it is bad. You can't just assemble paintings in a building like you assemble furniture in

your house and call it a museum that supposedly serves the public." The debates surrounding the Istanbul Modern were fueled further when its director, Oya Eczacıbaşı, described her transition from the business to the art world by stating, "There is no actual difference between the art business and any other business; only that the products are artworks" (cited in Artun 2011, 125). Even in its most unequivocally commoditized form, i.e., in the art market, the commodity character of art invokes discomfort, a discomfort that deepens once art enters the museum. To equate museum works with "products" steers too far from the mediating discourse of the greater good to be acceptable for most art world actors.

8. As of summer 2008, Çalıkoğlu has returned to the Istanbul Modern as chief curator.

9. The title played on Betty Mahomoody's bestseller *Not without My Daughter* (1988).

10. *Aufarbeitung* is generally attributed to Adorno's 1959 lecture "What Does Coming to Terms with the Past Mean?," where he maps a kind of working through the past that informs both the present and the future. In contrast, *Vergagenheitsbewältigung*, denoting a mastering or overcoming of the past, gained increasing currency throughout the 1980s in Germany's efforts at "normalization" (Olick 1998).

11. This purge resulted in the 1937 "Degenerate Art" exhibition that featured 650 artworks confiscated by the Nazi regime, spanning styles from expressionism, impressionism, Dadaism, and Neue Sachlichkeit to surrealism and cubism. Touring twelve cities, it drew over three million visitors (Levi 1998). It is one of the ironies of history that it attracted three times more visitors than the simultaneously organized "Great German Art" exhibition, which presented officially sanctioned art (Koldehoff 2014, 89).

12. Most famously among them was Propaganda Minister Joseph Goebbels, who retained a love for modernism, hoping it would be salvageable in the form of what he called "Nordic expressionism." This brought him into frequent conflict with the Kampfbund der deutschen Kultur (Militant League for German Culture), the cultural arm of the Nazi Party.

13. The importance given to art by the Nazis poses somewhat of a conundrum for Germany to this day. "At least the Nazis had culture" is as much a stereotypical phrase as it is a widely used one (Lepenies 2006).

14. The restitution process was marred with difficulties for Maria Altmann, Adele Bloch-Bauer's niece and sole inheritor to her estate, who carried the case to the US Supreme Court. Although the Austrian government obliged in the end, commentators qualified the "loss" of the painting as a "total meltdown" for the Austrian art world and "a blow against Austrian culture" (Haas 2006). Shortly after its return, Altmann sold the painting for $135 million to the cosmetics heir Ronald Lauder, an avid restitution activist who had supported her quest. The piece that Lauder calls "my Mona Lisa" is now on view at his Neue Galerie, New York.

15. They were mainly concerned with the restitution of non-German owned works and unable to locate all of the looted artworks, such as those that "disappeared" into

personal holdings or into what was to become the Eastern Bloc. For an overview of the Monuments Men, see http://www.monumentsmen.com.

16. Founded in 1928, the Protestant Art Service (Evangelischer Kunstdienst) focused on new liturgical art. After 1933, it represented Nazi cultural policy interests abroad. Experts from its ranks also took part in the selection committee of the "Degenerate Art" exhibition. Dismantled after 1945, many of its former employees subsequently held positions as art historians and appraisers in the Federal Republic and abroad (Koldehoff 2014).

17. For the development of the German notion of indemnification (*Wiedergutmachung*) and how it relates to ideas of forgiveness and justice, see Barkan (2000).

18. Flick delegated the responsibility of compensation payments to Deutsche Bank (DB), the majority shareholder of the Flick conglomerate. DB eventually paid the equivalent of 5 million DM into the compensation fund in 1999. Because of inflation (incurred by the currency switch to the euro) and the additional number of eligible survivors after 1989, the actual amount of compensation allocated per person decreased considerably (Kessen 2004, 67).

19. Flick's sister, Dagmar Ottmann, long critical of her brother's resistance against commissioning a full investigation into the family business during the Third Reich, initiated such a study when the debate first erupted in 2004. It was published 2009 (see Frei et al. 2009).

20. The neue Gesellschaft für Bildende Kunst (nGbK) was founded in 1969. Located in Berlin's Kreuzberg district, the association, consisting of artists and cultural workers, functions through a grassroots democracy model in which members vote on proposals to allocate funding. Its exhibition space is curated on the same principle.

21. The circulation of these posters was aided by an anonymous group of donors who, upon learning of Stih and Schnock's initiative, contributed funds so the artists could rent advertising trucks. It was also through these donors that the artists learned that Schröder was planning to soon step down from office and take on an advisory position in the Ringier publishing house, in Zurich, secured by Flick's financial advisor von Kroeber. One year later, Schröder did indeed step down and proceed in the manner foretold.

22. For a reprint of Chancellor Schröder's speech, see *Blätter für deutsche und internationale Politik* 11 (2004): 1398–1400.

23. Between 2005 and 2007, Götz Aly and Adam Tooze conducted a public exchange of blows, first on the pages of German newspapers and then in their academic publications, as they disagreed about the extent to which the war was financed by the German people or paid for by the dispossession of the occupied territories. For the initial exchange see Tooze (2005a, 2005b) and Aly (2005b).

24. Members of the Thyssen family have for several generations adopted similar practices to the Flicks by changing citizenship for tax purposes, which aided them

in maintaining and expanding what is now the Thyssen-Bornemisza collection (Litchfield 2006).

25. The Berggruen Collection was sold to the city of Berlin and does not pose the problems outlined here. For a full list of the museum network's institutions, see http://www.smb.museum/en/museums-and-institutions.html.

26. While this acquisition policy is generally portrayed as "bringing back" works formerly belonging to German institutions, it seems that availability and affordability on the international market were major factors in this process. I am still researching the specifics of how German modernism was thus constituted in retrospect.

27. Bastian resigned from his position in 2007. Citing irreconcilable differences for his decision, he charged the museum directorate with lack of vision and artistic mismanagement.

28. Many of these works were formerly part of the collection of the Palace of the Republic (built in 1976), the seat of the GDR parliament. After lengthy debate, the building was demolished in early 2006. While some cited asbestos contamination as the reason, others saw this decision as nothing short of yet another attempt to erase East German history. In its place, the Berlin Senate decided to rebuild the Berliner Stadtschloss (city castle) that, formerly at the same site, had been largely destroyed during World War II and then demolished by the GDR as a symbol of Prussian imperialism. In the early 2000s, the Palace of the Republic housed a series of interim art projects that functioned as a stand-in for a much needed but nonexisting *Kunsthalle*, i.e., a public space for contemporary art produced in Berlin. The rebuilt city castle will be at the center of the Humboldt Forum museum project, which I will turn to in the conclusion.

29. The GDR section of the show was subdivided into "official" and "unofficial," i.e., state-sanctioned and dissident art. However, this did little to mitigate the artists' distress. Incensed by the manner of display, one of the artists shown in the "unofficial" section tried to remove his work from the exhibition and was arrested in the process (Osmond 2000, 500).

30. The 1959 Bitterfeld conference was a turning point in GDR cultural policy. It marked a concerted effort to bind artists to the state structure and popularized the idea of transforming the GDR into a "literary society," i.e., into both the creators and audiences of East German national literature (Stephan et al. 1974, 86). This vision bears striking similarities to the Turkish notion of building "a republic of the fine arts" (see Chapter 3). In this process, the East German Artists League and its president, Johannes Becher, were sidelined. An expressionist poet and émigré to Moscow, Becher had facilitated dialogues with churches in the GDR and other émigré artists who returned to West Germany. He also convinced Thomas Mann to take part in the Goethe and Schiller celebrations in 1949 and 1955 in East Germany.

31. For an artistic intervention on the interconnections between contemporary art and the weapons industry in Turkey and beyond, see Hito Steyerl's performance-lecture "Is the Museum a Battlefield?" (2013), at https://vimeo.com/76011774.

32. For a more detailed discussion of Winchester's work, see Karaca (2019).

33. Widely reported at the time, this move fueled hopes that the exhibition, or parts of it, would become integrated into the permanent display of the museum. Upon further inquiry, however, I learned that the exhibition was merely stored at the museum for five years (2004–2009) and then taken over by the Hamburg Institute for Social Research.

34. For details on the attack, see Ergener (2009). The mob was led by the lawyer Kemal Kerinçsiz, who gained notoriety in the mid-2000s for bringing court cases against journalists and writers, among them Hrant Dink, Elif Shafak, and Orhan Pamuk, all for "denigrating Turkishness" (see Chapter 5). Kerinçsiz and his associates also targeted minority religious rituals and conferences numerous times. Much less known is that they regularly "frequented" exhibitions dealing with the Armenian genocide at Depo, an independent arts space in Istanbul. Kerinçsiz received an aggravated life sentence for plotting to overthrow the government in the controversial Ergenekon trial but was released in early 2014, with the verdict overturned in 2019.

5. The Politics of Art and Censorship

1. In the United States, free speech is generally understood as an unfettered right in the "liberal tradition." Germany and Turkey, however, constitutionally guarantee freedom of expression but also clearly delimit speech. Although beyond the scope of the present inquiry, I should note that all three contexts share regulations on public decency, e.g., pertaining to the protection of minors—which are highly normalized, and for good reason. As demonstrated by Marjorie Heins (2001), however, censorship becomes much more broadly acceptable when arguing that the depictions in question may harm or exploit those most vulnerable, i.e., children and minors. This move at times presents entry points for broader infringements upon freedom of expression than one might assume at first sight.

2. A grossly reinterpreted adaptation of Lion Feuchtwang's novel (1925) by the same title, the film was directed by Veit Harlan (also known as "Hitler's favorite filmmaker"). Himmler declared the film compulsory viewing for the SS and the police forces. Although Harlan was cleared through a denazification panel in 1947, he was the only director to be tried for his artistic work during the Third Reich. The Hamburg State Prosecutor indicted him for crimes against humanity, but Harlan was acquitted as the jury deemed "the charges that the extermination of the Jews was a result of the film . . . not 'provable'" (Tegel 2000, 216).

3. Conceptualized as arising from Germany's responsibility for its Nazi past, these offenses are bundled under Article 130 of the German penal code. The glorification of National Socialism, for example, is forbidden under paragraph 3 of Article 130. What constitutes glorification has repeatedly been questioned but in principle applies to any portrayal that does not unequivocally condemn Nazism. Incitements of the masses are understood as offenses against the public order

(*Straftaten gegen die öffentliche Ordnung*) and as such have precedence over the constitutionally stipulated freedom of the arts and sciences (Article 5, paragraph 3, of the German constitution, *Grundgesetz*). Ruth Gavinson (1998) argues that incitement laws assume a problematic causality between an inciting speech and an action and hence carry the risk of self-censorship rather than addressing the circumstances that give rise to hate speech. The German stance on the issue, however, is that nonintervention in inciting speech produces the impression of (tacit) approval by the state.

4. The same was long true for Adolf Hitler's *Mein Kampf*, which was not available in Germany but could be acquired in many neighboring countries as well as overseas. While *Mein Kampf* was considered banned in Germany, the facts on the ground were slightly more complicated. Its reproduction had been prevented by the Free State of Bavaria, which claimed the book's rights (as part of Adolf Hitler's estate from his Munich residence) after World War II and sued all publishers that printed the book, with the exception of those that had acquired international publishing rights before 1945. The copyright restrictions expired in 2015 (the seventieth year after its author's death), placing *Mein Kampf* in the public domain. The Institut für Zeitgeschichte, Munich, published a "critical annotated edition" in 2017. An unannotated edition of *Mein Kampf* would have certainly been banned because of its overtly anti-Semitic content.

5. The criminalization of Holocaust denial in Germany was enacted in 1985 as an addition to Article 130 of the penal code. A fact that is largely forgotten today is that this law—referred to as a measure against the *Auschwitzlüge* (Auschwitz lie)—only passed parliament after the addition, at the insistence of the conservative CDU/CSU majority, of a stipulation that also criminalized the denial of the forced expulsion of Germans from Eastern Europe.

6. Many believe that Ignatz Bubis, a Westend-based real estate developer who served as president of the Central Council of Jews in Germany (1992–1999), to be the real-life inspiration for the character. Markovits (Markovits et al. 1986, 6) notes that "Zwerenz strongly objected to Fassbinder's creation of the 'Rich Jew,'" whereupon Fassbinder promised to rewrite the role, calling the new character "'Rich Poor Jew' to convey that after Auschwitz even the richest Jew remained poor as well." This rewrite was never realized, as the scandal broke out before Fassbinder could return to the play.

7. The visit to the Bitburg military cemetery by Reagan and Kohl was originally billed as a symbolic act of German-American reconciliation. When it became known that the cemetery not only hosted the remains of fallen American service men but also those of members of the Waffen-SS, the armed wing of the Nazi party responsible for countless massacres of civilians, protests erupted. A hastily added concentration camp visit did little to assuage the scandal. For a comprehensive overview of the Bitburg controversy, see Hartmann (1986).

8. In fact, *Garbage* was performed for a closed audience of theater critics in Frankfurt in 1985, billed as a dress rehearsal. Previously, an amateur club at Ruhr

University had showcased the play in 1979, unbeknownst to and unauthorized by its publishers.

9. Initially the student arm of the Social Democratic Party (Sozialdemokratische Partei, SPD), the SDS became part of the extraparliamentarian opposition after the SPD excluded all SDS members in 1961 over rifts regarding Germany's rearmament program.

10. After working as a curator at KW (1998–2005), Blumenstein coestablished the independent curatorial collectives the Office and the Salon Populaire in Berlin and then served as director of KW from 2013 to 2016. Ensslin, the son of the RAF's founding member Gudrun Ensslin, grew up in foster care after his mother went underground in 1969. He is an independent curator, playwright, and dramaturge and in 2009 was appointed as professor for aesthetics and art mediation at the Stuttgart State Academy of Art and Design. Biesenbach, who is the founding director of both KW and the Berlin Biennial, has been serving as the director of MoMA PS1 since 2004, alongside his position of chief curator at large at the Museum of Modern Art, New York City.

11. Authored by Stefan Aust, the book widely popularized the thesis that the deaths of Baader, Ensslin, Jan-Carl Raspe, and Irmgard Möller at Stammheim prison were not suicides but executions staged as such. In 2007, secret recordings of the inmates' communications emerged that indicated that they planned to take their lives in order to animate their movement. Since these recordings were made by state agencies, the question remains why no attempts were made to prevent the alleged suicides.

12. During the Third Reich, Schleyer advanced through the ranks of the Nazi Party's Protection Squadron (SS) and from 1943 onward was responsible for the economy in the Protectorate of Bohemia and Moravia (Hachmeister 2004). He returned to Germany after being a prisoner of war in 1948. Taking on various business executive roles and coming into the public eye with his controversial lockout of striking workers in 1963, he was elected president of the German Employers' Association in 1973. The RAF kidnapped him on September 5, 1977, demanding the release of all its imprisoned members. When the German government refused, the Popular Front for the Liberation of Palestine hijacked the German aircraft *Landshut* to back their demands. After the hostages were freed when the *Landshut* landed in Mogadishu, Baader, Ensslin, and Raspe were found dead in their cells in Stammheim prison (Irmgard Möller survived her stab wounds), and the kidnappers assassinated Schleyer on October 19, 1977, shooting him three times. It was never ascertained who pulled the trigger, and surviving RAF members have remained silent on the issue to this day.

13. A former RAF attorney, Schily rose to political fame as a member of the Green Party in the 1980s. Switching to the Social Democrats in 1989, he attracted much attention because of his conservative stance on questions of *innere Sicherheit* (inner or national security—a concept akin to that of homeland security in the United States) in his function as minister of the interior (1998–2005).

14. *Bild* thus reprised the role it played for much of the years between the late 1960s and the 1980s in the "hunt for sympathizers" (*Jagd auf Sympathisanten*). Its founder, Axel Springer, became a target first of the student movement and then of the RAF, not least because of the paper's sway over German public opinion. Accusing Springer of right-wing populism, the RAF placed bombs in the paper's headquarters in Hamburg in 1972.

15. Members of the review committee that awarded the application along with Goehler were Undersecretary for Culture and Media Christina Weiss (independent), Berlin Senate's Administration for Culture's Thomas Flierl (Party of Democratic Socialism), Berlin's mayor Klaus Wowereit (Social Democratic Party of Germany), and Volker Ratzman (Alliance 90/Greens).

16. Established in 1952, the Federal Agency for Civic Education was to further the "reorientation" of the German population initiated by the Allied forces after 1945. Rather than merely facilitating the denazification process, its stated goal was to overcome authoritarian tendencies in society, to "recivilize" Germany (Jarausch 2006). Throughout the past decades, the Nazi past has remained a staple in the agency's citizenship education. During the Cold War, socialism and communism were frequent subjects; more recently multiculturalism and issues of religious freedom have moved to the fore.

17. Since then, a range of movies focusing on perpetrators, victims, and different generations of the RAF has appeared (Trnka 2007) along with scholarly engagements with the militant left.

18. Foreign Minister Joschka Fischer (1990–2005), like Schily a former RAF lawyer, never commented publicly on the exhibition. The fact that he was engaged behind the scenes, however, indicates that the exhibition raised concerns regarding Germany's image abroad. Goehler interpreted Chancellor Schröder's silence on the matter as a tacit approval of the pressure exerted on the Capital Cultural Fund and the exhibition organizers.

19. *October 18, 1977* is part of Richter's *Atlas* series. A number of the paintings from this series are based on photographs of Richter's family during the Third Reich, with each person representing a different position in the continuum between victim and perpetrator (Jaskot 2012, 67–75).

20. The RAF frequently employed the motifs of prisoners of war and Nazi victims in order to underscore the continuity between the Third Reich and the Federal Republic. Historically speaking, the mobilization of Nazi imagery has not been exclusive to the RAF. It has also served as a "metonym, signifying the congruence of the fascist regime with the contemporary German state and its enormous police force and right-wing political spectrum," for various oppositional movements throughout the 1980s (Linke 1997, 146).

21. The historian Klaus Neumann explains the distinction between different kinds of monuments in the German context as follows: The *Denkmal* serves "merely" as a reminder of the past, whereas "the term *Mahnmal* is a composite of the verb *mahnen*, 'to admonish,' 'to warn,' or 'to remind,' and the noun *Mal*, 'sign'

or 'mark.'" The *Ehrenmal* (based on the verb *ehren*, to honor), on the other hand, serves to honor something or someone (Neumann 2000, 10).

22. Here Biesenbach plays on formalistic understandings of art that maintain a separation between form and content, with the aesthetic as the primary ground on which artworks ought to be judged. He expresses this position through the shorthand "to the true, the good and the beautiful" (*Dem Wahren, Schönen, Guten*) that, taken from a Goethe poem, has been popularized in the German context.

23. Most notable is the case of Verena Becker, once a member of the leftist militant Movement June 2, who was allegedly recruited by the Federal Office for the Protection of the Constitution (Germany's domestic intelligence service) to infiltrate the RAF. Suspicions have been raised that Becker shot and killed Federal Prosecutor General Sigfried Buback in 1977 (Kraushaar 2010).

24. The fact that some RAF members are still at large and that the state has not solved any of the open RAF cases since 1985 has further contributed to the silence on left-wing militancy. That some RAF members sought refuge in the GDR has likewise remained unaddressed. The unease surrounding the RAF was exacerbated by the high rate—at least 50 percent—of women militants who made up their ranks. Patricia Melzer (2009, 36) posits that by troubling gender conventions these women were regarded as doubly deviant, i.e., "a deviance (violent female actors) within an already deviant framework (terrorism)." Clare Bielby (2010) shows that in the 1970s the high percentage of women in the RAF was frequently portrayed as the result of excessive emancipation and used to sensationalize left-wing violence (144). She argues that today feminization and sexualization of the RAF serve to "distance this period of history from contemporary Germany" (139).

25. While the article originally criminalized "denigrating Turkishness," the wording has been amended to the denigration of the "Turkish nation." Paragraph 2 of Article 301 criminalized "alienating" the public from the military (*askerden soğutmak*), whereas in the new version "only" the denigration of the Turkish military remains an offense. The maximum penalty was lowered from three to two years, and opening a case on the basis of 301 requires permission by the Ministry of Justice as of April 30, 2008. Criticism has persisted, however, since "the change signifies a clarification in the wording, but not in the content, and so does not contribute to expanding the enjoyment of freedom of expression" (Algan 2008, 2241).

26. The writer Orhan Pamuk and the singer Bülent Ersoy were tried for statements made outside artistic forums. Pamuk referred to the Armenian genocide, not by label but by number of people murdered, and stated that thirty thousand people had been killed in the war between the government and the PKK in an interview with the Swiss daily *Der Tages-Anzeiger* in 2005. Ersoy was charged for proclaiming during a live TV broadcast in 2008 that if she had a son, she would not send him to compulsory military service. The writer Elif Shafak was charged for statements that characters in her novel *The Bastard of Istanbul* (2006) utter about the Armenian genocide. All three cases ended in acquittals yet were successful in their discouraging function.

27. Entitled *Coyote II*, Tekand's painting was itself a nod to Joseph Beuys's 1974 performance *Coyote*, which Altındere was commenting on.

28. For a reprint of the affidavit, see Evren (2008, 81).

29. The Saturday Mothers is a group of mothers (and next of kin) that has protested the enforced disappearances of their children from May 1995 onward. Growing police repression forced them to discontinue their weekly vigils in 1998. Taking up their protests again in 2009, they met every Saturday on a small square next to Galatasaray High School in Istanbul (as well as in Diyarbakir) until August 2018, when they had to move to the street in front of the Human Rights Association's Beyoğlu office due to renewed police pressure. For a more detailed analysis of their protest through the lens of memory, see Ahıska (2019).

30. For a reprint of the decision, see Tüzünoğlu (2005, 102). The lawyer for the defense, Murat Altındere, argued with regard to Murat Tosyalı's work that "the military insignia integrate with the body, that actually people carry these insignia in their civilian life. There is thus a coalescence between insignia and the body. But there is no insult" (cited in Ergün 2005).

31. The Ministry of Culture and Tourism rarely if ever intervenes on behalf of artists. One notable exception was Fikri Sağlar, who after taking office in 1991 openly addressed the restrictions of freedom of expression and lifted bans on literary works instated by the 1980 military junta (Sağlar 1992, 34–35).

32. In an interview I conducted with Yazar in 2011, he both denied these statements and argued that they had been taken out of context.

33. At the time, Newroz (Kurdish New Year) celebrations were banned by the state. Officially fifty-seven people were killed during the uprising and many more injured. Bêrîvan herself, then seventeen years old, was taken into custody and severely tortured.

34. Another screening of *Bêrîvan*, this time at the Malatya Film Festival, was hindered on account of a technicality. Orak had applied but not yet received an "operating certificate" (*eser işletme belgelesi*) for the film. This certificate regulates copyright and commercial distribution of films but is usually not required for nonprofit screenings. Up until 2014 film festivals in Turkey did not request this certificate. The Malatya governor used his discretionary power to resort to a loophole in the regulation to hinder the screening of the film. Ultimately, Orak's application for the certificate was rejected by the Ministry of Culture and Tourism, supposedly because it features "separatist propaganda." Orak then made the film available free, "for pirating." "This way," he noted, "even more people get to see it than if it was regularly released." It seems that copyright protection mechanisms overseen by the ministry are increasingly used to control the dissemination of content (see Başaran 2014).

35. An exception was municipalities led by Barış ve Demokrasi Partisi (Freedom and Democracy Party, BDP), putting them often at odds with respective provincial governors.

36. The 2010 convictions of thirteen artists affiliated with the Bahar Cultural Center (Batman) are instructive in this regard, as they were prohibited from taking

part in any artistic or cultural events for five years. The deferred sentences not only aimed at isolating artists active in the Kurdish rights struggle but have consequences for the transmission of Kurdish artistic repertoires in the future. This point was impressively made by a Kurdish composer based in Adana who noted that his musical creations were all registered with the national copyright office. Having paid his copyright fees, he was unable to perform some of his pieces, which have been deemed "unconstitutional." In this case, censorship not only delimits which expressions are allowed to circulate without restriction but enables the Turkish state to profit from foreclosed artistic expressions while making them (and their producers) invisible.

37. While dropped from the amended version of 301, this was also the rationale for initially augmenting punishment by one-third for offenses that were "perpetrated" abroad.

38. While some suggest that nonfunding expresses hegemonic preferences as to what is regarded as culturally or socially important (Fenner 1995, 4), others argue that funding preferences rather than suppression constitute the operative realm of censorship (Levinson 1998). Censorship in Germany is further obscured as increasingly individuals, rather than state institutions, initiate legal proceedings by claiming that an artwork is violating their right to privacy and personal dignity (Ohmer 2004). The banning of Maxim Biller's novel *Esra* in 2007 is such a landmark case. Chronicling the relationship between the narrator and his relationship with Esra, the work was found to injure the dignity of Biller's former real-life partner. In Turkey, Prime Minister Erdoğan has opened thousands of cases against, for instance, cartoonists, based on alleged personal injury.

6. Enterprising Art, Aestheticizing Business

1. The invited artists were Ai Weiwei, from China; the French Iranian Romuald Karmakar; Santu Mofokeng, from South Africa; and Dayanita Singh, from India. To mitigate any potential criticism, German authorities made sure to emphasize the close ties that all the artists have to Germany.

2. Until recently, Kortun served as the director of SALT (established by Garanti Bank). Esche is the director of Van Abbemuseum (Eindhoven), which featured a contemporaneous exhibition entitled *Istanbul* during the biennial.

3. Cattelan rose to fame with provocative works that reference the art market, including the organization of the Sixth Caribbean Biennial (1999), for which he, together with Jens Hoffman, invited ten friends to take a break from the art world on the island of St. Kitts. Gioni is now artistic director of the New Museum, New York, and Subotnick is curator at the Hammer Museum at the University of California–Los Angeles. Together they founded the Wrong Gallery in 2002–2005, "the smallest exhibition space in New York," which they described as "the back door to contemporary art" that "is always locked." The project has since then popped up in different locations and iterations.

4. The Berlin Biennial was mainly funded by the Federal Cultural Fund and BMW and to a lesser extent by the Allianz insurance corporation. The Istanbul event received in-kind support from the municipality and the Ministry of Culture and Tourism through permits, while financial and material support was raised from a wide mix of private sponsors, including Koç Holding, which has since become the main corporate sponsor of the Istanbul Biennial. Both biennials were notably financed in part by Culture 2000, a cultural funding program operated by the European Union. In both cases, the biennials were established through private initiatives and not by the state or by the respective municipalities—a fact that speaks once again to the division of labor between the state and the private sector in cultural matters, which is especially contoured in the Turkish case. The subsequent Istanbul Biennial (2007) obtained government money through the Foreign Ministry's promotional fund, the *tanitim fonu*, which covered 4 percent of the biennial budget—most probably thanks to the international acclaim that its predecessor generated.

5. For an analysis of the dynamics of and imaginations surrounding "pioneering" in processes of gentrification, see Smith (1996).

6. As Charles Esche self-reflexively commented, the organizers and curators had not been "brave enough" to truly make a biennial for all of Istanbul, which would have required further inclusion of more remote or "underserved" parts of the city.

7. While then federal government commissioner for culture and the media Bernd Neumann highlighted these factors in his opening speech for the BB4, he did not refer to the fate of this very Jewish community only a few years later.

8. The case of the Jewish Girls School is striking not only because of the multiple processes of dispossession that it experienced. It was also subject to different dynamics of redistribution, first confiscation under National Socialists, then socialist redistribution that made it public, and finally postsocialist restitution to the Jewish community.

9. There is another kind of spatial history that develops from these artistic forays. The former tobacco warehouse has since been transformed into the permanent nonprofit arts and culture space Depo, and IKSV—the organizer of the Istanbul Biennial—has moved into the Deniz Palace, showing that gestures of artistic pioneering can initiate long-term stays and with it changes to the fabric of the neighborhoods into which arts organizations venture. IKSV's presence in Şişhane has underwritten changes in the neighborhood, with restaurants and bars following suit, not dissimilar to Auguststrasse in Mitte, which was substantially transformed by the presences of KW, the institutional organizer of the Berlin Biennial founded in the early 1990s and hence a vital actor in the transformation of Mitte. More recent installments of both biennials have retreated to already existing arts spaces explicitly in order to avoid complicities in these dynamics.

10. The BB4 curatorial team also published a second catalogue under the title *Checkpoint Charlie*. Conceptualized as a democratization of the biennial, it featured black-and-white reproductions of artworks collected during the extensive

studio visits they conducted throughout Germany. This move caused controversy because the catalogue was apparently printed without the artists' consent, or at least so the story goes. Those who protested against it noted its low quality: The paper used and its layout resembled that of a fanzine rather than a glossy art catalogue.

11. The workshop had invited up-and-coming curators from fifteen countries, along with a handful of internationally well-known senior curators; the event culminated in a public panel discussion which I attended.

12. During our interview, Girst noted that BMW periodically employed the services of consulting agencies in order to measure the effect of both regular advertising and the company's culture and arts sponsoring on the public perception of the brand. He stated, "In the end there is no way of ascertaining what is more advantageous in terms of impact on consumers: a two-page advertisement in *Der Spiegel* or supporting the biennial," implying that eventual economic benefits arising from sponsoring are but fortunate byproducts. In contrast, Birol Özalp, the director of the Pera Museum, proposed a direct and measurable correlation between cultural sponsoring activities, corporate profiles, and increases in business. Özalp had formerly worked for Yapı Kredi Bank and Publishing, a frequent sponsor of art events in Istanbul.

13. The establishment by the BB4 curators of a pirated version of Gagosian Gallery, which appropriated the name of the well-known international gallery network without permission and ran as a parallel event to the biennial, might speak to this irony.

14. According to the biennial organizers as well as those from the commercial Art Forum, the clientele is largely the same, although this is empirically hard to trace. Surely, the writeups in art magazines are similar, regarding the extent of the given coverage, with some art fairs like London's Frieze being even more broadly reported on than both the Istanbul and Berlin biennials. The visitors' numbers for BB4 and Art Forum both hovered around 44,000 in 2006, while IB9 recorded 50,000 visitors in 2005, with numbers rising every year since.

15. The organizers of Art Forum stayed notably mum about their reasons for discontinuing the art fair. This is all the more notable because they had been planning to merge with Art Contemporary Berlin, a platform initiated by Berlin-based galleries to show international contemporary artistic production in the city.

16. For a similar assessment of art fairs and particularly Art Basel Miami Beach of 2006, see Schjeldahl (2006).

17. Given a lack of funding, the Second Berlin Biennial could not take place as planned in 2000 and only resumed in 2001.

18. The Christian Democratic politician Monika Grütters frequently noted that culture is the foremost contributing factor to tourism in the case of Berlin. Since 2013, Grütters has served as federal government commissioner for culture and the media.

19. Berlin's 2002/2003 state and municipal budgets were deemed unconstitutional because of the large imbalance between debt accumulation and investment allocations, high unemployment rates, and lack in economic growth.

20. Directors of nonprofit arts organizations in Berlin tended to describe market interests as a positive aspect by highlighting the benefits for their own institution rather than emphasizing the long-term effects that the commercial cooptation of art might have on them.

21. Private entities such as the real estate and gallery sector have a vested interest in this development for the reasons just sketched. In Istanbul as in Berlin commercial gallery weekends are organized, featuring coordinated programs and simultaneous openings that overlap spatially and timewise with the cities' respective biennials.

22. Since its inception, the term "service economy" has been plagued by a certain vagueness. While it first referred to the realms of finance, insurance, and real estate, it has been extended to comprise highly paid executives in these sectors as well as restaurant workers, for instance.

23. For the discussion of similar processes of urban redevelopment and urban design to symbolize the bourgeois class project in fin-de-siècle Vienna, see Schorske (1961, 24–115).

24. In both cities there is a push by policy makers and city planners to privatize and homogenize (see Boyer 1992, Sorkin 1992) public space, not least through exclusionary practices inscribed in the aesthetics of the architectural environment that are frequently expressed through policing techniques and, in the case of Istanbul, the expansion of gated communities.

25. In their discussion of the gentrification of New York City's Lower East Side, Deutsche and Ryan (1984) criticize the lack of awareness of the local art scene, which in their opinion did not try hard enough to resist commercial monopolization and failed to create solidarity with the residents with whom they shared the neighborhood.

26. Huyssen presents a, historically speaking, longer view on these voids, counterposing the huge construction sites that characterized Berlin in the 1990s against the nineteenth-century collapse of the bourgeoisie diagnosed by Ernst Bloch, the landscape of ruins that was Berlin in 1945, and the division of the city, which left new voids adjacent to the wall. He notes that, viewed from East Berlin, the space occupied by the western part of the city presented yet another kind of void for the duration of the division.

27. Read against this background, the choice of the Feriköy Greek School or the Greek School in Karaköy as locations for the Istanbul Biennial of 2009 and 2011 might appear coincidental. Their "vacancy," however, is not.

28. In practice, this shift has not only entailed fundamental changes in day-to-day decision-making processes and operations of arts organizations but also led to artists being largely replaced in the administration of these organizations by marketing and management majors or graduates of the arts management programs that have sprung up at universities in Istanbul and Berlin.

29. It is important to note that while Florida in his much-cited *The Rise of the Creative Class* (2002) distinguishes between technological creativity (innovation),

economic creativity (entrepreneurship), and artistic or cultural creativity, the vernacular usage of his arguments in the realm of cultural policy making and political discourses tends to conflate these distinct categories. Equating these different realms with the conceptions of artistic creativity and cultural goods serves to legitimize the transfer of public funds to support private business and the application of cultural protectionist policies to circumvent international trade agreements that govern the exchange of "strictly" economic goods. This is especially significant in the framework of the European Union as well as for its accession candidates (such as Turkey), as state sovereignty in "cultural matters" has become an embattled issue in the EU integration process with regard to cultural goods, both in their symbolic and economic dimensions. To justify public expenditure for private profit, "creative industries policies [have been] portrayed as democratizing and anti-elitist instead of elitist cultural production that could meet its cost through the market" (Hesmondalgh and Pratt 2005, 5).

30. The establishment of other large-scale festivals by IKSV falls notably in the same time period. Their international film festival was established, and notably so, while the military junta was still in power, in 1982. The theater festival was inaugurated in 1989 and the jazz festival in 1994 at the height of the armed conflict between the Turkish military and the PKK.

31. Hans Haacke's *Shapolsky et al. Manhattan Real Estate Holdings, a Real Time Social System, as of May 1, 1971*, comes to mind, for instance. Critically documenting the relationship between art and power, and especially urban real estate speculation, the piece led to the cancellation of his planned solo show at the Guggenheim in 1971. Today it is part of the collection of the Whitney Museum for American Art, from which it continues to speak to both the institutionalization of critique (highlighted by Iversen) and the role of art in gentrification processes.

Instead of a Conclusion: Meeting, Again

1. Similarly themed exhibitions and formats had already established what seemed to become an increasingly normative pattern, among them *In den Schluchten des Balkans* (2003, Fridericanum, Kassel), *Call me Istanbul ist mein Name* (2004, ZKM, Kassel), and the Şimdi/Now Festival in Berlin 2004—to name but three examples from the early 2000s.

2. The motif of "infighting" not only presents an Orientalist trope but also glosses over the very real critique voiced by participants over Tannert and Lang's initial invitation of Şakir Eczacıbaşı (1929–2010) to contribute to the exhibition. Then chair of IKSV, Eczacıbaşı was a photographer by passion. Rumor has it that this invitation was animated not by artistic considerations but in the hopes of securing additional financial support. In the end, Eczacıbaşı did not take part in the show, but IKSV was one of the co-sponsors.

3. In response to these experiences, Özcan created a series of works that take up the discontents and stereotypes perpetuated in such "cultural exchange programs."

The series included a video entitled *Transfer Visiting* (2007), in which the artist's home renovation is portrayed as preparation for the impending visit of German curators to Istanbul and hence as a heightened play on the trope of "Turkish hospitality."

4. Pondering the vagueness of the notion of "intercultural dialogue," Joachim Sartorius, the former director of the German Goethe Institute, remarked during our interview: "After all these years, the idea of cultural exchange has become questionable to me. Take Germany and France, for example: Since the end of World War II we have the highest density of exchange, and yet I ask myself how well do we actually know each other?" Still, there seems to me a notable difference in that the kinds of questions described by Özcan are rarely asked in West-West encounters because they are marked by presumptions of familiarity, regardless of actual knowledge.

5. Like Scarry, I am leaving aside the division between the beautiful and the sublime that has marked aesthetic theory since Kant, not least because these concepts are frequently merged in the day-to-day shorthand discourses on art.

6. Public assemblies of feminist and LGBTI+ groups have also been regularly curtailed and met with police violence, and queer arts and film festivals have been de facto banned. For a detailed report on the restrictions of freedom of expression and censorship in the arts, see Joint Stakeholder Submission to the Universal Periodic Review of Turkey (2019, prepared by the author).

7. For details on Osman Kavala's arrest and its effect on the arts scene in Turkey, see Günal (2017).

8. The initiative is organized by the Initiative Schwarze Menschen in Deutschland Bund e.V., glokal e.V., Berliner Entwicklungspolitische Ratschlag (BER), AfricAvenir International, AFROTAK TV cyberNomads, Berlin Postkolonial, and Artefakte//anti-humboldt. For their mission statement, see http://www.no-humboldt21.de.

9. For the official mission statement of the project, see https://www.dainst.org/en/projekt/-/project-display/1869856.

References

Abu El-Haj, Nadia. 2001. *Facts on the Ground: Archaeological Practice and Territorial Self-Fashioning in Israeli Society*. Chicago: University of Chicago Press.

Ada, Serhan, and Ayça İnce. 2010. *Türkiye'de Kültür Politikaları'na Giriş*. Istanbul: Bilgi Üniversitesi Yayınları.

Adorno, Theodor W. 1967 [1949]. *Prisms*. Cambridge, MA: MIT Press.

——. 1997 [1959]. "Was bedeutet: Aufarbeitung der Vergangenheit." In *Kulturkritik und Gesellschaft II*, 555–72. Suhrkamp: Frankfurt/Main.

——.1991. *The Culture Industry: Selected Essays on Mass Culture*. London: Routledge.

——. 1997 [1960]. "Kultur und Verwaltung." In *Soziologische Schriften*, 8:122–46. Frankfurt/Main: Suhrkamp.

Adorno, Theodor W., and Max Horkheimer. 1969. *Dialektik der Aufklärung. Philosophische Fragmente*. Frankfurt/Main: Suhrkamp.

Ahearne, Jeremy. 2003. "Cultural Policy in the Old Europe: France and Germany." *International Journal of Cultural Policy* 9(2): 127–31.

Ahıska, Meltem. 2003. "Occidentalism: The Historical Fantasy of the Modern." *South Atlantic Quarterly* 102(2/3): 351–79.

——. 2010. *Occidentalism in Turkey: Questions of Modernity and National Identity in Turkish Radio Broadcasting*. London: I. B. Tauris.

——. 2019. "Memory as Encounter: The Saturday Mothers in Turkey." In *Women Mobilizing Memory*, ed. Ayşe Gül Altinay, María José Contreras, Marianne Hirsch, et al., 133–51. New York: Columbia University Press.

Akay, Ali, Levent Çalıkoğlu, and Haşim Nur Gürel. 2004. *Gözlem, Yorum, Çeşitlilik*. Exhibition catalogue. Instanbul: Istanbul Modern.

Akçam, Taner. 1996. *Armenien und der Völkermord: Die Istanbuler Prozesse und die türkische Nationalbewegung*. Hamburg: Hamburger Edition.

——. 2004. *From Empire to Republic: Turkish Nationalism and the Armenian Genocide*. New York: Zed.

Akcan, Esra. 2012. *Architecture in Translation: Germany, Turkey, and the Modern House*. Durham, NC: Duke University Press.

Aköz, Emre. 2004. "Yüzlerce eser nasıl yok oldu?" *Sabah*, April 15. https://www.sabah.com.tr/yazarlar/akoz/2004/04/15/yuzlerce_eser_nasil_yok_oldu.

Aksoy, Asu, and Burcu Yasemin Şeyben. 2014. "Storm over the State Cultural Institutions: New Cultural Policy Direction in Turkey." *International Journal of Cultural Policy*. https://doi.org/10.1080/10286632.2014.890605.

Aktar, Ayhan. 2002. *Varlık Vergisi ve 'Türkleştirme' Politikaları*. Istanbul: İletişim Yayınları.

——. 2009. "'Turkification' Policies in the Early Republican Era." In *Turkish Literature and Cultural Memory: "Multiculturalism" as a Literary Theme after 1980*, ed. Catherine Duft, 29–62. Wiesbaden: Harrassowitz Verlag.

Algan, Bülent. 2008. "The Brand-New Version of Article 301 of the Turkish Penal Code and the Future of Freedom of Expression Cases in Turkey." *German Law Journal* 9(12): 2237–52.

Altay, Can, et al. 2005. "An Open Letter Written by Some Artists and Curators from Istanbul to All Concerned Artists Regarding the Exhibition *Urban Realities: Focus Istanbul*." In *Urbane Realitäten: Fokus Istanbul*, ed. Christpher Tannert and Peter Lang, 22–24. Berlin: Künstlerhaus Bethanien.

Aly, Götz. 2005a. *Hitlers Volksstaat. Raub, Rassenkrieg und nationaler Sozialismus*. Frankfurt/Main: Fischer.

——. 2005b. "Nicht falsch, sondern anders gerechnet." *TAZ*, March 13, 2005. https://taz.de/!635089/.

And, Metin. 1984. "Atatürk and the Arts, with Special Reference to Music and Theater." In *Atatürk and the Modernization of Turkey*, ed. Martin Landau, 215–32. Boulder, CO: Westview.

Anderson, Benedict. 1983. *Imagined Communities: Reflections on the Origin and Spread of Nationalism*. New York: Verso.

Anderson, Margaret Lavinia. 2007. "'Down in Turkey, Far Away': Human Rights, the Armenian Massacres, and Orientalism in Wilhelmine Germany." *Journal of Modern History* 79(1): 80–111.

Anderson, Richard L. 1992. "Do Other Cultures Have 'Art'?" *American Anthropologist* 94(4): 926–29.

Andrews, Peter Alford, and Rüdiger Benninghaus, eds. 1989. *Ethnic Groups in the Republic of Turkey*. Wiesbaden: Reichert.

Andrews, Walter G., and Mehmet Kalpaklı. 2005. *The Age of Beloveds: Love and the Beloved in Early Modern Ottoman and European Culture and Society*. Durham, NC: Duke University Press.

Antmen, Ahu. 1993. "Ressamlar Evren'i 'fırçaladı.'" *Cumhuriyet*, October 7.

——. 2005. "Golsüz bir serbest vuruş." *Radikal*, September 21. radikal.com.tr/haber.php?haberno=164661.

Apperly, Eliza. 2019. "The Far Right Is Taking On Cultural Institutions." *Atlantic*, October 28. https://www.theatlantic.com/international/archive/2019/10/germany-far-right-culture-war/598978/

Appadurai, Arjun. 1996. *Modernity at Large: Cultural Dimensions of Globalization*. Minneapolis: University of Minnesota Press.

Applegate, Celia. 1990. *A Nation of Provincials: The German Idea of Heimat*. Berkeley: University of California Press.

Applegate, Celia, and Pamela Potter. 2002. "Germans as the 'People of Music': Genealogy of an Identity." In *Music and German National Identity*, ed. Celia Applegate and Pamela Potter, 1–35. Chicago: University of Chicago Press.

Artun, Ali. 2002. "The Museum That Cannot Be." Unpublished manuscript.

——. 2011. *Çağdaş Sanatın Örgütlenmesi Estetik Modernizmin Tasfiyesi*. Istanbul: İletişim.

Asad, Talal. 2002. "Muslims and European Identity: Can Europe Represent Islam?" In *The Idea of Europe: From Antiquity to the European Union*, ed. Anthony Pagden, 209–27. Cambridge: Cambridge University Press.

Asad, Talal, and Roger Owen. 1980. "The Critique of Orientalism: A Reply to Professor Dodd." *Bulletin (British Society for Middle Eastern Studies)* 7(1): 33–38.

Asad, Talal, Wendy Brown, Judith Butler, and Saba Mahmood. 2013. *Is Critique Secular? Blasphemy, Injury, and Free Speech*. New York: Fordham University Press.

Asad, Talal, et al. 1999. "Provocation of European Ethnology." *American Anthropologist* 99(4): 713–30.

Assmann, Aleida and Ute Frevert. 1999. *Geschichtsvergessenheit/Geschichtsversessenheit: Vom Umgang mit der deutschen Vergangenheit nach 1945*. Stuttgart: Deutschland Verlagsanstalt.

Atasoy, Yildiz. 1996. "Islamic Revivalism and the Nation-State Project. Competing Claims for Modernity." http://wwww.bsos.umd.edu/CSS97/papers/competin.html.

Aust, Stefan. 1985. *Der Baader Meinhof Komplex*. Hamburg: Hoffmann und Campe.

Ayata, Bilgin. 2016. "Silencing the Present. Die Aufarbeitung der NSU aus Postkolonialer Perspektive." In *Postkoloniale Politikwissenschaft. Theoretische und empirische Zugänge*, ed. Aram Ziai, 211–35. Bielefeld: Transcript Verlag.

Bahrani, Zainab, Zeynep Çelik, and Edhem Eldem, eds. 2011. *Scramble for the Past: A Story of Archaeology in the Ottoman Empire, 1753–1914*. Istanbul: SALT.

Bali, Rıfat N. 1999. *Cumhuriyet yıllarında Türkiye Yahudileri. Bir Türkleştirme serüveni (1923–1945)*. Istanbul: İletişim.

——. 2005. *The "Varlık Vergisi" Affair: A Study of Its Legacy—Selected Documents*. Istanbul: Isis.

——. 2012. *Varlık Vergisi: Hatıralar—Tanıklıklar*. Istanbul: Libra.

Balibar, Étienne. 1991a. "Is There a 'Neo-Racism'?" In *Race, Nation, Class: Ambiguous Identities*, ed. Étienne Balibar and Immanuel Wallerstein, 17–28. London: Verso.

——. 1991b. "The Nation Form: History and Ideology." In *Race, Nation, Class, Ambiguous Identities*, ed. Étienne Balibar and Immanuel Wallerstein, 86–106. London: Verso.
Baltacıoğlu, İsmail Hakkı. 1934. "Güzel Sanatlar Cumhuriyeti." *Yeni Adam* 3:6.
Balz, Hanno. 2006. "Der 'Sympathisanten'-Diskurs im Deutschen Herbst." In *Terrorismus in der Bundesrepublik: Medien, Staat und Subkulturen in den 1970er Jahren*, ed. Klaus Weinhauer, Jörg Requate, and Heinz Gerhard Haupt, 320–50. Frankfurt/Main: Campus.
Bardakçı, Murat. 2013. *İttihadçı'nın Sandığı*. Istanbul: İş Bankası Kültür Yayınları.
Bargu, Banu. 2018. "Year One: Reflections on Turkey's Second Founding and the Politics of Division." *Critical Times* 1(1): 23–48.
Barkan, Elazar. 2000. *The Guilt of Nations: Restitution and Negotiating Historical Injustices*. Baltimore, MD: John Hopkins University Press.
Barnett, David. 2004. "The Simulation of a Reception, or, Rainer Werner Fassbinder's *Der Müll, die Stadt und der Tod* in Germany, Holland, and Israel." *Contemporary Theater Review* 12(2): 29–40.
Barron, Stephanie. 2009. "Blurred Boundaries: The Art of Two Germanys between Myth and History." In *Art of Two Germanys/Cold War Cultures*, ed. Stephaine Barron, Sabine Eckmann, and Eckhart Gillen, 12–33. New York: Abrams.
Bartu, Ayfer. 2001. "Rethinking Heritage Politics in a Global Context: A View from Istanbul." In *Hybrid Urbanism: On Identity Discourse and the Built Environment*, ed. Nezar AlSayyad, 131–55. Westport, CT: Praeger.
Başaran, Ezgi. 2008. "Ailesi dört nesildir resim topluyor o 650 parçalık koleksiyonun varisi Ahmet Merey." *Hürriyet*, February 10. http://www.hurriyet.com.tr/pazar/8200826.asp.
Başaran, Pelin. 2014. "Devlet Desteği ve Sansür." *Altyazi*, February 5. http://www.altyazi.net/yazilar/dosya-devlet-destegi-ve-sansur/.
Baudrillard, Jean. 1994 [1968]. "The System of Collecting." In *The Cultures of Collecting*, ed. Roger Cardinal and Roger Cardinal, 7–24. London: Reaktion.
Bauman, Zygmunt. 1989. *Modernity and the Holocaust*. Ithaca, NY: Cornell University Press.
Baxandall, Michael. 1972. *Painting and Experience in Fifteenth-Century Italy: A Primer in the Social History of Pictorial Style*. Oxford: Oxford University Press.
Becker, Howard Saul. 1982. *Art Worlds*. Berkeley: University of California Press.
Bek Arat, Güler. *1970–1980 Yılları Arasında Türkiye'de Kültürel ve Sanatsal Ortam*. Istanbul: SALT. https://saltonline.org/tr/762/1970-1980-yillari-arasinda-turkiyede-kulturel-ve-sanatsal-ortam.
Belfiore, Elenora, and Oliver Bennet. 2008. *The Social Impact of the Arts: An Intellectual History*. Houndsmills: Palgrave Macmillan.
Bell-Villada, Gene H. 1996. *Art for Art's Sake and Literary Life: How Politics and Markets Helped Shape the Ideology and Culture of Aestheticism, 1790–1990*. Lincoln: University of Nebraska Press.

Belting, Hans. 1998. *The Germans and Their Art: A Troublesome Relationship*. New Haven, CT: Yale University Press.
——. 2003. *Art History after Modernism*. Chicago: University of Chicago Press.
——. 2010. "The Double Perspective: Arab Mathematics and Renaissance Art." *Third Text* 24(5): 521–27.
Benjamin, Walter. 1968 [1931]. "Unpacking My Library: A Talk about Book Collecting." In *Illuminations*, 59–68. New York: Schocken.
——.1968 [1940]. "Theses on the Philosophy of History." In *Illuminations*, 253–64. New York: Schocken.
——. 2003 [1936]. *Das Kunstwerk im Zeitalter seiner technischen Reproduziertbarkeit*. Frankfurt/Main: Suhrkamp.
Berdahl, Daphne. 1999. *Where the World Ended: Re-Unification and Identity in the German Borderland*. Berkeley: University of California Press.
Berger, Stefan. 1995. "Historians and Nation-Building in Germany after Reunification." *Past and Present* 148: 187–222.
Berghahn, Volker R. 1994. *Imperial Germany, 1871–1918: Economy, Society, Culture, and Politics*. Providence, RI: Berghahn.
Berk, Nurullah. 1938. *Sanat ve Devlet* 1(12): 5.
——. 1937. "Sanat Sorunları: Resim Üstüne Tartışma." *Varlık* 795 (Aralık): 13.
Berman, Tressa, ed. 2012. *No Deal! Indigenous Arts and the Politics of Possession*. Santa Fe, NM: School of Advanced Research Press.
Beşikçi, İsmail. 1990. *Devletlerarası sömürge: Kürdistan*. Istanbul: Alan Yayıncılık.
Bevilacqua, Alexander, and Helen Pfeifer. 2013. "Turquerie: Culture in Motion, 1650–1750." *Past and Present* 221: 75–118.
Bielby, Clare. 2010. "Remembering the Red Army Faction." *Memory Studies* 3(2): 137–50.
Bishop, Claire. 2012. *Artificial Hells: Participatory Art and the Politics of Spectatorship*. London: Verso.
Blackbourn, David, and Geoff Eley. 1984. *The Peculiarities of German History: Bourgeois Society and Politics in Nineteenth-Century Germany*. Oxford: Oxford University Press.
Boas, Franz. 1955. *Primitive Art*. New York: Dover.
Böer, Ingeborg, Ruth Haerkötter, Petra Kappert, and Sabine Adatepe. 2002. *Türken in Berlin 1871–1945. Eine Metropole in den Erinnerungen osmanischer und türkischer Zeitzeugen*. Berlin: Walter de Gruyter.
Böll, Heinrich. 1972. "Will Ulrike Gnade oder freies Geleit?" *Der Spiegel* 3: 54–57.
Booth, W. James. 2001. "The Unforgotten: Memories of Justice." *American Political Science Review* 95(4): 777–91.
Borneman, John. 1992. *Belonging in the Two Berlins: Kin, State, Nation*. Cambridge: Cambridge University Press.
Böröcz, József. 2006. "Goodness Is Elsewhere: The Rule of European Difference." *Comparative Studies in Society and History* 48(1): 110–38.

Bourdieu, Pierre. 1984. *Distinction: A Social Critique of the Judgment of Taste.* Cambridge, MA: Harvard University Press.
Boyer, Christine M. 1992. "Cities for Sale: Merchandising History at South Street Seaport." In *Variations on a Theme Park: The American City and the End of Public Space*, ed. Michael Sorkin, 181–204. New York: Hill and Wang.
Bozdoğan, Sibel. 2001. *Modernism and Nation Building: Turkish Architectural Culture in the Early Republic.* Seattle: Washington University Press.
Bozdoğan, Sibel, and Reşat Kasaba. 1997. "Introduction." In *Rethinking Modernity and National Identity in Turkey*, ed. Sibel Bozdoğan and Reşat Kasaba, 3–14. Seattle: University of Washington Press.
Brink-Danan, Marcy. 2011. *Jewish Life in Twenty-First-Century Turkey: The Other Side of Tolerance.* Bloomington: Indiana University Press.
Brown, Wendy. 1998. "Freedom's Silences." In *Censorship and Silencing: Practices of Cultural Regulation*, ed. Richard C. Post, 313–27. Los Angeles: Getty Research Institute for the History of Art and the Humanities.
Bruinessen, Martin van. 1994. "Genocide in Kurdistan? The Suppression of the Dersim Rebellion in Turkey (1937–38) and the Chemical War against the Iraqi Kurds (1988)." In *Conceptual and Historical Dimensions of Genocide*, ed. G. J. Andreopoulos, 141–70. Philadelphia: University of Pennsylvania Press.
Buğra, Ayşe. 1994. *State and Business in Modern Turkey: A Comparative Study.* Binghamton: SUNY Press.
Burns, Rob, and Wilfried van der Will. 2003. "German Cultural Policy: An Overview." *International Journal of Cultural Policy* 9(2): 133–52.
Burt, Richard, ed. 1994. *The Administration of Aesthetics: Censorship, Political Criticism, and the Public Sphere.* Minneapolis: University of Minnesota Press.
Büsing, Nicole, and Heiko Klaas. 2005. "Der Terror und die Kunst." http://www.kunstmarkt.com/pagesmag/kunst/_id74434-/ausstellungen_berichtdetail.html?_q=%20.
Butler, Judith. 1998. "Ruled Out: Vocabularies of the Censor." In *Censorship and Silencing: Practices of Cultural Regulation*, ed. Richard C. Post, 247–59. Los Angeles: Getty Research Institute for the History of Art and the Humanities.
Cattelan, Maurizio, Massimiliano Gioni, and Ali Subotnik. 2006. "Of Mice and Men." In *Of Mice and Men* (BB4 Catalogue). Berlin: Haje Cantz.
Çelik, Zeynep. 1992. *Displaying the Orient: Architecture of Islam at Nineteenth-Century World's Fairs.* Berkeley: University of California Press.
Certeau, Michel de. 1984. *The Practice of Everyday Life.* Berkeley: University of California Press.
Chakrabarty, Dipesh. 2000. *Provincializing Europe: Postcolonial Thought and Historical Difference.* Princeton, NJ: Princeton University Press.
Chatterjee, Partha. 1986. *Nationalist Thought and the Colonial World: A Derivative Discourse.* Minneapolis: University of Minnesota Press.
Clifford, James, and George E. Marcus, eds. 1986. *Writing Culture: The Poetics and Politics of Ethnography.* Berkeley: University of California Press.

Cohen, Roger. 1999. "Exhibiting the Art of History's Dustbin: Dictators' Treasures Stir German Anger." *New York Times*, August 17.
Collingwood, Robin. 1969 [1945]. "The Artist and the Community." In *Philosophy of Arts and Aesthetics: From Plato to Wittgenstein*, ed. Frank A. Tillman and Steven M. Cahn, 484–95. New York: Harper and Row.
Conrads, Martin, and Ulrich Gutmair. 2002. "Schluss mit Lustig. Die Kunst-Werke und die Wehrmacht." *Texte zur Kunst*, March 2002, https://www.textezurkunst.de/45/schlu-mit-lustig-die-kunst-werke-und-die-wehrmach/.
Crapanzano, Vincent. 2004. *Imaginative Horizons: An Essay in Literary-Philosophical Anthropology*. Chicago: University of Chicago Press.
Crowley, David, and Susan Reid, eds. 2000. *Style and Socialism: Modernity and Material Culture in Post-War Eastern Europe*. Oxford: Berg.
Cunningham, Stuart. 1992. *Framing Culture: Criticism and Policy in Australia*. North Sydney: Allen & Unwin.
Çaylı, Eray. 2019. "Making Violence Public: Spatializing (Counter)publicness through the 1993 Sivas Arson Attack, Turkey." *International Journal of Urban and Regional Research* 43(6): 1106–22.
Dahlhaus, Friedrich. 1990. *Möglichkeiten und Grenzen auswärtiger Kultur- und Pressepolitik dargestellt am Beispiel der deutsch-türkischen Beziehungen 1914–1928*. Frankfurt/Main: Lang.
Danto, Arthur. 1964. "The Artworld." *Journal of Philosophy* 61(19): 571–84.
Davidian, Vazken. 2015 "Reframing Ottoman Art Histories: Bringing Silenced Voices Back into the Picture." *Études Arméniennes Contemporaines* 6: 7–17.
Deakin, Annie. 2008. "Do We Need Art Galleries Anymore?" *Independent*. October 16. http://www.independent.co.uk/life-style/house-and-home/interiors/do-we-need-art-galleries-anymore-962496.html.
Debord, Guy. 1994 [1967]. *The Society of the Spectacle*. New York: Zone.
Deeb, Lara, and Jessica Winegar. 2012. "Anthropologies of Arab-Majority Societies." *Annual Review of Anthropology* 41: 537–58.
Der Matossian, Bedross. 2011. "The Taboo within the Taboo: The Fate of the 'Armenian Capital' in the End of the Ottoman Empire." *European Journal of Turkish Studies* [online]. https://ejts.revues.org/4411.
Deringil, Selim. 1998a. *The Well-Protected Domains: Ideology and the Legitimation of Power in the Ottoman Empire, 1876–1909*. London: I. B. Tauris.
——. 1998b. "From Ottoman to Turk: Self-Image and Social Engineering in Turkey." In *Making Majorities: Constituting the Nation in Japan, Korea, China, Malaysia, Fiji, Turkey, and the United States*, ed. Dru C. Gladney, 217–26. Stanford, CA: Stanford University Press.
——. 2003. "They Live in a State of Nomadism and Savagery: The Late Ottoman Empire and the Post-Colonial Debate." *Comparative Studies in Society and History* 45(2): 311–42.
——. 2007. "The Turks and 'Europe': The Argument from History." *Middle Eastern Studies* 43(5): 709–23.

Deutsche, Rosalyn, and Cara G. Ryan. 1984. "The Fine Art of Gentrification." *October* 31: 91–111.

Devereaux, Mary. 1995. "Protected Space: Politics, Censorship, and the Arts." In *Ethics and the Arts: An Anthology*, ed. David E. Fenner, 41–58. New York: Garland.

Dewey, John. 1995 [1934]. "Art and Civilization." In *The Philosophy of Art: Readings Ancient and Modern*, ed. A. Neil and A. Ridley, 522–25. Boston: McGraw Hill.

Dickie, George. 1995 [1984]. "The New Institutional Theory of Art." In *The Philosophy of Art: Readings Ancient and Modern*, ed. A. Neil and A. Ridley, 213–23. Boston: McGraw Hill.

Douglas, Lawrence. 1998. "Policing the Past: Holocaust Denial and the Law." In *Censorship and Silencing: Practices of Cultural Regulation*, ed. Richard C. Post, 67–87. Los Angeles: Getty Research Institute for the History of Art and the Humanities.

Duft, Catherine, ed. 2009. In *Turkish Literature and Cultural Memory: "Multiculturalism" as a Literary Theme after 1980*. Wiesbaden: Harrassowitz Verlag.

Dündar, Can. 2003. *Bir Yaşam İksiri: Dr. Nejat F. Eczacıbaşı*. Istanbul: İş Bankası Kültür Yayınları.

Dunning, Eric, and Stephen Mennell. 1998. "Elias on Germany, Nazism, and the Holocaust: On the Balance between 'Civilizing' and 'Decivilizing' Trends in the Social Development of Western Europe." *British Journal of Sociology* 49(3): 339–57.

Eagleton, Terry. 1990. *The Ideology of the Aesthetic*. Malden: Blackwell.

El-Tayeb, Fatima. 2016. *Undeutsch: Die Konstruktion des Anderen in der postmigrantischen Gesellschaft*. Bielefeld: Transcript Verlag.

Eldridge, Richard. 1995 [1985]. "Form and Content: An Aesthetic Theory of Art." In *The Philosophy of Art: Readings Ancient and Modern*, ed. Alex Neil and Aaron Ridley, 240–53. Boston: McGraw Hill.

Eley, Geoff. 1988. "Nazism, Politics, and the Image of the Past: Thoughts on the West German Historikerstreit, 1986–1987." *Past & Present* 121:171–208.

Elias, Norbert. 1969. *The Civilizing Process: The History of Manners*. New York: Urizen.

Eller, Thomas W. 2005. "Ästhetischer Vampirismus." http://www.artnet.de/magazine/kommentar/eller/eller01-31-05.asp.

Emre, Gültekin, ed. 2003. *Türk Edebiyatında Berlin*. Istanbul: Yapı Kredi Yayınları.

Engel, Kathrin. 2003. *Deutsche Kulturpolitik im besetzten Paris 1940–1944: Film und Theater*. München: R. Oldenbourg.

Ergener, Balca. 2009. "On the Exhibition 'Incidents of September 6–7 on Their Fiftieth Anniversary' and the Attack on the Exhibition." *Red Thread*. http://www.red-thread.org/en/article.asp?a=25.

Ergün, Demet Bilge. 2005. "Katalog toplatıldı. Bienale '301' gölgesi." *Radikal*, October 27. http://www.radikal.com.tr/haber.php?haberno=168190.

Erol, Turan. 1998. *Yurt Gezileri ve Yurt Resimleri (1938–1943)*. Istanbul: Milli Reasürans.

Ertürk, Nergis. 2011. *Grammatology and Literary Modernity in Turkey*. Oxford: Oxford University Press.
Esche, Charles, and Vasıf Kortun. 2005. "Introduction." In *The 9th International Istanbul Biennial (Guide)*, 1–9. Istanbul: IKSV.
Evren, Süreyyya. 2008. *Halil Altındere. Kayıplar Ülkesiyle Dans*. Istanbul: Yapı Kredi Yayınları.
Ewing, Katherine Pratt. 2008. *Stolen Honor: Stigmatizing Muslim Men in Berlin*. Stanford, CA: Stanford University Press.
Fabian, Johannes. 1983. *Time and the Other. How Anthropology Makes Its Object*. New York: Columbia University Press.
———. 1996. *Remembering the Present: Painting and Popular History in Zaire*. Berkeley: University of California Press.
Fanizadeh, Andreas. 2005. "Die Toten Ruhen nicht. Zur Vorstellung des Terrors. Die RAF-Ausstellung in den Kunst-Werken, Berlin." http://www.textezurkunst.de/57/die-toten-ruhen-nicht/.
Feldman, Hannah. 2014. *From a Nation Torn: Decolonizing Art and Representation in France, 1945–1962*. Durham, NC: Duke University Press.
Feliciano, Hector. 1998. *The Lost Museum: The Nazi Conspiracy to Steal the World's Greatest Works of Art*. New York: Basic Books.
Fenner, David E. W. 1995. "Introduction." In *Ethics and the Arts: An Anthology*, ed. David Fenner, 1–25. New York: Garland.
Ferguson, Bruce, Reesa Greenberg, and Sandy Nairne. 2005. "Mapping International Exhibitions." In *The Manifesta Decade: Debates on Contemporary Art Exhibitions and Biennials in Post-Wall Europe*, ed. Barbara Vanderlinden and Elena Filipovic, 47–56. Cambridge, MA: MIT Press.
Flood, Finbarr Barry. 2013. "Lost Histories of a Licit Figural Art." *International Journal of Middle East Studies* 45(3): 566–69.
Florida, Richard. 2002. *The Rise of the Creative Class and How It's Transforming Work, Leisure, Community, and Everyday Life*. New York: Basic Books.
Fox, Richard G. 1990. "Introduction." In *Nationalist Ideologies and the Production of National Cultures*, ed. Richard G. Fox, 1–14. American Ethnological Society Monograph Series 2.
Fraser, Andrea. 2005. "From the Critique of Institutions to an Institution of Critique." *Artforum* 44(1): 100–6.
Frehner, Matthias, and Urs Steiner. 2001. "Ich glaube, dass man Verantwortung erbt." NZZ, April 27. http://www.nzz.ch/2001/04/27/fe/article7CQCD.html.
Frei, Norbert, Ralf Ahrens, Jörg Osterloh, and Tim Schanetzky. 2009. *Flick. Der Konzern, die Familie, die Macht*. München: Karl Blessing Verlag.
Fricke, Harald, and Rolf Lautenschläger. 2005. "Kunst leistet Trauerarbeit." *TAZ*, July 28. https://taz.de/!734783/.
Fuhrmann, Malte. 2011. "'I would rather be in the Orient': European Lower Class Immigrants into the Ottoman Lands." In *The City in the Ottoman Empire:*

Migration and the Making of Urban Modernity, ed. Ulrike Freitag et al., 228–241. London: Routledge.
Gamboni, Dario. 1997. *The Destruction of Art: Iconoclasm and Vandalism since the French Revolution*. New Haven, CT: Yale University Press.
Gaonkar, Dilip Parameshwar. 2001. *Alternative Modernities*. Durham, NC: Duke University Press.
Garnham, Nicholas. 2005. "From Cultural to Creative Industries." *International Journal of Cultural Policy* 11(1): 15–29.
Gavinson, Ruth. 1998. "Incitement and the Limits of the Law." In *Censorship and Silencing: Practices of Cultural Regulation*, ed. Richard C. Post, 43–65. Los Angeles: Getty Research Institute for the History of Art and the Humanities.
Geertz, Clifford. 1975. *The Interpretation of Culture*. London: Hutchinson.
Gell, Alfred. 1998. *Art and Agency: An Anthropological Theory*. Oxford: Clarendon.
Gerlis, Melanie. 2013. "Art Fund Industry Struggles to Emerge from the Gloom." *Art Newspaper* 250 (October).
Gerndt, Helge, ed. 1987. *Volkskunde und Nationalsozialismus: Referate und Diskussionen*. München: Münchener Vereinigung für Volkskunde.
Glaser, Hermann. 1997. *Deutsche Kultur. Ein historischer Überblick von 1945 bis zur Gegenwart*. München: Carl Hanser Verlag.
Glaser, Hermann, and Karl Heinz Stahl. 1974. *Die Wiedergewinnung des Ästhetischen. Perspektiven und Modelle einer neuen Soziokultur*. München: Juventa.
Goehler, Adrienne. 2006. *Verflüssigungen. Wege und Umwege vom Sozialstaat zur Kulturgesellschaft*. Frankfurt/Main: Campus.
Gökalp, Ziya. 1959. *Turkish Nationalism and Western Civilization*. New York: Columbia University Press.
Grasskamp, Walter, and Wolfgang Ullrich, eds. 2001. *Mäzene, Stifter und Sponsoren. Fünfzig Jahre Kulturkreis der deutschen Wirtschaft im BDI—ein Modell der Kulturförderung*, Ostfildern-Ruit: Hatje Cantz.
Graw, Isabelle. 2005. "Regarding Terror: The RAF Exhibition." *Artforum* 43(8): 181.
——. 2008. *Der grosse Preis Kunst zwischen Markt und Celebrity Kultur*. Köln: DuMont.
Greenberg, Clement. 1961. *Art and Culture: Critical Essays*. Boston: Beacon.
Grimshaw, Anna, and Amanda Ravetz. 2004. *Visualizing Anthropology: Experimenting with Image-Based Ethnography*. Bristol: Intellect.
Gross, Hermann. 1979. "Die deutsch-türkischen Wirtschaftsbeziehungen." In *Die Türkei in Europa*, ed. Klaus-Detlev Grothusen, 167–91. Göttingen: Vandenhoeck & Ruprecht.
Groys, Boris. 2005. "The Fate of Art in the Age of Terror." In *Making Things Public: Atmospheres of Democracy*, ed. Bruno Latour and Peter Weibel, 970–77. Cambridge, MA: MIT Press.
Güçlü, Yücel. 2000. "Turkish-German Relations on the Eve of World War Two." *Turkish Studies* 1(2): 73–94.
Guggenheim, Peggy. 1960. *Confessions of an Art Addict*. New York: Macmillan.

Guilbaut, Serge. 1983. *How New York Stole the Idea of Modern Art: Abstract Expressionism, Freedom, and the Cold War.* Chicago: University of Chicago Press.
Günal, Asena. 2017. "'Cultural Hegemony' by Means of the Police." *Red Thread* 4. http://red-thread.org/en/cultural-hegemony-by-means-of-the-police/.
Gürbilek, Nurdan. 1992. *Vitrinde Yaşamak. 1980'lerin Kültürel İklimi.* Istanbul: Metis.
Gürpınar, Doğan. 2013. "Historical Revisionism vs. Conspiracy Theories: Transformations of Turkish Historical Scholarship and Conspiracy Theories as a Constitutive Element in Transforming Turkish Nationalism." *Journal of Balkan and Near Eastern Studies* 15(4): 412–33.
Guttstadt, Corry. 2008. *Die Türkei, die Juden und der Holocaust.* Berlin: Assoziation A Verlag.
Güven, Dilek. 2005. *Cumhuriyet dönemi azınlık politikaları ve stratejiler bağlamında 6–7 Eylül olayları.* Istanbul: İstanbul Tarih Vakfı.
Haas, Daniel. 2006. "Legendäres Klimt-Porträt: Langsame Heimkehr." *Spiegel*, June 19.
Hachmeister, Lutz. 2004. *Schleyer: Eine deutsche Geschichte.* München: C. H. Beck Verlag.
Hagen, Gottfried. 2004. "German Heralds of Holy War: Orientalists and Applied Oriental Studies." *Comparative Studies of South Asia, Africa, and the Middle East* 24(2): 145–62.
Hall, Stuart. 1996. "The West and the Rest: Discourse and Power." In *Modernity: An Introduction to Modern Societies*, ed. Stuart Hall, David Held, Don Hubert, and Kenneth Thompson, 184–227. Malden, MA: Blackwell.
Halman, Talat. 2006. "From Global Pillage to Pillars of Collaboration." In *Imperialism, Art, and Restitution*, ed. John H. Merryman, 37–46. Cambridge: Cambridge University Press.
Hamilton, Peter. 1996. "The Enlightenment and the Birth of the Social Sciences." In *Modernity: An Introduction to Modern Societies*, edited by Stuart Hall, David Held, Don Hubert, and Kenneth Thompson, 19–54. Malden, MA: Blackwell.
Hannerz, Ulf. 1996. *Transnational Connections: Culture, People, Places.* London: Routledge.
Hartmann, Geoffrey. 1986. *Bitburg in Moral and Political Perspective.* Bloomington: Indiana University Press.
Harutyunyan, Angela, Aras Ozgün, and Eric Goodfield. 2011. "Event and Counter-Event: The Political Economy of the Istanbul Biennial and Its Excesses." *Rethinking Marxism* 23(4): 478–95.
Harvey, David. 2001. "The Art of Rent." In *Spaces of Capital: Towards a Critical Geography*, 394–411. New York: Routledge.
——. 2004. "The 'New' Imperialism: Accumulation by Dispossession." *Socialist Register* 40: 63–87.
Haskins, Casey. 1989. "Kant and the Autonomy of Art." *Journal of Aesthetics and Art Criticism* 4(1): 43–54.

Hayes, Peter. 1998. *Profits and Persecution: German Big Business and the Holocaust.* Washington, DC: US Holocaust Memorial Museum, Center for Advanced Holocaust Studies.

Heins, Marjorie. 2001. *Not in Front of the Children: "Indecency," Censorship, and the Innocence of Youth.* New York: Hill and Wang.

Herf, Jeffrey. 1984. *Reactionary Modernism: Technology, Culture, and Politics in Weimar and the Third Reich.* Cambridge: Cambridge University Press.

Herstatt, Claudia. 2006. "Warhol, Richter und andere Blue Chips. Neu aufgelegte Kunstfonds versprechen hohe Renditen. Lohnt sich die Investition?" *Die Zeit*, June 29. http://www.zeit.de/2006/27/Kunstmarkt-27.

Herwig, Holger H. 1987. "Patriotic Self-Censorship in Germany after the Great War." *International Security* 12(2): 5–44.

Herzfeld, Michael. 1982. *Ours Once More: Folklore, Ideology, and the Making of Modern Greece.* Austin: University of Texas Press.

———. 2003. *The Body Impolitic: Artisans and Artifice in the Global Hierarchy of Value.* Chicago: University of Chicago Press.

Herzog, Samuel. 2007. "Sich elegant verdauen lassen." NZZ, September 12. https://www.nzz.ch/sich_elegant_verdauen_lassen-1.553999.

Hesmondalgh, David, and Andy C. Pratt. 2005. "Cultural Industries and Cultural Policy." *International Journal of Cultural Policy* 11(1): 1–13.

Hirsch, Marianne. 2012. *The Generation of Postmemory: Writing and Visual Culture after the Holocaust.* New York: Columbia University Press.

Hirschon, Renée, ed. 2003. *Crossing the Aegean: An Appraisal of the 1923 Compulsory Population Exchange between Greece and Turkey.* New York: Berghahn.

Hobsbawm, Eric. 1992. "Introduction: Inventing Traditions." In *The Invention of Tradition*, ed. Eric Hobsbawm and Terence Ranger, 1–14. Cambridge: Cambridge University Press.

Hobsbawm, Eric, and Terence Ranger, eds. 1992. *The Invention of Tradition.* Cambridge: Cambridge University Press.

Hoffmann, Hilmar. 1979. *Kultur für Alle. Perspektiven und Modelle.* Frankfurt/Main: Fischer.

Hohmann, Silke. 2005a. "Der Wille zur Bewegung." *Frankfurter Rundschau*, January 1.

———. 2005b. "Euphorie in Moll." *Frankfurter Rundschau*, September 5.

Huyssen, Andreas. 2003. *Presents Pasts: Urban Palimpsests and the Politics of Memory.* Stanford, CA: Stanford University Press.

———. 2010. "German Painting in the Cold War." *New German Critique* 37(2): 209–27.

Iğsız, Aslı. 2015. "Palimpsests of Multiculturalism and Museumization of Culture: Greco-Turkish Population Exchange Museum as an Istanbul 2010 European Capital of Culture Project." *Comparative Studies of South Asia, Africa, and the Middle East* 35(2): 324–45.

———. 2018. *Humanism in Ruins: Entangled Legacies of the Greek-Turkish Population Exchange.* Stanford, CA: Stanford University Press.

İlengiz, Çiçek. 2019. "Erecting a Statue in the Land of the Fallen: Gendered Dynamics of the Making of Tunceli and Commemorating Seyyid Rıza in Dersim." *L'Homme ZFG–European Journal of Feminist History* 2:75–92.
Illich, Niles Stefan. 2007. "German Imperialism in the Ottoman Empire: A Comparative Study." PhD diss., University of Texas.
İnce, Elif. 2017. "Turkey's State of Emergency Puts Kurdish Theatre in a Chokehold." *Ifex*, January 5. https://www.ifex.org/turkey/2017/01/05/kurdish_theatre/.
Isaacson, Walter, James O. Jackson, and Christopher Ogden. 1989. "Is One Germany Better Than Two?" *Time*, November 20. http://www.time.com/time/magazine/article/0,9171,959068,00.html.
Iversen, Trude. 2007. "What Now for Institutional Critique." In *The New Administration of Aesthetics*, ed. Trude Iversen and Tone Hansen, 7–12. Oslo: Torpedo.
Jameson, Frederic. 1991. *Postmodernism, or, the Cultural Logic of Late Capitalism*. Durham, NC: Duke University Press.
Jarausch, Konrad H. 2006. *After Hitler: Recivilizing the Germans, 1945–1995*. New York: Oxford University Press.
Jardine, Lisa, and Jerry Brotton. 2000. *Global Interests: Renaissance Art between East and West*. Ithaca, NY: Cornell University Press.
Jaskot, Paul B. 2012. *The Nazi Perpetrator: Postwar German Art and the Politics of the Right*. Minneapolis: University of Minnesota Press.
Judt, Tony. 1996. *A Grand Illusion? An Essay on Europe*. New York: Hill and Wang.
Kahn, Joel. 2001. "Anthropology and Modernity." *Current Anthropology* 42(5): 651–80.
Kaiser, Hilmar. 1997. *Imperialism, Racism, and Development Theories: The Construction of a Dominant Paradigm on Ottoman Armenians*. Ann Arbor: Gomidas Institute.
Kant, Immanuel. 1987 [1790]. *Critique of Judgment*. Indianapolis, IN: Hackett.
Kant, Marion. 2004. "German Dance and Modernity. Don't Mention the Nazis." In *Rethinking Dance History: A Reader*, ed. Alexandra Carter, 107–18. London: Routledge.
Kantarcıoğlu, Selçuk. 1987. *Türkiye Cumhuriyeti Hükûmet Programlarinda Kültür*. Ankara: Kültür Bakanlığı Yayınları.
Kaplan, Sam. 2006. *The Pedagogical State: Education and the Politics of National Culture in Post-1980 Turkey*. Stanford, CA: Stanford University Press.
Karaca, Banu. 2009. "Governance of or through Culture? Cultural Policy and the Politics of Culture in Europe." *Focaal—European Journal of Anthropology* 55: 27–40.
———. 2010. "The Art of Integration: Probing the Role of Cultural Policy in the Making of Europe." *International Journal of Cultural Policy* 16(2): 1–17.
———. 2013. "Europeanization from the Margins? Istanbul's Cultural Capital Initiative and the Formation of European Cultural Policies." In *The Cultural Politics of Europe*, ed. Kiran Klaus Patel, 157–75. New York: Routledge.

———. 2019a. "When Everything Has Been Said Before . . . : Dispossession and the Politics of Art in Turkey." In *Women Mobilizing Memory*, ed. Ayşe Gül Altinay et al., 285–302. New York: Columbia University Press.

———. 2019b. *Joint Stakeholder Submission to the Universal Periodic Review (UPR) of Turkey at the UN Human Rights Council on Artistic Freedom by P24 and Freemuse*. http://susma24.com/wp-content/uploads/2020/01/SUSMA-JOINT-UPR-SUBMISSION-TURKEY-2020.pdf.

Kasaba, Reşat. 1997. "Kemalist Certainties and Modern Ambiguities." In *Rethinking Modernity and National Identity in Turkey*, ed. Sibel Bozdoğan and Reşat Kasaba, 15–36. Seattle: University of Washington Press.

Kempers, Bram. 1987. *Painting, Power, and Patronage: The Rise of the Professional Artist in the Italian Renaissance*. London: Penguin.

Kester, Grant H. 2011. *The One and the Many: Contemporary Collaborative Art in a Global Context*. Durham, NC: Duke University Press.

Kessen, Peter. 2004. *Die Kunst des Erbens. Die "Flick Collection" und die Berliner Republik*. Berlin: Philo.

Keyder, Cağlar. 1997. "Wither the Project of Modernity? Turkey in the 1990s." In *Rethinking Modernity and National Identity in Turkey*, ed. Sibel Bozdoğan and Reşat Kasaba, 37–51. Seattle: University of Washington Press.

Kirişci, Kemal. 1998. "Minority/Majority Discourse: The Case of the Kurds in Turkey." In *Making Majorities: Constituting the Nation in Japan, Korea, China, Malaysia, Fiji, Turkey, and the United States*, ed. Dru C. Gladney, 227–45. Stanford, CA: Stanford University Press.

Knoblich, Tobias. 2001. "Das Prinzip Soziokultur." *Aus Politik und Zeitgeschehen* B11: 7–14.

Koçak, Orhan. 2010. "Westernisation against the West: Cultural Politics in the Early Turkish Republic." In *Turkey's Engagement with Modernity*, ed. Celia Kerslake, Kerem Öktem, and Philip Robins, 305–22. Houndsmills: Palgrave.

Kocka, Jürgen. 1999. "Asymmetrical Historical Comparison: The Case of the German Sonderweg." *History and Theory* 38(1): 40–50.

Köksal, Duygu. 2004. "Art and Power in Turkey: Culture, Nationalism, and Aesthetics during the Single Party Era." *New Perspectives on Turkey* 31: 91–119.

Koldehoff, Stefan. 2014. *Die Bilder sind unter uns. Das Geschäft mit der NS-Raubkunst und der Fall Gurlitt*. Berlin: Galiani.

Konuk, Kader. 2010. *East West Mimesis: Auerbach in Turkey*. Stanford, CA: Stanford University Press.

Kortun, Vasıf, and Erden Kosova. 2004. *Szene Türkei. Abseits, aber Tor!* Köln: Walther König.

Kortun, Vasif, and Hou Hanru. 2003. *How Latitudes Become Forms: Art in the Global Age*. Minneapolis, MN: Walker Art Center.

Kosnick, Kira. 2007. *Migrant Media: Turkish Broadcasting and Multicultural Politics in Berlin*. Bloomington: Indiana University Press.

Kosova, Erden. 2007. "Eleştirel İhanet—Burak Delier ile Söyleşi." http://everestmylord.blogspot.com/2007/10/eletirel-ihanet-burak-delier-ile-sylei.html.
Kramer, Jane. 1996. *The Politics of Memory: Looking for Germany in the New Germany*. New York: Random House.
Kraushaar, Wolfgang. 2010. *Verena Becker und der Verfassungschutz*. Hamburg: Hamburger Editionen.
Kürkman, Garo. 2004. *Armenian Painters in the Ottoman Empire, 1600–1923*. 2 vols. Istanbul: Matüsalem Uzmanlik ve Yayincilik.
Kuyucu, Tuna, and Özlem Ünsal. 2010. "Urban Transformation as State-Led Property Transfer: An Analysis of Two Cases of Urban Renewal in Istanbul." *Urban Studies* 47(7): 1479–99.
Lamb, Stephen, and Anthony Phelan. 1995. "Weimar Culture: The Birth of Modernism." In *German Cultural Studies: An Introduction*, ed. Rob Burns, 53–99. Oxford: Oxford University Press.
Lash, Scott, and John Urry. 1994. *Economies of Signs and Space*. London: Sage.
Latour, Bruno. 2001. *We Have Never Been Modern*. Cambridge, MA: Harvard University Press.
Lepenies, Wolf. 2006. *The Seduction of Culture in German History*. Princeton, NJ: Princeton University Press.
Leslie, Esther. 2008. *Walter Benjamin*. London: Reaktion.
Levi, Neil. 1998. "'Judge for Yourselves!' The 'Degenerate Art' Exhibition as Political Spectacle." *October* 85 (Summer): 41–64.
Levinson, Sanford. 1998. "The Tutelary State: 'Censorship,' 'Silencing,' and the 'Practices of Cultural Regulation.'" In *Censorship and Silencing: Practices of Cultural Regulation*, ed. Richard C. Post, 195–219. Los Angeles: Getty Research Institute for the History of Art and the Humanities.
Levy, Daniel, and Natan Sznaider. 2006. *Human Rights and Memory*. Philadelphia: University of Pennsylvania Press.
Lewis, Reina. 2004. *Rethinking Orientalism: Women, Travel, and the Ottoman Harem*. New Brunswick, NJ: Rutgers University Press.
Linke, Uli. 1997. "Fantasizing Violence." *City & Society* 9(1): 135–58.
———. 1999. *German Bodies: Race and Representation after Hitler*. London: Routledge.
Litchfield, David R. L. 2006. *The Thyssen Art Macabre*. London: Quartet.
Lorch, Catrin. 2005. "Eigentlich suche ich noch ein ausgestopftes Krokodil: Die Sammlung Olbricht im Leverkusener Museum Morsbroich." *FAZ*, December 6.
Lowe, Lisa. 2015. *The Intimacies of Four Continents*. Durham, NC: Duke University Press.
Lukács, Georg. 1955. *Probleme des Realismus*. Berlin: Aufbau Verlag.
MacClancy, Jeremy. 1997. "Anthropology, Art, and Contest." In *Art, Politics, and Identity in the Modern World*, ed. Jeremy MacClancy, 1–25. Oxford: Berg.
Macdonald, Sharon. 2009. *Difficult Heritage: Negotiating the Nazi Past in Nuremberg and Beyond*. London: Routledge.

Mack, Rosamond E. 2002. *Bazaar to Piazza: Islamic Trade and Italian Art, 1300–1600*. Berkeley: University of California Press.
MacMurray, Jonathan S. 2001. *Distant Ties: Germany, the Ottoman Empire, and the Construction of the Baghdad Railway*. Westport, CT: Prager.
Madley, Benjamin. 2005. "From Africa to Auschwitz: How German South West Africa Incubated Ideas and Methods Adopted and Developed by the Nazis in Eastern Europe." *European History Quarterly* 35(3): 429–64.
Mah, Harold. 1990. "The French Revolution and the Problem of German Modernity: Hegel, Heine, and Marx." *New German Critique* 50: 3–20.
Makdisi, Ussama. 2002. "Rethinking Ottoman Imperialism: Modernity, Violence, and the Cultural Logic of Ottoman Reform." In *The Empire and the City*, ed. Jens Hanssen, Thomas Philipp, and Stefan Weber, 29–48. Beirut: Ergon.
Mandel, Ruth. 2008. *Cosmopolitan Anxieties: Turkish Challenges to Citizenship and Belonging in Germany*. Durham, NC: Duke University Press.
Marchand, Laure, and Guillaume Perrier. 2014. *Türkiye ve Ermeni Hayaleti Soykırımın İzinde Adımlar*. Istanbul: İletişim.
Marchand, Suzanne. 1996a. "Orientalism as Kulturpolitik: German Archaeology and Cultural Imperialism in Asia Minor." In *Volksgeist as Method and Ethic*, ed. George W. Stocking, 298–336. Madison: University of Wisconsin Press.
——. 1996b. *Down from Olympus: Archaeology and Philhellenism in Germany, 1750–1970*. Princeton, NJ: Princeton University Press.
Marcus, George E., and Fred R. Myers, eds. 1995. *The Traffic in Culture: Refiguring Art and Anthropology*. Berkeley: University of California Press.
Marcuse, Herbert. 2007 [1937]. "The Affirmative Character of Culture." In *Art and Liberation*, 82–112. Abingdon: Routledge.
Mardin, Şerif. 2002. "Playing Games with Names." In *Fragments of Culture: The Everyday of Modern Turkey*, ed. Deniz Kandiyoti and Ayse Saktanber, 115–27. New Brunswick, NJ: Rutgers Unsiversity Press.
Markovits, Andrei S., Seyla Benhabib, and Moishe Postone. 1986. "Rainer Werner Fassbinder's *Garbage, the City and Death*: Renewed Antagonisms in the Complex Relationship between Jews and Germans in the Federal Republic of Germany." *New German Critique* 30: 3–27.
Mazower, Mark. 1998. *Dark Continent: Europe's Twentieth Century*. New York: Vintage.
Mazzarella, William. 2013. *Censorium: Cinema and the Open Edge of Mass Publicity*. Durham, NC: Duke University Press.
McMeekin, Sean. 2010. *The Berlin–Baghdad Express: The Ottoman Empire and Germany's Bid for World Power, 1898–1918*. London: Penguin.
Meeker, Michael. 2002. *Nation of Empire: The Ottoman Legacy of Turkish Modernity*. Berkeley: University of California Press.
Mehlig, Holger. 2005. "Zur Vorstellung des Terrors. RAF-Ausstellung in Berlin." *Stern*. http://www.stern.de/unterhaltung/fotografie/535899.html?nv=cb.

Melzer, Patricia. 2009. "'Death in the Shape of a Young Girl': Feminist Responses to Media Representations of Women Terrorists during the 'German Autumn' of 1977." *International Feminist Journal of Politics* 11(1): 35–62.
Michaud, Eric. 2004. *The Cult of Art in Nazi Germany*. Stanford, CA: Stanford University Press.
Miller, Arthur. 1990. "Uneasy about the Germans." *New York Times*. May 6.
Miller, Toby, and George Yúdice. 2002. *Cultural Policy*. London: Sage.
Mills, Amy. 2010. *Streets of Memory: Landscape, Tolerance, and National Identity in Istanbul*. Athens: University of Georgia Press.
Mirza, Munira. 2005. "The Therapeutic State: Addressing the Emotional Needs of the Citizen through the Arts." *International Journal of Cultural Policy* 11(3): 261–73.
Mitchell, Timothy. 2000. "The Stage of Modernity." In *Questions of Modernity*, ed. Timothy Mitchell, 1–34. Minneapolis: University of Minnesota Press.
———. 2009. "Orientalism and the Exhibitionary Order." In *The Art of Art History: A Critical Anthology*, ed. Donal Preziosi, 409–23. Oxford: Oxford University Press.
Moeller, Robert G. 1996. "War Stories: The Search for a Usable Past in the Federal Republic of Germany." *American Historical Review* 101(4): 1008–48.
Mollenkopf, John H., and Manuel Castels, eds. 1991. *Dual Cities: Restructuring New York*. New York: Russell Sage Foundation.
Mommsen, Wolfgang J. 1994. *Bürgerliche Kultur und Künstlerische Avangarde 1870–1918. Kunst und Kultur im Kaiserreich*. Frankfurt/Main: Propyläen.
———. 2000. *Bürgerliche Kultur und politische Ordnung. Künstler Schriftsteller und Intellektuelle in der deutschen Geschichte 1830–1933*. Frankfurt/Main: Fischer.
———. 2004. "Eine wunderbare Katastrophe." *Frankfurter Rundschau*, July 30.
Monod, David, 2005. *Settling Scores: German Music, Denazification, and the Americans, 1945–1953*. Chapel Hill: University of North Carolina Press.
Morphy, Howard, and Morgan Perkins, eds. 2006. *The Anthropology of Art: A Reader*. Malden, MA: Blackwell.
Mortensen, Preben. 1997. *Art in the Social Order: The Making of the Modern Conception of Art*. Albany: SUNY Press.
Mosse, George L. 1985. *Nationalism and Sexuality: Respectability and Abnormal Sexuality in Modern Europe*. New York: Howard Fertig.
Muka, Edi. 2004. "The A-Factor, or, The New Prolets of the Art-World." In *Die Schluchten des Balkans*, ed. René Block, 12–13. Kassel: Kunsthalle Fridericianum Kassel.
Myers, Fred. 2002. *Painting Culture: The Making of Aboriginal High Art*. Durham, NC: Duke University Press.
Narayan, Kirin. 1993. "How Native Is a 'Native' Anthropologist?" *American Anthropologist* 95(3): 671–86.
Naumann, Michael. 2001. *Die schönste Form der Freiheit. Reden und Essays zur Kultur der Nation*. Berlin: Siedler.

Navaro-Yashin, Yael. 2002. *Faces of the State: Secularism and Public Life in Turkey.* Princeton, NJ: Princeton University Press.

———. 2012. *The Make-Believe Space: Affective Geography in a Post-War Polity.* Durham, NC: Duke University Press.

Nehamas, Alexander. 2000. "The Return of the Beautiful: Morality, Pleasure, and the Value of Uncertainty." *Journal of Aesthetics and Art Criticism* 58(4): 393–403.

Neumann, Klaus. 2000. *Shifting Memories: The Nazi Past in the New Germany.* Ann Arbor: University of Michigan Press.

New York State Council on the Arts. 1997. *You Gotta Have ART! Profile of a Great Investment for New York State.* New York: NYSCA.

Neyzi, Leyla. 2011. *Nasıl Hatırlıyoruz? Türkiye 'de Bellek Çalışmaları.* Istanbul: İş Bankası Kültür Yayınları.

Nicholas, Lynn H. 1994. *The Rape of Europa: The Fate of Europe's Treasures during the Third Reich and Second World War.* New York: Random House.

Nickel, Gunther, and Johanna Schrön. 2002. *Carl Zuckmayers Geheimreport.* Göttingen: Wallstein.

Nipperdey, Thomas. 1996. *Germany from Napoleon to Bismarck: 1800–1866.* Princeton, NJ: Princeton University Press.

Obrist, Hans-Ulrich. 2008. *A Brief History of Curating.* Zurich: JRP Ringier.

Ohmer, Anja. 2004. "Literatur vor Gericht. Zensur in Deutschland." http://www.eurozine.com/articles/2004-03-22-ohmer-de.html.

Olick, Jeffrey. 1998. "What Does It Mean to Normalize the Past? Official Memory in German Politics since 1989." *Social Science History* 22(4): 547–71.

Onaran, Nevzat. 2010. *Osmanlı'da Ermeni ve Rum Mallarının Türkleştirilmesi (1914–1919). Emval-i Metrukenin Tasfiyesi.* 2 vols. Istanbul: Evrensel Basım Yayın.

Öncü, Ayşe. 2010. "Narratives of Istanbul's Ottoman Heritage." In *Spatial Conceptions of the Nation: Modernizing Geographies in Greece and Turkey*, ed. Nikiforos Diamandouros, Thalia Dragonas, and Çağlar Keyder, 205–28. New York: Tauris Academic Studies.

Önderoğlu, Erol. 2008. "Kültür Bakanlığı 'Gitmek'i Festival Programından Çıkarttı." *Bianet*, November 3. http://bianet.org/biamag/bianet/110616-kultur-bakanligi-gitmeki-festival-programindan-cikartti.

Öndin, Nilüfer. 2003. *Cumhuriyet'in Kültür Politikası ve Sanat 1923–1950.* Istanbul: İnsancıl Yayınları.

Osmond, Jonathan. 2000. "Looking German: Exhibitions and Collections at the Turn of the Century." *German History* 18(4): 495–508.

Özgül, Ceren. 2014. "Legally Armenian: Tolerance, Conversion, and Name Change in Turkish Courts." *Comparative Studies in Society and History* 56(3): 622–49.

Özmen, Şener. 2005. "Serbest Vuruş'ta 'star sanatçı' yok! Peki şimdi ne olacak?" *Birgün.* October 2. http://www.birgun.net/sunday_index.phpnews_code=1128239551&year=2005&month=10&day=02.

Özsezgin, Kaya. 1998. *Cumhuriyetimizin 75. Yılında Türk Resmi.* Istanbul: Türkiye İş Bankası Kültür Yayınları.

Öztürkmen, Arzu. 2002. "I Dance Folklore." In *Fragments of Culture: The Everyday of Modern Turkey*, ed. Deniz Kandiyoti and Ayse Saktanber, 128–46. New Brunswick, NJ: Rutgers University Press.
Özyürek, Esra. 2006. *Nostalgia for the Modern: State Secularism and Everyday Politics*. Durham, NC: Duke University Press.
———. 2007. *The Politics of Public Memory in Turkey*. Syracuse, NY: Syracuse University Press.
Ozment, Steven. 2004. "Deutschland, du kannst das besser." *Die Zeit*, August 5. http://zeus.zeit.de/text/2004/31/Esssay_Ozment.
Parla, Taha. 1985. *The Social and Political Thought of Ziya Gökalp, 1876–1924*. Leiden: Brill.
———. 2007. *Türk Sorunu Üstüne Yazılar 1998–2007*. Istanbul: Ürün Yayınları.
Parla, Taha, and Andrew Davison. 2004. *Kemalist Turkey: Progress or Order?* Syracuse, NY: Syracuse University Press.
Pearce, Susan. 1995. *On Collecting: An Investigation into Collecting in the European Tradition*. London: Routledge.
Perels, Joachim. 2006. "Der Mythos von der Vergangenheitsbewältigung." *Die Zeit* 61(5): 51.
Peters, Butz. 2005. "Korrekturen." *Artnet*. February 9. http://www.artnet.de/magazine/kommentar/peters/peters02-09-05.asp.
Peterson, Anya Royce. 2004. *Anthropology of the Performing Arts: Artistry, Virtuosity, and Interpretation in a Cross-Cultural Perspective*. Walnut Creek, CA: Alta Mira.
Petropoulos, Jonathan. 1996. *Art as Politics in the Third Reich*. Chapel Hill: University of North Carolina Press.
Pfitzenmaier, Pascal. 2005. "Geschichtsklippe 'Rote Armee Fraktion.'" *Deutsche Welle*, January 29. http://www.dw-world.de/dw/article/0,1564,1472291,00.html.
Pieprzak, Katarzyna. 2010. *Imagined Museums: Art and Modernity in Postcolonial Morocco*. Minneapolis: University of Minnesota Press.
Plattner, Stuart. 1996. *High Art Down Home: An Economic Ethnography of a Local Art Market*. Chicago: University of Chicago Press.
Polatel, Mehmet, Nora Mıldanoğlu, Özgür Leman Eren, and Mehmet Atılgan. 2012. *2012 Declaration: The Seized Properties of Armenian Foundations in Istanbul*. Istanbul: Hrant Dink Foundation.
Pommerin, Reiner. 1996. *Culture in the Federal Republic of Germany, 1945–1995*. Oxford: Berg.
Potuoğlu-Cook, Öykü. 2006. "Beyond the Glitter: Belly Dance and Neoliberal Gentrification in Istanbul." *Cultural Anthropology* 21(4): 633–60.
Post, Robert C. 1998. "Censorship and Silencing." In *Censorship and Silencing: Practices of Cultural Regulation*, ed. Richard C. Post, 1–12. Los Angeles: Getty Research Institute for the History of Art and the Humanities.
Preiß, Achim. 1999. *Abschied von der Kunst des 20. Jahrhunderts*. Weimar: VDG.
Price, Sally. 2007. *Paris Primitive: Jacques Chirac's Museum on the Quai Branly*. Chicago: University of Chicago Press.

Quataert, Donald. 2005. *The Ottoman Empire, 1700–1922*. Cambridge: Cambridge University Press.
Radikal. 2008. "Terör varsa aşk yok." *Radikal*, November 5. http://www.radikal.com.tr/2008/11/05/.
Ramge, Thomas. 2004. *Die Flicks—Eine deutsche Familiengeschichte über Geld, Macht und Politik*. Frankfurt/Main: Campus.
Rancière, Jacques. 2004. *The Politics of Aesthetics*. London: Continuum.
———. 2010. *Dissensus: On Politics and Aesthetics*. London: Continuum.
Rauterberg, Hanno. 1999. "Kesseltreiben in Weimar." *Die Zeit*, May 27. http://www.zeit.de/1999/22/199922..b7._fortsetzung.xml.
Reich, Cary. 1996. *The Life of Nelson A. Rockefeller: Worlds to Conquer, 1908–1958*. Vol. 1. New York: Doubleday.
Reichelt, Matthias. 2005. "Niemandem weh tun." *Junge Welt*. January 1. http://www.jungewelt.de/2005/01-31/018.php.
Reinecke, Stefan. 2003. "Neue Phantombilder." *TAZ*, July 25. https://taz.de/!735654/.
Reisman, Arnold. 2006. *Turkey's Modernization: Refugees from Nazism and Atatürk's Vision*. Washington, DC: New Academia Publishing.
Repp, Kevin. 2000. *Reformers, Critics, and the Paths of German Modernity: Antipolitics and the Search for Alternatives, 1890–1914*. Cambridge, MA: Harvard University Press.
Rogoff, Irit. 2002. "Hit and Run: Museums and Cultural Difference." *Art Journal* 61(3): 63–73.
Rothman, Nathalie E. 2011. *Brokering Empire: Trans-Imperial Subjects between Venice and Istanbul*. Ithaca, NY: Cornell University Press.
Rush, Richard H. 1961. *Art as an Investment: How to Buy and Sell Works of Art for Profit and Pleasure—an Analysis of the Art Market and Collector's Guide*. Englewood Cliffs, NJ: Prentice Hall.
Sağlar, Fikri. 1994. *Ulusaldan evrensele çağdaş kültür*. Ankara: T. C. Kültür Bakanlığı Yayınları.
Said, Edward. 2003 [1978]. *Orientalism*. New York: Vintage.
Saldern, Adelheid von. 2002. *The Challenge of Modernity: German Social and Cultural Studies, 1890–1960*. Ann Arbor: University of Michigan Press.
———. 2004. "Volk and Heimat Culture in Radio Broadcasting during the Period of Transition from Weimar to Nazi Germany." *Journal of Modern History* 76(2): 312–46.
Saltzman, Lisa. 2005. "Gerhard Richter's Stations of the Cross: On Martyrdom and Memory in Postwar German Art." *Oxford Art Journal* 28(1): 25–44.
Sassen, Saskia. 1991. *The Global City*. Princeton, NJ: Princeton University Press.
Scarry, Elaine. 1999. *On Beauty and Being Just*. Princeton, NJ: Princeton University Press.
Schauer, Frederick. 1998. "The Ontology of Censorship." In *Censorship and Silencing: Practices of Cultural Regulation*, ed. Robert C. Post, 147–68. Los Angeles: Getty Research Institute for the History of Art and the Humanities.

Schjeldahl, Peter. 2006. “Temptations of the Fair. Miami Virtue and Vice.” *New Yorker*, December 25. http://www.newyorker.com/magazine/2006/12/25/temptations-of-the-fair.

Schneider, Arnd. 2006. *Appropriation as Practice: Art and Identity in Argentina*. New York: Palgrave.

Schneider, Arnd, and Christopher Wright. 2010. *Between Art and Anthropology: Contemporary Ethnographic Practice*. Oxford: Berg.

Schorske, Carl E. 1961. *Fin-De-Siècle Vienna: Politics and Culture*. New York: Vintage.

Schug, Alexander, ed. 2007. *Palast der Republik: politischer Diskurs und private Erinnerung*. Berlin: Berliner Wissenschafts-Verlag.

Scott, David. 1999. *Refashioning Futures: Criticism after Postcoloniality*. Princeton, NJ: Princeton University Press.

Seitz, Norbert. 2002. “Nicht ohne meinen Nazi.” *Die Zeit*, December 18. http://www.zeit.de/2002/52/Nicht_ohne_meinen_Nazi.

Serra, Richard. 1995. “Art and Censorship.” In *Ethics and the Arts: An Anthology*, ed. David E. W. Fenner, 29–39. New York: Garland.

Shafak, Elif. 2006. “Wollt Ihr uns gebrochen sehen?” *Die Welt*, February 3. http://www.welt.de/print-welt/article195273/Wollt_ihr_uns_gebrochen_sehen.html.

Shaw, Wendy M. K. 2003. *Possessors and Possessed: Museums, Archaeology, and the Visualization of History in the Late Ottoman Empire*. Berkeley: University of California Press.

———. 2011. *Ottoman Painting: Reflections of Western Art from the Ottoman Empire to the Turkish Republic*. London: I. B. Tauris.

Shusterman, Richard. 1995. “Aesthetic Censorship: Censoring Art for Art’s Sake.” In *Ethics and the Arts: An Anthology*, ed. David E. W. Fenner, 59–74. New York: Garland.

Slyomovics, Susan. 2012. *How to Accept German Reparations*. Philadelphia: University of Pennsylvania Press.

Smith, Anthony. 2013. *The Nation Made Real: Art and National Identity in Western Europe, 1600–1850*. Oxford: Oxford University Press.

Smith, Neil. 1996. *The New Urban Frontier: Gentrification and the Revanchist City*. London: Routledge.

Spreen, Dierk. 2005. “Leuchtreklame für den Terror.” *Artnet Online*. March 9, 2005. http://www.artnet.de/magazine/reviews/spreen/spreen03-09-05.asp.

Sönmez, Ayşegül. 2005. “İstanbul Calling.” *Miliyet Sanat* 559 (126301): 7–10.

Soldt, Rüdiger. 2019. “AfD provoziert Kunstbetrieb in Baden-Württemberg.” *FAZ*, June 28. https://www.faz.net/aktuell/politik/inland/anfrage-zu-nationalitaeten-afd-provoziert-kunstbetrieb-in-baden-wuerttemberg-16259908.html.

Sorkin, Michael, ed. 1992. *Variations on a Theme Park: The American City and the End of Public Space*. New York: Hill and Wang.

Stallbaumer, Lisa M. 1995. “Strictly Business? The Flick Concern and ‘Aryanizations’: Corporate Expansion in the Nazi Era.” PhD diss., University of Wisconsin–Madison.

Stange, Raimar. 2006. "Geheimnisvoll, Psychologisch, Intim." *Zitty* 3: 81.
Stephan, Alexander, Sara Lennox, and Frank Lennox. 1974. "Johannes R. Becher and the Cultural Development of the GDR." *New German Critique* 2: 72–89.
Stevenson, Mark. 1999. "German Cultural Policy and Neo-Liberal Zeitgeist." *PoLAR: Political and Legal Anthropology Review* 22(2): 64–79.
Stokes, Martin. 1992. *The Arabesk Debate: Music and Musicians in Modern Turkey*. Oxford: Clarendon.
———. 2010. *The Republic of Love: Cultural Intimacy in Turkish Popular Music*. Chicago: University of Chicago Press.
Stolcke, Verena. 1995. "Talking Culture: New Boundaries, New Rhetorics of Exclusion in Europe." *Current Anthropology* 36(1): 1–24.
Stoler, Ann. 1992. "Sexual Affronts and Racial Frontiers: European Identities and the Cultural Politics of Exclusion in Colonial South East Asia." *Comparative Studies in Society and History* 34(2): 514–51.
———. 2006. *Haunted by Empire: Geographies of the Intimate in North American History*. Durham, NC: Duke University Press.
Storr, Robert. 2000. *Gerhard Richter: October 18, 1977*. New York: MoMA.
Svašek, Maruška. 2002. "Contacts: Social Dynamics in the Czechoslovak State-Socialist Art World." *Contemporary European History* 11(1): 67–86.
Tambar, Kabir. 2014. *The Reckoning of Pluralism: Political Belonging and the Demands of History in Turkey*. Stanford, CA: Stanford University Press.
Tan, Pelin. 2006. "Self-Initiated Collectivity: Artist-Run Spaces and Artists' Collectives in Istanbul." *Artpapers*, July/August, 21–23.
Tannert, Christoph. 2005. "Antwort auf einen Offenen Brief." In *Urbane Realitäten: Fokus Istanbul*, ed. Christoph Tannert and Peter Lang, 18–21. Berlin: Künstlerhaus Bethanien.
Tansuğ, Sezer. 1986. *Çağdaş Türk Sanatı*. Istanbul: Remzi Kitabevi.
Tatzkow, Monika, and Gunnar Schnabel. 2008. *The Story of Street Scene: Restitution of Nazi-Looted Art*. Case and Controversy. Berlin: Proprietas.
Tegel, Susan. 2000. "The Demonic Effect: Veit Harlan's Use of Jewish Extras in Jud Süss (1940)." *Holocaust and Genocide Studies* 14(2): 215–41.
Tekelioğlu, Orhan. 2001. "Modernizing Reforms and Turkish Music in the 1930s." *Turkish Studies* 2(1): 93–108.
Thomas, Nicholas. 1999. *Possessions: Indigenous Art, Colonial Culture*. London: Thames & Hudson.
Thomsen, Henrike. 2007. "Neue Philosophie des Kunstmarkts." *TAZ*, September 29. http://www.taz.de/index.php?id=digitaz-artikel&ressort=ku&dig=2007/09/29/a0175.
Thornton, Sarah. 2008. *Seven Days in the Art World*. New York: Norton.
Till, Karen E. 2005. *The New Berlin: Memory, Politics, Place*. Minneapolis: University of Minnesota Press.
Toksoy, Nurcan. 2007. *Halkevleri. Bir Kültürel Kalkınma Modeli Olarak*. Istanbul: Orion Yayınevi.

Tolen, Rachel. 1991. "Colonizing and Transforming the Criminal Tribesman: The Salvation Army in British India." *American Ethnologist* 18(1): 106–25.
Topuz, Hıfzı. 1998. *Dünyada ve Türkiye'de kültür politikaları*. Istanbul: Adam.
Tooze, Adam. 2005a. "Einfach verkalkuliert." *TAZ*, March 12. https://taz.de/!635819/.
———. 2005b. "Doch falsch gerechnet—weil falsch gedacht." *TAZ*, March 16. https://taz.de/!634818/.
Trnka, Jamie H. 2007. "'The Struggle Is Over, the Wounds Are Open': Cinematic Tropes, History, and the RAF in Recent German Film." *New German Critique* 34(2): 1–26.
Trouillot, Michel-Rolph. 1995. *Silencing the Past: Power and the Production of History*. Boston: Beacon.
Tüzünoğlu, Azra. 2005. "Free Kick ve sonrası." *art-ist* 2(4): 101–5.
Ulrich, Wolfgang. 2007. "Lust am Spektakel, Kitzel der Spekulation." *Literaturen* 6/7: 78–83.
Uluç, Ömer, et al. 2006. "Türkiye'deki Sanat Ortamı Üzerine Bir Tartışma." *Sanatdünyamız* 98: 60–77.
Üngör, Uğur Ümit. 2011. *The Making of Modern Turkey: Nation and State in Eastern Anatolia, 1913–1950*. Oxford: Oxford University Press.
Üngör, Uğur Ümit, and Mehmet Polatel. 2011. *Confiscation and Destruction: The Young Turk Seizure of Armenian Property*. London: Bloomsbury.
Ural, Murat. 1998. *Avni Arbaş*. Istanbul: Millî Reasürans Sanat Galerisi.
Üstel, Füsun. 1997. *İmparatorluktan Ulus-Devlete Türk Milliyetçiliği: Türk Ocakları, 1912–1931*. Istanbul: İletişim.
———. 2009. "Cultural Policies in Europe: Debates and Dilemmas. Introduction to Cultural Policy in Turkey." In *Introduction to Cultural Policy in Turkey*, ed. Serhan Ada and Ayça İnce, 7–25. Istanbul: Istanbul Bilgi University Press.
Varon, Jeremy. 2004. *Bringing the War Home: The Weather Underground, the Red Army Faction, and Revolutionary Violence in the Sixties and Seventies*. Berkeley: University of California Press.
———. 2008. "Stammheim Forever and the Ghosts of Guantanamo: Cultural Memory and the Politics of Incarceration." In *Baader-Meinhof Returns: History and Cultural Memory of German Left-Wing Terrorism*, ed. Gerrit-Jan Berendse and Ingo Cornils, 303–25. Amsterdam: Rodopi.
Waldinger, Ernst. 1940. "Von der Heimatkunst zur Blut- und Bodendichtung." *German Quarterly* 13(2): 83–87.
Weber, Max. 1958 [1915]. "The Esthetic Sphere." In *From Max Weber: Essays in Sociology*, ed. Hans Heinrich Gerth and C. Wright Mills, 340–43. New York: Oxford University Press.
Werneburg, Brigitte. 2004. "Unerträgliche Täuschung." *TAZ*, May 6. http://www.taz.de/index.php?id=archivseite&dig=2004/05/06/a0235.
———. 2005. "An den Gescheiterten gescheitert." *TAZ*, January 29. http://www.taz.de/index.php?id=archivseite&dig=2005/01/29/a0166.

Werneburg, Brigitte, and Harald Fricke. 2005. "Die Zumutung darf sehr weit gehen." *TAZ*, January 24. http://www.taz.de/index.php?id=archivseite&dig=2005/01/24/a0227.
Winegar, Jessica. 2006. *Creative Reckonings: The Politics of Art and Culture in Contemporary Egypt*. Stanford, CA: Stanford University Press.
Wolbert, Barabra. 2001. "De-Arranged Places: East German Art in the Museum of Unified Germany." *Anthropology of East Europe Review* 19(1): 57–64.
Wolf, Eric. 1999. "National Socialist Germany." In *Envisioning Power: Ideologies of Dominance and Crisis*, 197–273. Berkeley: University of California Press.
Woodmansee, Martha. 1994. *Art, the Author, and the Market: Rereading the History of Aesthetics*. New York: Columbia University Press.
Wright, Susan. 1998. "The Politicization of 'Culture.'" *Anthropology Today* 14(1): 7–15.
Wu, Chin-Tao. 2002. *Privatising Culture: Corporate Art Intervention since the 1980s*. New York: Verso.
——. 2009. "Biennials without Borders." *New Left Review* 57: 107–15.
Wulff, Helena. 1998. *Ballet across Borders: Career and Culture in the World of Dancers*. Oxford: Berg.
Yardımcı, Sibel. 2005. *Küreselleşen İstanbul'da Bienal. Kentsel Değişim ve Festivalizm*. Istanbul: İletişim.
Yúdice, George. 1999. "The Privatization of Culture." *Social Text* 17(2): 17–34.
——. 2003. *The Expediency of Culture: Uses of Culture in the Global Era*. Durham, NC: Duke University Press.
Zolberg, Vera. 1990. *Constructing a Sociology of the Arts*. Cambridge: Cambridge University Press.
Zukin, Sharon. 1982. *Loft Living: Culture and Capital in Urban Change*. New Brunswick, NJ: Rutgers University Press.
——. 1995. *The Cultures of the Cities*. Cambridge: Cambridge University Press.
Zürcher, Erik-Jan. 2004. *Turkey: A Modern History*. London: Tauris.

Index

Banu Karaca is a fellow at the Foundation for Arts Initiatives in New York and an Assistant Professor and EUME Fellow of the Volkswagen Foundation at the Forum Transregionale Studien in Berlin.

Lightning Source UK Ltd.
Milton Keynes UK
UKHW042233140121
376727UK00029B/370

9 780823 290215